JEWISH AND CHRISTIAN TEXTS IN
CONTEXTS AND RELATED STUDIES

Series
Executive Editor
James H. Charlesworth

Editorial Board of Advisors
Motti Aviam, Michael Davis, Casey Elledge, Loren Johns, Amy-Jill Levine, Lee McDonald, Lidia Novakovic, Gerbern Oegema, Henry Rietz, Brent Strawn

The Glory of the Invisible God

*Two Powers in Heaven Traditions
and Early Christology*

Andrei A. Orlov

LONDON • NEW YORK • OXFORD • NEW DELHI • SYDNEY

T&T CLARK
Bloomsbury Publishing Plc
50 Bedford Square, London, WC1B 3DP, UK
1385 Broadway, New York, NY 10018, USA
29 Earlsfort Terrace, Dublin 2, Ireland

BLOOMSBURY, T&T CLARK and the T&T Clark logo are
trademarks of Bloomsbury Publishing Plc

First published in Great Britain in 2019
Paperback edition first published 2021

Copyright © Andrei A. Orlov, 2019

Andrei A. Orlov has asserted his right under the Copyright,
Designs and Patents Act, 1988, to be identified as Author of this work.

All rights reserved. No part of this publication may be reproduced or
transmitted in any form or by any means, electronic or mechanical,
including photocopying, recording, or any information storage or retrieval
system, without prior permission in writing from the publishers.

Bloomsbury Publishing Plc does not have any control over, or responsibility for,
any third-party websites referred to or in this book. All internet addresses given
in this book were correct at the time of going to press. The author and publisher
regret any inconvenience caused if addresses have changed or sites have
ceased to exist, but can accept no responsibility for any such changes.

A catalogue record for this book is available from the British Library.

A catalog record for this book is available from the Library of Congress.

ISBN: HB: 978-0-5676-9223-8
PB: 978-0-5677-0209-8
ePDF: 978-0-5676-9224-5
eBook: 978-0-5676-9268-9

Series: Jewish and Christian Texts, volume 31

Typeset by Deanta Global Publishing Services, Chennai, India

To find out more about our authors and books visit
www.bloomsbury.com and sign up for our newsletters.

No one has ever seen God. It is God the only Son, who is close to the Father's heart, who has made him known.

Gospel of John 1:18

... the glory of Christ, who is the image of God.

2 Cor 4:4

For
Ian Arthur Fair

Contents

Abbreviations	xi
Preface	xiv
Introduction	1
Part One Two Powers in Heaven Traditions in Jewish Accounts	5
"Two Powers" Appearances in Early Jewish Accounts	9
Daniel 7	10
Book of the Similitudes	16
Primary Adam Books	24
The *Exagoge* of Ezekiel the Tragedian	28
2 Enoch	32
Apocalypse of Abraham	38
Ladder of Jacob	54
Angelic Opposition	58
Theophanic Molds in Rabbinic and Hekhalot Two Powers Debates	62
Story of the Four	71
Conclusion	77
Part Two Two Powers in Heaven Traditions in Early Christian Accounts	79
Kavod on the Mountain: The Transfiguration Account	83
Order of Two Powers Appearances	87
Mosaic Settings of the Transfiguration Story	89
The Extra-Biblical Mosaic Developments	95
Moses' Enthronement	95
Moses' Glorification at His Death/His Translation to Heaven	97
Moses' Angelification and Divinization	100
The Afterlife of Biblical Mosaic Traditions in Other	
Second Temple Mediatorial Trends	105
Mosaic Features of the Transfiguration Story	108
Timing of the Story	108
Chosen Companions	109

Motif of the Mountain	110
Mountain as the Throne of the Divine Glory	111
Secrecy	114
Jesus' Metamorphosis	115
Jesus' Garment	118
Jesus' Luminous Face	123
Elijah and Moses	128
Three Dwellings	129
The Fear Motif	130
Veneration Motif?	133
Imagery of the Cloud	136
The Divine Voice Traditions	137
"Listen to Him"	139
Conclusion	143
Kavod on the River: The Baptism Account	145
Theophanic Settings of the Account	145
Jesus as a Visionary	148
The Motif of Water	151
Fire and Light in Water	154
Robe of Glory in the Jordan	157
The Glorification of Jesus at the Jordan	160
The Motif of the Torn Heaven	163
Topological Peculiarities	166
Cosmological Ramifications	167
Likeness Language	173
Acquisition of the Spirit as the Restoration of the Image of God	174
The Divine Voice Traditions	175
The Dove Symbolism	177
Pteromorphic Glory	179
The Image of God Traditions and the Temptation Story	182
Conclusion	188
Conclusion	190
Bibliography	193
Texts and Translations	193
Secondary Literature	197
Index of Names	210
Index of Subjects	214
Index of References	218

Abbreviations

AAWG	Abhandlungen der Akademie der Wissenschaften in Göttingen
AB	Anchor Bible
AC	*Anthropology of Consciousness*
ACW	Ancient Christian Writers
AGAJU	Arbeiten zur Geschichte des antiken Judentums und des Urchristentums
AnBib	Analecta Biblica
ArBib	Aramaic Bible
AUSS	*Andrews University Seminary Studies*
BAC	Bible in Ancient Christianity
BAR	*Biblical Archaeology Review*
BBR	*Bulletin for Biblical Research*
BECNT	Baker Exegetical Commentary on the New Testament
BibInt	*Biblical Interpretation*
BJRL	*Bulletin of the John Rylands Library*
BJS	Brown Judaic Studies
BSJS	Brill's Series in Jewish Studies
BZAW	Beihefte zur Zeitschrift für die alttestamentliche Wissenschaft
BZNW	Beihefte zur Zeitschrift für die neutestamentliche Wissenschaft und die Kunde der älteren Kirche
CBQ	*Catholic Biblical Quarterly*
CEJL	Commentaries on Early Jewish Literature
ConBOT	Coniectanea Biblica. Old Testament series
CRINT	Compendia Rerum Iudaicarum ad Novum Testamentum
CSCO	Corpus Scriptorum Christianorum Orientalium
CTSI	Catholic Theological Studies of India
DSD	*Dead Sea Discoveries*
EB	Eichstätter Beiträge
ECR	*Eastern Churches Review*
EE	*Estudios eclesiásticos*
EJL	Early Judaism and Its Literature
EKKNT	Evangelisch-katholischer Kommentar zum Neuen Testament
EstBib	*Estudios Biblicos*
ETS	Erfurter theologische Studien
FAT	Forschungen zum Alten Testament

FRLANT	Forschungen zur Religion und Literatur des Alten und Neuen Testaments
FTS	Frankfurter theologische Studien
GCS	Die griechischen christlichen Schriftsteller der ersten drei Jahrhunderte
GOTR	*Greek Orthodox Theological Review*
HTKNT	Herders theologischer Kommentar zum Neuen Testament
HTR	*Harvard Theological Review*
HTS	Harvard Theological Studies
HUCA	*Hebrew Union College Annual*
ICC	International Critical Commentary on the Holy Scriptures of the Old and New Testaments
Imm	*Immanuel*
JAOS	*Journal of the American Oriental Society*
JBL	*Journal of Biblical Literature*
JCPS	Jewish and Christian Perspectives Series
JETS	*Journal of the Evangelical Theological Society*
JJS	*Journal of Jewish Studies*
JSHRZ	Jüdische Schriften aus hellenistisch-römischer Zeit
JSJ	*Journal for the Study of Judaism in the Persian, Hellenistic and Roman Period*
JSJSS	Journal for the Study of Judaism in the Persian, Hellenistic and Roman Period: Supplement Series
JSNTSS	Journal for the Study of the New Testament. Supplement Series
JSOTSS	Journal for the Study of the Old Testament. Supplement Series
JSP	*Journal for the Study of the Pseudepigrapha*
JTS	*Journal of Theological Studies*
LAB	Biblical Antiquities of Ps.-Philo
LCJP	Library of Contemporary Jewish Philosophers
LCL	Loeb Classical Library
LNTS	Library of New Testament Studies
LXX	Septuagint
NHMS	Nag Hammadi and Manichaean Studies
NHS	Nag Hammadi Studies
NICNT	New International Commentary on the New Testament
NIGTC	New International Greek Testament Commentary
NovT	*Novum Testamentum*
NovTSup	Supplements to Novum Testamentum
NSBT	New Studies in Biblical Theology
NTAbh	Neutestamentliche Abhandlungen
NTOA	Novum Testamentum et Orbis Antiquus
NTS	*New Testament Studies*

NTTS	New Testament Tools and Studies
OC	*Oriens Christianus*
PA	Philosophia Antiqua
PNTC	Pillar New Testament Commentary
PTS	Patristische Texte und Studien
PVTG	Pseudepigrapha Veteris Testamenti Graece
RB	*Revue biblique*
RechRib	Recherches bibliques
RTL	*Revue théologique de Louvain*
SANT	Studien zum Alten und Neuen Testaments
SBLDS	Society of Biblical Literature Dissertation Series
SBLSP	Society of Biblical Literature Seminar Papers
SBLTT	Society of Biblical Literature Texts and Translations
SC	Sources chrétiennes
SHR	Studies in the History of Religions
SJ	Studia Judaica
SJLA	Studies in Judaism in Late Antiquity
SJS	Studia Judaeoslavica
SNTSMS	Society for New Testament Studies Monograph Series
SP	*Studia Patristica*
SPhA	*Studia Philonica Annual*
SSEJC	Studies in Scripture in Early Judaism and Christianity
STAC	Studien und Texte zu Antike und Christentum
STDJ	Studies on the Texts of the Desert of Judah
SVTP	Studia in Veteris Testamenti Pseudepigrapha
TCS	Text-Critical Studies
TG	Tesi Gregoriana
ThZ	*Theologische Zeitschrift*
TNTC	Tyndale New Testament Commentary
TS	*Theological Studies*
TSAJ	Texte und Studien zum antiken Judentum
VC	*Vigiliae Christianae*
VCS	Vigiliae Christianae Supplements Series
VTSup	Supplements to Vetus Testamentum
YJS	Yale Judaica Series
WBC	Word Biblical Commentary
WUNT	Wissenschaftliche Untersuchungen zum Neuen Testament
ZECNT	Zondervan Exegetical Commentary on the New Testament
ZNW	*Zeitschrift für die neutestamentliche Wissenschaft und die Kunde der älteren Kirche*

Preface

Several people helped me in my work on this project. I am especially grateful to my research assistants—David Burnett, Hans Moscicke, and Patrick Bowman—who worked very hard through various versions of this book to help improve the text in grammar, style, and substance. Their meticulous editing has saved me from numerous errors. All remaining mistakes are solely my own responsibility.

I also extend my gratitude to my colleague at Marquette University's Theology Department, Prof. Julian Hills, who read the entire manuscript and offered numerous valuable suggestions.

I am grateful to Prof. James H. Charlesworth for accepting this study for T&T Clark's Jewish and Christian Texts Series.

Sincere thanks are also due to Dominic Mattos, Sarah Blake, and the editorial team of Bloomsbury Publishing Plc for their help, patience, and professionalism during the preparation of this book for publication.

I dedicate this book to my dear teacher, mentor, and friend, a former dean of the College of Biblical Studies at Abilene Christian University, Prof. Ian Fair. It was in Ian's class on apocalyptic literature, almost thirty years ago, where I first learned about the Jewish pseudepigrapha and the Enochic writings. I am grateful for Ian's guidance and help.

Andrei Orlov
Milwaukee
Feast of the Theophany of our Lord and Savior Jesus Christ, 2019

Introduction

The treatise *Hagiga* of the Babylonian Talmud unveils the story of a rabbinic apostate, Elisha ben Avuyah. Known also as Aher, "the Other," he received a vision of the great angel Metatron, who sat in heaven and recorded the merits of Israel. When the infamous visionary saw Metatron, whose celestial posture was strikingly reminiscent of the posture of the divine *Kavod*, he opened his mouth and uttered the following: "It is taught as a tradition that on high there is no sitting and no emulation, and no back, and no weariness. Perhaps,—God forfend!—There are two divinities!"[1] This heretical statement, which challenged God's sovereignty, would not remain unpunished. Accordingly, God banished Aher beyond the boundaries of the Tradition. As the *Hagiga* says, "a *bat qol* went forth and said: Return, ye backsliding children—except Aher. [Thereupon] he said: Since I have been driven forth from yonder world, let me go forth and enjoy this world. So Aher went forth into evil courses."[2]

This enigmatic episode, a crucial narrative connected with the so-called 'two powers in heaven' controversy, has been repeatedly invoked in scholarly debates about early Christology and monotheism. At first glance, it seems that bringing this relatively late rabbinic passage into a discussion about ancient Christian texts would be anachronistic. These scholarly efforts, however, are not completely inappropriate, since Aher's vision of Metatron provides important methodological lessons for the study of early Christological developments, yielding as it were an unexpected key that could elucidate the construction of Jesus' exalted identity as representing God's Glory (or *Kavod*) in the synoptic gospels. Although the rabbinic story is separated by several centuries from the New Testament Christological accounts, the Aher episode exhibits some interesting similarities.

First, as in early Christian developments where the Father and the Son are predestined to coexist within a single monotheistic framework, later rabbinic sources indicate that the appearance of the "second divinity" did not abolish the presence of the first. As shown above, Aher's paradoxical statement postulates a simultaneous existence of *two* powers.

Second, according to early Christian evidence, Jesus' promotion to the rank of divinity was overlaid with distinctive polemical concerns of those who attempted to uphold the old model of monotheism. Within the latter rabbinic traditions, similar distinctive polemical overtones are also markedly present.

The third and most important similarity is that both rabbinic and Christian traditions employ distinctive theophanic features within the depictions of their

---

[1] I. Epstein, *The Babylonian Talmud. Hagiga* (London: Soncino, 1935–1952), 15a.
[2] Epstein, *The Babylonian Talmud. Hagiga*, 15a.

respective second powers. Both traditions, moreover, attempt to construe the second power's authority on the basis of its possession of the theophanic attributes of the deity.

To be sure, it is not merely any theophanic feature that ultimately defines the second power. It is, rather, the peculiar ocularcentric attributes associated with the description of the divine Glory in various biblical and extra-biblical materials where the divine *Kavod* served as a normative manifestation of the deity. Thus, Elisha ben Avuyah makes his conclusion about Metatron's "divinity" on the basis of his possession of the divine seat, the famed hallmark of the divine Glory, epitomized in the symbolism of the divine Chariot. Metatron's divine status is both constructed and confused on the basis of this peculiar theophanic feature. As will become clear later in this study, early Christian accounts, including the transfiguration narratives found in the synoptic gospels, often define Jesus' identity through his possession of the ocularcentric attributes of the divine Glory.

Another important connection found in both Christian and rabbinic accounts is that the "first power" is no longer rendered according to its normative visual aesthetics, namely, as a manifestation of the divine Glory, but instead as the aural expression—the *bat qol* or the divine Voice. It is this divine Voice that both reprimands Elisha ben Avuyah in the *Hagiga* passage and confirms Jesus' role as the Son of God in the gospels' baptism and transfiguration accounts, where for the first time certain attributes of the divine Glory are transferred to him. This transferal is not coincidental, since the withdrawal of the first power into the aural invisible mode frees the symbolic space for the theophanic apotheosis of the second power. In rabbinic traditions such withdrawal has a distinct polemical flavor intended to deconstruct the second power's visual attributes. In the Christian tradition, however, it provides unique Christological opportunities for the second power's induction into the realm of the deity.

Finally, another similar feature involves a pronounced emphasis on the visionary experience in the construction of the second power's identity in both Christian and rabbinic accounts. In *Hagiga*'s passage it is Aher's apprehension, or his vision, of Metatron that creates a fatal mistake about the status of the second power. Some scholars have argued that in early Christian tradition, the religious experience, which included the visionary experience, also played a crucial role in the construction of Jesus' divine identity.[3]

With respect to the paramount importance of theophanic traditions in both rabbinic and early Christian accounts of the "two powers," it is shocking that this particular symbolic dimension has not played a significant role in recent scholarly debates about the methodological value of the two powers traditions for our understanding of early Christological developments. Often scholars fail to note that in both corpora the two powers are portrayed in a similar way, appearing in two theophanic modes:

---

[3] Larry Hurtado has suggested that "if we seek a factor to account for the striking innovation constituted by the incorporation of Christ into a binitarian devotional pattern, that is, if we seek an answer to the question of why Christ-devotion assumed the proportions it did and so quickly, I propose that we have to allow for the generative role of revelatory religious experiences." L. Hurtado, *Lord Jesus Christ: Devotion to Jesus in Earliest Christianity* (Grand Rapids: Eerdmans, 2005), 74.

the manifestation of the first is portrayed as an epiphany of the aniconic Voice, while the second appears as the celestial Form, frequently bearing attributes of the divine Glory.

In my recent book, *Yahoel and Metatron: Aural Apocalypticism and the Origins of Early Jewish Mysticism*,[4] I offered a new perspective on the two powers, arguing that these debates depict a historical tension between ocularcentric and aural theophanic paradigms. My study attempted to demonstrate that in rabbinic and Hekhalot materials dealing with the two powers controversy, the second power is often portrayed with the theophanic attributes of the visual *Kavod* paradigm, while the first power, representing the true deity, is depicted as completely stripped of such attributes.

The affirmation of tension between visual and aniconic trends in the two powers in heaven materials may provide crucial lessons not only for understanding Jewish mystical traditions, but also for clarifying some of the earliest Christological developments. These traditions could especially aid our understanding of the construction of Christ's novel divine attributes and functions within the framework of Jewish monotheism.

---

[4] A. A. Orlov, *Yahoel and Metatron: Aural Apocalypticism and the Origins of Early Jewish Mysticism* (TSAJ 169; Tübingen: Mohr Siebeck, 2017).

Part One

Two Powers in Heaven Traditions in Jewish Accounts

Rabbinic traditions regarding the two powers in heaven, along with their alleged relevance for understanding the formation of early Christology, have been the subject of vigorous discussion in the last several decades. Setting the stage for these recent debates was the seminal study of Alan Segal, "Two Powers in Heaven."[1] Reflecting on the essence of the rabbinic debates about two powers or authorities, Segal proposed that "the basic heresy involved interpreting scripture to say that a principal angelic or hypostatic manifestation in heaven was equivalent to God."[2]

Segal argued for the early existence of these conceptual currents, suggesting that they were "a very early category of heresy, earlier than Jesus, if Philo is a trustworthy witness, and one of the basic categories by which the rabbis perceived the new phenomenon of Christianity."[3] Throughout his study, Segal consistently argued for the early roots of these traditions, claiming that "the extra-rabbinic evidence allowed the conclusion that the traditions were earlier than the first century."[4]

Postulating an early date for the two powers controversy, Segal advocated the importance of these debates for our understanding of early Christological developments. He argued that "the relationships between these traditions of angelic mediation and Christianity are significant enough to call for a more complete study of the problem as background for Christology than has yet been attempted."[5] Notably,

---

[1] A. F. Segal, *Two Powers in Heaven: Early Rabbinic Reports about Christianity and Gnosticism* (SJLA 25; Leiden: Brill, 1977).

[2] Segal, *Two Powers in Heaven*, x.

[3] Segal, *Two Powers in Heaven*, ix. Segal argues that "apparently, even within Christianity the 'two powers' controversy was evidenced" and "the language of the 'two powers' controversy becomes especially important within the church's struggle to refine Christology." Segal, *Two Powers in Heaven*, 215. He further notes that "there is warrant to believe that 'two powers' heresy was manifested in some kinds of Christianity in the first century." Segal, *Two Powers in Heaven*, 218. Yet, Segal doubts if the terminology "two powers in heaven" should be applied to early Christian developments: "perhaps the term 'two powers' is anachronistic as applied to the first century." Segal, *Two Powers in Heaven*, 215.

[4] Segal, *Two Powers in Heaven*, x.

[5] Segal, *Two Powers in Heaven*, 208. Elsewhere in his monograph, Segal notes that "besides the obvious relevance of these findings for understanding the rabbinic movement, this study has ramifications for Christian historians in two important areas: (1) the development of Christology

his hypothesis attracted the attention of several contemporary experts of early Judaism and Christian origins.[6]

Another scholar who has likewise acknowledged the importance of the two powers traditions for understanding of early Jewish and Christian accounts is Daniel Boyarin. According to Boyarin, "there is significant evidence (uncovered in large part by Segal) that in the first century many—perhaps most—Jews held a binitarian doctrine of God."[7] Like Segal, who advocated early pre-Christian roots of the two powers traditions, Boyarin maintains that the concept of a second and independent divine agent can be traced to the Hebrew Bible.[8]

Another scholar who has engaged in dialogue with Segal's legacy is Larry Hurtado. Applying some of Segal's ideas to his research on early Christian devotion, Hurtado concludes that

> although we do not actually have first-century Jewish documents that tell us directly what Jewish religious leaders thought of Christian devotion, there seems to be every reason to assume that the attitude was probably very much like the one reflected in slightly later Jewish sources, which apparently reject cultic devotion to

---

and (2) the rise of Gnosticism. On the subject of Christology, the rabbinic information emphasizes the scriptural basis for Christological discussion." Segal, *Two Powers in Heaven*, x.

[6] J. Ashton, *Understanding the Fourth Gospel* (Oxford: Clarendon Press, 1991), 158; D. Boyarin, *Border Lines: The Partition of Judaeo-Christianity* (Philadelphia: University of Pennsylvania Press, 2004), 128–47; idem, "Two Powers in Heaven; Or, The Making of a Heresy," in: *The Idea of Biblical Interpretation: Essays in Honor of James L. Kugel* (ed. H. Najman and J. H. Newman; Leiden: Brill, 2004), 331–70; idem, "Beyond Judaisms: Meṭaṭron and the Divine Polymorphy of Ancient Judaism," *JSJ* 41 (2010): 323–65; J. D. G. Dunn, *The Partings of the Ways Between Christianity and Judaism and Their Significance for the Character of Christianity* (London: SCM, 1991), 228–29; A. Goshen-Gottstein, "Jewish-Christian Relations and Rabbinic Literature—Shifting Scholarly and Relational Paradigms: The Case of Two Powers," in: *Interaction Between Judaism and Christianity in History, Religion, Art, and Literature* (ed. M. Poorthuis, J. J. Schwartz, and J. Turner; JCPS 17; Leiden: Brill, 2009), 15–44; L. W. Hurtado, *One God, One Lord* (Philadelphia: Fortress, 1988); J. F. McGrath, *The Only True God: Early Christian Monotheism in Its Jewish Context* (Urbana: University of Illinois Press, 2012); J. F. McGrath and J. Truex, "Early Jewish and Christian Monotheism: A Select Bibliography," in: *Early Jewish and Christian Monotheism* (ed. L. T. Stuckenbruck and W. E. S. North; JSNTSS 263; London: T&T Clark, 2004), 235–42; E. Osborn, *The Emergence of Christian Theology* (Cambridge: Cambridge University Press, 1993), 24–29; J. Painter, *The Quest for the Messiah* (2nd ed.; Nashville: Abingdon, 1993), 225; A. Schremer, "Midrash, Theology, and History: Two Powers in Heaven Revisited," *JSJ* 39 (2008): 230–54; idem, *Brothers Estranged: Heresy, Christianity and Jewish Identity in Late Antiquity* (Oxford: Oxford University Press, 2010); S. Scott, "The Binitarian Nature of the Book of Similitudes," *JSP* 18 (2008): 55–78; M. S. Smith, *God in Translation: Deities in Cross-Cultural Discourse in the Biblical World* (FAT 57; Tübingen: Mohr Siebeck, 2008), 294; L. T. Stuckenbruck, *Angel Veneration and Christology: A Study in Early Judaism and in the Christology of the Apocalypse of John* (WUNT 2.70; Tübingen: Mohr Siebeck, 1995); Y. Y. Teppler, *Birkat HaMinim: Jews and Christians in Conflict in the Ancient World* (TSAJ 120; Tübingen: Mohr Siebeck, 2007), 345; R. M. M. Tuschling, *Angels and Orthodoxy: A Study in Their Development in Syria and Palestine from the Qumran Texts to Ephrem the Syrian* (STAC 40; Tübingen: Mohr Siebeck, 2007), 104–5; S. G. Wilson, *Related Strangers: Jews and Christians* (Minneapolis: Fortress, 1995), 79; M. de Jonge, *God's Final Envoy: Early Christology and Jesus' Own View of His Mission* (Grand Rapids: Eerdmans, 1998), 141.

[7] Boyarin, "Two Powers in Heaven; Or the Making," 334.

[8] Boyarin, "Two Powers in Heaven; Or the Making," 339–40.

Jesus as constituting an example of the worship of "two powers in heaven," that is, the worship of two gods.[9]

Several other scholars have followed suit, noting the ability of rabbinic debates concerning two powers to shed light on early Christological developments. James Davila effectively sums up these scholarly hopes by suggesting that the two powers traditions associated with the Metatron figure "might help us understand the rise of the worship of Jesus."[10]

While some experts think that the two powers traditions can provide us with crucial insights for understanding early Christological developments, others have expressed their reservations about the value of these later conceptual currents for understating early Christology. James McGrath surveys these doubts in his recent study "The Only True God." In it, McGrath offers nuanced skepticism about the relevance of the aforementioned rabbinic debates, suggesting "there is good reason to conclude that certain conceptualities later condemned as two powers heresy would not have been controversial in the first century."[11] He concludes by stating "it is anachronistic to interpret Jewish and Christian documents from this period as reflecting 'two powers' heresy."[12]

While one can certainly agree with McGrath that a straightforward application of later rabbinic debates to the Second Temple Jewish and Christian ideological environments appears problematic, the terminology of "two powers" can be methodologically useful in analyzing binitarian developments found in early Jewish and Christian angelology and pneumatology. This language is especially helpful for the study of early Jewish and Christian theophanic accounts in which God appears alongside a second mediatorial figure, who at times paradoxically emulates the deity's attributes. In this respect, the notion of the "second power" allows us to approach the attributes and functions of a novel mediator without assigning an exclusive divine status to this agent. These traditions, moreover, are crucial for understanding the earliest Christological developments, especially those that feature a sudden and paradoxical delegation of various functions and attributes of the deity to Jesus.

Furthermore, it should be noted that, in modern debates regarding the relevance of the two powers traditions for the study of early Judaism and Christian origins, the focus is often exclusively placed on the "oppositional" nature of the two powers traditions. This dimension is certainly prominent in later rabbinic and Hekhalot accounts, where the second power, in the form of the supreme angel Metatron, is clearly situated in polemical opposition to the first power represented by the deity. Scholars are often overfocused on this polemical tension between the two powers, having utilized it as an interpretive framework for understanding the long-lasting tensions between the

---

[9] Hurtado, *One God, One Lord*, 1–2.

[10] J. R. Davila, "Of Methodology, Monotheism and Metatron: Introductory Reflections on Divine Mediators and the Origins of the Worship of Jesus," in: *The Jewish Roots of Christological Monotheism: Papers from the St. Andrews Conference on the Historical Origins of the Worship of Jesus* (ed. C. C. Newman et al.; JSJSS 63; Leiden: Brill, 1999), 16.

[11] McGrath, *The Only True God*, 71.

[12] McGrath, *The Only True God*, 95–96.

adepts of Christian devotion and their opponents. These previous investigations often failed to ascertain the existence, and thus value, of other complementary interactions and relationships between the two respective powers, utilizing instead only the oppositional characterization.

Yet, already Alan Segal in his seminal study reflected on the nature of the relationships between the two powers, whether complementary or oppositional, noting that "the earliest heretics believed in two complementary powers in heaven while only later could heretics be shown to believe in two opposing powers in heaven."[13] Segal's attention to the complementary two powers template is significant for the study of early Christian accounts, precisely because it appears to play a major role in the construction of Jesus' divine identity.

While in the oppositional two powers template the second power is often deconstructed and demoted, in its complementary variation it is built up and exalted. In this respect it is not coincidental that in many New Testament accounts, including stories of Jesus' baptism and transfiguration, his exalted identity is constructed in conjunction with aural manifestations of the deity, who, through his assuring voice, affirms the mediator's distinctive stand. With this in mind, a close investigation of early occurrences of the complementary two powers template, as found in early Jewish and Christian evidence, could shed a unique light on early Christological developments. In short, these currents may provide an important methodological perspective that enables us to witness the construction of a new divinity.

Along this same trajectory, it is also significant that the early complementary appearances of the two powers, much like their later oppositional counterparts, unfold in the midst of peculiar theophanic imagery. In previous scholarly debates these theophanic peculiarities were largely neglected by the majority of disputants. As previously noted, Alan Segal proposed that the gist of the qualms surrounding the rabbinic two powers traditions was an issue of the second power being found equivalent to God.[14] While postulating such relationships, scholars often paid little to no attention to the means by which such equivalency was advanced in various earlier and later two powers traditions. Yet it is clear that many of the tools used to postulate equivalency are connected to special theophanic imagery applied to respective mediatorial agents, thereby demonstrating a sharing of attributes and functions. Moreover, such theophanic qualities, by which the second power is often inducted into the realm of the deity, by themselves often create boundaries between the respective powers, signaling their proper place in the divine hierarchy. This is especially noticeable in the dual or joint theophanies in which two powers appear together. As is often the case in such combined theophanies, each power is associated with a particular theophanic mold that attempts to underline its unique status while simultaneously distancing it from the other power, thus demonstrating its superior place in the celestial hierarchy. Regularly, subtle changes in the depiction of the theophanic attributes of the divine protagonists— that is, when the second power suddenly assumes the features formally attributed to the first power—are intended to signal the ever-changing status of this new authority,

---

[13] Segal, *Two Powers in Heaven*, x.
[14] Segal, *Two Powers in Heaven*, x.

paradoxically predestined for promotion into the realm of the deity. Sometimes the release of the authorial space guarded by the peculiar theophanic attributes is even more radical. In some accounts, the first power is completely withdrawn from the visual dimension of the ocularcentric theophany by assuming the aniconic aural mode. This latter pattern persists in early Christian accounts in which the deity is presented as the aniconic Voice while Jesus assumes the former anthropomorphic features of the deity. The exaltation of the new authority occurs when the first power surrenders its former symbolic space for a new guardian of the ocularcentric trend by withdrawing into the distinctive aural mode. This tradition is paramount for our understanding of early Christological innovations. In order to better grasp these Christological developments, we now turn to consider several early Jewish accounts in which two powers appear together in distinctive theophanic settings.

"Two Powers" Appearances in Early Jewish Accounts

In early Jewish sources, several theophanic accounts depict God alongside a second celestial manifestation that fashions or emulates his attributes. Such dual imagery is present in the Book of Daniel, the *Book of the Similitudes*, the *Exagoge* of Ezekiel the Tragedian, *2 Enoch*, the *Apocalypse of Abraham*, and the *Ladder of Jacob*, as well as other biblical and extra-biblical narratives. Features of some of these accounts, like the one found in the Book of Daniel, and possibly the memories of others, were often invoked in later rabbinic and Hekhalot two powers debates.[15] Such allusions indicate that the rabbinic authors intuitively saw early seeds of the two powers controversy rooted in these early visionary accounts.

Nevertheless, the application of the two powers terminology to early Jewish texts is regarded by some as an anachronistic application that could distort the intended original meaning of these sources. Others might argue, as I intend to do here, that such a move could provide a novel methodological framework that would enable a better understanding of "joint theophanies" and their divine protagonists. In this respect, the notion of the *second* "power" or "authority" appears to be especially helpful, since it provides a new perspective and an additional exegetical dimension often intentionally marginalized or eradicated in the traditional "orthodox" lines of interpretation. Applying the terminology of "power" to the second manifestation, in my opinion, represents a helpful provisional category for exploring early Jewish and Christian "dual" theophanies. In these accounts an exact status of the second mediator who appears along with the deity often remains uncertain, and it is difficult to establish

---

[15] Segal points out that Daniel 7 became pivotal in several rabbinic texts that dealt with two powers in heaven traditions. He suggests it happened because "two different manifestations of God present in Daniel's vision might trouble the rabbis." Segal, *Two Powers in Heaven*, 43. Elsewhere, Segal notes that "a common proof-text against the heresy is Dan 7:9ff. However, it is also likely to be the locus of an heretical argument since the passage describes two different figures in heaven in Daniel's night vision." A. F. Segal, "Judaism, Christianity and Gnosticism," in: *Anti-Judaism in Early Christianity, Vol. 2, Separation and Polemic* (ed. S. G. Wilson; Waterloo: Wilfrid Laurier University Press, 1986), 136.

whether he represents a divine, angelic, or corporeal entity. In this respect, the category of the second power can provide a helpful conceptual framework for the mediatorial protagonist's enigmatic identity. In the light of these benefits, I will use the "powers" terminology in my analysis of the dual theophanies found in the pertinent early Jewish and Christian texts. Additionally, the two powers terminology is useful because within these accounts one can see peculiar transferals of power and authority between the theophanic dyad, whereby crucial attributes of divine sovereignty and authority represented by the divine throne or crown are suddenly transferred from the first power to the second.

The theophanic settings of early two powers accounts are indeed fluid. In some, the deity appears as an anthropomorphic being, in others, he is presented as an aniconic voice. Of course, the deity's appearances as visual or audial representations are not entirely surprising here, since already in the earliest biblical theophanies God had revealed himself both as the anthropomorphic extent[16] and as the divine voice.[17] Moreover, in some paradigmatic Exodus accounts, the deity chooses to reveal himself simultaneously in various theophanic modes, both aural and ocularcentric. On the surface, the deity's revelation in aural and ocularcentric modes appears to be very similar to Jewish and Christian joint theophanies that attest to the simultaneous existence of both theophanic molds. What is different, however, in comparison to the Exodus accounts, is that in the dual theophanies these molds are no longer associated with one God but are instead applied to the respective powers. Often in such accounts God becomes confined solely to the aural mode, while the second power absorbs the whole legacy of the ocularcentric trend formerly possessed by the deity. We should now proceed to a close investigation of these conceptual developments.

Daniel 7

One of the foundational witnesses to the two powers in heaven traditions is found in the Hebrew Bible. Thus, chapter 7 of the Book of Daniel narrates the appearance of two enigmatic celestial figures—the first under the name Ancient of Days, and the second bearing the title Son of Man. In later rabbinic discourses this theophany will be seen as a controversial symbolic well that generated a panoply of heretical opinions. Dan 7:9–14 reads:

> As I watched, thrones were set in place, and an Ancient One took his throne, his clothing was white as snow, and the hair of his head like pure wool; his throne was fiery flames, and its wheels were burning fire. A stream of fire issued and flowed out from his presence. A thousand thousands served him, and ten thousand times ten thousand stood attending him. The court sat in judgment, and the books were opened. I watched then because of the noise of the arrogant words that the horn was speaking. And as I watched, the beast was put to death,

---

[16] Ezek 1; Isa 6.
[17] 1 Kgs 19:11–13.

and its body destroyed and given over to be burned with fire. As for the rest of the beasts, their dominion was taken away, but their lives were prolonged for a season and a time. As I watched in the night visions, I saw one like a human being coming with the clouds of heaven. And he came to the Ancient One and was presented before him. To him was given dominion and glory and kingship that all peoples, nations, and languages should serve him. His dominion is an everlasting dominion that shall not pass away, and his kingship is one that shall never be destroyed.[18]

Scholars have noted that despite its use of unique mythological imagery, the theophanic language of this passage is nevertheless deeply rooted in prophetic and apocalyptic traditions. For example, John Collins says "the scene as a whole belongs to the tradition of biblical throne visions, attested in such passages as 1 Kgs 22:19; Isaiah 6; Ezekiel 1; 3:22–24; 10:1 and paralleled in writings of the Hellenistic period such as *1 Enoch* 14:18–23; 60:2; 90:20."[19] Yet while some features of the account certainly perpetuate familiar conceptual lines found in other earlier biblical and extra-biblical theophanies, it also manifests a striking departure from these earlier patterns by attempting to depict the deity *in conjunction* with another celestial "power." Such novelty in the portrayal of the deity along with the second mediatorial figure, upon whom divine attributes are also conferred, can be understood as a portentous paradigm shift in the history of the Jewish theophanic tradition.

An important symbolic dimension that still ties the Danielic account to the long-lasting tradition of Jewish biblical and extra-biblical theophanies is its explicit anthropomorphic tendencies. In order to better understand this portentous symbolic dimension, a short excursus on its conceptual origins is necessary.[20]

Scholars have noted that biblical anthropomorphism received its most forceful expression in the Israelite Priestly ideology,[21] where God is depicted in "the most tangible corporeal similitudes."[22] Already in the initial chapters of the Pentateuch one

---

[18] All biblical quotations are taken from the New Revised Standard Version (NRSV) unless otherwise indicated.

[19] J. J. Collins, *Daniel* (Hermeneia; Minneapolis: Fortress, 1993), 300.

[20] The conceptual origins of the biblical anthropomorphism cannot be determined with certainty. Some scholars argue that the anthropomorphic position was not entirely an invention of the Priestly tradition, but stemmed from early pre-exilic sacral conceptions regarding divine corporeal manifestations, influenced by ancient Near Eastern materials.

[21] James Barr observes that

because the priestly *Kabod* conception is thus connected naturally with the circumstances in which the cult operated, we can see that it is not just a part of the developed priestly thought as found in P, but goes back to an earlier time; and in particular we note this kind of divine manifestation in the old story from the very beginning of the Solomonic temple (1 Kgs 8:12–13).

J. Barr, "Theophany and Anthropomorphism in the Old Testament," in: *Congress Volume: Oxford 1959* (ed. G. W. Anderson; VTSup 7; Leiden: Brill, 1960), 35.

[22] M. Weinfeld, *Deuteronomy and the Deuteronomic School* (Oxford: Clarendon Press, 1972), 191.

can clearly see a significant presence of this corporeal symbolism. Commenting on these developments, Benjamin Sommer posits that

> in Genesis 2:7 God blows life-giving breath into the first human—an action that might suggest that God has a mouth or some organ with which to exhale. Less ambiguously, in Genesis 3:8, Adam hears the sound of God going for a stroll in the Garden of Eden at the breezy time of the day. A being who takes a walk is a being who has a body—more specifically, a body with something closely resembling legs.[23]

Sommers further discerns that these portrayals of the deity point toward the possibility of the possession of a body, since the divine body portrayed in these texts is located at a particular place and at a particular time.[24]

Already in the first chapter of the Book of Genesis, the concept of divine corporeality is closely intertwined with the etiology of humankind itself. According to E. R. Wolfson, "a critical factor in determining the biblical (and, by extension, subsequent Jewish) attitude toward the visualization of God concerns the question of the morphological resemblance between the human body and the divine."[25] The Priestly ideology proposes the deity created humanity in his own image (Gen 1:27) and is therefore frequently described as possessing a human-like form.[26] As will become clear later, the correspondence between the deity's form and the human body made in the divine image becomes a crucial stratagem in the construction of several "second powers" by early Christians and Jews.

Another important aspect of early Jewish anthropomorphism is its sacerdotal aspect. Early on in the Hebrew Bible, formative portrayals of the divine anthropomorphic extent, often labeled as the divine Glory or *Kavod*, are surrounded with depictions of celestial and earthly worship. Notably, these early accounts attempt to envision the

---

[23] B. D. Sommer, *The Bodies of God and the World of Ancient Israel* (New York: Cambridge University Press, 2009), 2.

[24] Sommer, *The Bodies of God*, 2.

[25] E. R. Wolfson, *Through a Speculum That Shines: Vision and Imagination in Medieval Jewish Mysticism* (Princeton: Princeton University Press, 1994), 20.

[26] Ludwig Köhler and Moshe Weinfeld argue that the phrase, "in our image, after our likeness" precludes the anthropomorphic interpretation that the human being was created in the divine image. L. Köhler, "Die Grundstelle der Imago-Dei-Lehre, Genesis i, 26," *ThZ* 4 (1948): 16; Weinfeld, *Deuteronomy and the Deuteronomic School*, 199. In relation to these conceptual developments, Wolfson notes that

> it seems that the problem of God's visibility is invariably linked to the question of God's corporeality, which, in turn, is bound up with the matter of human likeness to God. . . . Although the official cult of ancient Israelite religion prohibited the making of images or icons of God, this basic need to figure or image God in human form found expression in other ways, including the prophetic visions of God as an anthropos, as well as the basic tenet of the similitude of man and divinity. The biblical conception is such that the anthropos is as much cast in the image of God as God is cast in the image of the anthropos. This is stated in the very account of the creation of the human being in the first chapter of Genesis (attributed to P) in the claim that Adam was created in the image of God.
>
> Wolfson, *Through a Speculum*, 20–21.

deity not simply as an anthropomorphic manifestation,²⁷ but rather as a crucial nexus of cultic devotion and worship. Such veneration of the divine glorious Form takes place not only in heaven, where the divine *Kavod* is surrounded by angelic worship, but also on earth, where the symbolic presence of the divine Form between the two cherubim of the Holy of Holies becomes the very center of the sacrificial cult. We will see the afterlife of these sacerdotal traditions in various early two powers accounts where the second power's invitation into the divine realm will usually coincide with the motif of angelic veneration. Moreover, in the course of such induction, the second power will often be associated with the *Kavod* or its symbolic cognates, like *panim* or *iqonin*.

Early roots of this *Kavod* imagery in Jewish lore are traceable to the mythological imagery found in the first chapter of the Book of Ezekiel, which becomes a long-lasting inspiration for generations of apocalypticists and mystics. The *Kavod* tradition, found in Ezekiel and the Priestly Source, promulgates a distinctive "visual" or "ocularcentric" theophanic mode that becomes influential in many biblical and apocalyptic depictions of God, including Daniel 7. The *Kavod* thus becomes a symbol of the theophanic ideology that presupposes visual apprehension of the divine presence. T. N. D. Mettinger has previously noted that "the *Kavod* is used in Ezekiel as a central theological term in texts where visual contact with God is important."²⁸

It is also significant that already in the earliest specimens of the *Kavod* imagery found in Ezek 1 the anthropomorphic extent of the deity is closely tied to the symbolism of the divine throne, which functions as a symbol of authority and power.²⁹ Mettinger argues that, already in the Priestly ideology, the *Kavod* "is conceived of as referring to the complete manifestation of divine majesty, both to the chariot-throne

---

[27] James Barr notes that
> anthropomorphism in the understanding of theophanic occurrences is no exclusive Israelite phenomenon. The interest which it evokes in Israelite contexts is much greater because iconic representations of the deity are, if not unknown, at any rate abnormal or not regulative for the general trend of thought. The God whom Israel worships appears, if he wills to appear at all, in living human likeness. Anthropomorphism in the strict sense, in the sense of the appearance of God in human shape, depends for Israel in the earliest stages we can trace on the memory of the ancestors and the meeting of their God with them.
> Barr, "Theophany and Anthropomorphism," 37–38.

[28] T. N. D. Mettinger, *The Dethronement of Sabaoth: Studies in the Shem and Kabod Theologies* (ConBOT 18; Lund: Wallin & Dalholm, 1982), 106. Mettinger asserts that
> Ezekiel's choice of the word *kavod* was dictated by the earlier use of the term in the theophanic tradition. It was here those connotations were preserved which underlie the usage in the Priestly traditions. Ezekiel's visions of the divine majesty exhibit the striking combination of *kavod* with the throne, and this combination epitomizes, with emblematic density, the whole theology of Ezekiel's visions.
> Mettinger, *The Dethronement of Sabaoth*, 123.

[29] In relation to the throne symbolism, Richard Bauckham notes that "in Second Temple Judaism, the throne of God in the highest heaven became a key symbol of monotheism, representative of one of the essential characteristics definitive of the divine identity. While a few traces of other enthroned figures associated with God's rule can be found, the subordination of such figures to God's rule is almost always stressed." R. J. Bauckham, "The Throne of God and the Worship of Jesus," in: *The Jewish Roots of Christological Monotheism* (ed. C. C. Newman, J. R. Davila, and G. S. Lewis; JSJSS 63; Leiden: Brill, 1999), 43–69 at 53.

and to God himself."³⁰ These theophanic settings of the ocularcentric *Kavod* paradigm will become an important blueprint for apocalyptic visions reflected in early Enochic accounts, including Enoch's ascents to the heavenly throne room in *1 Enoch* 14 and *1 Enoch* 71.

Anthropomorphic symbolism also appears to play a special role in the context of Daniel 7, where the text's antagonists are fashioned in their distinctive theriomorphic shapes. In the cryptic symbolic code of the Danielic account, the anthropomorphism of the Ancient of Days and the Son of Man signals authority and dominion.³¹ The same tendency is discernible both in Gen 1, where the anthropomorphic shape of the prelapsarian Adam endows him with authority over the animals, and in Ezek 1, where the "animals" of the upper realm—the Living Creatures or the *Hayyot*—are envisioned as servants who hold the foundation of the divine throne. Scholars have suggested that those traditions might constitute the background of Daniel 7.³² They argue that Daniel 7 is "closely connected to Gen 1:26–28, in which the human form resembles the divine and is also connected to ruling power."³³ According to Amy Merrill Willis these traditions "situate divine anthropomorphic features in a hierarchy of bodily forms in which the human form resides at the pinnacle and signals dominion over the beasts of air, land, and sea."³⁴ In this context the anthropomorphism of the Son of Man can be seen as a divine attribute bestowed on the second power. Merrill Willis perceptively argues that the Son of Man "is visually aligned with divine righteous rule through his shape. . . . Unlike the first beast, who must be made humanlike in a process that is never completed,³⁵ this figure possesses the divine image from the beginning."³⁶

The important aspect of the two powers traditions found in Daniel 7 is that, unlike later rabbinic testimonies in which two powers are often depicted in polemical opposition, here in Daniel they are predestined to complement one another. Such complementarity expresses itself in the transference of divine attributes from the first

---

30 Mettinger, *The Dethronement of Sabaoth*, 107.

31 In this context, the metamorphoses of some Danielic theriomorphic antagonists, including the first beast who attempts to emulate a human posture by standing on two feet, can be seen as arrogations against the divine authority. On this see A. C. Merrill Willis, *Dissonance and the Drama of Divine Sovereignty in the Book of Daniel* (Library of Hebrew Bible/Old Testament Studies; London: T&T Clark, 2010), 76.

32 Amy Merrill Willis points out that

> Daniel's description of the Ancient of Days signals incomparable honor, glory, and power. Daniel clearly borrows from Ezek 1:26–28 where the description of the deity emphasizes Yahweh's holiness and glory, which is seated on a mobile throne and surrounded by hybrid creatures. Moreover, one finds in the vision cycle Ezekiel's language of brilliant light, fire, and the wheeled throne (Ezek 1:15, 27–28/Dan 7:9–10).
>
> Merrill Willis, *Dissonance and the Drama of Divine Sovereignty in the Book of Daniel*, 74–75.

33 Merrill Willis, *Dissonance and the Drama of Divine Sovereignty in the Book of Daniel*, 75.

34 Merrill Willis, *Dissonance and the Drama of Divine Sovereignty in the Book of Daniel*, 75.

35 Dan 7:4: "The first was like a lion and had eagles' wings. Then, as I watched, its wings were plucked off, and it was lifted up from the ground and made to stand on two feet like a human being; and a human mind was given to it."

36 Merrill Willis, *Dissonance and the Drama of Divine Sovereignty in the Book of Daniel*, 76.

power to the second—the same process that occurs in other early Jewish and Christian accounts.

In Dan 7:14 the transfer happens when the Son of Man receives "dominion, glory and kingship." Important to note is that while the text mentions the transferal of "glory" to the second power, such attributes are markedly absent in the description of the first power, represented by the deity. Although scholars often argue for the formative influence of the Ezekielian vision of the divine Glory on the Danielic theophany, the text does not assign the *Kavod* attributes to the first power in the form of the Ancient of Days. Instead, some of these attributes are implicitly transferred to the Son of Man. Thus, Merrill Willis noted that "as the deity bestows on the humanlike one dominion and glory, divine prerogative becomes visible. Though the passive voice obscures—grammatically speaking—divine activity, the humanlike one *brings to full visibility, in the sight of the nations, the glory of the Most High*."[37] This insightful comment accentuates one of the essential features of the joint theophanies, when the "visibility" of the deity is gradually transferred to the second power, who will eventually become the image of the invisible God. Of course, at the starting point of this important conceptual trajectory, in Daniel 7, the deity is still far away from being invisible. Yet the first steps, especially in relation to the portentous symbol of the ocularcentric ideology—the divine *Kavod*, are already made. In this respect Merrill Willis perceptively notes that in the Son of Man "the reader encounters the language of honor or glory that was notably missing from the use of Ezek 1 to speak of the Ancient of Days. Ironically, the humanlike one, as the undistorted embodiment of divine glory, one who is totally dependent upon the divine, underscores the incomparability of the divine."[38]

The notion of transferred glory represents a portentous aspect of the two powers traditions. This conceptual development will play a formative role not only in Jewish sources, but also in early Christian materials, such as the transfiguration accounts. In the latter Jesus is endowed with the ocularcentric glorious attributes of the *Kavod*, while God is withdrawn in the aniconic void of his aural manifestation.

Vital for our study, however, is that the roots of such a process go back to the very first example of the two powers tradition in early Jewish lore: the theophany of Dan 7. Here the attributes of the divine *Kavod* are for the first time transferred to the second power in the form of the Son of Man.

Another crucial "gift" that newly endowed second powers receive in Jewish apocalyptic and mystical accounts is the attribute of the divine seat, which, by its essential role in the *Kavod* iconography, signals the unique celestial status of its owner.[39] It is therefore not coincidental that such attributes become the main

---

[37] Merrill Willis, *Dissonance and the Drama of Divine Sovereignty in the Book of Daniel*, 77, emphasis is mine.

[38] Merrill Willis, *Dissonance and the Drama of Divine Sovereignty in the Book of Daniel*, 77.

[39] Darrell Hannah states,

> a Rabbinic baraita holds that "on high there is no sitting and no emulation, no back and no weariness" (*b. Hag.* 15a; cf. *3 Enoch* 18:24). To drive this point home some of the rabbis asserted that angels have no knees and so could not sit even if they so wished (*y. Ber.* 1:12c; *Gen. Rab.* 65:21; *Lev. Rab.* 6:3; *Pes. Rab.* 22:6). Now it is just possible that this idea, that

stumbling block for Aher in later rabbinic and Hekhalot materials, forcing him to take the enthroned angel for the second divinity or power. Already in Daniel 7 one detects an occurrence of the divine seat motif in the construction of the second power.

Recall now, the Danielic theophany begins with an announcement that multiple thrones "were set in place" (Dan 7:9). Although this account does not assign the heavenly seat explicitly to the second power—the door for such an interpretation is left open, as later Jewish exegetes amply illustrate. It has been noted that "from an early time, v. 9 was taken to refer to two thrones, one for the Ancient of Days and one to be occupied later by the 'one like a son of man.'"[40] With respect to this tradition, Daniel Boyarin notes that "although in Daniel read on its own, it certainly seems that the thrones are multiple and set up for the Court, it is clear from here as well as from other passages that late-ancient Jews read the thrones as two, one for the Ancient of Days and one for the One Like a Son of Man."[41]

Other details of the account, including a reference to the Son of Man's endowment with the kingdom, provide further evidence for his possible possession of the seat. In relation to these developments John Collins suggests that "the 'one like a human being' who appears in v. 13 is given a kingdom, so it is reasonable to assume that he is enthroned, even though his enthronement is not actually described."[42] Collins further concludes the analysis of the multiple thrones theme by suggesting that "there is plenty of evidence, then, that the plural 'thrones' was understood to accommodate a second heavenly being, who is represented in Daniel as 'one like a human being,' although originally there was probably a more inclusive reference to the divine council."[43]

Book of the Similitudes

Another instance of the "dual theophany" where both powers appear in their complementary relationships can be found in the extra-biblical Jewish apocalypse known to us as the *Book of the Similitudes*, where the Ancient of Days and the Son of Man are again depicted as anthropomorphic manifestations. Although this Enochic text is not found among the Qumran fragments of the Enochic writings, the current

---

angels are not able to sit, is actually much earlier than the rabbinic period. For example, a fragmentary text from the *Songs of the Sabbath Sacrifice* may state categorically that angels do not sit.

D. D. Hannah, "The Throne of His Glory: The Divine Throne and Heavenly Mediators in Revelation and the Similitudes of Enoch," *ZNW* 94 (2003): 68–96 at 89.

[40] Collins, *Daniel*, 301.
[41] Boyarin, "Beyond Judaisms," 337.
[42] Collins, *Daniel*, 301.
[43] Collins, *Daniel*, 301.

scholarly consensus holds that the book was likely composed before the second century CE.⁴⁴ *1 Enoch* 46:1–2⁴⁵ provides the following description of two powers:

> And there I saw one who had a head of days, and his head (was) white like wool; and with him (there was) another, whose face had the appearance of a man, and his face (was) full of grace, like one of the holy angels. And I asked one of the holy angels who went with me, and showed me all the secrets, about that Son of Man, who he was, and whence he was, (and) why he went with the Head of Days.⁴⁶

Although this description draws heavily from Daniel 7, several other important details are added. Analyzing this account, George Nickelsburg and James VanderKam note that in this joint theophany the deity is not enthroned and the reference to his enthronement is deferred to chapter 47.⁴⁷ The author prefers to focus solely on the two figures, and in vv. 2–3 on the identity of the human-like figure. In this respect the text differs from Dan 7:13, where his identity is taken for granted.⁴⁸

Another important dimension of the *Similitudes*' account in comparison with Daniel 7 is the text's prolonged attention to the functions and offices of the second

---

⁴⁴ In his conclusion to the Enoch Seminar's volume devoted to the *Book of the Similitudes*, Paolo Sacchi writes: "In sum, we may observe that those scholars who have directly addressed the problem of dating the *Parables* all agree on a date around the time of Herod. Other participants of the conference not addressing the problem directly nevertheless agree with this conclusion." P. Sacchi, "The 2005 Camaldoli Seminar on the Parables of Enoch: Summary and Prospects for Future Research," in: *Enoch and the Messiah Son of Man: Revisiting of the Book of Parables* (ed. G. Boccaccini; Grand Rapids: Eerdmans, 2007), 510. See also D. Suter, "Enoch in Sheol: Updating the Dating of the Book of Parables," in: *Enoch and the Messiah Son of Man: Revisiting the Book of Parables* (ed. G. Boccaccini; Grand Rapids: Eerdmans, 2007), 415–43; G. W. E. Nickelsburg and J. C. VanderKam, *1 Enoch 2: A Commentary on the Book of 1 Enoch: Chapters 37–82* (Hermeneia; Minneapolis: Fortress, 2012), 58–63.

⁴⁵ Regarding this passage Hurtado notes,
> the effects of the heavenly divine agent concept may be seen especially in *1 Enoch* 46:1–3, where, employing imagery from Dan 7:9–14, the writer pictures the "Son of Man"/"Chosen One" in a heavenly scene, prominently associated with God, possessing an angelic aspect, and privy to all heavenly secrets. In this theophanic scene, the writer pictures God and "another," manlike in appearance, whose face was "full of grace, like one of the holy angels," who "will reveal all the treasures of that which is secret." The writer of *1 Enoch* 46 apparently saw the figure in Dan. 7:13–14 as a real being bearing heavenly (angelic) qualities and as God's chosen chief agent of eschatological deliverance. Whether this interpretation reflects the meaning intended by the author of Daniel 7 or was a later development, in either case I suggest that such an interpretation is evidence of the concept of a heavenly divine agent, a figure next to God in authority who acts as God's chief representative.
>
> Hurtado, *One God, One Lord*, 54.

⁴⁶ M. Knibb, *The Ethiopic Book of Enoch: A New Edition in the Light of the Aramaic Dead Sea Fragments* (2 vols.; Oxford: Clarendon, 1978), 2.131–32.

⁴⁷ *1 Enoch* 47:3: "And in those days I saw the Head of Days sit down on the throne of his glory, and the books of the living were opened before him, and all his host, which (dwells) in the heavens above, and his council were standing before him." Knibb, *The Ethiopic Book of Enoch*, 2.133.

⁴⁸ Nickelsburg and VanderKam, *1 Enoch 2*, 156.

power, which permeate the *angelus interpres*' explanations following the theophany.[49] As Nickelsburg and VanderKam indicate,

> Enoch does not inquire about the Head of Days but only about "that Son of Man." The audience knows who the deity is. However, Enoch's Son of Man, who is so central to his text, is different from the Danielic figure and must be explained to the author's audience. He is the judge of the kings and the mighty—a function that Daniel 7 does not ascribe to him—and as such he is the object of the audience's faith and hope.[50]

This emphasis on the Son of Man figure in the dual theophany is noteworthy, since he distinctly absorbs some traits of the first power. One of the intriguing features of his description is a reference to his "face (which was) full of grace."[51] This attention to the "face" of the second power does not appear to be coincidental. The imagery of the face, or the *panim*, also plays an important role in other early two powers theophanies, often serving as a symbolic correlate to notions of the divine *Kavod* and the divine *Tselem* (Image). In the *Similitudes*, it is also possible that the imagery of the face appears as a divine attribute. Reflecting on the Son of Man's face, Nickelsburg and VanderKam note that the text further "expands the description of the figure's face, likening it to that of one of the holy angels (v. 1d). That is, the deity is accompanied by another divine figure. The expression 'full of grace' is not used here theologically but denotes a physical characteristic."[52] Comparable to Dan 7, it is possible that the second power in *1 Enoch* 46:1–2 absorbs the features of the divine Glory. This transferal is more readily apparent in other parts of the *Similitudes*. In these sections the "Throne of Glory," also depicted

---

[49] *1 Enoch* 46: 3–8 reads:

> And he answered me and said to me: "This is the Son of Man who has righteousness, and with whom righteousness dwells; he will reveal all the treasures of that which is secret, for the Lord of Spirits has chosen him, and through uprightness his lot has surpassed all before the Lord of Spirits for ever. And this Son of Man whom you have seen will rouse the kings and the powerful from their resting-places, and the strong from their thrones, and will loose the reins of the strong, and will break the teeth of the sinners. And he will cast down the kings from their thrones and from their kingdoms, for they do not exalt him, and do not praise him, and do not humbly acknowledge whence (their) kingdom was given to them. And he will cast down the faces of the strong, and shame will fill them, and darkness will be their dwelling, and worms will be their resting-place; and they will have no hope of rising from their resting-places, for they do not exalt the name of the Lord of Spirits. And these are they who judge the stars of heaven, and raise their hands against the Most High, and trample upon the dry ground, and dwell upon it; and all their deeds show iniquity . . . and their power (rests) on their riches, and their faith is in the gods which they have made with their hands, and they deny the name of the Lord of Spirits. And they will be driven from the houses of his congregation, and of the faithful who depend on the name of the Lord of Spirits."
>
> Knibb, *The Ethiopic Book of Enoch*, 2.132.

[50] Nickelsburg and VanderKam, *1 Enoch 2*, 157.

[51] Nickelsburg and VanderKam bring attention to this feature by noting that, in comparison with Dan 7:13, *1 Enoch* 46:1 mentions the *face* of the Son of Man. Nickelsburg and VanderKam, *1 Enoch 2*, 156.

[52] Nickelsburg and VanderKam, *1 Enoch 2*, 157.

as an attribute of the deity, is transferred to the second power, who is described by the author with several designations, including the appellation Elect One/Chosen One. As *1 Enoch* 45:3 recounts, "the Chosen One will sit on the throne of glory."[53] Darrell Hannah comments on this striking transferal, arguing that "in the *Similitudes* the Son of Man or Elect One, who is also identified as the Messiah (48:10; 52:4), is said to sit on the throne of Glory, which must mean for our author God's own throne."[54] Moreover, Hannah notes that

> significantly, in 47:3 and 60:2 of the *Similitudes* the phrase "the throne of his glory" is used with reference to the Lord of Spirits. In these two passages it is the Lord of Spirits, or the Chief of Days, as he is there termed, who sits "on the throne of his glory." So the precise phrase "the throne of his glory" is used both for the Son of Man and for the Lord of Spirits, without any indication that a different reality is intended. One cannot help concluding that our author speaks of one reality, the one throne of glory.[55]

As discerned in the present study, already in the earliest instances of the *Kavod* symbolism there exists a curious symbiosis between the deity's anthropomorphic shape and the divine seat as they often appear as a single inseparable entity. Given this, it is possible that the second power, through the possession of the seat of glory, becomes an embodiment of the deity's glory. Jarl Fossum argues that "in the *Similitudes* the 'Elect One' or 'Son of Man' who is identified as the patriarch Enoch, is enthroned upon the 'throne of glory'. If 'glory' does not qualify the throne but its occupant, Enoch is actually identified with the Glory of God."[56] Fossum also suggests a connection to other Jewish two powers accounts, including the tradition of Jacob's *iqonin*,[57] arguing

---

[53] Knibb, *The Ethiopic Book of Enoch*, 2.131. On the throne of glory see also *1 Enoch* 51:1; 55:4; 61:8; 62:5; 69:27, 29.

[54] Hannah, "The Throne of His Glory," 82. In relation to these traditions Laszlo Gallusz notes that
> it is necessary to discern the difference between the passages indicating the throne occupancy by the Elect One and the scene of his enthronement. In this sense, 45.3; 51.3 and 55.4 can be considered as anticipatory references to the enthronement, an event of major significance taking place in 61.8, towards which the whole book is progressing. Not only has the identity of the throne's occupant been questioned; the ultimate ownership of the "throne of glory" has also been the subject of debate ... Moreover, in 47.3 and 60.2 the "throne of glory" is used also in reference to God, who as "the Antecedent of Time" appears as its occupant. There is no indication in the text that this "throne of glory" is different from the "throne of glory" occupied by the Elect One.
> L. Gallusz, *The Throne Motif in the Book of Revelation* (LNTS 487; London: T&T Clark, 2014), 63–64.

[55] Hannah, "The Throne of His Glory," 86.

[56] J. Fossum, *The Image of the Invisible God: Essays on the Influence of Jewish Mysticism on Early Christology* (NTOA 30; Fribourg: Universitätsverlag Freiburg Schweiz; Göttingen: Vanderhoeck & Ruprecht, 1995), 145.

[57] On *iqonin* as the Aramaic transliteration of εἰκών/εἰκόνιον see M. Jastrow, *A Dictionary of the Targumim, the Talmud Babli and Yerushalmi, and the Midrashic Literature* (New York: Judaica Press, 1996), 60 and 297; S. N. Bunta, "The Likeness of the Image: Adamic Motifs and *Tselem* Anthropology in Rabbinic Traditions about Jacob's Image Enthroned in Heaven," *JSJ* 37 (2006): 55–84 at 62–63.

that "the 'Similitudes of Enoch' present an early parallel to the targumic description of Jacob being seated upon the 'throne of glory.'"[58]

As in the Book of Daniel, where the attribute of the glory is transferred to the Son of Man in the deity's presence, some arguing by God himself, in the *Book of the Similitudes* the Elect is also placed on the throne of glory by the deity who is designated as the Lord of Spirits.[59] Regarding the installment of the second power, Hannah notes that

> in 61:8-9 the Lord of Spirits in explicitly portrayed installing the Son of Man on the throne and investing him with the authority to pronounce eschatological judgment: "And the Lord of Spirits placed the Elect One on the throne of glory." . . . The Ethiopic verb here is the equivalent of a Hebrew causative verb: The Lord of Spirits causes the Elect One to sit on the throne of glory.[60]

Here in the *Similitudes* the transference of the attribute of the throne of glory functions complementarily, as in the Book of Daniel. Hurtado notes the complementary nature of the second power in the *Similitudes* by observing that the Son of Man

> seems to act as judge on God's behalf ("in the name of the Lord of Spirits," e.g., 1 Enoch 55:4) and in this capacity sits upon a throne that is closely linked with God: "On that day the Chosen One will sit on the throne of Glory" (45:3; see also 51:3; 55:4; 61:8; 62:2, 3, 5-6; 70:27). The meaning of this is not that the figure rivals God or becomes a second god but rather that he is seen as performing the eschatological functions associated with God and is therefore God's chief agent, linked with God's work to a specially intense degree.[61]

In our ongoing analysis of the two powers' complementary template contained in early Jewish and Christian accounts, it is essential not only to note the gradual endowment of the second power with attributes of the deity, but also the first power's steady abandonment of its previous roles and functions. In this respect, alongside the transference of attributes of the divine authority and power in the form of the divine seat and Glory to the Son of Man/Chosen One in the *Similitudes*, one detects another related process, namely, the deity's withdrawal from his traditional ocularcentric "visible" offices to invisibility. Observing these changing roles of the deity in the *Similitudes*, George Nickelsburg and James VanderKam note that despite God being found in every subsection of the book except one, either by name or by implication

> he *is never described in any detail*, and he is *rarely depicted as doing anything himself*. Almost everything that is ascribed to him takes place by means of agents.

---

[58] Fossum, *The Image of the Invisible God*, 145.

[59] *1 Enoch* 61:8 reads: "And the Lord of Spirits set the Chosen One on the throne of his glory, and he will judge all the works of the holy ones in heaven above, and in the balance he will weigh their deeds." Knibb, *The Ethiopic Book of Enoch*, 2.149.

[60] Hannah, "The Throne of His Glory," 86–87.

[61] Hurtado, *One God, One Lord*, 53.

Various angels function as mediators with the human world, interceding for the suffering righteous and exacting punishment on the sinners, both in ancient times in the flood and in the future after the great assize. The chief agent of this future judgment is the Son of Man, the Righteous One and God's Chosen and Anointed One, the second-most dominating figure in the *Parables*. Thus, for example, the Lord is not the divine warrior whose epiphany is described in the introduction to the Book of the Watchers (*1 Enoch* 1); rather it is the Chosen and Anointed One whose appearance melts the mountains like wax (52:4, 6, 9; 53:6–7; cf. 38:2, "the Righteous One"). Thus, the deity dominates the narrative world of the Parables and at the same time is himself absent from the world that is inhabited by its chief actors, the righteous and chosen, the kings and the mighty, and the demonic hordes of Azazel.[62]

Another important feature of the *Similitudes* is that the second power in this text is explicitly linked to its earthly counterpart in the form of the seventh antediluvian patriarch, Enoch. This development manifests a new step in comparison with Daniel 7 where the Son of Man is not openly linked to his earthly correlative. This understanding of the second power as the heavenly counterpart of a human seer plays a significant role in many other early two powers theophanies, including the *Exagoge*, *2 Enoch*, and the *Ladder of Jacob*.[63]

The heavenly counterpart tradition serves as the formative blueprint for early Christian developments, where the Son of Man figure becomes a designation for the heavenly identity of the Christian exemplar.[64] The seeds of this understanding—that is, of the second power as a heavenly counterpart of an earthly seer—is already present in *1 Enoch* 71:9–14, in which Enoch is identified as the second power in the form of the Son of Man. The metamorphosis is described as follows:

> And Michael and Raphael and Gabriel and Phanuel, and many holy angels without number, came out from that house; and with them the Head of Days, his head white and pure like wool, and his garments indescribable. And I fell upon my face, and my whole body melted, and my spirit was transformed; and I cried out in a loud voice in the spirit of power, and I blessed and praised and exalted. And these blessings which came out from my mouth were pleasing before that Head of Days. And that Head of Days came with Michael and Gabriel, Raphael, and Phanuel, and thousands and tens of thousands of angels without number. And he [that angel] came to me, and greeted me with his voice, and said to me: "You are the Son of

---

[62] Nickelsburg and VanderKam, *1 Enoch 2*, 42, emphasis is mine.

[63] Some later Hekhalot accounts continue this tradition by envisioning Enoch as the earthly counterpart of the second power in the form of the supreme angel Metatron.

[64] Some scholars entertain the connections between the synoptic transfiguration accounts and the *Book of the Similitudes*. On this see C. H. T. Fletcher-Louis, *Luke-Acts: Angels, Christology and Soteriology* (WUNT 2.94; Tübingen: Mohr Siebeck, 1997), 44–45; S. S. Lee, *Jesus' Transfiguration and the Believers' Transformation: A Study of the Transfiguration and Its Development in Early Christian Writings* (WUNT 2.265; Tübingen: Mohr Siebeck, 2009), 42–43.

Man who was born to righteousness, and righteousness remains over you, and the righteousness of the Head of Days will not leave you."[65]

With respect to this passage, Nickelsburg and VanderKam see connections with other two powers accounts (both apocalyptic and rabbinic), suggesting that "the identification of Enoch as the Son of Man can be read as a first step toward the angelification of the seer in *2 Enoch* 22 and of his identification with Metatron in *3 Enoch*."[66] When compared to the Danielic joint theophany and the dual theophany reflected in *1 Enoch* 46:1–2, one can detect not only a simultaneous presentation of the two powers, but also a description of the human being's initiatory endowment to the office of the second power.

Another important aspect of the *Similitudes* is its tendency to portray the human protagonist both as a visionary who contemplates the second power and as the second power himself. Such a tendency in the simultaneous depiction of Enoch both as a recipient of the vision and the object of the vision is present in one of the earliest Enochic booklets—the *Book of the Watchers*. There, in one of his visions reflected in *1 Enoch* 14, the seventh antediluvian hero enters into the heavenly temple as an angelic priest. In Helge Kvanvig's analysis of this account, the dream about the celestial temple "is told by Enoch from two perspectives. The first tells the whole series of events, emphasizing that Enoch stays on the earth during the entire dream. . . . The second perspective focuses on Enoch as the protagonist of the dream itself, and he is carried away to the heavenly temple."[67] If Kvanvig is correct, the seer appears to be in both realms: dreaming in his sleep on the earth while at the same time functioning as the sacerdotal servant in the heavenly temple. As will be shown below, depictions of the double identity of a human adept is widespread in various accounts of the two powers traditions.

Kvanvig sees these early Enochic developments as a crucial conceptual step in shaping the subsequent tradition of Enoch's identification with his heavenly persona in the form of the Son of Man in the *Book of the Similitudes*. Accordingly, "in *1 Enoch* 13–14 Enoch sees himself as a visionary counterpart in heaven. In [the *Similitudes*] 70–71 Enoch is actually taken to heaven to be identified as the Son of Man."[68] Both perspectives occur in the *Similitudes*: Enoch first describes the Son of Man's mighty deeds and is later identified with this celestial figure.[69] Kvanvig claims that "the two perspectives thus constitute two ways of reporting a dream experience where the dreamer sees himself. In the first the dreamer reports what happened in retrospect, depicting how he sees himself

---

[65] Knibb, *The Ethiopic Book of Enoch*, 2.166.

[66] Nickelsburg and VanderKam, *1 Enoch 2*, 328.

[67] H. Kvanvig, "The Son of Man in the Parables of Enoch," in: *Enoch and the Messiah Son of Man: Revisiting of the Book of Parables* (ed. G. Boccaccini; Grand Rapids: Eerdmans, 2007), 181.

[68] Kvanvig, "The Son of Man in the Parables of Enoch," 182. For criticism of this position see J. Collins, "Enoch and the Son of Man: A Response to Sabino Chialà and Helge Kvanvig," in: *Enoch and the Messiah Son of Man: Revisiting of the Book of Parables* (ed. G. Boccaccini; Grand Rapids: Eerdmans, 2007), 218.

[69] Helge Kvanvig has argued that "Enoch sees the Son of Man in visions of the future, not in disclosures of the present. He is seeing what he will become." Kvanvig, "The Son of Man in the Parables of Enoch," 201.

acting in the dream; in the second he remains in the dream experience itself, where only one of the figures is involved, the figure seen in the dream."[70]

The portrayal of the protagonist as both contemplating and becoming the divine mediator is especially significant, since this narrative device is present in many Jewish and Christian two powers in heaven accounts. Thus, in the *Exagoge* of Ezekiel the Tragedian Moses first sees the divine figure enthroned on the mountain, after which he himself becomes this figure. In the *Ladder of Jacob*, Jacob sees a vision of his own heavenly identity in the form of his *iqonin* installed in heaven. Along these lines, the baptism and transfiguration accounts found in the synoptic gospels also seem to depict Jesus as a visionary and the center of the theophany.

Another relevant aspect of the *Similitudes* is that, in the course of the two powers theophany of *1 Enoch* 71, we also have a revelation of the celestial voice, although the speaker's identity is not entirely clear. In some manuscripts, it is an angel who speaks; in others, it is the voice of the deity.[71] If the utterance comes from the mouth of the deity, the aural affirmation of the second power's newly acquired status is significant. As we will see, such affirmations of the first power regarding the heavenly status of the second power play an essential role in early Christian accounts, where the deity is entirely withdrawn from the visual plane. Another striking feature of this initiatory scene is the peculiar form of the address, which recalls the deity's utterances in the baptism and transfiguration accounts where Jesus is endowed—for the first time in the Christian tradition—with the ocularcentric attributes of the deity.

In conclusion, a summary might be helpful regarding the order of the two powers' appearances in the *Similitudes*' theophanies. As we remember in Dan 7, the first power in the form of the Ancient of Days appears first; only after this does the text recount the epiphany of the second power, represented by the Son of Man. A similar procession of two powers are also reflected in the *Book of the Similitudes*, where the theophanies of the first power (rendered there as the Head of Days) are routinely followed by the appearances of the Son of Man. Some of these accounts represent "visionary reports," where the order is often established through the successive descriptions of the "reporter." As we recall in *1 Enoch* 46:1, the seer reports the advent of the Head of Days before describing the second figure represented by the Son of Man.[72] In *1 Enoch* 71:9–14, the text again attests to the same order of processions—first, we have the

---

[70] Kvanvig, "The Son of Man in the Parables of Enoch," 181.
[71] Nickelsburg and VanderKam note that
> in v. 14a the MSS. differ as to who is speaking to Enoch. Instead of "and he" (*waweetu*) some MSS. read "and that angel" (*waweetu mal'ak*). This looks like an attempt either to identify the vague "he" or to keep the text from saying that the deity spoke directly to the seer. If "that angel" is original, the text is vague as to which angel is speaking to Enoch. However, if the author can depict God as actually approaching Enoch, there seems to be no reason why the Head of Days should not address him directly, although the third person reference to the Head of Days seems odd if the Head of Days is speaking.
> Nickelsburg and VanderKam, *1 Enoch 2*, 327–28.

[72] "And there I saw one who had a head of days, and his head (was) white like wool; and with him (there was) another, whose face had the appearance of a man, and his face (was) full of grace, like one of the holy angels." Knibb, *The Ethiopic Book of Enoch*, 2.131.

appearance of the Head of Days, and only after do we find the report about Enoch's transformation into the Son of Man.

Primary Adam Books

An important pseudepigraphical testimony relevant to our exploration of the two powers traditions is the story of Adam's exaltation and angelic veneration found in the Armenian, Georgian, and Latin versions of the *Primary Adam Books*.[73] Although the macroforms of these books are products of later Christian milieus, these Christian compositions undoubtedly contain earlier Adamic traditions. Our further study will demonstrate that the motif of the angelic veneration of the protoplast was well known to some authors within the Jewish literature of the Second Temple period, including *2 Enoch*.[74]

Chapter 13 of the Armenian, Georgian, and Latin versions of the *Primary Adam Books* describes the protoplast's creation. There is a curious addition to the protological account in Genesis regarding a motif concerned with Adam's face that is attested in the Georgian and Latin versions. For example, the Georgian version of the text recounts that God breathed a spirit onto the protoplast's face.[75] However, this tradition is not entirely novel. While in the Hebrew text of Gen 2:7 Adam's *panim* is not mentioned, in the Septuagint's rendering of that passage, the deity breathed the breath of life in Adam's *face*.[76] In the Latin *Vita* 13:2 the face motif appears again, this time conveying the novel tradition that the protoplast's countenance was made in God's image: "when God blew into you the breath of life and your countenance (*vultus*) and likeness were made in the image of God."[77] This passage appears to entertain a conceptual link between the protoplast's *panim* and the *tselem*, a connection that will play a paramount role in later two powers traditions.

The motif of the second power's *panim*, already discernible in the earliest accounts of Jewish dual theophanies such as Dan 7, will play a prominent role in later Metatron lore, where this particular second power is envisioned as the hypostatic face of God. The memory of the second power's identification with the *panim* will not be forgotten: it is present in *2 Enoch*, where Adam will be created in the face of God, as well as in the lore about Jacob's *iqonin*.

According to the *Primary Adam Books*, after the protoplast's creation the archangel Michael brought the human into the divine presence and forced him to bow down

---

[73] For the original texts and English translation of various versions of the *Primary Adam Books* see G. Anderson and M. Stone, *A Synopsis of the Books of Adam and Eve: Second Revised Edition* (EJL 17; Atlanta: Scholars, 1999).

[74] Crispin Fletcher-Louis in his recent study revisits some early evidence for the angelic veneration of Adam arguing for early Second Temple roots of such a motif. On this see C. Fletcher-Louis, *Jesus Monotheism, Vol. 1, Christological Origins: The Emerging Consensus and Beyond* (Eugene: Cascade Books, 2015), 262–63.

[75] Anderson and Stone, *A Synopsis of the Books of Adam and Eve*, 16E.

[76] LXX version of Gen 2:7 reads: "And God formed man, dust from the earth, and breathed into his face (εἰς τὸ πρόσωπον αὐτοῦ) a breath of life, and the man became a living being."

[77] Anderson and Stone, *A Synopsis of the Books of Adam and Eve*, 16–16E.

before God.[78] Adam's veneration of the deity implicitly indicates that God may be present in the account as the visible anthropomorphic manifestation. The description of the first power's form is conveyed in our account through several obscure references, which, besides the protoplast's act of veneration of the deity, also includes God's address after the ritual obeisance. In this address, as it appears in the Latin *Vita*, the deity tells Adam that his body was created in the likeness of the divine Form: "Behold, Adam, I have made you in our image and likeness."[79] In the Georgian version God's address is directed not to the protoplast but instead to the archangel Michael: "And God told Michael, 'I have created Adam according to (my) image and my divinity.'"[80]

The curious avoidance of the direct description of the deity, who prefers to express himself through addresses and utterances, demonstrates the aural proclivities of our account in which the deity is steadily withdrawn into the aural mode. The tendency toward God's invisibility may also be supported by Adam's function as an icon through which the angels can now worship the deity. As clarified by the text, all the angels are ordered to bow down to this human "icon."[81] A significant feature is that Michael, who summons all celestial citizens to the act of veneration, does not instruct them to venerate *Adam*, but instead commands them to bow down before *the image and likeness of God*. In the Georgian version his command takes the following form: "Bow down before the likeness and the image of the divinity."[82] The Latin version is similar: "Worship the image of the Lord God, just as the Lord God has commanded."[83] So, too, in the Armenian version, Adam's name is omitted and the newly created "second power" is portrayed as the divine manifestation: "Then Michael summoned all the angels, and God said to them, 'Come, bow down to god whom I made.'"[84]

The results of Michael's order to venerate the "icon" of the divinity are mixed. While some angels obey the command, others, including Satan, refuse. In the Latin version the tradition of God's image is reiterated when Michael personally invites Satan to "worship the image of God Jehovah."[85] In comparison with Michael's command, which

---

[78] The Latin version of the *Primary Adam Books* 13:2 reads: "When God blew into you the breath of life and your countenance and likeness were made in the image of God, Michael led you and made you worship in the sight of God." The Armenian version of the *Primary Adam Books* 13:2 reads: "When God breathed his spirit into you, you received the likeness of his image. Thereupon, Michael came and made you bow down before God." Anderson and Stone, *A Synopsis of the Books of Adam and Eve*, 16E.

[79] Anderson and Stone, *A Synopsis of the Books of Adam and Eve*, 16E.

[80] Anderson and Stone, *A Synopsis of the Books of Adam and Eve*, 16E.

[81] The Latin version of the *Primary Adam Books* 13:2–14:1 reads: "The Lord God then said: 'Behold, Adam, I have made you in our image and likeness.' Having gone forth Michael called all the angels saying: 'Worship the image of the Lord God, just as the Lord God has commanded.'" The Armenian version of the *Primary Adam Books* 13:2–14:1 reads: "God said to Michael, 'Behold I have made Adam in the likeness of my image.' Then Michael summoned all the angels, and God said to them, 'Come, bow down to god whom I made.'" Anderson and Stone, *A Synopsis of the Books of Adam and Eve*, 16E.

[82] Anderson and Stone, *A Synopsis of the Books of Adam and Eve*, 16E.

[83] Anderson and Stone, *A Synopsis of the Books of Adam and Eve*, 16E.

[84] Anderson and Stone, *A Synopsis of the Books of Adam and Eve*, 16E.

[85] "*adora imaginem dei Jehova.*" Anderson and Stone, *A Synopsis of the Books of Adam and Eve*, 16–16E. See also Latin *Vita* 15:2: "Worship the image of God. If you do not worship, the Lord God will grow angry with you." Anderson and Stone, *A Synopsis of the Books of Adam and Eve*, 17E.

does not invoke Adam's name but rather refers to him as the "image of God," Satan's refusal to worship now specifically mentions Adam's name, seeing him not as an icon but as a creature that is "younger" or "posterior" to the antagonist.[86] In Satan's refusal to venerate Adam one also finds a portentous theme of "opposition" to the second power. Yet, in the complementary two powers framework of the *Primary Adam Books*, such opposition is not intended to deconstruct the divine agent envisioned as God's image. Instead, it serves as a reaffirmation of his unique position.

In this respect it would not be an exaggeration to say that angelic veneration is integral to the construction of Adam's unique upper identity, apparently revealing the process of the protoplast's paradoxical deification.[87] Angelic veneration, therefore, shepherds the human protagonist into his new supra-angelic ontology, when he becomes an "icon" or "face" of the deity; the conditions often established both via angelic obeisance and the seers' own veneration of the deity. Here as in other two powers accounts, the identity of the second power is constructed through the concept of the divine Image. We will see similar conceptual developments in Enoch's and Jacob's traditions where the exaltation of these patriarchal figures will also be executed through the concept of the divine Image. The same initiatory device will manifest itself in early Christological currents where Jesus will be envisioned as the Image of the invisible God.

As mentioned previously, scholars of the two powers debates note that while in some accounts the two powers complement each other, in other accounts they oppose each other. Segal, for example, says that early accounts often exhibit complementary relationships between two powers while later ones are often filled with polemical overtones. An example of this shift occurs in the evolution of the aforementioned story of Adam's elevation and veneration by angels. While in early pseudepigraphical accounts, God favors the protoplast's exaltation and veneration, in later rabbinic accounts he opposes such obeisance by the celestial citizens.[88]

---

[86] The Latin version of the *Primary Adam Books* 14:2–15:1 reads:

> Michael himself worshipped first then he called me and said: "Worship the image of God Jehovah." I answered: "I do not have it within me to worship Adam." When Michael compelled me to worship, I said to him: "Why do you compel me? I will not worship him who is lower and later than me. I am prior to that creature. Before he was made, I had already been made. He ought to worship me." Hearing this, other angels who were under me were unwilling to worship him.

The Armenian version of the *Primary Adam Books* 14:2–15:1 reads:

> Michael bowed first. He called me and said "You too, bow down to Adam." I said, "Go away, Michael! I shall not bow [down] to him who is posterior to me, for I am former. Why is it proper [for me] to bow down to him?" The other angels, too, who were with me, heard this, and my words seemed pleasing to them and they did not prostrate themselves to you, Adam.

Anderson and Stone, *A Synopsis of the Books of Adam and Eve*, 16E–17E.

[87] Thus, the deification of Adam is especially evident in the Armenian *PAB* 14:1: "Then Michael summoned all the angels, and God said to them, 'Come, bow down *to god* whom I made.'" Anderson and Stone, *A Synopsis of the Books of Adam and Eve*, 16E.

[88] Reflecting on these rabbinic renderings of the angelic veneration story, Gary Anderson notes that

> rabbis were familiar with such a motif and took an active role in subverting it. One can see evidence of this subversive energy in the numerous rabbinic stories that polemicize against any act of veneration toward Adam. A particularly good example of this is the

An important feature of the aforementioned accounts is that in the *Primary Adam Books* the story of Adam's exaltation and angelic veneration comes from the mouth of Satan. It is he who conveys to Adam the account of his own demotion for refusing to venerate the newly created image of God. Thus, in the Latin *Vita* 12:1 the adversary exclaims that he was expelled and alienated from his glory, which he had in heaven in the midst of the angels.[89] Notably, in both the Latin and Armenian versions Satan's former condition is described as a "dwelling of light," where he was endowed with "glory."[90] In the Latin and the Georgian version of 13:2, his demotion is described as a casting out from the face of God.[91] Satan also appears to be associated with the attribute of the divine throne. In the Armenian version of 12:1, he utters the following enigmatic statement: "I was alienated from the throne of the Cherubim who, having spread out a shelter, used to enclose me." The antagonist's initial endowment with attributes of glory and the divine seat suggests that he was a former favorite of the deity before Adam's creation and he himself may be envisioned in our text as a demoted "second power." Christian traditions reflected in the synoptic accounts of Jesus' temptation in the wilderness may indicate an interaction between the former, demoted, second power in the form of Satan and the new holder of this office represented by Jesus. These developments will be explored more fully a bit later.

For now, suffice it to say that in the *Primary Adam Books* one witnesses a unique process of the "rotation" of the second powers when the former vice-regent became demoted and replaced by the new favorite of the deity. Although in the complementary framework of the *Primary Adam Books* it is Satan who opposes the veneration of God's image, within the later non-complementary two powers developments this function of opposition is often transferred to the deity himself. In these accounts, it is God who disapproves of the veneration of the newly created protoplast and shows the angelic hosts that his beloved creature does not deserve the obeisance reserved solely for their Creator. This demonstrates that two motifs, the angelic veneration and the angelic opposition, stem from a single conceptual root already present in early Jewish accounts, serving as important devices for the construction and deconstruction of the second power in Jewish lore.

---

story found in *Gen. Rab.* 8.10 in which the angels mistake Adam for God and almost shout "Holy" before him. God averts this error by casting a deep sleep on Adam so that his mortal nature would be evident. This example is then compared by R. Hoshaya to a parable in which a king and his governor go forth in a chariot together. The subjects of the king wish to acclaim the king as Dominus. But the king, anxious about his citizens mistaking the governor for him, quickly pushes the governor from the chariot. Hence there was no ambiguity about just who was to be proclaimed lord.

G. Anderson, "The Exaltation of Adam and the Fall of Satan," in: *Literature on Adam and Eve: Collected Essays* (ed. G. Anderson, M. Stone, and J. Tromp; SVTP 15; Brill: Leiden, 2000), 92.

[89] Anderson and Stone, *Synopsis*, 15–15E.
[90] Anderson and Stone, *Synopsis*, 18E.
[91] See Latin *Vita* 13:2: "ego proiectus sum a facie dei...." Anderson and Stone, *Synopsis*, 16.

The *Exagoge* of Ezekiel the Tragedian

Exagoge 67–90 of Ezekiel the Tragedian contains another early account of the two powers theophany in which both the deity and the second power (here in the form of Moses) share ocularcentric attributes.[92] Preserved in fragmentary form by several ancient sources,[93] the text reads:

> Moses: I had a vision of a great throne on the top of Mount Sinai and it reached till the folds of heaven. A noble man was sitting on it, with a crown and a large scepter in his left hand. He beckoned to me with his right hand, so I approached and stood before the throne. He gave me the scepter and instructed me to sit on the great throne. Then he gave me a royal crown and got up from the throne. I beheld the whole earth all around and saw beneath the earth and above the heavens. A multitude of stars fell before my knees and I counted them all. They paraded past me like a battalion of men. Then I awoke from my sleep in fear.
>
> Raguel: My friend, this is a good sign from God. May I live to see the day when these things are fulfilled. You will establish a great throne, become a judge and leader of men. As for your vision of the whole earth, the world below and that above the heavens—this signifies that you will see what is, what has been and what shall be.[94]

Given its quotation by Alexander Polyhistor (ca. 80–40 BCE), this Mosaic account has been taken as a witness to traditions of the second century BCE.[95] The text exhibits a tendency to adapt some Enochic motifs and themes into the framework of the Mosaic tradition.[96]

---

[92] Scholars have suggested that Moses may be conceptualized in the *Exagoge* as the second power. Reflecting on Moses' endowment with the attributes of the throne, diadem, and scepter, Wayne Meeks argues that "the meaning of this divine investiture is probably no different from the more common apocalyptic imagery in which the ascended hero is seated at God's left or right or shares God's throne, that is, Moses becomes God's vice-regent." W. A. Meeks, *The Prophet-King: Moses Traditions and the Johannine Christology* (NovTSup 14; Leiden: Brill, 1967), 148. Pieter van der Horst compares Moses' exaltation in the *Exagoge* with Enoch's metamorphosis into Metatron, pointing out that "the similarities are clearly striking. But there is also a striking difference. In Moses' vision, there is only one throne, God's. And Moses is requested to be seated on it, not at God's side, but all alone. God leaves his throne. This scene is unique in early Jewish literature and certainly implies a deification of Moses." P. van der Horst, "Moses' Throne Vision in Ezekiel the Dramatist," *JJS* 34 (1983): 21–29 at 25.

[93] The Greek text of the passage was published in several editions, including A.-M. Denis, *Fragmenta pseudepigraphorum quae supersunt Graeca* (PVTG 3; Leiden: Brill, 1970), 210; B. Snell, *Tragicorum Graecorum fragmenta I* (Göttingen: Vandenhoeck & Ruprecht, 1971), 288–301; H. Jacobson, *The Exagoge of Ezekiel* (Cambridge: Cambridge University Press, 1983), 54; C. R. Holladay, *Fragments from Hellenistic Jewish Authors* (3 vols.; SBLTT 30; Pseudepigrapha Series 12; Atlanta: Scholars, 1989), 2.362–66.

[94] Jacobson, *The Exagoge of Ezekiel*, 54–55.

[95] Meeks, *The Prophet-King*, 149. See also Holladay, *Fragments*, 2.308–12.

[96] On the Enochic motifs in the *Exagoge*, see van der Horst, "Moses' Throne Vision in Ezekiel the Dramatist," 21–29; A. A. Orlov, *The Enoch-Metatron Tradition* (TSAJ 107; Tübingen: Mohr Siebeck, 2005), 262–68; K. Ruffatto, "Polemics with Enochic Traditions in the *Exagoge* of Ezekiel the

With respect to the present study, the most salient feature of the account is the transfer of distinctive celestial attributes, including the attribute of the divine seat, to the second power. Notably, the first power appears to execute the transferal when he orders the new guardian to take the seat he previously occupied. The enthroned celestial figure then vacates his heavenly seat and hands his royal attributes to the son of Amram. This extra-biblical Mosaic account therefore provides a unique opportunity to behold the transferal of the attributes from the first power to the second. While in other accounts we are often privy only to the final outcome of such transferals, here in the *Exagoge* we are able to witness the entire process.

Another portentous detail of the initiatory encounter is the motif of the deity's hand—a prominent theme in other early Jewish two powers theophanies, including the ones attested in *2 Enoch* and in later Jacobian accounts, where human adepts are also embraced by the deity in heaven. Recall how the text of the *Exagoge* relates that during the prophet's vision of the *Kavod*, a noble man sitting on the throne beckoned him with his right hand (δεξιᾷ δέ μοι ἔνευσε).[97] Such close contact between the deity and the second power is found only within two powers accounts where both the deity and the second power are envisioned as anthropomorphic beings.

In *2 Enoch* 39, another pivotal two powers in heaven theophany, the motif of the deity's right hand appears again. The hand there is described as having gigantic size and filling heaven.[98] Similar to the *Exagoge*, the motif of God's hand fulfills several functions. While certainly reaffirming the hierarchical relationships between the respective powers it also serves as an important initiatory device in which the deity invites the second power into the unique realm of his existence.

As in Daniel 7 and the *Similitudes*, in the *Exagoge* the second power receives the attribute of the celestial seat. Some scholars also establish a connection between Moses' acquisition of the divine seat in the *Exagoge* and the enthronement of the Son of Man in Daniel and the *Similitudes*. Analyzing these similarities, Howard Jacobson points out that in "Daniel 7:9ff the divine being sits on his throne in great splendor and then 'one like a man comes with the clouds of heaven.' Like Moses in Ezekiel, the man approaches the throne and is given sovereignty, glory and kingly power."[99] Christopher Rowland and Christopher Morray-Jones draw attention to another set of parallels, this time with the Son of Man traditions found in the *Book of the Similitudes*, noting that "in Ezekiel the Tragedian God places Moses on a throne with a crown on his head and a sceptre in his hand. In the *Similitudes of Enoch* the Son of Man or Elect One sits on the throne of glory (e.g. *1 Enoch* 69:29). Elsewhere in the text the throne

---

Tragedian," *JSP* 15 (2006): 195–210; idem, "Raguel as Interpreter of Moses' Throne Vision: The Transcendent Identity of Raguel in the Exagoge of Ezekiel the Tragedian," *JSP* 17 (2008): 121–39.

[97] Jacobson, *The Exagoge of Ezekiel*, 54.

[98] *2 Enoch* 39:5: "But you, my children, see the right hand of one who helps you, a human being created identical to yourself, but I have seen the right hand of the Lord, helping me and filling heaven." F. Andersen, "2 (Slavonic Apocalypse of) Enoch," in: *The Old Testament Pseudepigrapha* (ed. J. H. Charlesworth; 2 vols.; New York: Doubleday, 1983–1985), 1.162.

[99] Jacobson, *The Exagoge of Ezekiel*, 91.

is occupied by God."[100] Larry Hurtado also sees connections with the *Similitudes*; he argues that

> the seating of Moses on a divinely appointed throne is paralleled in the description of the "Chosen One" of *1 Enoch*, who is to be seated similarly in the eschatological judgment (e.g., 45:3; 51:3; 55:4; 61:8). The cosmic insight given to Moses (lines 77–78, "the whole earth . . . beneath the earth and above the heavens") is similar to the descriptions of the revelation of heavenly secrets given to Enoch (e.g., *Jub.* 4:21; *1 Enoch* 14–36; 72–82). This is a further indication that the vision reflects a view of Moses as divinely chosen and equipped to take a prominent role in God's rule of the creation.[101]

The motif of God vacating the throne and transferring occupancy to another has long puzzled scholars. Some have suggested that Moses' endowment with the heavenly seat signifies the prophet's deification.[102] Pieter van der Horst has proposed that in the *Exagoge* Moses becomes "an anthropomorphic hypostasis of God himself."[103] Kristine Ruffatto offers a similar argument, noting that "Moses does not merely ascend and have a vision of God's throne: God bids Moses to sit on his divine throne. Moses is given God's own scepter and crown, God's insignia. Moses shares God's throne: he is divinized. Moses thus not only sees God's throne, as did Enoch: he rules from God's own throne."[104]

Other scholars are less enthusiastic in supporting the view of Moses' deification, while accepting the assignment of divine attributes to the son of Amram could hint at his role as a divine agent, or in the nomenclature of this study, the "second power." In this vein, Hurtado argues that "the *Exagoge* of Ezekiel can be taken as another indication of a pre-Christian Jewish presentation of Moses in terms of divine agency. Whether the enthroned figure in the vision is God or a heavenly figure, such as a principal angel, representing God, in either case Moses is given a divinely appointed position as ruler, together with the appropriate symbols of such status, the scepter and the crown."[105] For Hurtado, then, "the *Exagoge* is at least indirect evidence of a tradition that Moses was viewed as God's chief representative in heaven."[106]

---

[100] C. Rowland and C. R. A. Morray-Jones, *The Mystery of God: Early Jewish Mysticism and the New Testament* (CRINT 12; Leiden: Brill, 2009), 70.

[101] Hurtado, *One God, One Lord*, 59.

[102] On Moses' exaltation in the *Exagoge*, see J. J. Collins, *The Scepter and the Star: The Messiahs of the Dead Sea Scrolls and Other Ancient Literature* (New York: Doubleday, 1995), 144–46; Meeks, *The Prophet-King*, 147–50; idem, "Moses as God and King," in: *Religions in Antiquity: FS Erwin Ramsdall Goodenough* (ed. J. Neusner; SHR 14; Leiden: Brill, 1968), 354–71 at 358–59; van der Horst, "Moses' Throne Vision in Ezekiel the Dramatist," 21–29; idem, "Some Notes on the Exagoge of Ezekiel," *Mnemosyne* 37 (1984): 354–75.

[103] van der Horst. "Some Notes on the *Exagoge*," 364.

[104] Ruffatto, "Polemics with Enochic Traditions," 204.

[105] Hurtado, *One God, One Lord*, 59.

[106] Hurtado, *One God, One Lord*, 59.

I have previously argued that Moses' enthronement in the *Exagoge* could be interpreted via the heavenly counterpart imagery. It is particularly relevant that in many early Jewish accounts the second powers are conceptualized as the *doppelgängers* of human seers. This motif is present in the *Book of the Similitudes* as well as in *2 Enoch* and the *Ladder of Jacob*. Furthermore, it is clear that in the *Exagoge*, as in the previously explored accounts of the protoplast's elevation from the *Primary Adam Books*, the reader appears to witness the initiatory ritual of the second power's endowment, which in the Adamic story coincides with the angelic veneration. Such angelic veneration is most likely also present in the *Exagoge*.[107] As one recalls, the account portrays the "multitude of stars" falling on their knees before Moses.[108] Considering the Enochic influences on the *Exagoge*, where the stars often designate angelic beings,[109] the multitude of stars kneeling before the seer may be a reference to angelic veneration. Some scholars, therefore, consider it possible that the kneeling stars represent angelic hosts. Thus, with respect to the obeisance of the stars, Larry Hurtado suggests that "they may represent the acceptance by the heavenly hosts of Moses' appointed place as God's chief agent. Stars are a familiar symbol for angelic beings in Jewish tradition (e.g., Job 38:7) and are linked with divine beings in other religious traditions as well."[110]

---

[107] On the possibility of angelic veneration of Moses in the *Exagoge* see S. N. Bunta, *Moses, Adam and the Glory of the Lord of the Lord in Ezekiel the Tragedian: On the Roots of a Merkabah Text* (PhD diss.; Marquette University, 2005), 167–83. Bunta argues for four similarities between the portrayal of Moses in the *Exagoge* and traditions about the angelic veneration of Adam: (1) In both traditions the human heroes are appropriately venerated by angels; (2) In both traditions the veneration reflects the human's attainment of a privileged status within the divine entourage; (3) Both traditions reflect an ironic polemic against angels; (4) Within this imagery, both traditions construct a complex dialectic of identity that emphasizes the dichotomous condition of humanity. On one hand, humanity is reminded of its earthliness, its mortal substance, and, on the other hand, the body's divine likeness deserves angelic veneration. Bunta, *Moses, Adam and the Glory of the Lord*, 183.

[108] Jacobson, *The Exagoge of Ezekiel*, 54–55.

[109] John Collins notes that "the stars had long been identified with the angelic host in Israelite tradition. . . . Ultimately this tradition can be traced back to Canaanite mythology where the stars appear as members of the divine council in the Ugaritic texts." J. J. Collins, *The Apocalyptic Vision of the Book of Daniel* (Harvard Semitic Monographs 16; Missoula: Scholars, 1977), 136. See for example, Judg 5:20: "The stars fought from heaven, from their courses they fought against Sisera"; Job 38:7: "When the morning stars sang together and all the heavenly beings shouted for joy?"; Dan 8:10: "It grew as high as the host of heaven. It threw down to the earth some of the host and some of the stars, and trampled on them"; *1 Enoch* 86:3–4:

> And again I saw in the vision and looked at heaven, and behold, I saw many stars, how they came down and were thrown down from heaven to that first star, and amongst those heifers and bulls; they were with them, pasturing amongst them. And I looked at them and saw, and behold, all of them let out their private parts like horses and began to mount the cows of the bulls, and they all became pregnant and bore elephants and camels and asses.
> Knibb, *The Ethiopic Book of Enoch*, 2.197;

> *1 Enoch* 88:1: "And I saw one of those four who had come out first, how he took hold of that first star which had fallen from heaven, and bound it by its hands and its feet, and threw it into an abyss; and that abyss was narrow, and deep, and horrible, and dark."
> Knibb, *The Ethiopic Book of Enoch*, 2.198;

> *1 Enoch* 90:24: "And the judgment was held first on the stars, and they were judged and found guilty; and they went to the place of damnation, and were thrown into a deep (place), full of fire, burning and full of pillars of fire."
> Knibb, *The Ethiopic Book of Enoch*, 2.215.

[110] Hurtado, *One God, One Lord*, 59.

If this motif is present in our text, it is important to acknowledge that here, as in other two powers accounts where angelic veneration takes place, Moses is implicitly envisioned as the personification of the divine image.[111] In the later targumic accounts Moses' shining face was often interpreted as his *iqonin*. These conceptual currents will be explored later in our study.

2 Enoch

In another early Jewish apocalypse, *2 Enoch*, the two powers, the deity and his newly appointed vice-regent (i.e., the transformed seventh antediluvian patriarch) again appear as two distinctively ocularcentric manifestations. The storyline of this text, probably written before the destruction of the Second Jerusalem Temple,[112] concerns Enoch's heavenly journey to the throne of God. There the hero of faith undergoes a luminous transformation into a celestial being, a being that strikingly shares a conglomeration of divine characteristics with the deity.

The first important nexus of theophanic traditions relevant to our study occurs in chapters 21–22, which depict Enoch's transformation and his endowment into the office of a celestial power. In this cryptic portrayal, one finds several motifs reminiscent of Adam's and Moses' initiations in the previously explored two powers accounts. According to the text, angels bring Enoch to the edge of the seventh heaven. At God's command, the archangel Gabriel invites the seer to stand perpetually in front of the deity. When Enoch agrees, he is taken to the deity's Face and does obeisance to God. God then repeats the invitation to Enoch to stand before him forever. Following this invitation, the archangel Michael brings the patriarch before God's Face. The deity then

---

[111] It is possible that Moses' coronation in the *Exagoge* represents a reference to his endowment with the divine image. Wayne Meeks points out that in some Jewish and Samaritan traditions Moses' crown was envisioned as the divine image. He notes that Moses'

> crown of light was nothing less than the visual symbol for the image of God. Jacob Jervell, moreover, has shown that in Jewish Adam-speculation the image of God was typically regarded as "gerade auf dem Antlitz eingepraßt." Jervell argues that this conception of the *imago* was especially connected with the notion that Adam had been God's vice-regent, the first "king of the world." When the *imago* is identified with Moses' divine crown of light, it is quite clear that the same kind of connection is implied. The similarity is not accidental, for further examination of the enthronement traditions about Moses shows that these stories link Moses very closely with Adam.
>
> Meeks, "Moses as God and King," 363.

On this tradition, also see M. Smith, "The Image of God: Notes on the Hellenisation of Judaism with Especial Reference to Goodenough's Work on Jewish Symbols," *BJRL* 40 (1958): 473–512; J. Jervell, *Imago Dei: Gen 1, 26f. im Spätjudentum, in der Gnosis und in den paulinischen Briefen* (FRLANT 76; Göttingen: Vandenhoeck & Ruprecht, 1960), 45.

[112] On the date of *2 Enoch*, see R. H. Charles, and W. R. Morfill, *The Book of the Secrets of Enoch* (Oxford: Clarendon Press, 1896), xxvi; R. H. Charles and N. Forbes, "The Book of the Secrets of Enoch," in: *The Apocrypha and Pseudepigrapha of the Old Testament* (ed. R. H. Charles; 2 vols.; Oxford: Clarendon Press, 1913), 2.429; J. T. Milik, *The Books of Enoch* (Oxford: Clarendon Press, 1976), 114; C. Böttrich, *Das slavische Henochbuch* (JSHRZ 5; Gütersloh: Gütersloher Verlaghaus, 1995), 813; Orlov, *The Enoch-Metatron Tradition*, 323–28; idem, "The Sacerdotal Traditions of 2 Enoch and the Date of the Text," in: *New Perspectives on 2 Enoch: No Longer Slavonic Only* (ed. A. A. Orlov, G. Boccaccini, and J. Zurawski; SJS 4; Leiden: Brill, 2012), 103–16.

summons his angels with a resounding call: "Let Enoch join in and stand in front of my face forever!" In response to this address, the Lord's glorious ones do obeisance to Enoch saying, "Let Enoch yield in accordance with your word, O Lord!"[113]

Michael Stone suggests that this story recalls the account of Adam's elevation and veneration by angels found in the Armenian, Georgian, and Latin versions of the *Primary Adam Books*.[114] Along with the motifs of Adam's elevation and veneration, the author of *2 Enoch* appears to be aware of the motif of angelic disobedience and refusal to venerate the first human. In support, Stone draws the reader's attention to the phrase "sounding them out," found in *2 Enoch* 22:6, which another translator of the Slavonic text rendered as "making a trial of them."[115] It may be that the expression "sounding them out" or "making a trial of them" implies that the obedience of the angels is being tested.[116]

Stone proposes that the order of events in *2 Enoch* follows the same progression of the *Primary Adam Books*, since both sources are familiar with the three steps of Adam's initiation:[117]

I. *Primary Adam Books*: Adam is created and placed in heaven.
   2 Enoch: Enoch is brought to heaven.
II. *Primary Adam Books*: The archangel Michael brings Adam before God's face. Adam does obeisance to God.
   2 Enoch: The archangel Michael brings Enoch before the Lord's Face. Enoch does obeisance to the Lord.
III. *Primary Adam Books*: God commands the angels to bow down. Some of the angels do obeisance. Satan and his angels disobey.
   2 Enoch: "The rebellion in the Adam events is assumed. God tests whether this time the angels will obey. The angels are said to bow down and accept God's command."[118]

Stone concludes that the author of *2 Enoch* 21–22 was cognizant of the traditions resembling[119] those found in the Armenian, Georgian, and Latin versions of the

---

[113] Andersen, "2 Enoch," 1.138.

[114] The Adamic story of the angelic veneration of Adam and Satan's disobedience is attested in many Jewish, Christian, and Muslim materials. See, for example, the Slavonic version of *3 Baruch* 4; *Gos. Bart.* 4; Coptic *Enthronement of Michael*, *Cave of Treasures* 2:10–24; Qur'an 2:31–39; 7:11–18; 15:31–48; 17:61–65; 18:50; 20:116–23; 38:71–85.

[115] Charles and Morfill, *The Book of the Secrets of Enoch*, 28.

[116] M. E. Stone, "The Fall of Satan and Adam's Penance: Three Notes on the *Books of Adam and Eve*," in: *Literature on Adam and Eve: Collected Essays* (ed. G. Anderson, M. Stone, and J. Tromp; SVTP 15; Leiden: Brill, 2000), 43–56 at 47.

[117] Stone, "The Fall of Satan and Adam's Penance: Three Notes on the *Books of Adam and Eve*," 48.

[118] Stone, "The Fall of Satan and Adam's Penance: Three Notes on the *Books of Adam and Eve*," 48.

[119] Stone's argument was later supported and developed by Gary Anderson. Anderson observes that "one cannot imagine that the tradition in the Enoch materials was created independently from the tradition found in the *Vita*." Anderson, "The Exaltation of Adam and the Fall of Satan," 101.

Primary Adam Books.[120] He emphasizes that these traditions did not enter *2 Enoch* from the Slavonic *Life of Adam and Eve*, because this form of tradition does not occur in the Slavonic recension of the *Primary Adam Books*.[121]

The presence of the angelic veneration motif is important for our study since here, like in the Adamic lore (and possibly in the *Exagoge*), it serves as a portentous indicator that allows for the singling out of these particular accounts from the bulk of other biblical and extra-biblical Jewish visions, where the translated human characters are not regarded as the "second powers."

The next pivotal articulation of the two powers traditions is situated in *2 Enoch* 39. Here the anthropomorphic extents of both powers are rendered through the imagery of the *Panim*. Thus, *2 Enoch* 39:3–6 depicts the patriarch upon his brief return to earth, revealing to his children his earlier dramatic encounter with the divine Face. The shorter recension contains the following:

> You, my children, you see my face, a human being created just like yourselves; I am one who has seen the face of the Lord, like iron made burning hot by a fire, emitting sparks. For you gaze into my eyes, a human being created just like yourselves; but I have gazed into the eyes of the Lord, like the rays of the shining sun and terrifying the eyes of a human being. You, my children, you see my right hand beckoning you, a human being created identical to yourselves; but I have seen the right hand of the Lord, beckoning me, who fills heaven. You see the extent of my body, the same as your own; but I have seen the extent of the Lord, without measure and without analogy, who has no end.[122]

This passage portrays the deity's Form with massive dimensions: "without measure and without analogy." While the goal is to argue that God's extent transcends any analogy, the account of Enoch's vision of the deity seems to represent a set of paradoxical analogies in which the descriptions of the patriarch's face and body are compared to the divine Face and Body. This element of the Enochic account also hints at the transferal of the deity's features and the attributes of the divine Form that resemble the second power's extent. Several experts of Jewish apocalyptic and mystical lore, including Gershom Scholem, have argued that the text appears to suggest such a transferal as Enoch becomes envisioned as the measurement of the divine body or its *Shiʿur Qomah*.[123]

For the first time in the Enochic tradition, through the analogical descriptions introduced in chapter 39, a significant bond is established between the deity's form and

---

[120] Stone, "The Fall of Satan and Adam's Penance: Three Notes on the *Books of Adam and Eve*," 48.

[121] Stone, "The Fall of Satan and Adam's Penance: Three Notes on the *Books of Adam and Eve*," 48.

[122] Andersen, "2 Enoch," 1.163.

[123] In his commentary on the text, Scholem draws the reader's attention to the expression "the extent of my stature." He notes that earlier Abraham Kahana in his Hebrew translation of *2 Enoch* rendered this expression as *shiʿur qomati*. Scholem further suggests that despite the late date of the known rabbinic *Shiʿur Qomah* materials, the *Shiʿur Qomah* terminology might be already evident in the account drawn from *2 Enoch* 39, where Enoch describes God's gigantic limbs. G. Scholem, *On the Mystical Shape of the Godhead* (New York: Schocken, 1976), 29.

Enoch's transformed body. This bond will later occupy a prominent role in rabbinic and Hekhalot accounts about the paradigmatic second power, the supreme angel Metatron.

Our study has already demonstrated that the two powers often share corporeal attributes in such a way that the second power becomes, or appears to be, a visible manifestation of the deity. In *2 Enoch* it seems that the translated human has become a visible representation or an icon of the deity, which, in a way that is similar to the divine *Kavod*, is able to glorify its beholders. In the later chapters of the Slavonic apocalypse, the elders of the earth will approach the transformed Enoch in order to be glorified before the patriarch's "face." This motif is clearly reminiscent of the Mosaic traditions.

This brings us to another important conceptual trajectory found in *2 Enoch* 39 regarding the presence of distinctive Mosaic allusions, inclusive of the motifs concerning the divine Face and the face of the visionary. The authors of the Slavonic apocalypse employ these familiar themes, associated with the son of Amram's story, in order to build up the exalted identity of their own celestial "power." These "Mosaic" strategies in the construction of a second power will also play a prominent role in early Christian literature especially within the transfiguration account, where many "Mosaic" features are bestowed upon Jesus.

Within *2 Enoch*'s portrayals of the two powers, one can easily recognize the familiar theophanic imagery appropriated from the Exodus accounts.[124] In *2 Enoch* 39, as in Exod 33, the Face is closely associated with the divine extent. The association between the divine Face and the divine Form in *2 Enoch* 39:3–6 alludes to the biblical tradition found in Exod 33:18–23 where the divine *Panim* is mentioned in connection with the glorious divine form, God's *Kavod*.

These terminological correspondences, which are related to the concept of the divine image, are crucial in constructing the heavenly identities of various second powers. Similarly in *2 Enoch*, the symbolism of the divine image, or, more precisely, its conceptual correlative in the form of the deity's *Panim*, becomes a pivotal conduit in the creation of the patriarch's upper identity. Scholars have noted that the divine face symbolism in *2 Enoch* is closely intertwined with the notion of the divine image.[125] Although the Slavonic apocalypse does not explicitly mention the divine image in the description of the creation of Enoch's heavenly identity, it constantly refers to another pivotal celestial entity, the divine Face. This entity plays a paramount role in the process of the seer's initiation into the second power's role. It is also noteworthy that the angelic veneration of the hero takes place in immediate proximity to the divine Face, the entity that becomes a crucial pattern for the patriarch's metamorphosis.

In the light of these connections, it is possible that in *2 Enoch*, as in some later rabbinic and Hekhalot accounts,[126] the divine *Panim* performs the role of the divine

---

[124] See Exod 19:9; Exod 19:16–18; Exod 34:5.

[125] Andersen, "2 Enoch," 1.171; N. Deutsch, *The Gnostic Imagination: Gnosticism, Mandaeism, and Merkabah Mysticism* (Leiden: Brill, 1995), 102.

[126] The interchangeability between the notions of *tselem* and *panim* is observable, for example, in later Jewish lore about Jacob's image engraved on the divine throne. Several texts replace the notion of Jacob's *tselem* with the imagery of his *panim*. For example, *Hekhalot Rabbati* (*Synopse* §164):

Tselem, since the divine Countenance represents the cause and prototype after which Enoch's new celestial identity was formed. The new creation after the divine Visage signifies the return to the prelapsarian condition of Adam, who, surprisingly, was also modeled after the face of God, according to the Slavonic apocalypse. Support for this view can be found in *2 Enoch* 44:1, where one learns that the protoplast was also created after the *Panim* of God. The text reads: "the Lord with his own two hands created humankind; in a facsimile of his own face, both small and great, the Lord created [them]."[127] Strikingly, *2 Enoch* departs here from the canonical reading attested in Gen 1:26–27, where Adam was created not after the face of God, but after his image (*tselem*).[128] Francis Andersen observes that *2 Enoch*'s "idea is remarkable from any point of view.... This is not the original meaning of *tselem*.... The text uses *podobie lica* [in the likeness of the face], not *obrazu* or *videnije*, the usual terms for 'image.'"[129]

> And testify to them. What testimony? You see Me—what I do to the visage of the face of Jacob your father which is engraved for Me upon the throne of My glory. For in the hour that you say before Men "Holy," I kneel on it and embrace it and kiss it and hug it and My hands are on its arms three times, corresponding to the three times that you say before Me, "Holy," according to the word that is said, Holy, holy, holy (Isa 6:3).
> J. R. Davila, *Hekhalot Literature in Translation: Major Texts of Merkavah Mysticism* (SJJTP 20; Leiden: Brill, 2013), 86; P. Schäfer, with M. Schlüter and H. G. von Mutius, *Synopse zur Hekhaloth-Literatur* (TSAJ 2; Tübingen: Mohr Siebeck, 1981), 72.

Here, the deity embraces and kisses Jacob's heavenly identity engraved on his Throne. Yet, the striking difference here in comparison with other rabbinic accounts is that now it is not the image, but instead Jacob's face, or more precisely a cast of the patriarch's face, that is said to be engraved on the throne. It appears that this shift is not merely a slip of a Hekhalot writer's pen but a deliberate conceptual turn, since it is also attested in other rabbinic materials. For example, a testimony is found in *Pirke de Rabbi Eliezer* 35, which also attempts to replace the *tselem* imagery with the symbolism of Jacob's *panim*, by arguing that the angels went to see the face of the patriarch and that his heavenly countenance was reminiscent of a visage of one of the Living Creatures of the divine throne:

> Rabbi Levi said: In that night the Holy One, blessed be He, showed him all the signs. He showed him a ladder standing from the earth to the heaven, as it is said, "And he dreamed, and behold a ladder set up on the earth, and the top of it reached to heaven" (Gen 28:12). And the ministering angels were ascending and descending thereon, and they beheld the face of Jacob, and they said: This is the face—like the face of the *Chayyah*, which is on the Throne of Glory. Such (angels) who were (on earth) below were ascending to see the face of Jacob among the faces of the *Chayyah*, (for it was) like the face of the *Chayyah*, which is on the Throne of Glory.
> *Pirke de Rabbi Eliezer* (tr. G. Friedländer; New York: Hermon Press, 1965), 265.

Such peculiar terminological exchanges between *tselem* and *panim* are significant for our study.

[127] Andersen, "2 Enoch," 1.170.

[128] In relation to this passage, Nathaniel Deutsch says

> the key to understanding this passage has been provided by F. I. Andersen, who notes in his edition of *2 Enoch*, that its form imitates that of Gen 1:27, which states that "God created man in his image, in the image of God he created him, male and female he created them." Instead of the "image" of God, in *2 Enoch* we find God's "face," and in place of "male and female He created them," we read "small and great the Lord created." In the light of the Jewish, Gnostic, and Mandaean traditions, which treated the image of God in Gen 1:27 hypostatically, often identifying it with the Cosmic Adam, the substitution of the divine image in Gen 1:27 with the divine face is early evidence that God's face was perceived hypostatically, as well.
> Deutsch, *Gnostic Imagination*, 102.

[129] Andersen, "2 Enoch," 1.171, note b. As previously indicated, in other Jewish materials the concept of the divine image is often rendered through the symbolism of the divine face. See M. Idel,

However, it is clear that this reading did not arise in the Slavonic environment but belonged to the original argument of *2 Enoch*, where the creation of the luminous first human after the deity's Face corresponded to a similar angelic creation of the seventh antediluvian patriarch.

In the light of these terminological parallels it is possible that the second power tradition attested in *2 Enoch* is also associated with the *tselem* concept. As we will learn later in our study, this rendering of *tselem* imagery through the formulae of the divine Countenance, or *Panim*, will continue to exercise its formative influence in later pseudepigraphical and rabbinic accounts about Jacob's heavenly identity.

Another important motif that plays a significant role in other early Jewish two powers traditions is the theme of Enoch's possession of the seat in heaven. Although in some two powers accounts, as in Dan 7, possession of such an attribute is rendered only implicitly—through a reference to installations of thrones—the Slavonic apocalypse recounts Enoch's seating in heaven with great detail. In chapters 23 and 24, Enoch is twice offered a seat, first by the angel Vrevoil (Uriel) in relation to the patriarch's scribal role, and second by God himself, this time in relation to his duties as the second power. The second invitation is especially momentous, as the deity offers Enoch a special place next to him, "closer than that of Gabriel," in order to share with him the information that remains hidden even from the angels. The longer recension of *2 Enoch* 22:10–24:4 reads:

> And I looked at myself, and I had become like one of his glorious ones, and there was no observable difference. And the Lord summoned one of the archangels, Vrevoil by name, who was swifter in wisdom than the other archangels, and who records all the Lord's deeds. And the Lord said to Vrevoil, "Bring out the books from my storehouses, and fetch a pen for speed-writing, and give it to Enoch and read him the books." . . . And he [Vrevoil] was telling me the things of heaven and earth. . . . And Vrevoil instructed me for 30 days and 30 nights, and his mouth never stopped speaking. . . . And [then] . . . Vrevoil said to me, "These things, whatever I have taught you . . . you sit down and write". . . . And I sat down for a second period of 30 days and 30 nights, and I wrote everything accurately. And I wrote 366 books. . . . And the Lord called me; and he said to me, "Enoch, sit to the left of me with Gabriel." And I did obeisance to the Lord. And the Lord spoke to me: "Enoch [Beloved], whatever you see and whatever things are standing still or moving about were brought to perfection by me. And I myself will explain it to you. Before anything existed at all, from the very beginning, whatever exists I created from the non-existent, and from the invisible the visible. [Listen, Enoch, and pay attention to these words of mine!] For not even to my angels have I explained my secrets . . . as I am making them known to you today."[130]

"The Changing Faces of God and Human Dignity in Judaism," in: *Moshe Idel: Representing God* (ed. H. Tirosh-Samuelson and A. W. Hughes; LCJP 8; Leiden: Brill, 2014), 103–22.

[130] Andersen, "2 Enoch," 1.138–42.

Note especially the invitation of the deity, who calls upon the visionary to sit to his left with Gabriel.[131] The shorter recension of *2 Enoch* 24 puts even greater emphasis on the unique nature of this offer, as God places the patriarch "to the left of himself, closer than Gabriel."[132] Scholars have attempted to compare such enthronement traditions with later rabbinic and Hekhalot two powers developments. Following this trajectory, Crispin Fletcher-Louis argued that Enoch's possession of the seat next to God "suggests some contact with the rabbinic Enoch/Metatron tradition."[133] Michael Mach also suggests that this motif is closely connected with the Metatron imagery, noting "the exaltation to a rank higher than that of the angels as well as the seating at God's side have their parallels and considerable development in Enoch's/Metatron's transformation and enthronement as depicted in *3 Enoch*."[134]

Apocalypse of Abraham

Our previous analysis of the dual theophanies found in early Jewish accounts demonstrates that, for a majority of these narratives, both powers were envisioned as anthropomorphic ocularcentric manifestations. Within the comparable theophanic episodes, the respective functions and delegation of authority to the second power were mainly indicated through the possession or transferal of peculiar ocularcentric aspects of the deity. These features, such as attributes of the divine throne or the divine Glory, are often transferred to the various second powers who become the new guardians of these divine qualities.

Yet, in some other early Jewish accounts, which will be explored later, the two powers appear as two distinct manifestations belonging to two entirely different symbolic worlds, one visual and the other aural. Such theophanic contrast in its most obvious form occurs in the *Apocalypse of Abraham*,[135] a Jewish pseudepigraphon most likely written in the second century CE, soon after the destruction of the Second Jerusalem Temple. In this text the deity is no longer present in his "human" shape, like the Ancient of Days in Daniel 7 or the "Noble Man" in the *Exagoge*'s dual theophany. Instead, the anthropomorphism of the first power has been completely abandoned as the deity prefers to manifest himself as the divine voice streaming from the heavenly furnace. Of course, such emphasis on the aural manifestation of the deity was not an invention that first appeared here within the second-century Jewish apocalyptic

---

[131] The assigning of the left side to the vice-regent instead of the right may appear puzzling. Martin Hengel suggests that this situation can be explained as the "correction" of the Christian scribe(s) who reserved the right side for Christ. Hengel points to a similar situation in the *Ascension of Isaiah* where the angel of the Holy Spirit is placed at the left hand of God. M. Hengel, *Studies in Early Christology* (Edinburgh: T&T Clark, 1995), 193.

[132] Andersen, "2 Enoch," 1.143.

[133] Fletcher-Louis, *Luke-Acts*, 154.

[134] M. Mach, "From Apocalypticism to Early Jewish Mysticism," in: *The Encyclopedia of Apocalypticism* (ed. J. J. Collins; 3 vols.; New York: Continuum, 1998), 1.229–64 at 1.251.

[135] As Wolfson observes, in the *Apocalypse of Abraham*, "the anthropomorphic imagery is displaced from the visual to the auditory realm." Wolfson, *Through a Speculum*, 32.

account; instead, it represents a conceptual development deeply rooted in the Hebrew Bible. Attention to these conceptual roots will now be given.

As previously mentioned, corporeal ideologies play a prominent role in the Hebrew Bible. Despite its forceful promulgation of anthropomorphic currents, the Hebrew Bible also bears witness to polemical narratives that challenge corporeal portrayals of the deity and offer quite different representations of the divine presence. Researchers have long noted the sharp opposition of the Book of Deuteronomy and the so-called Deuteronomic school to early anthropomorphic conceptions of the deity. Moshe Weinfeld points out that "the Deuteronomic conception of the cult is . . . vastly different from that reflected in the other Pentateuchal sources; it represents a turning point in the evolution of the religious faith of Israel."[136] The exact reasons for this polemical attitude cannot be determined with certainty. Scholars usually trace the introduction of this ideology to specific historical occasions, such as "the centralization of the cult, the loss of the ark from the northern kingdom, or the destruction of the temple."[137]

The Deuteronomic school is widely thought to have initiated the polemic against the ocularcentric and anthropomorphic conceptions of the deity, which the prophets Jeremiah and Deutero-Isaiah subsequently adopted.[138] Attempting to marginalize ancient anthropomorphic beliefs, the Book of Deuteronomy and the Deuteronomic

---

[136] Weinfeld, *Deuteronomy and the Deuteronomic School*, 190.

[137] I. Wilson, *Out of the Midst of the Fire: Divine Presence in Deuteronomy* (SBLDS 151; Atlanta: Scholars, 1995), 6–7. It is possible that the Deuteronomic paradigm shift was relying on already existing auricular developments. Elliot Wolfson notes that

> while the epistemic privileging of hearing over seeing in relation to God is attested in various biblical writers, including many of the classical prophets, the aversion to iconic representation of the deity can be traced most particularly to the Deuteronomist author who stressed that the essential and exclusive medium of revelation was the divine voice and not a visible form. . . . Whatever the "original" rationale for the prohibition on the iconic representation of God in ancient Israelite culture, whether theological or socio-political, it seems likely that the Deuteronomist restriction on the visualization of God is a later interpretation of an already existing proscription.
>
> Wolfson, *Through a Speculum*, 14.

[138] Weinfeld, *Deuteronomy and the Deuteronomic School*, 198. In relation to the developments found in Deutero-Isaiah, Wolfson notes that

> a significant element in the biblical tradition, as we have seen in the case of the Deuteronomist, opposes physical anthropomorphism, emphasizing the verbal/auditory over the iconic/visual. Positing that God addresses human beings through speech does not affect the claim to divine transcendence, that is, the utter incomparability of God to anything created, humanity included. The most extreme formulation of such a demythologizing trend occurs in Deutero-Isaiah: "To whom, then, can you liken God, what form (*demut*) compares to him?" (Isa 40:18; cf. 40:25, 46:5). In this verse one can perceive, as has been pointed out by Moshe Weinfeld, a direct polemic against the Priestly tradition that man is created in God's image. This tradition implies two things: first that God has an image (*demut*), and, second, that in virtue of that image in which Adam was created there is a basic similarity or likeness between human and divine. The verse in Deutero-Isaiah attacks both of these presumptions: since no image can be attributed to God it cannot be said that the human being is created in God's image. From this vantage point there is an unbridgeable and irreducible gap separating Creator and creature.
>
> Wolfson, *Through a Speculum*, 24–25.

school propagated the anti-corporeal "aural" ideology[139] of the divine Name[140] with its conception of the earthly temple[141] as the exclusive dwelling place of God's Name.[142] Gerhard von Rad argues that the Deuteronomic formula, "to cause his Name to dwell" advocates a new understanding of the deity, challenging the popular ancient conviction that God is truly present in the sanctuary.[143] In this Deuteronomi(sti)c ideology, apparitions of the deity are often depicted through the non-visual, aural symbolism of the divine Voice.[144] Tryggve Mettinger asserts that, "by way of contrast, the

---

[139] Wilson notes that scholars usually derive the Name theology "from two sets of texts, namely references to YHWH's Name dwelling, or being in some other sense present, at the sanctuary (e.g. in Deut 12–26 and throughout the Deuteronomistic History) and those to YHWH himself dwelling or being in heaven (e.g. Deut 4:36; 26:15, and 1 Kgs 8, in Solomon's prayer of dedication of the temple)." Wilson, *Out of the Midst of the Fire*, 3.

[140] For modern reconstructions of the ideology of the divine Name in Deuteronomy and other biblical materials, see S. Richter, *The Deuteronomic History and the Name Theology: lešakkēn šemô šām in the Bible and the Ancient Near East* (BZAW 318; Berlin: Walter de Gruyter, 2002), 26–39.

[141] Similar to the *Kavod* paradigm, the *Shem* ideology is also permeated by distinctive sacerdotal concerns that will maintain their powerful grip on the onomatological imagery long after the destruction of the Second Jerusalem temple. Wilson asserts that "despite the resulting Deuteronomistic emphasis on the transcendence of YHWH in the *Shem* ideology, the sanctuary retains its importance for the Israelite worshiper, since the presence there of the Name is seen as providing indirect access to that of the deity himself." Wilson, *Out of the Midst of the Fire*, 7.

[142] Mettinger observes that in the *Shem* theology "God himself is no longer present in the Temple, but only in heaven. However, he is represented in the Temple by his Name." Mettinger, *The Dethronement of Sabaoth*, 124. See also Weinfeld, *Deuteronomy and the Deuteronomic School*, 193.

[143] Weinfeld, *Deuteronomy and the Deuteronomic School*, 193. Elsewhere Weinfeld notes

> this attempt to eliminate the inherent corporeality of the traditional imagery also finds expression in Deuteronomy's conception of the Ark. The specific and exclusive function of the Ark, according to the book of Deuteronomy, is to house the tablets of the covenant (10:1–5); no mention is made of the Ark's cover (כפרת) or of the cherubim that endow the Ark with the semblance of a divine chariot or throne.... The Ark does not serve as God's seat upon which he journeys forth to disperse his enemies (Num 10:33–36), but only as the vessel in which the tablets of the covenant are deposited.
>
> M. Weinfeld, *Deuteronomy 1–11* (AB 5; New York: Doubleday, 1991), 39.

According to von Rad

> in Deuteronomy, it [the name] may be established in a particular place, the conception is definite and within fixed limits; it verges closely upon a hypostasis. The Deuteronomic theologumenon of the name of Jahweh clearly holds a polemic element, or, to put it better, is a theological corrective. It is not Jahweh himself who is present at the shrine, but only his name as the guarantee of his will to save; to it and it only Israel has to hold fast as the sufficient form in which Jahweh reveals himself. Deuteronomy is replacing the old crude idea of Jahweh's presence and dwelling at the shrine by a theologically sublimated idea.
>
> G. von Rad, *Studies in Deuteronomy* (London: SCM Press, 1953), 38–39.

In a similar vein, Ronald Clements postulates that "by the concept of the name of God the Deuteronomic authors have sought to avoid too crude a notion of the idea that God's presence could be located at the sanctuary. They have sought to emphasize the fact that God's true place of habitation could only be in heaven.

R. E. Clements, *Deuteronomy* (Old Testament Guides; Sheffield: JSOT, 1989), 52.

[144] Wolfson points out that

> while the figural representation of the deity is deemed offensive or even blasphemous, the hearing of a voice is an acceptable form of anthropomorphic representation, for, phenomenologically speaking, the voice does not necessarily imply an externalized concrete shape that is bound by specific spatial dimensions.... The voice admits no spatial reference in the external world and is therefore presumed to be immediately present.... It is appropriate to speak of a voice of God rather than a visible form because

Deuteronomistic theology is programmatically abstract: during the Sinai theophany, Israel perceived no form (*temuna*); she only heard the voice of her God (Deut 4:12, 15).[145] The Deuteronomistic preoccupation with God's voice and words represents an auditive, non-visual theme."[146]

As in the anthropomorphic ideology, where its ocularcentric features became manifested not only in the deity's epiphany, but also in the peculiar features of its recipients, the auricularcentric trend likewise profoundly affects the experiences of its adepts. One cluster of such metamorphoses is reflected in Moses' changing roles in Deuteronomy, where the Israelite prophet also adopted features of the aural trend. While in the ocularcentric passages Moses frequently emulates the features of the deity's form, including its luminosity, in the respective aural traditions he is predestined to mediate God's voice. Analyzing this paradigm shift, Steven Weitzman notes that

> Moses' role, it turns out, is to buffer God's voice, to mediate it through the filter of his voice. Deuteronomy did not invent this role for the prophet any more than it invented the ban against images (cf. Exod 20:19); its contribution is to reframe this tradition in ways that make it a significant turning point in the history of the senses we have been tracing. Departing from the version in Exodus, the Deuteronomic Moses tells Israel that God himself approved its proposal: "The Lord heard your words when you spoke to me, and the Lord said to me: 'I heard the voice of the words of this people, which they have spoken to you. They have done well in what they have spoken ... You, stand here by me, and I will tell you all the commandments, the statutes and the ordinances so that you may teach them.'" (5:25–28) This is the first time in Deuteronomy that God is said to have heard Israel in an approving way.[147]

One can observe that, as in the visual paradigm where Moses functions as an ocularcentric mediator whose luminous face reflects the visual features of the deity, in the Deuteronomic traditions his voice becomes a revelatory device. In other words, a mediated vision becomes a mediated audition. Deliberating on these differences, scholars argue that

> the sensory material in Deuteronomy 1–5 rules out the direct perception of God: seeing God is impossible because he does not reveal himself in a visible form; hearing God is possible but it is too overwhelming to bear for long. What is sustainable is the former implies a sense of phenomenological immediacy without necessitating spatial or worldly exteriority.
>
> Wolfson, *Through a Speculum*, 14–15.

---

[145] Weitzman notes that
   although the God of Deuteronomy cannot be seen, he can be heard: "The Lord spoke to you from the midst of a fire. The sound of words you were hearing ... only a voice" (4:12). This experience of God's voice is not available to other peoples; it is revealed to Israel alone: "Has anything so great as this ever happened, or has its like ever been heard of? Has a people heard the voice of God speaking out of a fire, as you have heard and lived?" (4:32).
   S. Weitzman, "Sensory Reform in Deuteronomy," in: *Religion and the Self in Antiquity* (ed. D. Brakke, M. L. Satlow, and S. Weitzman; Bloomington: Indiana University Press, 2005), 123–39 at 129.

[146] Mettinger, *The Dethronement of Sabaoth*, 46.

[147] Weitzman, "Sensory Reform in Deuteronomy," 131.

precisely the kind of mediated audition that Deuteronomy purports to record—the indirect audition of God's voice through the filter of Moses. The sensory history that we have been tracing, in other words, may be an attempt to cast Deuteronomy itself as an alternative to direct sensory experience, a kind of auditory compromise like the visual compromise achieved by Moses in Deuteronomy 3 that balances between too much raw sensation and no sensation at all.[148]

Furthermore, as with the visual *Kavod* tradition in which the corporeal imagery of the earthly sanctuary with their cherubim emulates the angelic retinue of the heavenly Temple, the aural paradigm is not confined solely to the revisions of the earthly shrine[149] but also promulgates a novel audial understanding of the heavenly Chariot and its divine Charioteer. As Mettinger observes, the concept of God advocated by the Deuteronomistic theology is strikingly abstract. "The throne concept has vanished and the anthropomorphic characteristics of God are on the way to oblivion."[150]

While the Deuteronomi(sti)c *Shem* ideology does not totally forsake terminology related to the concept of the divine Glory (*Kavod*),[151] it is noteworthy that, in the *Apocalypse of Abraham*, it markedly voids any corporeal associations, at least in relation to the deity. With respect to this paradigm shift, Weinfeld notes that "the expression '*kavod*,' when occurring in Deuteronomy, does not denote the being and substantiality of God as it does in the earlier sources but his splendor and greatness," implying "abstract and not corporeal qualities."[152]

An early example of the polemical interaction between the corporeal ideology of the divine form (*Kavod*), which is often labeled in some theophanic accounts as the divine Face (*Panim*), and the incorporeal theology of the divine Name, appears in Exodus 33, where, upon Moses' supplication to view the divine *Kavod*, the deity offers an aural option, promising to reveal to the prophet his Name:

> Moses said, "Show me your glory, I pray." And he said, "I will make all my goodness to pass before you, and I will proclaim before you the name, the Lord … but," he said, "you cannot see my face; for no one shall see me and live."

This account highlights the opposition between visual/corporeal and aural/aniconic disclosures, concentrating on the possibility of experiencing the divine not only

---

[148] Weitzman, "Sensory Reform in Deuteronomy," 131.

[149] Wilson notes that

> the presence of the Name at the cult-place is not regarded as an isolated phenomenon, but is linked to a whole complex of new ideas involving changes in the conception of the ark (from being YHWH's footstool or throne to being a mere container for the law) and of the temple (from being YHWH's dwelling-place and therefore a place of sacrifice to being a place of prayer).
>
> Wilson, *Out of the Midst of the Fire*, 8.

[150] Mettinger, *The Dethronement of Sabaoth*, 124.

[151] This tendency to polemically re-interpret the imagery of the rival paradigm is also observable in the *Kavod* tradition, which in turn employs the symbolism of the divine Voice along with other aspects of the *Shem* symbolism.

[152] Weinfeld, *Deuteronomy and the Deuteronomic School*, 206.

through vision but also through sound.¹⁵³ One mode of revelation often comes at the expense of the other—the idea hinted at in Exodus 33 and articulated more unequivocally in Deuteronomy 4:12, through the expression "you heard the sound of words, but saw no form." Scholars point to a paradigm shift in Deuteronomy's switch of the revelatory axis from the visual to the aural plane¹⁵⁴ by noting that

> Deuteronomy makes its transition to hearing subtly, moving away from the visual motifs it has been employing (though not abandoning them) in favor of aural motifs: "they hear all these statutes" (4:6); "I will cause them to hear my words" (4:10). The switch is even apparent in small rhetorical gestures such as Moses prefacing his speech in this section with the command "Hear" in contrast to the previous section where his addresses begin with "See!" (1:21; 2:31). All this occurs in tandem with the text's increasing emphasis on hearing as a conduit between God and Israel, an emphasis detectable in how it reworks material known from Exodus.¹⁵⁵

In this new theo-*phonic* conception, as opposed to the theo-*phanic* conception, even God's revelation to Moses on Mount Sinai in Exodus 19—an important nexus of the visual paradigm—is reinterpreted in terms of its aural counterpart. Deut 4:36 renders the Sinai theophany as hearing the celestial Voice: "Out of heaven he let you hear his voice, that he might discipline you; and on earth he let you see his great fire and you heard his words out of the midst of the fire." Here the disclosure is received not in the form of tablets, the media that may implicitly underline the corporeality of the deity; rather, "the commandments were heard from out of the midst of the fire … uttered by the deity from heaven."¹⁵⁶ This aniconic nature of the deity's revelation, now manifested as a formless voice in the fire, wipes out any requirement for its corporeal representation in the form of the anthropomorphic Glory of God. In relation to this paradigm shift Steven Weitzman notes that

> Deuteronomy's version of the commandments themselves is more or less parallel with Exodus 20, but it offers a slightly different account of what it was like to receive them. In Exod 20:18–19, in a passage that appears just after the commandments, the people are said to have been frightened by a mixture of sounds and sights that

---

¹⁵³ In relation to this passage Amy Merrill Willis observes that
> even in the Hebrew Bible itself one finds significant tensions between anthropomorphic traditions of representation and aniconic ones. Though Exod 20:4 and Deut 4:12–24 deny that God has a form, Exod 24:9–11 says that God and the leaders of the Israelites met face to face. Sometimes the tensions manifest themselves within a single passage. Exodus 33 is a case in point. Here, Moses asks to see both the embodied face of the divine and also the formless *kavod*.
> A. C. Merrill Willis, "Heavenly Bodies: God and the Body in the Visions of Daniel," in: *Bodies, Embodiment, and Theology of the Hebrew Bible* (ed. S. T. Kamionkowski and W. Kim; New York: T&T Clark, 2010), 13–37 at 17.

¹⁵⁴ Weinfeld observes that "Deuteronomy has … taken care to shift the centre of gravity of the theophany from the visual to the aural plane." Weinfeld, *Deuteronomy and the Deuteronomic School*, 207.

¹⁵⁵ Weitzman, "Sensory Reform in Deuteronomy," 129.

¹⁵⁶ Weinfeld, *Deuteronomy and the Deuteronomic School*, 207. For criticism of Weinfeld's methodology in this comparative analysis, see Wilson, *Out of the Midst of the Fire*, 90ff.

follow God's speech: "All the people, seeing the thunder and lightning, the sound of the trumpet, and the mountain smoking, were afraid and trembled and stood at a distance, and they said to Moses, 'You speak with us, and we will listen, but do not let God speak with us lest we die.'" Deut 5:22–27 also notes the fire and smoke, but its version focuses much more attention on the terror of hearing God.... Whereas Israel saw nothing of God's form, (Deut 5:22–27) makes it very clear that it did enjoy a direct experience of God's voice, an experience so intense, in fact, that Israel wonders that it survived the experience and turns to Moses to mediate God's words.[157]

The portrayal of the deity's activity and presence as the voice in the fire thus becomes one of the distinctive markers of the aural ideology.[158] The exemplary case of such symbolism is the Deuteronomistic record of God's appearance to Elijah on Mount Horeb in 1 Kgs 19:11–13:

> He said, "Go out and stand on the mountain before the Lord, for the Lord is about to pass by." Now there was a great wind, so strong that it was splitting mountains and breaking rocks in pieces before the Lord, but the Lord was not in the wind; and after the wind an earthquake, but the Lord was not in the earthquake; and after the earthquake a fire, but the Lord was not in the fire; and after the fire a sound of sheer silence. When Elijah heard it, he wrapped his face in his mantle and went out and stood at the entrance of the cave. Then there came a voice to him that said, "What are you doing here, Elijah?"

Comparable to the ocularcentric paradigm where the vision of God poses imminent risk to its beholder, the aural trend contains its own "danger motif" by depicting the adept protecting his face against fiery[159] utterances of the deity.[160]

---

[157] Weitzman, "Sensory Reform in Deuteronomy," 129–30.

[158] Mettinger remarks that "it is not surprising that the Name of God occupies so central a position in a theology in which God's words and voice receive so much emphasis." Mettinger, *The Dethronement of Sabaoth*, 124.

[159] With respect to this, Weinfeld notes that

> Deuteronomy has, furthermore, taken care to shift the center of gravity of the theophany from the visual to the aural plane. In Exod 19 the principal danger confronting the people was the likelihood that they might "break through to the Lord to gaze" (v. 21); it was to prevent this that there was need to "set bounds for the people round about" (v. 12) and to caution them not to ascend the mountain. Indeed, the pre-Deuteronomic texts invariably speak of the danger of seeing the deity: "For man shall not see me and live" (Exod 33:20), and similarly in Gen 32:31: "For I have seen God face to face, and yet my life is preserved" (cf. Judg 13:22; Isa 6:5). The book of Deuteronomy, by contrast, cannot conceive of the possibility of seeing the Divinity. The Israelites saw only "his great fire," which symbolizes his essence and qualities (4:24: "for YHWH your God is a consuming fire, an impassioned God," cf. 9:3), whereas God himself remains in his heavenly abode. The danger threatening the people here, and the greatness of the miracle, is that of hearing the voice of the Deity: "Has any people heard the voice of God speaking from the midst of a fire, as indeed you have, and survived?" (4:33; cf. 5:23).
>
> Weinfeld, *Deuteronomy 1–11*, 38–39.

[160] In relation to these conceptual developments Weitzman notes that "while God has allowed Israel unprecedented sensory access to him, hearing his voice poses dangers of its own, Moses marveling that Israel has survived the experience: 'Has a people heard the voice of God ... and

Scholars have argued that the Deuteronomi(sti)c aniconism exercised profound influence on later Jewish and Christian accounts. With respect to early Christian traditions, Markus Bockmuehl reminds us that "fierce resistance to any human visual representations of God . . . the theme that 'no one has ever seen God' is widely picked up in post-biblical Jewish literature and in the New Testament (John 1:18; cf. Rom 1:20; Col 1:15; 1 Tim 1:17)."[161]

The aforementioned Deuteronomi(sti)c aural traditions also play a prominent role in select Jewish apocalyptic accounts, including the pivotal theophanic description found in chapter 8 of the *Apocalypse of Abraham*. There the deity is described as "the voice of the Mighty One coming down from the heavens in a stream of fire."

The striking distinction, however, is that while in the Pentateuch aural and visual manifestations are both firmly associated with one God, in the *Apocalypse of Abraham* and some other Jewish and Christian writings these two theophanic expressions are now divided between two powers, one of which assumes the visible ocularcentric shape while the other is confined exclusively to the aural aniconic mode. We now turn to examine such theophanic bifurcation in the *Apocalypse of Abraham*.

Unlike previously explored accounts, in which the deity assumed a visible anthropomorphic shape, the *Apocalypse of Abraham* fashions God according to the Deuteronomi(sti)c "aural" template.[162] Already in the inaugural vision of the text (chapter 8), the divine presence is portrayed as "the voice of the Mighty One," which

---

lived?' Deuteronomy 4–6 seeks to mitigate the danger of hearing God by instituting a kind of virtual hearing, an indirect way to hear his voice." Weitzman, "Sensory Reform in Deuteronomy," 129.

[161] M. N. A. Bockmuehl, "'The Form of God' (Phil 2:6): Variations on a Theme of Jewish Mysticism," *JTS* 48 (1997): 1–23 at 13. Bockmuehl also reminds us that

> at the same time, however, the Old Testament also shows evidence of a persistent contrary tradition. The Lord God walks in the garden in the cool of the evening (Gen. 3:8); he meets with Abraham (Genesis 18, esp. v. 13 ff.); the seventy Elders ascend Mount Sinai to see him and eat and drink in his presence (Exod. 24:10f.). This has often been regarded as indicative of a primitive anthropomorphism later abandoned in the course of increasing religious sophistication. Visions of God (or of his throne, heaven, etc.) extend in fact from the earliest to the latest traditions in the Old Testament: from Jacob's Ladder in Genesis 28 or the hem of the Lord's robe filling the Temple in Isaiah 6 all the way to Ezekiel's vision of the throne chariot (Ezekiel 1) or Daniel's daring vision of the Ancient of Days (Daniel 7). Gershom Scholem and students of apocalyptic after him have frequently argued for a continuity of mystical tradition from the throne visions of the Old Testament and of *1 Enoch* 14:18–24 (cf. e.g. *Life of Adam and Eve* 25:3) to those of later apocalyptic and rabbinic Judaism. And even if we must now reject Scholem's argument for the early date of many texts of merkabah mysticism, the heavenly liturgies contained in Qumran's *Songs of the Sabbath Sacrifice* now seem to confirm his instincts about a basic continuum of tradition from the earlier to the later visions of God's celestial glory.

Bockmuehl, "The Form of God," 13–14.

[162] The affinities with the Deuteronomic/Deuteronomistic materials can also be seen in the implicit and explicit connections between the vision of Abraham and Moses' Sinai encounter. In this respect, David Halperin notes that the author of the *Apocalypse of Abraham* "gives us several clues that he is modeling Abraham's experience after Moses' at Sinai. The most obvious of these is his locating the experience at Mount Horeb, the name that Deuteronomy regularly uses for Sinai." D. Halperin, *The Faces of the Chariot: Early Jewish Response to Ezekiel's Vision* (TSAJ 16; Tübingen: Mohr Siebeck, 1988), 109–10.

comes in a stream of fire.¹⁶³ The manifestation of God as a formless voice rather than an angelic or divine form becomes standard; it is adopted by the authors of the Slavonic *Apocalypse* in order to convey a theophany of the deity.¹⁶⁴ Emphasis on the deity's auditory revelation recalls several prominent Deuteronomi(sti)c scenes, including the previously mentioned encounter between Elijah and God on Mount Horeb (1 Kgs 19:11–13).

Tendencies toward the aural manifestation of the deity saturate the narrative of the Slavonic pseudepigraphon, as the celestial Voice appears pervasively throughout the story. Accordingly, in *Apoc. Ab.* 9, the voice of "the primordial and mighty God" orders Abraham to bring sacrifices. In the following chapter the aural manifestation designates the angel Yahoel as the celestial guide of the exalted patriarch.

The identification of the deity with the Voice in the *Apocalypse of Abraham* also impacts the way in which this divine manifestation ought to be approached and worshiped. An aural God requires a corresponding audial response from its subjects. In this regard, the *Apocalypse of Abraham* underlines the significance of praise as a parallel process of the audial expression of creation in relation to its Creator.¹⁶⁵ The *Apocalypse* also seems to view the praise of God as a mystical routine that in many ways replicates the visionary praxis of the *Kavod* paradigm, wherein the adept often mirrors the *Kavod* in the process of his transformation, assuming the theophanic features of the divine Form. In this regard it is notable that references to "bodily" transformations are markedly missing in the *Apocalypse of Abraham*, an element that has often baffled researchers accustomed to the traditional apocalyptic stories influenced by visual ideology.

As in the *Kavod* paradigm in which the anthropomorphic extent of the deity represents a celestial projection of the seer's own body, in the auricularcentric model human praise paradoxically fashions the deity. Scholars have observed the significance of invocation, or "calling upon," in the *Shem* paradigm, which functioned as an act of actualizing the presence of God.¹⁶⁶

The aural ideology achieves one of its highest symbolic expressions in *Apoc. Ab.* 18, where the seer encounters the divine Chariot. The most striking detail in the description of the divine throne in this chapter, which radically differs from the ocularcentric Ezekielian account, is the climactic moment of the hero's encounter with the divine Chariot; here the text does not give any indication of the presence of the anthropomorphic Glory of God, as in Ezekiel 1:26, where it is described as "something

---

¹⁶³ *Apoc. Ab.* 8:1 reads: "The voice (глас) of the Mighty One came down from heaven in a stream of fire, saying and calling, 'Abraham, Abraham!'" A. Kulik, *Retroverting Slavonic Pseudepigrapha: Toward the Original of the Apocalypse of Abraham* (TCS 3; Atlanta: Scholars, 2004), 16; B. Philonenko-Sayar and M. Philonenko, *L'Apocalypse d'Abraham. Introduction, texte slave, traduction et notes* (Semitica 31; Paris: Librairie Adrien-Maisonneuve, 1981), 54.

¹⁶⁴ See, for example, *Apoc. Ab.* 18:2: "And I heard a voice (глас) like the roaring of the sea, and it did not cease because of the fire." Kulik, *Retroverting Slavonic Pseudepigrapha*, 24; Philonenko-Sayar and Philonenko, *L'Apocalypse d'Abraham. Introduction, texte slave, traduction et notes*, 76.

¹⁶⁵ Andrea Lieber draws attention to similar developments in the aforementioned passage from 4Q405. See A. Lieber, "Voice and Vision: Song as a Vehicle for Ecstatic Experience in Songs of the Sabbath Sacrifice," in: *Of Scribes and Sages: Early Jewish Interpretation of Scripture* (ed. C. A. Evans; 2 vols.; London/New York: T&T Clark, 2004), 2.51–58 at 55.

¹⁶⁶ Mettinger, *The Dethronement of Sabaoth*, 125.

that seemed like a human form."¹⁶⁷ Instead of the Ezekielian anthropomorphic deity, the adept encounters the now familiar voice amidst flames and encompassed by the sound of the *qedushah*:

> While I was still standing and watching, I saw behind the Living Creatures a chariot with fiery Wheels. Each Wheel was full of eyes round about. And above the Wheels there was the throne which I had seen. And I was covered with fire and the fire encircled it round about, and an indescribable light surrounded the fiery people. And I heard the sound of their *qedushah* like the voice of a single man. And a voice came to me out of the midst of the fire (*Apoc. Ab.* 18:12–19:1).¹⁶⁸

David Halperin detects a paradigm shift from the visual to the aural plane in this passage; he points out that "Ezekiel's phrase 'like the appearance of a man,' becomes, in a concluding sentence, that which plainly draws on the end of Ezekiel 1:28, 'like the voice of a man.'"¹⁶⁹ Noting auricular proclivities of the text, Halperin also suggests that "the author of the apocalypse surrounds the *merkabah* with angelic chant."¹⁷⁰

Permeated with the aural ideology, the account of the seer's visitation to the throne room underscores the importance of the angelic praxis of praise. Thus, in the depictions of the Living Creatures (the *Hayyot*) and the Wheels (the *Ophannim*), the text emphasizes their aural activities:

> And as the fire rose up, soaring higher, I saw under the fire a throne [made] of fire and the many-eyed Wheels, and they are reciting the song. And under the throne [I saw] four singing fiery Living creatures (*Apoc. Ab.* 18:3).¹⁷¹

What is especially curious in this passage is that, rather than accentuating the role of the *Hayyot* as the foundation of the throne, the Slavonic *Apocalypse* focuses on the aural functions of the Living Creatures, depicting them as "singing the divine presence." Later in the text, when God reveals to Abraham the eschatological temple, we again see

---

¹⁶⁷ Christopher Rowland points out that,
> unlike Ezek 1, no mention is made whatsoever of any human form sitting on the throne of glory. All that the patriarch speaks of above the throne is "the power of invisible glory" (19:5). Abraham stresses that he saw no other being there apart from the angels. God's presence is located within the most holy part of heaven above the throne-chariot itself, but there is little sign of any anthropomorphism except for the divine voice.
> Rowland and Morray-Jones, *The Mystery of God*, 82–83.

Scholars often highlight a radical paradigm shift in the text's description of the deity, noting "a deliberate attempt . . . to exclude all reference to the human figure mentioned in Ezekiel 1." C. Rowland, *The Open Heaven: A Study of Apocalyptic in Judaism and Early Christianity* (New York: Crossroad, 1982), 86–87.

¹⁶⁸ Kulik, *Retroverting Slavonic Pseudepigrapha*, 24.
¹⁶⁹ Halperin, *The Faces of the Chariot*, 108.
¹⁷⁰ Halperin, *The Faces of the Chariot*, 108.
¹⁷¹ Kulik, *Retroverting Slavonic Pseudepigrapha*, 24.

striking reformulations of the traditional *Kavod* imagery with the distinctive audial mold:

> I saw there *the likeness of the idol of jealousy* (подобие идола ревнования), as *a likeness* (подобие) of a craftsman's [work] such as my father made, and its statue was of shining copper, and a man before it, and he was worshiping it; and [there was] an altar opposite it and youth were slaughtered on it before the idol. And I said to him, "What is this idol, and what is the altar, and who are those being sacrificed, and who is the sacrificer, and what is the beautiful temple which I see, art and beauty if your glory that lies beneath your throne?" And he said: "Hear Abraham! This temple and altar and the beautiful things which you have seen are my image of *the sanctification of the name of my glory* (святительства имени славы моея), where every prayer of men will dwell, and the gathering of kings and prophets, and the sacrifice which shall establish to be made for me among my people coming from your progeny. And the statue you saw is my anger, because the people who will come to me out of you will make me angry. And the man you saw slaughtering is he who angers me. And the sacrifice is the murder of those who are for me a testimony of the close of judgment in the end of the creation" (*Apoc. Ab.* 25:1–6).[172]

Here, as in the biblical Deuteronomistic reformulations, the *Kavod* symbolism is sealed with unmistakable aural imagery. Another conspicuous detail is that some prior ocularcentric symbols from earlier stories of the idolatrous practices of Abraham's parent are suddenly and explicitly invoked. The memory of the idols, like those made in the house of Terah, are now introduced in the narrative about the polluted temple. This idolatrous practice of worshiping a statue, described in the story as "a *likeness* (подобие) of a craftsman's work," appears to invoke the formula of "likeness" known from theophanic portrayals found in Genesis 1:26 and Ezekiel 1. The idolatrous practices are then contrasted to true worship, unsurprisingly rendered in the now recognizable aural symbolism. Here the future eschatological Temple is depicted as an abode, not for the anthropomorphic Form polemically represented by the detestable shining statue, but for "the image of the *sanctification of the name of my [God's] glory* (святительства имени славы моея), where *every prayer of men will dwell* (в нюже вселится всяка молба мужьска)."[173] It is evident that the authors are attempting to re-interpret the technical terminology of the ocularcentric *Kavod* paradigm by consolidating it within the formulae prominent in the aural ideology. However, there is no doubt that the authors' attitude about the anthropomorphic ideology remains polemical, as demonstrated by calling the shining statue an idol of jealousy.

In this complex aural reformulation of the traditional *Kavod* imagery, the familiar ocularcentric profile of the second power receives a novel reconfiguration. One of the crucial dimensions of this reformulation is the distinctive physiognomic attributes of the deity, which, although never previously transferred to anyone, are now given to the second power, who is refashioned into a mirror, or a visible "icon," of the deity.

---

[172] Kulik, *Retroverting Slavonic Pseudepigrapha*, 29; Philonenko-Sayar and Philonenko, *L'Apocalypse d'Abraham. Introduction, texte slave, traduction et notes*, 92.

[173] Philonenko-Sayar and Philonenko, *L'Apocalypse d'Abraham. Introduction, texte slave, traduction et notes*, 92.

Although the initial steps of such transferals have been detected, even in accounts where God retains his anthropomorphic shape, the aural trend with its even more withdrawn deity provides additional unparalleled opportunities.

Whereas in early ocularcentric accounts the attributes of the anthropomorphic Glory were shared by both powers, in later accounts the first power is no longer associated with this distinctive theophanic symbolism. The second power's complete assimilation of God's visual properties seems to have special significance in the portrayal of the *Apocalypse of Abraham*'s chief angelic protagonist—Yahoel. Paradoxical transferals taking place in the Slavonic *Apocalypse* greatly contribute to the blurriness of the boundaries between the deity and his envoy. The latter now assumes complete scope of the theophanic features, which were the distinctive markers of God in the ocularcentric Jewish accounts. This ambiguity adds to the perplexities and misconceptions associated with the interpretation of Yahoel's identity, serving as grounds for the unending scholarly deliberations that attempt to establish his exact status. We turn now to consider Yahoel's role as the second power in the *Apocalypse of Abraham*.

Important to note that Yahoel makes his first appearance in the course of the dual theophany. Unlike the previously explored two powers accounts, here in the *Apocalypse of Abraham* the first and the second powers are manifested in two separate and distinctive theophanic modes: one as the ocularcentric, visible manifestation, and the other as the aniconic voice.

As mentioned above, Yahoel's description in this dual theophany has long puzzled even the most advanced experts of Jewish mediatorial traditions. This is because the striking panoply of theophanic markers represents features that until now were reserved exclusively for the apparitions of God.

Yahoel's celestial shape represents an amalgam of theophanic elements of several essential biblical depictions of God. The angel assumes both the theophanic features of the Ancient of Days from Daniel 7 and the peculiar details of the *Kavod* from the first chapter of the Book of Ezekiel—two formative accounts of divine apparitions in the Hebrew Bible.[174] The *Apocalypse of Abraham* 11:2–3 recounts the following portrayal of the angel's form:

> The appearance of the griffin's body was like sapphire, and the likeness of his face like chrysolite, and the hair of his head like snow, and a turban on his head like the appearance of the bow in the clouds, and the closing of his garments [like] purple, and a golden staff [was] in his right hand.[175]

---

[174] One can see a similar constellation of theophanic motifs in the Book of Revelation.

[175] Kulik, *Retroverting Slavonic Pseudepigrapha*, 19. Daniel Harlow discerns that
> features of Yahoel's appearance resemble those attributed to God in biblical theophanies. His head looks like a man's, but his torso looks like that of an eagle or griffin, and in this respect he resembles the angel Serapiel in 3 Enoch. Yet his body is also "like sapphire," a detail that recalls the sapphire pavement under God's feet in Exod 24:10 and Ezek 1:26; and his hair is white as snow, like the Ancient of Days in Dan 7:9.
>
> D. Harlow, "Idolatry and Alterity: Israel and the Nations in the Apocalypse of Abraham," in: *The "Other" in Second Temple Judaism. Essays in Honor of John J. Collins* (ed. D. C. Harlow, M. Goff, K. M. Hogan, and J. S. Kaminsky; Grand Rapids: Eerdmans, 2011), 302–30 at 313.

Jarl Fossum proposes that this portrayal contains adaptations of various depictions of the divine Glory, ranging from Ezek 1:27 to the *Shiʿur Qomah* accounts.[176] Deliberating on these similarities, Fossum notes that "in the *Shiʿur Qomah* texts, there is frequent reference to the shining appearance of the body of the Glory, and chrysolite is even used expressly to describe it: 'His body is like chrysolite. His light breaks tremendously from the darkness.'"[177] Moreover, he observes a close similarity between Yahoel and the Ezekielian *Kavod*, especially in their rainbow-like appearance, arguing that "the rainbow-like appearance of Yahoel's turban is reminiscent of Ezek 1:28, which says that 'the appearance of the brightness round about' the Glory was 'like the appearance of the bow that is in the cloud on the day of rain.'"[178]

Para-biblical Mosaic theophanies may also contribute to Yahoel's enigmatic profile. Scholars have noticed similarities with another two powers theophany attested in the *Exagoge* of Ezekiel the Tragedian. According to Fossum, "the sceptre which Yahoel has in his right hand recalls the sceptre held by the *phōs* whom Moses saw upon the great throne in the drama of Ezekiel the Tragedian."[179] In the light of these similarities, he infers that, in the *Apocalypse of Abraham*, "Yahoel obviously is the Glory of God."[180]

Another prolific expert of mediatorial traditions—Christopher Rowland—also detects the transference of divine attributes to Yahoel, arguing that there is "a strong indication that this angel is closely linked with God himself."[181] He points out that "Revelation 1:13ff. and the angelophany in the *Apocalypse of Abraham* show some affinities with developments of Ezekiel 1:26f., particularly as they are found in Daniel 10:5f. The result is a theology of some complexity. Both works clearly think of the angelic figure as one who possesses divine attributes."[182] Rowland notes that the striking embellishment of the angelic mediator with the divine ocularcentric attributes coincides here with the removal of the anthropomorphic features from the deity. He points out, furthermore, that in both the *Apocalypse of Abraham* and the Book of Revelation,

> the reluctance to use anthropomorphic terminology in relation to God is matched by the development of an interest in an exalted angelic figure with divine attributes, who is, of course, given the form of a man. In the *Apocalypse of Abraham* we find that the angel Yahoel is said to have God's name dwelling in him, and in Rev 1:13ff. the description of the glorified Christ derives in part from the description of the angel who appears to Daniel in Dan 10:6, but he is also given attributes of God himself derived from Dan 7:9.[183]

---

[176] J. Fossum, *The Name of God and the Angel of the Lord: Samaritan and Jewish Concepts of Intermediation and the Origin of Gnosticism* (WUNT 36; Tübingen: Mohr Siebeck, 1985), 319–20.

[177] Fossum, *The Name of God*, 319–20.

[178] Fossum, *The Name of God*, 319–20. Similarly, Christopher Rowland remarks that "the mention of the rainbow is reminiscent of Ezekiel 1:28 (cf. Rev 4:3), where God's glory is compared to the bow in the clouds." Rowland, *The Open Heaven*, 102–3.

[179] Fossum, *The Name of God*, 320.

[180] Fossum, *The Name of God*, 320.

[181] Rowland, *The Open Heaven*, 102.

[182] Rowland, *The Open Heaven*, 102–3.

[183] C. Rowland, "The Visions of God in Apocalyptic Literature," *JSJ* 10 (1979): 137–54 at 153–54.

Another important cluster of Yahoel's attributes evokes the memory of the peculiar features of the Ancient of Days from the Book of Daniel.[184] The transferal of the deity's attributes from the latter will play a prominent role in a few other mediatorial streams; this includes various Jewish and Christian depictions of the Son of Man in which the second power of Daniel 7 procures the distinctive qualities of the first power. Several researchers have noted the transference of the peculiar characteristics of the Ancient of Days to Yahoel. Jarl Fossum contends that Yahoel's hair being white as snow is a clear reference to the representation of the Ancient of Days in Dan 7:9, *1 Enoch* 46:1,[185] and *1 Enoch* 71:10.[186] Although "it is perhaps astonishing that Yahoel in this respect is modeled upon the Ancient of Days and not upon the Son of Man,"[187] such transference has all the hallmarks of legitimacy, since, according to the aforementioned tendencies, in the aural structure of the text, features of the ocularcentric deity, and not the second power, must be transferred and emulated.

One feature of the *Apocalypse of Abraham* that has persistently bedeviled numerous scholars is situated in Abraham's vision of the Chariot in chapter 18. In this account the anthropomorphic Rider remains paradoxically absent. This non-appearance has frequently been interpreted as the possibility that Yahoel himself, with his striking divine qualities, represents the missing divine figure, who somehow abandoned the throne and manifested himself to Abraham. Christopher Rowland entertains such a possibility, noting that

> the description of God's throne in the *Apocalypse of Abraham* (ch. 18) is notable for the absence of any reference to a figure sitting on the throne. As we have seen, the description of the throne-chariot clearly owes much to Ezekiel 1, which makes the lack of any figure on the throne all the more significant. It is clear that Jaoel is the companion of the throne of glory. This close link between the two is confirmed by the words of the angel: "I am called Jaoel by him who moveth that which existeth with me." Such an identification may be confirmed by reference to Ezekiel 12, where movement is one of the characteristics pointed out by the prophet, as it is also in the throne-chariot firmament from Cave 4 at Qumran. At the very least it seems that Jaoel, like Wisdom (Wisd 9:4) was the companion of God's throne. While there is no explicit evidence from the *Apocalypse of Abraham* to suggest that Jaoel was the one whose seat was on the throne of God, it is not impossible that we have a theological description here which reflects that found

---

[184] The *Visions of Ezekiel* also depict Metatron as the *atiq yomin* or the Ancient of Days from Dan 7:9–10. On this tradition, see N. Deutsch, *Guardians of the Gate. Angelic Vice Regency in Late Antiquity* (BSJS 22; Leiden, Boston: Brill, 1999), 45.

[185] *1 Enoch* 46:1 reads: "And there I saw one who had a head of days, and his head (was) white like wool." Knibb, *The Ethiopic Book of Enoch*, 2.131; *1 Enoch* 71:10 reads: "... and with them the Head of Days, his head white and pure like wool, and his garments indescribable." Knibb, *The Ethiopic Book of Enoch*, 2.166.

[186] Fossum, *The Name of God*, 319–20. Rowland also argues that, "as in Revelation 1 the description of the angel takes up the reference to the Ancient of Days in Dan 7:9." Rowland, *The Open Heaven*, 102–3.

[187] Fossum, *The Name of God*, 319–20.

in Ezekiel 1 and 8, where the human figure on the throne leaves the throne to function as the agent of the divine will.[188]

Fossum also suggests that Yahoel may be the missing rider of the Chariot. In his assessment, "the throne is empty because Yahoel accompanies Abraham. Already in Ezekiel, the Glory is not bound to the throne upon the chariot and can appear apart from it."[189]

Fossum's and Rowland's speculations about Yahoel's identification provoked a critical reaction from some scholars. For instance, Richard Bauckham contended that a cautious examination of Yahoel's profile "makes wholly redundant scholarly speculations that Yahoel is some kind of embodiment of the divine glory or participant in divine nature or even a personification of the divine Name."[190] In Bauckham's judgment,

> Yahoel is wholly intelligible as a principal angel (one of at least two), who exercises a delegated authority on God's behalf as the angelic high priest, the heavenly and cosmic equivalent of the Aaronide high priest in the Jerusalem temple. He is neither included in the unique identity of YHWH, as understood by Jews of this period, nor any sort of qualification of or threat to it. Throughout the work he is, as a matter of course, distinguished from God and never confused with God.[191]

Another opponent of Fossum's and Rowland's theories, Larry Hurtado, likewise rejects the identification of Yahoel with the divine *Kavod*. While recognizing similarities between Yahoel's appearance and the depictions of the divine figures in the Books of Ezekiel[192] and Daniel,[193] he proposes that "Yahoel's white hair and his rainbow-like

---

[188] Rowland, *The Open Heaven*, 102–3.

[189] Fossum, *The Name of God*, 320. Alan Segal appears also to have supported such an identification, noting that "in various Jewish sects and conventicles the foremost name given to the figure on the throne is Yahoel." A. F. Segal, *Paul the Convert: The Apostolate and Apostasy of Saul the Pharisee* (New Haven: Yale University Press, 1990), 42.

[190] R. Bauckham, *Jesus and the God of Israel: God Crucified and Other Essays on the New Testament's Christology of Divine Identity* (Milton Keynes: Paternoster; Grand Rapids: Eerdmans, 2008), 227.

[191] Bauckham, *Jesus and the God of Israel*, 227.

[192] Hurtado points out that

> two details of the description of Yahoel are important: His hair is "like snow" and he holds a golden staff (or scepter) in his right hand. The first detail recalls the description of God in Dan 7:9 and may be an attempt to portray graphically Yahoel's status as second in command to God, which he holds by virtue of being indwelt by God's name. The net effect of this description is to suggest that here we have yet another important example of divine agency speculation. If, as most scholars hold, the *Apocalypse of Abraham* reflects early Jewish tradition, then in Yahoel we have an additional principal angel seen by ancient Jews as God's vizier or chief agent.
>
> Hurtado, *One God, One Lord*, 80.

[193] Hurtado notes that

> some of these details remind us of the visions recounted in Ezekiel (1:26–28) and Daniel (7:9; 10:5–6), although there is no exact duplication of any of the biblical visions. Rather

headdress may instead be intended to suggest a limited similarity between him and God, just enough to portray him as the divine vizier."[194]

Examining the previous speculation concerning Yahoel as a missing "charioteer," Hurtado suggests that "there is little justification for the idea that Yahoel represents some sort of separation of the divine figure from the throne."[195] In Hurtado's opinion

> both Rowland and Fossum make too much of the fact that in 18:1–5 there is no explicit description of a figure on the divine throne. To take the absence of a description of a figure on the throne as "the lack of any figure on the throne" is simply a non sequitur. The throne is not said to be empty. Granted, the author does not portray God in human form, and instead describes the divine manifestation as fire (17:1; 18:1–4, 13–14; 19:1).[196]

Hurtado's observations are important, pointing to the fact that, in Abraham's vision of the throne room, God isn't missing; rather, his presence is asserted through aural, aniconic means. He further notes that, in spite of the fact that

> the author does not engage in anthropomorphic description of God such as in Ezek 1:26–28 . . . this is hardly evidence of an empty divine throne. The *Apocalypse of Abraham* gives no physical description of God beyond the traditional theophanic image of fire, but the author refers to a voice coming from the divine fire above the throne (17:1; 18:1–3; 19:1), suggesting that the throne is occupied, although no description is given of the one speaking.[197]

Hurtado's thoughtfulness regarding the aural proclivities of the text is refreshing, since scholarly statements regarding the absence or presence of the divine form in the *Apocalypse of Abraham*, along with Yahoel's alleged attempt to mitigate this absence, are frequently made without proper recognition of the text's auricularcentric ideology and its crucial role in depictions of the angelic and divine manifestations.

The Yahoel tradition found in the *Apocalypse of Abraham* appears to unveil novel functions of the familiar divine characteristics drawn from the exemplary scriptural theophanies. While in the accounts influenced by the *Kavod* mold these features serve as the unambiguous markers of the deity, in the materials affected by the aural ideology they fulfill a quite different theophanic function. They now serve as the sign of the corporeal second power, clearly separated from the aniconic, aural God.

> than identifying Yahoel directly as any of the figures in these biblical passages, the writer may have intended to draw a more general comparison between Yahoel and the biblical figures.
>
> Hurtado, *One God, One Lord*, 80.

[194] Hurtado, *One God, One Lord*, 80.
[195] Hurtado, *One God, One Lord*, 80.
[196] Hurtado, *One God, One Lord*, 88–89.
[197] Hurtado, *One God, One Lord*, 88–89.

Ladder of Jacob

Another important narrative nexus, which often appears in scholarly discussions regarding the origins of the two powers debates, is the story of the patriarch Jacob. Later rabbinic lore offers an unprecedented amount of information about Jacob's exaltation. In these traditions he is often portrayed as the image of God, either engraved or enthroned on the divine seat. Some targumic and midrashic accounts also envision him as the cosmic ladder by which the angels achieve their parades from the upper to the lower realms. These targumic and midrashic stories do not merely represent late rabbinic inventions, but rather indicate deep roots within early Jewish accounts. One early legend about the exalted identity of Jacob comes from the *Prayer of Joseph*.[198] In this pseudepigraphical text Jacob is portrayed as "an angel of God and a ruling spirit" and is named as "the firstborn of every living thing to whom God gives life."[199]

Another early witness that recounts Jacob's heavenly identity is the *Ladder of Jacob*. Unlike the *Prayer of Joseph*, where the surviving portions of the text do not depict a simultaneous appearance of two powers, the *Ladder of Jacob* clearly portrays a dual theophany. Moreover, in the *Ladder* (as in the *Apocalypse of Abraham*), God assumes the role of the aural manifestation, while Jacob's heavenly identity is depicted with

---

[198] A total of nine Greek sentences of this pseudepigraphon were preserved in the writings of Origen (c.185–c.254 CE). Fragment A is quoted in Origen's *In Ioannem* II. 31.25. Fragment B, a single sentence, is cited in Gregory and Basil's compilation of Origen, the *Philokalia*. This fragment is also quoted in Eusebius, *The Preparation of the Gospel* and in the Latin *Commentary on Genesis* by Procopius of Gaza. Fragment C, which is also found in the *Philokalia*, quotes Fragment B and paraphrases Fragment A. J. Z. Smith, "Prayer of Joseph," in: *The Old Testament Pseudepigrapha* (ed. J. H. Charlesworth; 2 vols.; New York: Doubleday, 1983–1985), 2.699. Pieter van der Horst and Judith Newman note that "according to the ancient *Stichometry* of Nicephorus, the text originally contained 1100 lines. The extant portions totaling only nine Greek sentences or 164 words thus reflect a small fraction of the original composition." *Early Jewish Prayers in Greek* (ed. P. W. van der Horst and J. H. Newman; CEJL; Berlin: Walter de Gruyter, 2008), 249.

[199] Fragment A of the text reads:

> I, Jacob, who is speaking to you, am also Israel, an angel of God and a ruling spirit. Abraham and Isaac were created before any work. But, I, Jacob, who men call Jacob but whose name is Israel am he who God called Israel which means, a man seeing God because I am the firstborn of every living thing to whom God gives life. And when I was coming up from Syrian Mesopotamia, Uriel, the angel of God, came forth and said that "I (Jacob-Israel] had descended to earth and I had tabernacled among men and that I had been called by the name of Jacob." He envied me and fought with me and wrestled with me saying that his name and the name that is before every angel was to be above mine. I told him his name and what rank he held among the sons of God. "Are you not Uriel, the eighth after me? And I, Israel, the archangel of the power of the Lord and the chief captain among the sons of God? Am I not Israel, the first minister before the face of God? And I called upon my God by the inextinguishable name."
>
> Smith, "Prayer of Joseph," 2.713–14.

For the primary texts see Denis, *Fragmenta pseudepigraphorum quae supersunt Graeca*, 61–64; A. Resch, *Agrapha: Aussercanonische Schriftfragmente* (Leipzig: J. C. Hinrichs, 1906), 295–98; Origène, *Commentaire sur Saint Jean. Tome I* (Livres I–V) (ed. C. Blanc; SC 120; Paris: Cerf, 1966), 334–37; Origen, *Philocalia* (ed. J. A. Robinson; Cambridge: Cambridge University Press, 1893); Eusebius, *Praeparatio Evangelica* (ed. K. Mras; 2 vols.; GCS 43.1–2; Leipzig: J. C. Hinrichs, 1954–1956).

ocularcentric symbolism. *Lad. Jac.* 1:3–10 offers the following description of Jacob's vision:

> And behold, a ladder was fixed on the earth, whose top reaches to heaven. And the top of the ladder was the face as of a man, carved out of fire.[200] There were twelve steps leading to the top of the ladder, and on each step to the top there were two human faces, on the right and on the left, twenty-four faces (or busts) including their chests. And the face in the middle was higher than all that I saw, the one of fire, including the shoulders and arms, exceedingly terrifying, more than those twenty-four faces. And while I was still looking at it, behold, angels of God ascended and descended on it. And God was standing above its highest face, and he called to me from there, saying, "Jacob, Jacob!" And I said, "Here I am, Lord!" And he said to me, "The land on which you are sleeping, to you will I give it, and to your seed after you. And I will multiply your seed."[201]

Comparable to some previously explored accounts, one again encounters the presence of imagery associated with the *panim*. According to the text, the visionary sees twenty-four human faces with their chests, two of them on each step of the ladder. On the top rung, the seer beholds another human visage "carved out of fire"[202] with its shoulders and arms.[203] Compared to previous faces, this highest one is "exceedingly terrifying." In the light of the developments in *2 Enoch*, one might expect that this particular visage represents God's face. Curiously, however, the deity does not appear to be associated with this visible manifestation. Instead, the text explicitly states that God "was staying" above the highest countenance and called Jacob by name. This leaves the impression that God's voice was hidden behind the upper fiery face as a distinct divine manifestation,[204] and, from there,

---

[200] Reflecting on this verse, James Kugel notes that

anyone who knows the Hebrew text of Gen 28:12 will immediately recognize the source of this image. For though the Bible says that in his dream Jacob saw a ladder whose top reached to the Heavens, the word for "top," in Hebrew, *rosh*, is the same word normally used for "head." And so our Slavonic text—or, rather, the Hebrew text that underlies it—apparently takes the biblical reference to the ladder's "head" as a suggestion that the ladder indeed had a head, a man's head, at its very top. The fact, then, of this biblical text's wording—"a ladder set up on the earth, and its head reached to heaven"—engendered the heavenly "head" in our pseudepigraphon.

J. Kugel, *In Potiphar's House: The Interpretive Life of Biblical Texts* (San Francisco: Harper Collins, 1990), 118.

[201] H. G. Lunt, "Ladder of Jacob," *The Old Testament Pseudepigrapha* (ed. J. H. Charlesworth; 2 vols.; New York: Doubleday, 1983–1985), 2.407.

[202] Lunt, "Ladder of Jacob," 2.406.

[203] Elliot Wolfson points to a possible connection of this imagery to the conceptual developments found in the targumim. He notes that "it is worthwhile to compare the targumic and midrashic explanation of Gen 28:12 to the words of the apocryphal text the *Ladder of Jacob*. . . . 'And the top of the ladder was the face as of a man, carved out of fire.'" E. Wolfson, "The Image of Jacob Engraved upon the Throne," in: idem, *Along the Path: Studies in Kabbalistic Myth, Symbolism, and Hermeneutics* (Albany: SUNY, 1995), 114.

[204] James Charlesworth notes that in the *Ladder of Jacob*, as "in some of other pseudepigrapha, the voice has ceased to be something heard and has become a hypostatic creature." See Charlesworth's comment in: Lunt, "Ladder of Jacob," 2.406.

conveyed to the adept his audible revelation about the Promised Land. Moreover, one can see that, with respect to fashioning the first power with aural aniconic attributes, the *Ladder of Jacob* progresses even further than the *Apocalypse of Abraham*. While in the latter the divine Voice is still surrounded with ocularcentric theophanic markers, including the imagery of fire, in the former these theophanic details are completely abandoned, as the divine Voice proceeds in a more abstract and aniconic fashion.

Scholars have noted the *Ladder*'s hesitance to apply ocularcentric imagery to the deity. According to Alexander Kulik and Sergey Minov, "the fact that the text avoids the language of 'seeing' may reflect the author's belief that it is impossible for a human being to see God directly."[205] In their discussion of the aural proclivities of the text, Kulik and Minov also draw attention to the second chapter of the *Ladder*, where Jacob reflects on the deity's revelation as an auditory experience. *Lad. Jac.* 2:1–3 reads: "And when I heard (this) from on high, awe and trembling fell upon me. And I rose up from my dream and, the voice still being in my ears, . . ."[206] Notably, it is not the vision of the ladder but the memory of God's voice that is defined as the pinnacle of the patriarch's experience. Commenting on this passage, Kulik and Minov point out that the text "adds non-biblical details; for example, the echo of God's voice in the patriarch's ears immediately after he had awakened."[207] They further suggest that "this particular addition might reflect the tendency to present God's voice as a hypostasized agent for the transmission of revelatory knowledge from the deity to the seer."[208]

The imagery of the central ocularcentric manifestation in the form of the ladder's upper face also warrants attention. Researchers have already noted that in the *Ladder* the blazing Face not only exemplifies God's Glory,[209] but also represents the heavenly counterpart of Jacob.[210] Yet it has also been noted that the heavenly twin imagery in the *Ladder* appears to be garbled by the text's long transmission history.[211]

---

[205] A. Kulik and S. Minov, *Biblical Pseudepigrapha in Slavonic Tradition* (Oxford: Oxford University Press, 2016), 302–3.

[206] Lunt, "The Ladder of Jacob," 2.407.

[207] Kulik and Minov, *Biblical Pseudepigrapha in Slavonic Tradition*, 303.

[208] Kulik and Minov, *Biblical Pseudepigrapha in Slavonic Tradition*, 303.

[209] Kulik and Minov argue about the connection of the face with the *Kavod* imagery. They note that "the theophanic associations of the fiery face in 1:4–7 are strengthen even more by the fact that in several rabbinic sources the vision of the ladder of Jacob is explicitly linked to the notion of God's glory." Kulik and Minov, *Biblical Pseudepigrapha in Slavonic Tradition*, 301.

[210] Fossum, *The Image of the Invisible God*, 135–51, esp. 143.

[211] Böttrich notes that the complexity of the heavenly counterpart's imagery in the *Ladder of Jacob* posed some challenges for the transmitters of the text. He points out that "the whole idea is very complex and puzzling here. Perhaps it was already unintelligible for the Slavonic translators or redactors." C. Böttrich, "Apocalyptic Tradition and Mystical Prayer in the *Ladder of Jacob*," *JSP* 23 (2014): 290–306 at 296–97. Kulik and Minov also underline the ambiguity of the upper face imagery noting it "could be interpreted as related to God or to Jacob himself." Kulik and Minov, *Biblical Pseudepigrapha in Slavonic Tradition*, 300.

One of the scholars whose studies contributed most to the recovery of traces of Jacob's identity in the fiery face of the *Ladder* is James Kugel. While reflecting on the terminological peculiarities found in the first chapter of the text, he argues that the authors of the text were familiar with the tradition about Jacob's image or *iqonin* installed in heaven. In support, Kugel points to a remark made by a translator of the text, Horace Lunt, who, while conjecturing about the text's original language, noted that the word utilized to designate the great face on the ladder is to some degree unusual. According to Lunt, "no other Slavonic text has *lice*, 'face,' used to mean 'statue' or 'bust' (1:5 etc.), and there is no Semitic parallel."[212] On the other hand, Kugel claims that such a Semitic parallel can indeed be found. In his opinion, such a term is the Greek loan word into Mishnaic Hebrew—איקונין, which, in some rabbinic texts, did in fact come to mean "face."[213] Moreover, the basic meaning of *iqonin* as "portrait" or "bust"[214] is preserved in a number of rabbinic usages, and features prominently in the expression the *iqonin shel 'abiv* ("his Father's Countenance").[215] In the light of these connections, Kugel contended that "there is little doubt that our pseudepigraphon, in seeking to 'translate' the biblical phrase 'his/its head reached to Heaven,' reworded it in Mishnaic Hebrew as 'his [Jacob's] *iqonin* reached Heaven,' and this in turn gave rise to the presence of a heavenly bust or portrait of Jacob on the divine throne."[216]

Jarl Fossum also affirms[217] the presence of the *iqonin* tradition in the *Ladder*, arguing that "in the fiery bust of the terrifying man we are probably correct to see the heavenly 'image' of Jacob."[218] Christfried Böttrich calls attention to another significant detail, namely, an accentuated distance between the mysterious face and the deity. Deliberating on this feature, Böttrich notes that in the *Ladder*, "God is standing 'above its highest face' and seems to speak in hiding from behind it, so that

---

[212] Lunt, "The Ladder of Jacob," 2.403.

[213] Kugel, *In Potiphar's House*, 119.

[214] Rachel Neis observes that

> it is conceivable that the "face of Jacob" is used in a more generic sense for Jacob's image or likeness and could include a representation of his entire figure or bust. The bust, or portrait medallion, was ubiquitous in civic, funerary and religious art in Late Antiquity and Byzantine periods, and while emphasizing the face of the person portrayed could portray the upper torso and arms.
> R. Neis, "Embracing Icons: The Face of Jacob on the Throne of God," *Images: A Journal of Jewish Art and Visual Culture* 1 (2007): 36–54 at 42.

[215] Kugel, *In Potiphar's House*, 119.

[216] Kugel, *In Potiphar's House*, 119.

[217] See also C. C. Rowland, "John 1:51, Jewish Apocalyptic and Targumic Tradition," *NTS* 30 (1984): 498–507; C. H. von Heijne, *The Messenger of the Lord in Early Jewish Interpretations of Genesis* (BZAW 42; Berlin, New York: Walter de Gruyter, 2010), 177–78.

[218] Fossum, *The Image of the Invisible God*, 143, n. 30. I have also argued for the existence of the heavenly counterpart traditions in the *Ladder of Jacob*. For my arguments, see A. A. Orlov, "The Face as the Heavenly Counterpart of the Visionary in the Slavonic Ladder of Jacob," in: *Of Scribes and Sages: Early Jewish Interpretation and Transmission of Scripture* (ed. C. A. Evans; 2 vols.; SSEJC 9; London: T&T Clark, 2004), 2.59–76; idem, *The Greatest Mirror: Heavenly Counterparts in the Jewish Pseudepigrapha* (Albany: SUNY, 2017), 93–104.

the fiery face does appear only as a divine representation of God himself."[219] Here, as in many other two powers accounts, the second power is conceptualized as a visible divine manifestation.

In the light of the aforementioned deliberations, it is possible that, on the ladder, the seer encounters two celestial manifestations. One of them in the visible shape of his own heavenly *iqonin*, and the other as an audial representation of the divine Voice.

A few words must be said about the order of appearance of the two powers in the *Ladder of Jacob*. When compared with the accounts found in the Book of Daniel, the *Book of the Similitudes*, the *Primary Adam Books*, the *Exagoge*, and *2 Enoch*, in which both powers are portrayed as ocularcentric manifestations, in the *Ladder of Jacob* and in the *Apocalypse of Abraham*, one can see an inverse procession of the respective powers. While in the ocularcentric dual theophanies the primary power emerges first, here the narrative first describes the visual manifestation of the second power (in the form of the Angel Yahoel or Jacob's *iqonin*), which is then followed by the aural address of the deity. The same order is present in some early Christian accounts, where Jesus and the deity will appear together.

Angelic Opposition

Another important feature that supports the notion that the fiery face represents Jacob's heavenly image (*iqonin*), which became conceived in our text as the second power, is the presence of the motif of angelic opposition. This theme, as noted above, is often expressed in early Jewish two powers accounts.

In later rabbinic sources this theme often appears in the context of stories about Jacob's heavenly image engraved or installed on the Throne of Glory. An example of this tradition is found in *Genesis Rabbah* 68:12, a passage that speaks about the angelic exaltation of Jacob and opposition to this exaltation:

> R. Hiyya the Elder and R. Jannai disagreed. One maintained: They were ascending and descending the ladder; while the other said: They were ascending and descending on Jacob. The statement that they were ascending and descending the ladder presents no difficulty. The statement that they were ascending and descending on Jacob we must take to mean that some were exalting him and others degrading him, dancing, leaping, and maligning him.[220]

This account echoes the Adamic and Enochic traditions where a newly appointed "icon" of the deity encounters both the obeisance and opposition of the angelic hosts. In this regard, the salient feature of the text is the postulation that some angels opposed Jacob's heavenly image by "degrading . . . and maligning him," thus revealing a familiar motif of angelic rivalry already explored in our study. This theme is already reflected

---

[219] Böttrich, "Apocalyptic Tradition and Mystical Prayer," 297.

[220] H. Freedman and M. Simon, *Midrash Rabbah* (10 vols.; London: Soncino, 1961), 2.626.

in some talmudic materials that constitute the background of *Gen. Rab.* 68:12. Thus, *b. Hul.* 91b contains the following tradition:

> A Tanna taught: They ascended to look at the image above and descended to look at the image below. They wished to hurt him, when Behold, the Lord stood beside him (Gen 28:13). R. Simeon b. Lakish said: Were it not expressly stated in the Scripture, we would not dare to say it. [God is made to appear] like a man who is fanning his son.[221]

Elliot Wolfson notes that in these rabbinic sources the motif of the patriarch's heavenly image "is placed in the context of another well-known motif regarding the enmity or envy of the angels toward human beings. That is, according to the statements in *Genesis Rabbah* and *Bavli Hullin* the angels, who beheld Jacob's image above, were jealous and sought to harm Jacob below."[222]

The theme of angelic opposition also unfolds in chapter 5 of the *Ladder*, which deals with the interpretation of the seer's vision. There the interpreting angel reveals to the earthly Jacob the following meaning of the ladder:

> Thus he [*angelus interpres*] said to me [Jacob]: "You have seen a ladder with twelve steps, each step having two human faces which kept changing their appearance. The ladder is this age, and the twelve steps are the periods of this age. But the twenty-four faces are the kings of the ungodly nations of this age. Under these kings the children of your children and the generations of your sons will be interrogated. These will rise up against the iniquity of your grandsons. And this place will be made desolate by the four ascents ... through the sins of your grandsons. And around the property of your forefathers a palace will be built, a temple in the name of your God and of (the God) of your fathers, and in the provocations of your children it will become deserted by the four ascents of this age. For you saw the first four busts which were striking against the steps ... angels ascending and descending, and the busts amid the steps. The Most High will raise up kings from the grandsons of your brother Esau, and they will receive all the nobles of the tribes of the earth who will have maltreated your seed."[223]

Here the twelve steps of the ladder represent the twelve periods of "this age," while the twenty-four "minor" faces embody the twenty-four kings of the ungodly nations. Ascending and descending angels on the ladder are envisioned as the guardian angels belonging to the nations hostile to Jacob and his descendants. The angelic locomotion or "ascents" appear to be construed in the passage as arrogations against Israel. As previously noted, this historic revelation is influenced by the four-fold scheme of the antagonistic empires reflected in the Book of Daniel and also through the peculiar

---

[221] Epstein, *The Babylonian Talmud. Hullin,* 91b.
[222] Wolfson, "The Image of Jacob Engraved upon the Throne," 4.
[223] Lunt, "Ladder of Jacob," 2.409.

features of the Danielic empires, specifically the fourth kingdom of Rome, represented by Esau.[224]

Although the description found in the *Ladder* has been obscured by the text's long journey in various ideological milieus, a clearer presentation of the same constellation of peculiar details is present in several rabbinic accounts. James Kugel notes that several rabbinic passages dealing with Jacob's vision of the ladder attest to the similar motif of the ascending and descending angels as hostile nations.[225] Thus, for example, *Lev. Rab.* 29:2 offers the following description:

> R. Nahman opened his discourse with the text, Therefore fear thou not, O Jacob My servant (Jer 30:10). This speaks of Jacob himself, of whom it is written, And he dreamed, and behold, a ladder set up on the earth ... and behold the angels of God ascending and descending on it (Gen 28:12). These angels, explained R. Samuel b. Nahman, were the guardian Princes of the nations of the world. For R. Samuel b. Nahman said: This verse teaches us that the Holy One, blessed be He, showed our father Jacob the Prince of Babylon ascending seventy rungs of the ladder, the Prince of Media fifty-two rungs, the Prince of Greece one hundred and eighty, while the Prince of Edom ascended till Jacob did not know how many rungs. Thereupon our father Jacob was afraid. He thought: Is it possible that this one will never be brought down? Said the Holy One, blessed be He, to him: Fear thou not, O Jacob My servant. Even if he ascend and sit down by Me, I will bring him down from there! Hence it is written, Though thou make thy nest as high as the eagle, and though thou set it among the stars, I will bring thee down from thence. R. Berekiah and R. Helbo, and R. Simeon b. Yohai in the name of R. Meir said: It teaches that the Holy One, blessed be He, showed Jacob the Prince of Babylon ascending and descending, of Media ascending and descending, of Greece ascending and descending, and of Edom ascending and descending.[226]

---

[224] In relation to these connections Kugel observes that

> the same motif [of four empires] apparently underlies the *Ladder of Jacob*. Here too, it is Jacob's vision of the ladder that serves as the vehicle for a revelation of the "kings of the lawless nations" who will rule over Israel, and if this text does not specifically mention how many such nations there will be, it does go on to speak (as we have seen) of four "ascents" or "descents" that will bring Jacob's progeny to grief. Indeed, the continuation of our text alludes specifically to the last of the four empires, Rome: "The Most High will raise up kings from the grandsons of your brother Esau, and they will receive the nobles of the tribes of the earth who will have maltreated your seed." As is well known, Esau frequently represents Rome in Second Temple writings.
>
> J. Kugel, "The Ladder of Jacob," *HTR* 88 (1995): 209–27 at 214.

[225] Kugel, "The Ladder of Jacob," 214.

[226] Freedman and Simon, *Midrash Rabbah*, 4.370. See also *Exod. Rab.* 32:7:

> God showed Jacob the guardian angels of every empire, for it says, And he dreamed, and behold a ladder set up on the earth (Gen 28:12). He showed him how many peoples, governors, and rulers would arise from each kingdom, and just as He displayed their rise, so he showed their fall, as it says, And behold, the angels of God ascending and descending on it.
>
> Freedman and Simon, *Midrash Rabbah*, 3.411.

A similar understanding is found in *Midrash on Psalms* 78:6:

> R. Berechiah, R. Levi, and R. Simeon ben Jose taught in the name of R. Meir that the Holy One, blessed be He, let Jacob see a ladder upon which Babylon climbed up seventy rungs and came down, Media climbed up fifty-two rungs and came down, Greece climbed up a hundred and eighty rungs and came down. But when Edom climbed higher than these, Jacob saw and was afraid. The Holy One, blessed be He, said to him, Therefore fear thou not, O Jacob My servant (Jer 30:10). Even as the former fell, so will the latter fall.[227]

In these passages the similarities with the Danielic account are even more apparent than in the *Ladder*, since the familiar four-fold structure is now represented by Babylon, Media, Greece, and Edom, empires that, in the history of interpretation, are often associated with the four beasts of Daniel 7.[228] According to Kugel, "the four beasts [of Daniel's vision] are transformed into 'angels of God' said to go up and down Jacob's ladder."[229]

The peculiar theme of angelic hostility might provide additional evidence that the authors of the *Ladder* were cognizant of the motif of angelic opposition, which performs a pivotal role in the two powers in heaven lore.

---

[227] W. G. Braude, *The Midrash on Psalms* (2 vols.; YJS, 13; New Haven: Yale University Press, 1959), 2.26–27. *Pesiqta de-Rab Kahana* 23 contains an almost identical tradition:

> R. Nahman applied it to the episode in Jacob's life when He dreamed, and beheld a ladder ... and angels of God (Gen 28:12). These angels, according to R. Samuel bar R. Nahman, were the princes of the nations of the earth. Further, according to R. Samuel bar Nahman, this verse proves that the Holy One showed to our father Jacob the prince of Babylon climbing up seventy rungs of the ladder, then climbing down; the prince of Media climbing up fifty-two rungs and no more; the prince of Greece, one hundred and eighty rungs and no more; and the prince of Edom climbing and climbing, no one knows how many rungs. At the sight of Edom's climbing our father Jacob grew afraid, and said: Is one to suppose that this prince will have no come-down? The Holy One replied: Be not dismayed, O Israel (Jer 30:10): Even if—as though such a thing were possible!—thou were to see him seated next to Me, I would have him brought down thence.
>
> W. G. Braude and I. J. Kapstein, *Pesikta de-Rab Kahana. R. Kahana's Compilation of Discourses for Sabbaths and Festal Days* (Philadelphia: Jewish Publication Society of America, 1975), 353.

See also *Zohar* I.149b:

> And behold, the angels of God ascending and descending on it; this alludes to the Chieftains who have charge of all the nations, and who ascend and descend on that ladder. When Israel is sinful, the ladder is lowered and the Chieftains ascend by it; but when Israel are righteous, the ladder is removed and all the Chieftains are left below and are deprived of their dominion. Jacob thus saw in this dream the domination of Esau and the domination of the other nations. According to another explanation, the angels ascended and descended on the top of the ladder; for when the top was detached, the ladder was lowered and the Chieftains ascended, but when it was attached again, the ladder was lifted and they remained below.
>
> H. Sperling and M. Simon, *The Zohar* (5 vols.; London and New York: Soncino, 1933), 2.79–80.

[228] On this see J. Kugel, *Traditions of the Bible: A Guide to the Bible as It Was at the Start of the Common Era* (Cambridge: Harvard University Press, 1998), 363.

[229] Kugel, "The Ladder of Jacob," 215.

Theophanic Molds in Rabbinic and Hekhalot Two Powers Debates

Our study of early Jewish two powers traditions demonstrated that within these accounts the second power often played a complementary role in relation to the deity, frequently understood as God's visual "icon." Yet as Alan Segal and other scholars have rightly observed, in later rabbinic and Hekhalot milieus the two powers traditions were predestined to play a very different role, often serving as an important doctrinal warning. The interaction between the two theophanic molds—one ocular, the other aural—employed in early Jewish accounts to complement the unique functions of the respective powers, received a new polemical meaning in rabbinic traditions. Often in these later accounts the two theophanic molds were deliberately contrasted in order to underline the inauthenticity of the second power's corporeality and its inferiority to the true deity, now depicted with aniconic aural terminology. This paradigm shift is illustrated by the story of Aher's vision of Metatron, an oft-repeated theme in rabbinic and Hekhalot sources. The story recounts the infamous visionary Elisha ben Avuyah encountering the great angel Metatron during his ascent to heaven. The Babylonian Talmud (*b. Hag.* 15a)[230] relates the following rendering of Aher's story:

> Aher mutilated the shoots. Of him Scripture says: Suffer not thy mouth to bring thy flesh into guilt. What does it refer to? He saw that permission was granted to Metatron to sit and write down the merits of Israel. Said he: It is taught as a tradition that on high there is no sitting and no emulation, and no back, and no weariness. Perhaps, God forbid! There are two divinities! [Thereupon] they led Metatron forth, and punished him with sixty fiery lashes, saying to him: Why didst thou not rise before him when thou didst see him? Permission was [then] given to him to strike out the merits of Aher. A *Bat Qol* went forth and said: Return, ye backsliding children—except Aher. [Thereupon] he said: Since I have been driven forth from yonder world, let me go forth and enjoy this world. So Aher went forth into evil courses.[231]

Debates about this mysterious passage have perpetuated for centuries. Frequently missed, however, is a recognition of polemical interaction between different molds of theophanic symbolism. Thus, while the great angel is depicted with the divine attributes of the visionary trend, the true deity is delineated through the distinctive aural symbolism, namely, through the image of the heavenly Voice. Additionally, unlike in early Jewish accounts where the two theophanic modes complement each other, they are here presented in polemical tension as one mode is challenged by the nearness of the other. In symbolic juxtaposition, one manifestation becomes a mere phantom, a dangerous illusion. In this context the ocularcentric or visual mode, characterized by

---

[230] On the various manuscript versions of *b. Hag.* 15a, see P. Alexander, "3 Enoch and the Talmud," *JSJ* 18 (1987): 40–68; C. R. A. Morray-Jones, "Hekhalot Literature and Talmudic Tradition: Alexander's Three Test Cases," *JSJ* 22 (1991): 1–39.

[231] Epstein, *The Babylonian Talmud. Hagiga*, 15a.

the *Hagiga* passage as heretical, is clearly cast in an unfavorable light to the adept of this visionary praxis, Elisha ben Avuyah, or Aher.

This represents a striking contrast to the harmony of the dual theophanies found in early Jewish accounts, where the seer and the object of his vision often become united, thereby signaling the eschatological restoration of humankind. Unlike the latter, Aher's vision of Metatron does not end amicably, but rather in disarray, bringing with it the anger of the Creator.[232] The visual representation of the invisible God suddenly turned into a hazardous delusion that was bound to mislead the infamous visionary. One of the dire consequences of the encounter is that both the seer and the object of his erroneous vision were ruthlessly reprimanded by the deity. While Metatron was punished with sixty blazing lashes, Aher is reprimanded even more severely through his expulsion from the Tradition. Whereas in early Jewish accounts, all the actors of the theophany are lifted up, here they are unified through an overwhelming demotion.

The "divine" feature that clearly puzzles our infamous seer in *3 Enoch*'s story is the angel's sitting,[233] a motif that summons the memory of the divine seat, the Chariot, an iconic glyph of the ocularcentric ideology in the Hebrew Bible.[234] As previously noted, the feature of the divine seat was often transferred in early Jewish dual theophanies to various second powers without any tension or polemical overtones. Here, however, there is a defining moment of contention. The vision of Metatron's sitting in heaven is not corrected by the alternative *vision* of the genuine Chariot,[235] but rather by an *audition* of the celestial Voice (בת קול), portrayed here as the true manifestation of God.[236] Researchers frequently recognize the

---

[232] While in *b. Hag.* 15a and *3 Enoch* Metatron's figure is surrounded with controversy, in some Jewish mystical accounts he is envisioned as the complementary second power. Regarding these traditions, see Orlov, *The Enoch-Metatron Tradition*, 143–46.

[233] For some problems with this interpretation, see M. Miller, *The Name of God in Jewish Thought: A Philosophical Analysis of Mystical Traditions from Apocalyptic to Kabbalah* (New York: Routledge, 2015), 69ff. Miller points out that some manuscripts remove reference to Metatron's seated posture. Miller, *The Name of God*, 70.

[234] Reflecting on Aher's encounter with Metatron, Daniel Boyarin argues "that it was the combination of sitting, suggesting the enthronement . . . which leads to the idea of Two Sovereignties." Boyarin, "Beyond Judaisms," 350. In the same vein, Daniel Abrams earlier noted that "the heavenly enthronement or 'sitting' of Metatron, which was apparently a sign to Elisha that Metatron was himself divine, supports this understanding of Elisha's heresy." D. Abrams, "The Boundaries of Divine Ontology: The Inclusion and Exclusion of Metatron in the Godhead," *HTR* 87 (1994): 294.

[235] The polemical stand against the ocularcentric representation of the deity is also underlined by Aher's own reaction, namely, his doubt and his postulation concerning the possibility of "two authorities in heaven." In other words, he does not merely succumb to the anthropomorphic replica of the deity in the form of Metatron, but he doubts it.

[236] In the *Ascent of Elisha ben Avuyah* (*Synopse* §597), the vision of the ambiguous celestial form is also contrasted with the aural revelation of the deity:

> Elisha ben Avuyah said: When I ascended into paradise I saw 'KTRY'L YH God of Israel, YHWH of Hosts, who sits at the entrance of paradise, and one hundred twenty myriads of attending angels encircling him, as it is said, A thousand thousands served him and a myriad myriads stood before him (Dan 7:10). When I saw them, I was confounded and shaken, but I forced myself and I entered before the Holy One, blessed be he. I said before him: Lord of the world, it is written in Your Torah, Behold, to YHWH your God belong the heavens and the heaven of heavens (Deut 10:14). But it is written The

anthropomorphic[237] overtones of Aher's infamous vision, reflected in the seer's statement that "on high there is no sitting and no emulation, and no back, and no weariness." In his discussion of this dictum, Alan Segal notes that "the rabbis are determined to refute the whole idea of heavenly enthronement by stating that such things as 'sitting' and other anthropomorphic activities are unthinkable in heaven."[238] Philip Alexander likewise discerns the anthropomorphic overtones of Aher's utterance; he thinks the list suggests "God and the angels are without body parts or passions."[239] Scholars have also directed attention to the theophanic connotations in Elisha's announcement, arguing that every component of Aher's list seems to allude to a pivotal biblical passage that describes theophanic features of the deity. Daniel Boyarin notes that[240]

> each of the elements in the list refers to a verse: thus, for standing, we find Num 12:5, where the verse reads: "And YHWH came down on a column of cloud and stood in front of the Tent." . . . The crux, "back," is now neatly solved as well. Referring to the back of God that Moses allegedly saw [Exod 33:23], the text denies the literal existence of that as well.

In a Hekhalot version of the Aher story reflected in *Merkavah Rabbah* (*Synopse* §672), one finds a similar polemical juxtaposition of ocularcentric and aural markers:

> They said: When Elisha descended into to the chariot, he saw, with reference to Metatron, that he was given authority for one hour in the day to sit down and to write the merits of Israel. He said: The sages have taught: "On high there is no standing
>
> firmament tells the work of his hands (Ps 19:2)—one alone! He said to me: Elisha, my son, have you come for nothing but to discuss My consistency? Have you not heard the proverb that mortals tell?
>
> Davila, *Hekhalot Literature in Translation*, 355.

James Davila argues that "the passage seems to imply that this being is God rather than an angel, but this may be a subtle allusion to the tradition that Elisha ben Avuyah was led into a polytheistic heresy when he saw the angel Metatron enthroned in heaven." Davila, *Hekhalot Literature in Translation*, 355.

[237] Reflecting on the connections between anthropomorphism and ocularcentric visionary experience, Elliot Wolfson observes that

> the problem of visionary experience in Jewish mysticism cannot be treated in isolation from the question of God's form or image. The problem surrounding the claim for visionary experience invariably touches upon the larger philosophical-theological problem of God's having a visible form or body . . . to be sure, the issues of visionary experience and anthropomorphism are theoretically distinct. That is, from an analytical standpoint it is possible to conceive of a divine body that is nevertheless invisible to human beings. Conversely, God may be visible, but not in human form. It is nevertheless the case that the two are often intertwined in classical theological and philosophical texts in general and in the primary sources of biblical and postbiblical Judaism in particular.
>
> Wolfson, *Through a Speculum*, 23.

[238] Segal, *Two Powers in Heaven*, 61.

[239] Alexander, "3 Enoch and the Talmud," 60.

[240] Boyarin, "Beyond Judaisms," 347.

and no sitting, no jealousy and no rivalry, no pride and no humility." He conceived the thought that perhaps there are two authorities in heaven. At once he brought Metatron outside the curtain and struck him sixty times with blows of fire. And they gave Metatron authority to burn the merits of Elisha. There went out a heavenly voice and it said: Repent, returning sons (Jer 3:22), except for the Other One.[241]

Aher's scene in *3 Enoch* 16:1–5 (*Synopse* §20), now exclaimed from the mouth of Metatron, fashions the same contrast between the corporeal characteristics of the great angel and the auricular depiction of the deity:

At first I sat upon a great throne at the door of the seventh palace, and I judged all the denizens of the heights on the authority of the Holy One, blessed be he. I assigned greatness, royalty, rank, sovereignty, glory, praise, diadem, crown, and honor to all the princes of kingdoms, when I sat in the heavenly court. The princes of kingdoms stood beside me, to my right and to my left, by authority of the Holy One, blessed be he. But when Aher came to behold the vision of the chariot and set eyes upon me, he was afraid and trembled before me. His soul was alarmed to the point of leaving him, because of his fear, dread, and terror of me, when he saw me seated upon a throne like a king, with ministering angels standing beside me as servants and all the princes of kingdoms crowned with crowns surrounding me. Then he opened his mouth and said, "There are indeed two powers in heaven!" Immediately a divine voice came out from the presence of the Shekinah and said, "Come back to me, apostate sons—apart from Aher!" Then Anafiel YHWH, the honored, glorified, beloved, wonderful, terrible, and dreadful Prince, came at the command of the Holy One, blessed be he, and struck me with sixty lashes of fire and made me stand to my feet.[242]

While the sections from *Hagiga Bavli* and *Merkavah Rabbah* do not elaborate the full scope of Metatron's story, *3 Enoch* expounds more broadly on the origin of his chief angelic protagonist by tracing it back to the exaltation of Enoch in the antediluvian age. The conceptual steps of Enoch's elevation into the rank of the ocularcentric "second power" in *Sefer Hekhalot* are grandiose in nature. The tale of the hero's exaltation begins in chapter 6, where Anafiel YHWH removes Enoch from the midst of humankind and transports him to heaven in the fiery chariot. In chapter 7, Enoch-Metatron is installed near the throne of Glory. In the following chapter (8), he is endowed with the totality of heavenly knowledge bestowed upon him by the divinity himself. Chapter 9 describes the vast amplification of Metatron's body and his procurement of cosmic wings, the metamorphosis that transforms him into a celestial creature. In chapter 10, the deity makes a throne for his new beloved, spreading over his distinguished seat "a coverlet of splendor." Metatron is then enthroned by the deity on his celestial seat constructed for him. In chapter 11 God reveals to Metatron all the mysteries of the universe, while in

---

[241] Schäfer et al., *Synopse*, 246; Davila, *Hekhalot Literature in Translation*, 203.

[242] P. Alexander, "3 (Hebrew Apocalypse of) Enoch," in: *The Old Testament Pseudepigrapha* (ed. J. H. Charlesworth; 2 vols.; New York: Doubleday, 1983–1985), 1.268; Schäfer et al., *Synopse*, 10–11.

chapter 12 he further endows the great angel with a glorious robe and crown and names him the Lesser YHWH. In chapter 13 Metatron's crown is decorated with the letters of the Tetragrammaton. In chapter 14, Metatron is crowned and receives homage from the angelic hosts. In chapter 15, which immediately precedes Aher's story, the reader learns about the dramatic metamorphosis of Metatron's body into his celestial form.

An important detail that connects Metatron's exaltation with the early Jewish two powers in heaven traditions is the story of angelic veneration and angelic opposition to Enoch-Metatron found in *3 Enoch* 4:5–10. As we recall, such motifs of angelic rivalry and obeisance often accompany a human seer's initiation into a rank of the second power, as observed in the *Primary Adam Books*, *2 Enoch*, the *Ladder of Jacob*, and, possibly, the *Exagoge*. In *Sefer Hekhalot* 4:5–10, Enoch encounters the same reactions from the angelic host during the process of his elevation into the rank of the second power. *Synopse* §6 (*3 Enoch* 4:5–10) unveils the following tradition:

> And the Holy One, blessed be he, appointed me (Enoch) in the height as a prince and a ruler among the ministering angels. Then three of ministering angels, ʿUzzah, ʿAzzah, and ʿAzaʾel, came and laid charges against me in the heavenly height. They said before the Holy One, blessed be he, "Lord of the Universe, did not the primeval ones give you good advice when they said, do not create man!" The Holy One, blessed be he, replied, "I have made and I will sustain him; I will carry and I will deliver him." When they saw me they said before him, "Lord of the Universe, what right has this one to ascend to the height of heights? Is he not descended from those who perished in the waters of the Flood? What right has he to be in heaven?" Again the Holy One, blessed be he, replied and said to them, "What right have you to interrupt me? I have chosen this one in preference to all of you, to be a prince and a ruler over you in the heavenly heights." At once they all arose and went to meet me and prostrated themselves before me, saying, "Happy are you, and happy your parents, because your Creator has favored you." Because I am young in their company and a mere youth among them in days and months and years—therefore they call me "Youth."[243]

In this passage, as in the *Primary Adam Books*, the angelic opposition is provoked by an appeal to the inferior origins of the new favorite of God, chosen by the deity to be a prince and ruler over the celestial citizens in the heavenly heights. The shape of the tradition appears to be closer to the account related in *2 Enoch* than the version attested in the *Primary Adam Books*, since here the angels who initially opposed the exaltation of the newly appointed second power later offer their obeisance to Enoch.

As in early Adamic and Enochic traditions, the angelic veneration enhances Enoch-Metatron's exalted profile by transforming him into an "icon" of God. Assessing the angel's profile, Joseph Dan suggests that Metatron turns out to be "almost a miniature version of God himself."[244] However, the endowment of the second power with ocularcentric features is not surprising. As we have already demonstrated, a significant

---

[243] Alexander, "3 Enoch," 1.258–9; Schäfer et al., *Synopse*, 6–7.

[244] J. Dan, *The Ancient Jewish Mysticism* (Tel Aviv: MOD Books, 1993), 117.

number of such attributes were transferred to the second power in various delineations found in early Jewish accounts. What is novel here is the implicit polemical dimension observed in the tension, culminating in Metatron's subsequent demotion by fiery flagellation, and thereby accentuating the difference between him and the genuine deity.

Furthermore, when compared to the testimonies regarding Aher's apostasy found in *b. Hag.* 15a and *Merkavah Rabbah* (*Synopse* §672), *3 Enoch*'s record of Metatron's demotion is adorned with additional theophanic imagery. A careful reexamination of this puzzling account would be advantageous. *3 Enoch* 16:1–5 reads:

> R. Ishmael said: The angel Metatron, Prince of the Divine Presence, the glory of highest heaven, said to me: At first I sat upon a great throne at the door of the seventh palace, and I judged all the denizens of the heights on the authority of the Holy One, blessed be he. I assigned greatness, royalty, rank, sovereignty, glory, praise, diadem, crown, and honor to all the princes of kingdoms, when I sat in the heavenly court. The princes of kingdoms stood beside me, to my right and to my left, by authority of the Holy One, blessed be he. But when Aher came to behold the vision of the chariot and set eyes upon me, he was afraid and trembled before me. His soul was alarmed to the point of leaving him because of his fear, dread, and terror of me, when he saw me seated upon a throne like a king, with ministering angels standing beside me as servants and all the princes of kingdoms crowned with crowns surrounding me. Then he opened his mouth and said, "There are indeed two powers in heaven!" Immediately a divine voice came out from the presence of the Shekinah and said, "Come back to me, apostate sons—apart from Aher!" Then Anafiel YHWH, the honored, glorified, beloved, wonderful, terrible, and dreadful Prince, came at the command of the Holy One, blessed be he, and struck me with sixty lashes of fire and made me stand to my feet.

Unlike *b. Hag.* 15a and *Synopse* §672, where Metatron's seated position is explained via his role as celestial scribe,[245] here the great angel is depicted as the enthroned celestial ruler and arbiter dispatched to judge "all the denizens of the heights on the authority of the Holy One." The section provides additional insight into Metatron's status in the celestial court with regard to "the princes of kingdoms," particularly by announcing that "he *sat* in the heavenly court." In *3 Enoch*, in like manner, Aher encounters not just a seated scribe,[246] but rather the enthroned vice-regent, who is encompassed by a stunning

---

[245] *b. Hag.* 15a: "He saw that permission was granted to Metatron to sit and write down the merits of Israel"; *Synopse* §672: "he was given authority for one hour in the day to sit down and to write the merits of Israel."

[246] Concerning the differences between the *Hagiga* version and *3 Enoch* 16, Alexander notes that
> there is no reference in *3 Enoch* to Metatron as the heavenly scribe. In the Talmud Metatron sits in virtue of the fact that he is the celestial scribe; in *3 Enoch* he sits in virtue of the fact that he is the Lesser Lord. . . . Why does *3 Enoch* say nothing about Metatron as scribe? The answer probably is that the author of *3 Enoch* 16 was simply not interested in Metatron's scribal activity. He was interested in the fact that the Talmudic story spoke of Metatron sitting. He seized on this element and used it as a way of introducing material on Metatron's throne and retinue. His subsequent stress on Metatron's viceregal splendour left no place for Metatron's role as celestial scribe.
>
> Alexander, "3 Enoch and Talmud," 65.

entourage comprised of crowned princes.[247] In this regard it is not coincidental that the notorious list asserting there is no sitting in heaven is absent here, since other more exalted features of Metatron clearly take priority over this previously decisive hallmark.[248]

A vital aspect of 3 Enoch's story is its conceptual ties to early Jewish two powers accounts. Researchers have observed that the depiction of Metatron's court is reminiscent of elements found in the narrative of Dan 7:9–10.[249] As one recalls, these Danielic themes also played a crucial role in the construction of Yahoel's exalted personage in the *Apocalypse of Abraham*. Similarly, in *3 Enoch* 16, the memory of the eschatological judge in the form of the Ancient of Days becomes instrumental in fashioning Metatron's exalted position.

Furthermore, Metatron's interaction with his subjects in the form of the "princes of kingdoms," on whom he heaps "greatness, royalty, rank, sovereignty, glory, praise, diadem, crown, and honor," is reminiscent of God's activities in relation to the great angel earlier in the story. Subsequently, Metatron not only obtains the distinctive theophanic qualities himself, he now, like God, can share them with other subjects.

Aher's perception of Metatron likewise undergoes striking revisions in *Sefer Hekhalot*'s version of the story. First, the nature of mystical experience as ocular experience is underscored in *3 Enoch* 16 through the expression, "Aher came *to behold the vision of the chariot and set eyes upon me*." In contrast, both *b. Hag.* 15a and *Merkavah Rabbah* (Synopse §672) simply state that *he saw*. A second significant detail is Aher's unusual reaction to Metatron's epiphany. Metatron reports that Aher "was afraid and trembled before me. His soul was alarmed to the point of leaving him because of his fear, dread, and terror of me." Both *b. Hag.* 15a and *Merkavah Rabbah* do not specify such an emotional reaction. This reaction, however, enhances Metatron's theophanic status by directly associating it with the memory of biblical and pseudepigraphical accounts in which seers are portrayed as overpowered with fear upon encountering the divine Form.[250] The seer's dread, as in numerous other Jewish accounts, therefore serves as a mirror of the theophany.

---

[247] Christopher Morray-Jones remarks that,

> in *3 Enoch*, the cause of Aher's error is not the mere fact of Metatron's being seated, but his god-like and glorious appearance as the enthroned "Grand Vizier" of Heaven. No mention is made of Metatron's being the heavenly scribe: the whole . . . seems to be derived from the "Lesser Lord" tradition (which does not figure—at least explicitly—in the talmudic versions). This suggests that the original—and far more plausible—cause of Aher's heresy was that he mistook the "Lesser Lord" for a co-equal "Second Power" and hence fell into heresy.
>
> Morray-Jones, "Hekhalot Literature and Talmudic Tradition," 30.

[248] Yet, the memory of this important attribute has not been forgotten in *3 Enoch*, since in the course of demotion Anafiel places Metatron in a standing position: "Then Anafiel YHWH . . . made me stand to my feet." Alexander notes that "*3 Enoch* makes no mention of the teaching that there is 'no sitting, no rivalry, no neck, and no weariness' in heaven, but 'sitting' in its almost literal sense clearly plays an important part in its version of the story." Alexander, "3 Enoch and Talmud," 64.

[249] Nathaniel Deutsch remarks that in *3 Enoch* 16, Metatron is portrayed as the divine judge or *atiq yomin* of Dan 7:10, "although *3 Enoch* 16 . . . only implicitly draws on this *Vorlage*." Deutsch, *Guardians of the Gate*, 65.

[250] In the light of the influences that the Enochic traditions exercised in the shaping of Metatron's exalted profile, the tradition of Aher's fear is also possibly informed by some pseudepigraphical

These striking theophanic details, now imbedded into Aher's episode itself, again point to the fact that Metatron's demotion in *3 Enoch* represents no mere happenstance or later insertion of an "orthodox" editor; rather it constitutes an essential part of the original plot in which the ocularcentric theophanic traits of the second power are contrasted with the aniconic aural deity who appears as the divine Voice.[251] Moreover, in *3 Enoch* the "genuine" deity emerges as more aniconic and incorporeal than in *b. Hag.* 15a and *Synopse* §672, wherein it appears that God himself punishes Metatron with sixty blazing lashes. In *3 Enoch*, however, this role is now straightforwardly relegated to another otherworldly power in the form of Anafiel YHWH. It is thus conceivable that these two conspicuous appearances of this puzzling angelic figure serve as essential structural milestones, defining the limits of Metatron's story. Recall that in *3 Enoch* 6, Anafiel YHWH assumes a pivotal role in the initial step of Enoch-Metatron's elevation by transporting the hero in a fiery chariot to heaven.[252] The accounts of Metatron's elevation and demotion are thus additionally interconnected through this mysterious angelic operator, who features in the beginning of Enoch-Metatron's exaltation in chapter 6 and again at the end of his demotion in chapter 16, thereby solidifying this literary piece as a single unit. This literary schema reconfirms that the Aher scene does not represent a mere interpolation but rather constitutes an integral conceptual part of this Hekhalot macroform.[253] Situating the Anafiel YHWH—whose lofty designation,

---

developments. Thus in *1 Enoch* 14:9–14, which describes Enoch's entrance into the divine presence, Enoch is not simply frightened by his otherworldly experience, but he is literally "covered with fear."

[251] Hugo Odeberg sees various interconnections between the theophanic details of Metatron's exaltation and demotion, including similarities of the throne imagery found in chapters 10 and 16. Yet he is unable to recognize any real polemical meaning of such parallels, seeing them as the work of an "orthodox" editor who was not only responsible for the interpolation of chapter 16, but also for editing the section concerning Metatron's exaltation. Thus, he suggests that,

> in view of the subtle way in which the writer of ch. 16 veils his opposition against the excessive and dangerous developments (as he regards them) of the Metatron-conception by the use of terms and notions recognized by or congenial to the Metatron-tradition, it is not impossible to assume that the qualifying expression of ch. 10, referred to above, is an insertion made by the same hand who is responsible for ch. 16. There seems in fact to be a natural connection between 10 and 16, in so far as the former contains the logical presupposition for the statements of the latter.

H. Odeberg, *3 Enoch or the Hebrew Book of Enoch* (New York: KTAV, 1973), 87.

[252] *3 Enoch* 6:1 relates the following tradition:

> R. Ishmael said: The angel Metatron, Prince of the Divine Presence, said to me: When the Holy One, blessed be he, desired to bring me up to the height, he sent me Prince Anafiel YHWH and he took me from their midst, before their very eyes, and he conveyed me in great glory on a fiery chariot, with fiery horses and glorious attendants, and he brought me up with the Shekinah to the heavenly heights.

Alexander, "3 Enoch," 1.261.

[253] Hugo Odeberg notes that the reference to Anafiel as the executor of the punishment of Metatron

> seems to have been made with conscious allusion to ch. 6. The angel who according to ch. 6 was first sent to fetch Enoch from on earth, in order that he might be translated into Metatron, was well suited to be the superior angel who carried out Metatron's degradation. And it was thereby emphasized that just as Anafiel had been superior to Enoch at the time of his elevation he was also superior to Metatron at least from his degradation onwards.

Odeberg, *3 Enoch*, 86.

like Metatron's, incorporates the Tetragrammaton—in the beginning and at the end of Metatron's story also provides an important authorial protective framework, which underscores the polemical thrust of the composition.[254]

As previously mentioned, the overwhelming majority of researchers assume that Metatron's downgrade reflected in *b. Hag.* 15a and *3 Enoch* 16, represented an "orthodox" reaction to the challenges of the second power's exaltation, which the guardians of the faith were no longer able to overlook. Hugo Odeberg expresses this scholarly consensus, arguing that "the attack on Metatron as an enthroned vice-regent of the Most High has, it would seem, emanated from early opponents to the Metatron speculations of the mystics, probably at a time when the name and function of Metatron had entered to a certain degree even into popular belief and could no longer be flatly negated."[255] Such a reactive hypothesis has dominated the study of the Metatron tradition for almost a century. However, it is conceivable that in rabbinic and Hekhalot legends, Metatron's demotion was not a reactive development but rather an initiatory endeavor, which in turn provoked the facilitation of Metatron's exaltation. In which body of literature (rabbinic or Hekhalot) the tradition of Metatron's demotion arose remains uncertain and a point of debate,[256] however its paramount significance for the advancement of the Metatron tradition should not be underestimated. The story of Metatron's demotion appears to have served as a vital channel that secured the influx and development of early remnants of Enochic and Yahoel traditions into the mainstream rabbinic and Hekhalot lore. This was in order to elucidate further the controversial theophanic profile of the conceptual rival. Such aims are clearly discernible in *3 Enoch*, wherein the demotion represents an integral part of the narrative of exaltation, so that Enoch-Metatron's endowment with the exalted qualities is conceptually linked with their deconstruction through a set of mutually interconnected themes.

3 Enoch in its present shape is essentially a polemical commentary on *b. Hag.* 15a or a similar Hekhalot counterpart. Metatron's demotion therefore does not represent a later interpolation in *Sefer Hekhalot*, but rather can be viewed as its inspirational starting point. This further indicates that, within the Hekhalot macroform, the exaltation of Metatron itself represents a reaction or an auxiliary development in relation to his demotion and not the other way around.

The careful gaze of orthodoxy is present without a doubt in our text, as some distinguished scholars of Jewish mysticism have already noted. However, it is present not as a redaction, but rather as an original intention. From the point of view of such orthodox gatekeepers, the full story of the apostasy, exemplified by the hero of the ocularcentric, anthropomorphic ideology must be fully written out and clarified. This does not imply that all components of such an exaltation have been invented by the rabbinic or Hekhalot authors. Rather, they were likely re-utilizing already existing

---

[254] Anafiel's unique mediatorial status as Metatron's virtual double is hinted at in several Hekhalot passages. On these traditions see J. Dan, "Anafiel, Metatron and the Creator," *Tarbiz* 52 (1982): 447–57 [in Hebrew]; Deutsch, *Guardians of the Gate*, 45.

[255] Odeberg, *3 Enoch*, 86.

[256] The majority of scholars insist on the rabbinic origins in view of the testimony reflected in *b. Hag.* 15a, while some scholars argue, in light of *3 Enoch* 16, that the roots of the demotion motif lie in Hekhalot lore. On these debates, see Alexander, "3 Enoch and the Talmud," 40–68; Morray-Jones, "Hekhalot Literature and Talmudic Tradition," 1–39.

examples of the apocalyptic and mystical ocularcentric traditions, similar to those found in *2 Enoch* and the *Apocalypse of Abraham*. They utilized these traditions for their novel blend for which the second power's downgrade was just the beginning of the story.

Story of the Four

The record of Aher's vision is often fused in rabbinic materials with the so-called Story of the Four Rabbis who Entered Pardes. For our purposes, it is crucial to explore the theophanic idiosyncrasies of this broader narrative, since it often constitutes the immediate context for Aher's vision of Metatron. Some researchers argue that the earliest specimen of the Story of the Four is attested in *Tosefta*. *T. Hag.* 2.3–4, which unveils the following tradition:

> Four entered the garden [Paradise]: Ben Azzai, Ben Zoma, the Other [Elisha], and Aqiba. One gazed and perished, one gazed and was smitten, one gazed and cut down sprouts, and one went up whole and came down whole. Ben Azzai gazed and perished. Concerning him Scripture says, Precious in the sight of the lord is the death of his saints (Ps 116:15). Ben Zoma gazed and was smitten. Concerning him Scripture says, If you have found honey, eat only enough for you, lest you be sated with it and vomit it (Prov 25:16). Elisha gazed and cut down sprouts. Concerning him Scripture says, let not your mouth lead you into sin (Qoh 5:5). R. Aqiba went up whole and came down whole. Concerning him Scripture says, Draw me after you, let us make haste. The king has brought me into his chambers (Song of Songs 1:4).[257]

This account seems to feature a polemic against the ocularcentric ideology, a predisposition that has consistently escaped the attention of almost all modern interpreters of this passage.[258] The text depicts four adepts who entered the mysterious garden. The experience of three adepts, represented respectively by Ben Azzai, Ben Zoma, and Elisha ben Avuyah (Aher), are portrayed negatively and unfavorably. One of them died, another "was smitten," and the third became a heretic. A significant feature is found here as their common praxis in the "garden" is rendered in distinctively ocularcentric formulae, involving the term[259] הציץ—all three of them "gazed" or "peered."[260] In all three instances when reference to visionary praxis is made it

---

[257] J. Neusner, *The Tosefta: Translated from the Hebrew with a New Introduction* (2 vols.; Peabody: Hendrickson, 2002), 1.669.

[258] Some scholars have noted the stance against ocularcentric traditions. In his analysis of the Story of the Four, Alon Goshen Gottstein notes the polemics against the visionary praxis. He observes that "the editor's point is basic: visionary activity is a form of uncontrolled pleasure seeking, and whoever tries it is doing something other than studying Torah. The sages who engage in visionary activity therefore contradict their own teaching." A. Goshen Gottstein, *The Sinner and the Amnesiac: The Rabbinic Invention of Elisha ben Abuya and Eleazar Ben Arach* (Stanford: Stanford University Press, 2000), 56.

[259] On various occurrences of this term in rabbinic literature, see D. Halperin, *The Merkabah in Rabbinic Literature* (New Haven: Yale University Press, 1980), 93; P. Schäfer, *Hekhalot-Studien* (TSAJ 19; Tübingen: Mohr Siebeck, 1988), 241, n. 50.

[260] David Halperin notes that in rabbinic literature הציץ "is used for examining an infant; for peering into a pit (to examine a fetus thrown there); for the crowd's straining to catch a glimpse of the scarlet cloth hung inside the Temple vestibule; for peeping into other people's windows; for God's

repeatedly coincides with negative results: "one gazed and perished, one gazed and was smitten, one gazed and cut the sprouts."

Ben Azzai, Ben Zoma, and Elisha ben Avuyah thus belong to the chain of practitioners of the same visual paradigm, as their approach to the divine presence is repeatedly defined through the formula of "gazing." Yet in the case of the adept who ended his experience positively and favorably (Rabbi Akiva), the visionary praxis of "gazing" is not mentioned, and the corresponding terminology is not applied.

A similar contrast between the ocular terminology applied to the first three visionaries and a lack of such terminology in relation to an exemplary adept, R. Akiva, is attested in other versions of the story found in the Palestinian[261] and Babylonian[262] Talmuds,[263] *Shir ha-Shirim Rabbah*,[264] and Hekhalot literature.[265]

---

gazing down upon his people's suffering." He argues that the closest English equivalent to *hetzitz* is "to peer." Halperin, *The Merkabah in Rabbinic Literature*, 93. In relation to the Hekhalot tradition, Peter Schäfer observes that "few passages in the Hekhalot literature combine *hetzitz* with an object that relates to the Merkavah: God's robe, his beauty, and the vision of the Merkavah." P. Schäfer, *The Origins of Jewish Mysticism* (Tübingen: Mohr Siebeck, 2009), 198.

[261] *y. Hag.* 77b reads:

> Four entered the Garden, One peeked and was hurt; one peeked and died; one peeked and cut saplings, one entered in peace and left in peace. Ben Azzai peeked and was hurt; about him the verse says, if you found honey, eat your fill. Ben Zoma peeked and died, about him the verse says, dear in the Eternal's eyes is the death of his pious. Aher peeked and cut saplings.
>
> *The Jerusalem Talmud. Tractates Taʿaniot, Megillah, Hagigah and Moʿed Qatan. Edition, Translation and Commentary* (ed. H. W. Guggenheimer; SJ 85; Berlin: Walter de Gruyter, 2015), 421–22.

[262] *b. Hag.* 14b:

> Our Rabbis taught: Four men entered the "Garden," namely, Ben ʿAzzai and Ben Zoma, Aher, and R. Akiba. R. Akiba said to them: When ye arrive at the stones of pure marble, say not, water, water! For it is said: He that speaketh falsehood shall not be established before mine eyes. Ben ʿAzzai cast a look and died. Of him Scripture says: Precious in the sight of the Lord is the death of his saints. Ben Zoma looked and became demented. Of him Scripture says: Hast thou found honey? Eat so much as is sufficient for thee, lest thou be filled therewith, and vomit it. Aher mutilated the shoots. R. Akiba departed unhurt.
>
> Epstein, *The Babylonian Talmud. Hagiga*, 14b.

[263] For comparisons pertaining to the Tosefta and the Talmudic accounts, see Halperin, *The Merkabah in Rabbinic Literature*, 86–87.

[264] *Shir ha-Shirim Rabbah* 1:27 reads:

> Four entered the Garden, Ben ʿAzzai, Ben Zoma, Elisha b. Abuya, and R. Akiba. Ben ʿAzzai peered [into the mysteries] and became demented; and of him it is said, Hast thou found honey? Eat so much as is sufficient for thee (Prov 25:16). Ben Zoma peered and died; and of him it says, Precious in the sight of the Lord is the death of his saints (Ps 116:15). Elisha b. Abuya began to "lop the branches." How did he "lop the branches"? When he entered a synagogue or house of study and saw children making progress in the Torah, he uttered incantations over them which brought them to a stop; and of him it is said, Suffer not thy mouth to bring thy flesh into guilt (Eccl 5:5). R. Akiba entered in peace and came out in peace. He said: It is not because I am greater than my colleagues, but thus taught the Sages in the Mishnah: Thy deeds bring thee near [to heaven] and thy deeds keep thee far. And of him it is said, The King hath brought me into his chambers.
>
> Freedman and Simon, *Midrash Rabbah*, 9.46–47.

[265] *Hekhalot Zutarti* (*Synopse* §338) and *Merkavah Rabbah* (*Synopse* §671) read: "R. Akiva said: We were four who entered paradise. One peered in and died. One peered in and was struck down. One

Although researchers have traditionally considered the variants of the Pardes account reflected in the Tosefta and Talmuds as the earliest examples of this tradition, some scholars[266] argue that such priority ought to be given to the Hekhalot renderings of the Story of the Four. In their opinion the Hekhalot accounts are stratigraphically earlier and can be situated, at the latest, in the early fourth century CE.[267] *Hekhalot Zutarti* (*Synopse* §§338–48) and other parallels[268] offer the following rendering of the familiar account:

> R. Akiva said: We were four who entered paradise. One peered in and died. One peered in and was struck down. One peered in and cut the plants. I entered safely and I went forth safely. Why did I enter safely and go forth safely? Not because I was greater than my associates, but my works accomplished for me to establish what the sages taught in their Mishnah, Your works shall bring you near and your works shall make you far away. And these are they who entered paradise: Ben Azzay, Ben Zoma, the Other, and R. Akiva. Ben Azzay peered and died. Concerning him the Scripture says, Worthy in the eyes of YHWH is the death of his pious ones (Ps 116:15). Ben Zoma peered and was struck down. Concerning him the Scripture says, Have you found honey? Eat (only) your fill, lest you become sated and vomit it up (Prov 25:16). Elisha ben Avuyah peered and cut the plants. Concerning him the Scripture says, Do not let your mouth cause your flesh to sin (Qoh 5:5). R. Akiva entered safely and went forth safely. Concerning him the Scripture says,

---

peered in and cut the plants. I entered safely and I went forth safely." Davila, *Hekhalot Literature in Translation*, 202.

[266] See C. R. A. Morray-Jones, *A Transparent Illusion: The Dangerous Vision of Water in Hekhalot Mysticism: A Source-Critical and Tradition-Historical Inquiry* (JSJSS 59; Leiden: Brill, 2002), 17–19; J. R. Davila, "Review of *A Transparent Illusion: The Dangerous Vision of Water in Hekhalot Mysticism: A Source-Critical and Tradition-Historical Inquiry* by C. R. A. Morray-Jones," *JBL* 121 (2002): 585–88.

[267] Analyzing Morray-Jones' hypothesis regarding the priority of the Hekhalot evidence, James Davila offers the following reflection:

> Morray-Jones begins in the first two chapters by recapitulating the convincing case he has made elsewhere that the recension of the story of the four found in the Hekhalot texts known as the *Hekhalot Zutarti* (§§338–39) and the *Merkavah Rabbah* (§§671–73), when cleared of obvious redactional elements from another, third-person version, preserves a first-person account that clearly takes "paradise" to mean the heavenly realm and which predates the versions in the rabbinic "mystical collection." It follows that we must place this recension at the latest in the early fourth century. This early Hekhalot account did not include the warning about water, although a different version of it, the "water vision episode," appears elsewhere in the *Hekhalot Zutarti* (§§407–8), with a parallel version appearing in the *Hekhalot Rabbati* (§§258–59). In ch. 3 he argues, again convincingly, first that the latter version (in the *Hekhalot Rabbati*) is a garbled abbreviation of the former (in the *Hekhalot Zutarti*) and, second, that in manuscript New York 8128 aversion of the water vision episode has been secondarily combined with the story of the four in the *Hekhalot Zutarti* and the *Merkavah Rabbah* and that it is this combined passage that is assumed by the Babli, and not the other way around, strongly implying that the Hekhalot traditions are stratigraphically earlier. Indeed, other evidence, especially from the Qumran *Hodayot*, implies that the concept of hostile waters of chaos associated with the celestial temple may go back to the Second Temple period.
> Davila, "Review of *A Transparent Illusion*," 585–86.

[268] *Merkavah Rabbah* (*Synopse* §§671–74).

Draw me after you, let us run. The King has brought me into his chambers (Cant 1:4). R. Akiva said: In the hour that I ascended on high, I laid down more markings on the entrances of the firmament than on the entrances of my house. And when I arrived at the curtain, angels of violence went forth to do me violence. The Holy One, blessed be He, said to them: Leave this elder alone, for he is fit to gaze at Me. R. Akiva said: In the hour, that I ascended to the chariot a heavenly voice went forth from beneath the throne of glory, speaking in the Aramaic language. In this language what did it speak? Before YHWH made heaven and earth, he established a vestibule to the firmament, to enter by it and to go out by it. A vestibule is nothing but an entrance. He established the firm names to fashion by means of it the whole world.[269]

If this variant of the Pardes story narrated by Rabbi Akiva indeed represents the original version, as Christopher Morray-Jones[270] and James Davila argue, it is captivating that in addition to the already familiar depictions of the problematic ocular practices of the three adepts, one also encounters here a curious reference to Rabbi Akiva's own praxis depicted with peculiar aural markers. The first important detail in this regard is God's discourse that protects the adept against the threatening heavenly attendants. The deity *speaks* to his servants, asking them to leave Rabbi Akiva alone. The most essential element, nonetheless, is R. Akiva's own encounter with the divine presence, which is rendered in a distinctively "aural" manner, namely, as the epiphany of the heavenly Voice.[271] *Synopse* §348 reports the following: "R. Akiva said: In the hour that I ascended on high I heard a heavenly voice that went forth from beneath the throne of glory and was speaking in the Aramaic language."[272] In contrast to the aforementioned seers,

---

[269] Davila, *Hekhalot Literature in Translation*, 202–4. Schäfer et al., *Synopse*, 145.

[270] Reflecting on the priority of the rabbinic and Hekhalot accounts of the story, Christopher Morray-Jones argues that

> the Hekhalot sources have preserved a version of the Pardes story—the first-person narrative in *Hekhalot Zutarti/Merkavah Rabbah* A–C—which is different from and much simpler than that found in the talmudic sources and *Canticles Rabbah*. A subsequent redactor has expanded this first-person narrative by inserting third-person materials taken from the talmudic tradition in section B, but, when this additional material is discounted, it can be seen that the hekhalot version was originally a statement by or attributed to Aqiba that he and three unnamed individuals went into Pardes, that the other three met with disaster, and that he alone went in/up and came out/down safely, despite the opposition of the angels, through the merit of his deeds.... I conclude, therefore, that the version preserved in *Hekhalot Zutarti/Merkavah Rabbah* A–C represents the original form of the Pardes story and that the redactor of the mystical collection adapted this source to suit his purpose by adding the names of the three חכמים תלמידי, thereby turning it into an illustration of *m. Hag.* 2:1.... Thus, once the priority of the hekhalot version (A and C) has been established, it is clear that the story is concerned with a visionary ascent to the heavenly temple, in the face of fierce opposition on the part of the "angels of destruction." These angels seem to be the terrifying guardians of the gateways, who are described in other passages of the hekhalot literature and will be encountered again below.
>
> Morray-Jones, *A Transparent Illusion*, 17–19.

[271] On this tradition see G. Scholem, *Jewish Gnosticism, Merkabah Mysticism, and Talmudic Tradition* (2nd ed.; New York: Jewish Theological Seminary of America, 1965), 77–78.

[272] Davila, *Hekhalot Literature in Translation*, 204.

Rabbi Akiva does not "gaze," rather, he "hears." Furthermore, the symbolism of the divine Voice streaming from beneath the divine seat vividly reminds us of Abraham's encounter with the divine presence in the Slavonic apocalypse. As in the *Apocalypse of Abraham*, despite the fact that the throne is mentioned, the deity's epiphany is rendered as the Voice. The auricularcentric praxis of R. Akiva[273] thus represents a striking contrast to the ocularcentric practices of Ben Zoma, Ben Azzai, and Aher. The third crucial aural detail is the reference to the "names," by means of which the deity fashioned the whole world. Such onomatological features further solidify the aural proclivities of R. Akiva's report.

The previously mentioned tensions between ocularcentric and aural streams, identified in the Story of the Four,[274] are vital not only for our present examination, but also for continuing scholarly deliberations concerning the two powers in heaven controversy and its underlying foundations in early Jewish and Christian materials. In spite of the fact that past investigations have regularly recognized rabbinic discourse with regard to the two powers as directed against anthropomorphic understandings of the deity, these speculations rarely take into consideration the peculiar tensions existing between aural and ocular ideologies found in these materials. However, thoughtfulness regarding the existence and peculiarities of such interactions can contribute to our understanding of the conceptual dynamics of such debates. As demonstrated above, the materials relating to the two powers controversy frequently display a polemical strain between the aural depictions of the deity, regularly manifested in these accounts as the divine voice, and the ocular portrayals of the "second power," frequently endued with the theophanic qualities of the *Kavod* paradigm. In this regard, the two powers debate itself might represent one of the phases in the long-lasting interaction between the *Shem* and the *Kavod* streams, which receives its controversial afterlife in various rabbinic and Hekhalot contexts.[275]

Another good illustration of how the complementary intentions of the early Jewish two powers accounts received their new polemical afterlife in their later rabbinic counterparts can be seen in the tale of the exaltation and angelic veneration of Adam found in later rabbinic lore. While in early Adamic legends the protoplast is conceived as the divine image and visual symbol of the divinity, in later rabbinic stories he, in a similar way to Metatron in Aher's vision, became understood as a perilous apparition

---

[273] Morray-Jones compares Akiva's aural encounter with Paul's experience described in 2 Cor 12:1–12, noting that "Aqiba, like Paul, heard words when he ascended to paradise." C. Morray-Jones, "Paradise Revisited (2 Cor 12:1–12): The Jewish Mystical Background of Paul's Apostolate Part 2: Paul's Heavenly Ascent and its Significance," *HTR* 86 (1993): 265–92 at 280.

[274] This polemical tension between the aural and ocular praxis found in the Story of the Four appears to be further perpetuated in rabbinic lore concerning Ben Azzai, Ben Zoma, and Aher. For example, in *Genesis Rabbah*, two of the infamous seers offer an interpretation of the aural manifestation of the deity (divine Voice) as the vision of Metatron. From *Gen. Rab.* 5:4 we learn the following: "Levi said: Some interpreters, e.g. Ben 'Azzai and Ben Zoma, interpret: The voice of the Lord became Metatron on the waters, as it is written, 'The voice of the Lord is over the waters' (Ps 29:3)." Freedman and Simon, *Midrash Rabbah*, 1.36.

[275] Thus, Daniel Boyarin suggests that "Aher represents older theological traditions which have been anathematized as heresy by the authors of the story." D. Boyarin, "Is Metatron a Converted Christian," *Judaïsme Ancien/Ancient Judaism* 1 (2013): 13–62 at 41.

that is able to challenge God' sovereignty and authority. In order to prevent apostasy from the angelic hosts, God was forced to "distort" the divine likeness in his beloved creature by reducing his size or putting him to sleep. Jarl Fossum's research demonstrates that the motif of God's opposition to the veneration of Adam by the angels appears in several forms in rabbinic lore, where it is closely associated with the two powers in heaven traditions.[276] In contrast to early developments, where the relationship between the deity and the second power remains complementary, in rabbinic literature one can detect unmistakable polemical overtones. Fossum differentiates three major forms of this tradition:

1. The angels mistake Adam for God and want to exclaim "Holy" before him, whereupon God lets sleep fall upon Adam so it becomes clear that the latter is human.
2. All creatures mistake Adam for their creator and wish to bow before him, but Adam teaches them to render all honor to God as their true creator.
3. The angels mistake Adam for God and wish to exclaim "Holy" before him, whereupon God reduces Adam's size.[277]

An important similarity can be detected between these later Adamic traditions and the Metatron accounts. In *b. Hag.* 15a, for instance, God punished Metatron with sixty fiery lashes. Alan Segal observes that "just as Metatron needed correction for the false impression he gave Aher, so Adam needs correction for the false impression given the angels."[278]

In the Adamic two powers accounts, the protoplast is indeed disciplined in various ways, including the reduction of his stature. Thus, from *Gen. Rab.* 8:10 one learns that when God created man in his own image "the ministering angels mistook him [for a divine being] and wished to exclaim 'Holy' before him. . . . What did the Holy One, blessed be he, do? He caused sleep to fall upon him, and so all knew that he was [only

---

[276] An important similarity can be detected between these Adamic traditions and the Metatron accounts. In *b. Hag.* 15a, for instance, God punished Metatron with sixty fiery lashes. Alan Segal observes that "just as Metatron needed correction for the false impression he gave Aher, so Adam needs correction for the false impression given the angels." Segal, *Two Powers in Heaven*, 112. Indeed, in the Adamic "two powers" accounts, the protoplast is disciplined in various ways, including the reduction of his stature. Thus, *Gen. R.* 8:10 recounts that when God created man in his own image "the ministering angels mistook him [for a divine being] and wished to exclaim 'Holy' before him. . . . What did the Holy One, blessed be He, do? He caused sleep to fall upon him, and so all knew that he was [only a mortal] man." Freedman and Simon, *Midrash Rabbah*, 1.61. In the *Alphabet of Rabbi Akiba* the angels' erroneous behavior is explained through reference to Adam's gigantic body. *Pesikta de Rab Kahana* 1:1 reflects the same tradition: "Said R. Aibu, 'At that moment the first man's stature was cut down and diminished to one hundred cubits.'" *Pesiqta de Rab Kahana* (tr. J. Neusner; 2 vols.; BJS 122–23; Atlanta: Scholars, 1987), 1.1.

[277] J. Fossum, "The Adorable Adam of the Mystics and the Rebuttals of the Rabbis," in: *Geschichte-Tradition-Reflexion. Festschrift für Martin Hengel zum 70. Geburtstag* (ed. H. Cancik, H. Lichtenberger, and P. Schäfer; 3 vols.; Tübingen: Mohr Siebeck, 1996), 1.529–39.

[278] Segal, *Two Powers in Heaven*, 112.

a mortal] man."[279] In the *Alphabet of Rabbi Akiba*, the angels' erroneous behavior is explained through reference to Adam's gigantic body; it reads:

> This teaches that initially Adam was created from the earth to the firmament. When the ministering angels saw him, they were shocked and excited by him. At that time they all stood before the Holy One, blessed be he, and said to him; "Master of the Universe! There are two powers in the world, one in heaven and one on earth." What did the Holy One, blessed be he, do then? He placed his hand on him, and decreased him, setting him at one thousand cubits.[280]

Pesikta de Rab Kahana 1:1 reflects the same tradition: "Said R. Aibu, 'At that moment the first man's stature was cut down and diminished to one hundred cubits.'"[281]

It is intriguing that many of the strategies used by the deity for Adam's demotion in these accounts pertain to the alteration of his cosmic body, which becomes diminished or put in the horizontal position. Within this curious deconstruction, one can see the dismantling of the deity's visible "icon," prominent in many early two powers in heaven accounts.

Conclusion

This part has traced an important evolution of the theophanic imagery in Jewish two powers traditions in which the ocularcentric features of the first power were steadily transferred to their new guardians; these guardians were predestined to become visible representations of the deity. Various second powers of early and late Jewish accounts will eventually inherit the whole range of formative divine attributes, known from such foundational theophanic accounts of the Hebrew Bible as Ezekiel 1, Isaiah 6, and Daniel 7.

We also noted that the deity's gradual withdrawal from the visible ocularcentric mode coincided already in the earliest dual theophanies with his conferral to the aniconic, audial dimension in which he would express himself as the aniconic Voice. The process of gradual endowing of the second power with the ocularcentric attributes of the divine *Kavod* leads to the second power becoming understood as an image, or visual icon, of the deity. These peculiar dynamics within the theophanic symbolism become especially prominent in New Testament accounts, preparing a unique seedbed for the growth and development of early Christology. The second part of our study, which follows, provides a detailed analysis of these conceptual developments.

---

[279] Freedman and Simon, *Midrash Rabbah*, 1.61.

[280] M. Idel, "Enoch Is Metatron," *Imm* 24/25 (1990): 220–40 at 226. For the Hebrew text, see S. A. Wertheimer, *Batei Midrashot* (2 vols.; Jerusalem: Mossad Harav Kook, 1950–1953), 2.333–477.

[281] Neusner, *Pesiqta de Rab Kahana*, 1.1

Part Two

Two Powers in Heaven Traditions in Early Christian Accounts

Already within the earliest Christian testimonies preserved in the Pauline corpus, one can see clear tendencies toward the promulgation of the glory language. According to New Testament experts, "in its various forms, δόξα occurs some ninety-six times in the letters attributed to Paul."[1] Herein lies another important feature relevant to our study: the predisposition to transfer the attributes and functions of the divine Glory to Jesus. This tendency is present in the Pauline and Deutero-Pauline materials. We find here the exemplar of the Christian tradition absorbing peculiar traits that signal his reception and possession of attributes, which in the Hebrew Bible are associated with the deity.[2] 1 Cor 2:8 designates Christ as "the Lord of Glory" (ὁ κύριος τῆς δόξης), and Eph 1:17 declares that "the God of our Lord Jesus Christ" (ὁ θεὸς τοῦ κυρίου ἡμῶν Ἰησοῦ Χριστοῦ) is the "Father of glory" (ὁ πατὴρ τῆς δόξης), thus paralleling Jesus and the δόξα.[3] Alan Segal notes that, for Paul, Christ's unique role in relation to the deity is achieved through the Glory of the Lord, "a well-known technical term for the human apparition of God which followed the Israelites through the desert and was manifest

---

[1] C. C. Newman, *Paul's Glory-Christology: Tradition and Rhetoric* (NovTSup 69; Leiden: Brill, 1992), 3. Reflecting on the Pauline δόξα traditions, George Henry Boobyer observes that "a body of shining δόξα certainly was the form which the early Church thought Christ possessed in heaven." G. H. Boobyer, *St. Mark and the Transfiguration Story* (Edinburgh: T&T Clark, 1942), 19.

[2] Reexamining the usage of δόξα in the New Testament materials, C. A. A. Anderson Scott notes that

> the word owes its significance in many passages of the New Testament to the fact that (probably along with σκηνή) it stands for the Jewish conception of the *Shekinah*, the splendor or brilliance which is an effluence from the Deity, which can be seen though he himself is not visible, and which marks the place of his dwelling. In the Targums this word *Shekinah* is commonly employed as a substitute for "God" in the Hebrew text.
>
> C. A. A. Scott, *Christianity According to St. Paul* (Cambridge: Cambridge University Press, 1927), 268.

[3] Newman, *Paul's Glory-Christology*, 4. Looking at the same passages, Scott notes that

> in 1 Corinthians 2:8 we find him described as "the Lord of the Glory"; and in Ephesians 1:17 God is spoken of as "the Father of the Glory." If along with these passages we take James 2:1 ("Our Lord Jesus Christ, who is the Glory.") and 1 Peter 4:14 ("The Spirit of the Glory and of God"), it is difficult to resist the conclusion that for St Paul also the Glory was an equivalent for Christ.
>
> Scott, *Christianity According to St Paul*, 268.

to Moses at Sinai (Exod 23–34) and again with the exiles in Babylonian captivity (Ezek 1:26)."[4]

Indeed, in the Pauline corpus, the key events in Jesus' life became overlaid with glory language. For instance, we learn that "Christ was raised from the dead through the Glory (ἠγέρθη Χριστὸς ἐκ νεκρῶν διὰ τῆς δόξης, Rom 6:4; ἀνελήμφθη ἐν δόξῃ, 1 Tim 3:16),"[5] and

> as the resurrected and exalted Lord, Jesus possesses a body of Glory (σῶμα τῆς δόξης, Phil 3:21). The future *parousia* of Jesus, therefore, will be an apocalypse in Glory (φανερωθήσεσθε ἐν δόξῃ, Col 3:4; ἐπιφάνειαν τῆς δόξης, Tit 2:13), in which sinners will be judged and believers transformed (οἵτινες δίκην τίσουσιν ὄλεθρον αἰώνιον ἀπὸ προσώπου τοῦ κυρίου καὶ ἀπὸ τῆς δόξης τῆς ἰσχύος αὐτοῦ, ὅταν ἔλθῃ ἐνδοξασθῆναι ἐν τοῖς ἁγίοις, 2 Thess 1:9–10).[6]

Carey Newman points out that according to the Pauline corpus "Glory legitimized the new covenant established by Jesus' life, death and resurrection (ἡ διακονία . . . ἐν δόξῃ, 2 Cor 3:8, 9),"[7] and "this Glory possesses a final, eschatological character (ὑπερβαλλούσης δόξης, 2 Cor 3:10)."[8]

Another important theophanic dimension involves Jesus' role as the revealer and mediator of the Glory. According to the Pauline writings

> Jesus reveals and mediates Glory. The knowledge of Glory is discovered in Jesus (τῆς γνώσεως τῆς δόξης τοῦ θεοῦ ἐν προσώπῳ [Ἰησοῦ] Χριστοῦ, 2 Cor 4:6). The saving deeds of Jesus make known the mystery of Glory, hidden from the ages past, to all the nations (γνωρίσῃ τὸν πλοῦτον τῆς δόξης αὐτοῦ, Rom 9:23; γνωρίσαι τί τὸ πλοῦτος τῆς δόξης τοῦ μυστηρίου τούτου ἐν τοῖς ἔθνεσιν, Col 1:27a).[9]

Newman argues that the gospel that the Pauline corpus preaches—a gospel that features the death, resurrection, and future coming of Jesus—"is a 'gospel of glory' (τοῦ εὐαγγελίου τῆς δόξης τοῦ Χριστοῦ, 2 Cor 4:4; cf. τὸ εὐαγγέλιον τῆς δόξης, 1 Tim 1:11)."[10]

Furthermore, Paul's accounts of his own mystical experience are overlaid with the glory language. Relying on Alan Segal's insights,[11] Andrew Chester notes that "the 'glory of the Lord' in 2 Cor 3:18, both referring to Christ and also as a technical term

---

[4] A. F. Segal, "'Two Powers in Heaven' and Early Christian Trinitarian Thinking," in: *The Trinity: An Interdisciplinary Symposium on the Trinity* (ed. S. T. Davis, D. Kendall, and G. O'Collins; Oxford: Oxford University Press, 1999), 73–95 at 73.

[5] Newman, *Paul's Glory-Christology*, 4.

[6] Newman, *Paul's Glory-Christology*, 4–5.

[7] Newman, *Paul's Glory-Christology*, 5.

[8] Newman, *Paul's Glory-Christology*, 5.

[9] Newman, *Paul's Glory-Christology*, 5.

[10] Newman, *Paul's Glory-Christology*, 5.

[11] See Segal, *Paul the Convert*, 34–71; idem, "Paul and the Beginning of Jewish Mysticism," in: *Death, Ecstasy, and Other Worldly Journeys* (ed. J. Collins and M. Fishbane; Albany: SUNY, 1995), 95–122; idem, "Paul's Thinking about Resurrection in Its Jewish Context," *NTS* 44 (1998): 400–19.

for *kabod* (the human form of God appearing in biblical visions), implies that Paul, in 2 Corinthians 12, has seen Jesus as the image and glory of God in the heavenly world."[12] In Paul's mind, an encounter with the divine Glory in the form of Christ thus becomes the soteriological endeavor. Newman suggests that "Paul defines the eschatological goal of salvation as obtaining the Glory of the exalted Christ (οὓς δὲ ἐδικαίωσεν, τούτους καὶ ἐδόξασεν, Rom 8:30; εἰς περιποίησιν δόξης τοῦ κυρίου ἡμῶν Ἰησοῦ Χριστοῦ, 2 Thess 2:14)."[13]

With these developments in mind, scholars often postulate that, in the Pauline corpus and other New Testament literature, "δόξα" becomes a key Christological term, functioning synonymously with other crucial Christological terms, such as εἰκών and μορφή.[14] The scope of various applications of the glory language to Jesus in the Pauline Epistles is impressive. Yet, as we have already learned, the transference of certain functions and attributes of the divine Glory to another individual is not entirely novel; rather, this theme is apparent in various earlier Jewish accounts that seek to construct the exalted identities of the Son of Man, Enoch, Jacob, and Moses. Moreover, in early Christian literature, one detects another strategy reminiscent of these earlier Jewish accounts. This move involves a simultaneous withdrawal of the deity into an invisible aural mode, in which God is manifested as the aniconic voice. The majority of scholars have been reluctant to note correspondences between these two interconnected processes as the endowment of Jesus with the ocularcentric attributes of the divine Glory is placed in conspicuous parallel with God's marked withdrawal into the invisible aural dimension. As mentioned earlier, however, one can see the early roots of these developments already in the Pauline corpus, where the glory traditions are applied to Jesus for the first time. In these earliest Christian testimonies, one can also see the repeated affirmation about God's invisibility.[15] Already within the Pauline corpus, Jesus' endowment with the divine form becomes juxtaposed with the motif of God's hiddenness via the paradoxical dictum found in the Epistle to the Colossians, where Christ is designated as the image of the invisible God.[16]

The correlations between Jesus' endowment with the unique attributes of the deity and God's withdrawal into the aniconic dimension are even clearer in the

---

[12] A. Chester, *Messiah and Exaltation: Jewish Messianic and Visionary Traditions and New Testament Christology* (WUNT 207; Tübingen: Mohr Siebeck, 2007), 81–82.

[13] Newman, *Paul's Glory-Christology*, 5.

[14] Newman, *Paul's Glory-Christology*, 7.

[15] Rom 1:20; Col 1:15; 1 Tim 1:17.

[16] Chester suggests that

> there was originally a strong and powerful visionary tradition that constituted an important factor in the emergence of early (and very "high") Christology. That is, Christ was seen in transformed mode and appearance; no longer as simply human, but transcending human form, and in at least some cases being seen as set alongside God in the heavenly world, and having more a heavenly form and body. Indeed, Christ had been seen as reflecting the glory and appearance of God himself, and thus making the invisible God visible.
>
> Chester, *Messiah and Exaltation*, 92.

See also J. D. G. Dunn, *Jesus and the Spirit: A Study of the Religious and Charismatic Experience of Jesus and the First Christians as Reflected in the New Testament* (London: SCM, 1975), 62–65; L. E. Keck, "The Spirit and the Dove," *NTS* 17 (1970–1971): 41–67; Rowland, *The Open Heaven*, 358–63.

synoptic gospels. Present there are two crucial theophanic encounters associated with Jesus' baptism and his transfiguration in which the deity is manifested solely in his aniconic, aural mode. These events appear to share important similarities with the "joint theophanies" found in the previously explored Jewish accounts. In particular, the baptism and transfiguration are two crucial places where theophanic attributes of the deity are transferred to Jesus. In this respect it does not seem coincidental that the topological settings of both accounts, one of which occurs on the river and the other on the mountain, mimic two important *loci* for the unfolding of *Kavod* ideology in the Hebrew Bible, namely, Ezekiel's vision of the divine Chariot on the river Chebar and Moses' encounter with the divine Glory on Mount Sinai. That both the transfiguration story and the account of Jesus' baptism contain striking symbolic markers reminiscent of Ezekiel's encounter and Moses' ordeal are not happenstance.

In light of the multifaceted nature of the theophanic traditions reflected in the New Testament materials and the enormous bulk of secondary scholarship devoted to them, the present study focuses on a few passages where Jesus' endowment with theophanic attributes coincides with the manifestation of God.[17] Two crucial specimens of such joint theophanies can be found in the already mentioned accounts of Jesus' baptism and transfiguration, where "two powers" will appear as in previously mentioned early Jewish accounts in two strikingly different theophanic modes. We begin our investigation of the theophanic traditions in the New Testament with the exploration of the transfiguration account, where the juxtaposition of ocular and aural elements applied to respective powers is presented with clarity.[18]

---

[17] Alan Segal entertained the possibility that some Christian groups were aware of the two powers in heaven traditions. He noted that

> of all the forms of religion in Palestine in the first century, New Testament Christianity is the best documented, most controversial, and most often studied. Even so, there is little that can be said in certainty about the roots of Christian doctrines. This lack of sure knowledge will be especially frustrating in studying "two powers" tradition, as we shall see, because many traditions found heretical by the rabbis in the second century were intimately connected to the apostolic understanding of Jesus. Yet, it is a mistake to assume that Christianity was a unified social movement which contained a consistent, theological perspective, even in its earliest stages. The most we can say is that some kinds of Christianity found "two powers" traditions favorable to their perspective.
>
> Segal, *Two Powers in Heaven*, 205.

[18] Scholars have recognized the multifaceted nature of the theophanic imagery attested in the transfiguration story. For example, Ulrich Luz laments that

> the transfiguration narrative is difficult to interpret. It contains a multitude of possible associations and reminiscences of biblical and Jewish materials, but there is no key in the tradition that completely unlocks it. Repeatedly there are individual statements that do not fit a certain background or a certain expectation or that fit several of them. Thus one has the impression that the transfiguration story is distinctively "of manifold meanings."
>
> U. Luz, *Matthew 8–20* (Hermeneia; Minneapolis: Fortress, 2001), 395.

Luz further suggests that the transfiguration story can be seen as a "polyvalent" story that permits several possibilities of interpretation. Luz, *Matthew 8–20*, 397.

Kavod on the Mountain: The Transfiguration Account[19]

As previously mentioned, already in the Pauline corpus some distinctive features solely associated in the Hebrew Bible with the apparitions of the divine Glory became paradoxically applied for the first time to the figure of Jesus. This transference of the glory to the Christian exemplar finds its succinct presentation also in the synoptic gospels. Thus from Mk 8:34 and Matt 16:27 we learn that the Son of Man will come "in the glory of his Father," a tradition that was later rephrased in Luke as "in the glory of the Father" (Luke 9:26).

The transference of ocularcentric divine attributes to the Christian mediator is also laden with profound changes with respect to the theophanic profile of the deity. Similar to certain Jewish accounts, the refashioning of the second power's theophanic makeup goes hand-in-hand with the deity's abandonment of its visual, corporeal dimension and its withdrawal into the aniconic aural mode.[20] These changes can be seen as two inverse conceptual dynamics consisting first in "auralization" of the first power represented by the Father, and second in "visualization" of the second power, represented by the Son.[21] In the context of nascent Christianity, these two dynamics proved to be of paramount significance for the development of early Christology.

---

[19] The connections between the transfiguration account and the two powers in heaven traditions have been discussed by scholars. Already Alan Segal in his "Two Powers in Heaven," entertains such a connection by suggesting that "uses of 'two powers' traditions may be found in the synoptic gospels. For instance, the Sinai theophany, together with Dan 7:9 has often been suggested as the background for the synoptic account of the transfiguration, especially prominent in the Lukan version." Segal, *Two Powers in Heaven*, 209. On this see also F. H. Borsch, *The Son of Man in Myth and History* (London: SCM Press, 1967), 383; J. G. Davies, *He Ascended into Heaven: A Study in the History of Doctrine* (London: Lutterworth, 1958), 25, 185; G. Lohfink, *Die Himmelfahrt Jesu: Untersuchungen zu den Himmelfahrts- und Erhöhungstexten bei Lukas* (SANT 26; Munich: Kösel, 1971), 64, 191.

[20] John McGuckin reflects on the deity's withdrawal into the aural mode by noting that

> by a subtle redaction which has amounted to removing the radiant face motif, transforming the two angels of covenant into Moses and Elijah, relocating the awe of the disciples away from the cloud theophany towards the appearance of the prophets, introducing the correction of Peter by means of a patronizing excuse, and finally reintroducing the theophany words from God now as *bat qol* to throw all our attention specifically onto Jesus alone—by means of such editorial reworkings, then, Mark has effectively removed the last lingering vestiges of prophetic Christology from the story and pointed us quite clearly in the Christological direction.
>
> J. A. McGuckin, *The Transfiguration of Christ in Scripture and Tradition* (New York: Edwin Mellen, 1986), 18.

[21] Andrew Dearman observes that

> one sees the anti-anthropomorphic influences clearly in Philo of Alexandria, who spoke for many when he declared that "neither is God in human form nor is the human body God-like." And the New Testament continues in this vein with claims that no one has actually seen God (who is "spirit") and that God is invisible or veiled from human sight (John 1:18; 4:24; 1 Tim. 6:16; Col. 1:15). To be sure, second-temple Judaism did not intend to deny the revelatory significance of the OT theophanies, but their anthropomorphic aspects are understood in a spiritual and highly symbolic sense. The

The withdrawal of the deity into an incorporeal, aural mode provides a unique opportunity for the construction of what can be referred to as the ocularcentric or *Kavod* Christology, in which the second power, in the form of the Second Person, now almost instantaneously inherits the prominent legacy of the ancient theophanic tradition reflected in the Hebrew Bible and the Jewish pseudepigrapha, where the deity was traditionally portrayed as the divine Glory or *Kavod*. The abandonment of the deity's long-lasting theophanic heritage, that is, by surrendering it to its new guardian, appears to be an unexpected move that has not gone unnoticed by the experts. Some scholars of the earliest Christian traditions have reflected on the strange absence of the visual manifestations of God the Father in the New Testament materials. For example, Carl Davis laments that "apart from Jesus, the idea of God's theophany has all but disappeared in the New Testament. It is no longer God's *parousia* but Christ's. God did not reveal himself visibly in the new exodus, only Christ. Nor did God the Father reveal himself visibly to any human during Jesus' lifetime."[22]

One of the most striking features of the early Christian accounts is that, unlike the early Jewish two powers accounts, where the deity remains present in his ocularcentric shape during the transfer of the glory attributes to the second power, in the New Testament, God is suddenly and completely withdrawn into his invisible aural mode.

As one recalls in the complementary two powers template prominent in the Book of Daniel, the *Book of the Similitudes*, and the *Exagoge* of Ezekiel the Tragedian, the novel ocularcentric profile of the second power still remains closely overseen and controlled by the simultaneous appearance of the dominant first power, who remains visibly present. The first power in these episodes remains endowed with the loftiest *Kavod* attributes, which point to the inferiority of the second power's features, thus signaling their subordination to God. In these early Jewish accounts the deity still secures its firm grip upon the ancient tradition of the ocularcentric theophanies. Yet in the New Testament materials, where the first power is suddenly and permanently removed into the invisible, aural mode, its ancient ocularcentric legacy is now completely and unconditionally surrendered to the second power. From now on (in Christian tradition), the most striking attributes solely reserved in the Hebrew Bible for God himself are yielded to a new custodian of this theophanic inheritance—Jesus Christ.[23].

Scholars have often overlooked this monumental paradigm shift, which manifests itself in almost every early Christian theophany scene. Despite the fact that similar conceptual constellations are also found in early Jewish accounts, such as the *Apocalypse*

NT writers apparently accept this qualification of the theophanies, but then proceed in various other ways to reinterpret divine presence in Christological terms.
J. A. Dearman, "Theophany, Anthropomorphism, and the *Imago Dei*: Some Observations about the Incarnation in Light of the Old Testament," in: *The Incarnation: An Interdisciplinary Symposium on the Incarnation of the Son of God* (ed. S. T. Davis, D. Kendall, and G. O'Collins; Oxford: Oxford University Press, 2004), 43.

[22] C. J. Davis, *The Name and Way of the Lord: Old Testament Themes, New Testament Christology* (JSNTSS 129; Sheffield: Sheffield Academic Press, 1996), 165.

[23] In later Jewish accounts such role will be absorbed by Yahoel and Metatron.

of Abraham and the *Ladder of Jacob*, it is possible that a strict delineation between aural and visual modes in relation to the two respective powers was initially a Christological development; a conceptual turn that was adopted in the framework of Jewish apocalypticism only later in the second century CE, possibly under the influences of Christian currents.[24]

This profound paradigm shift, when the ancient theophanic heritage, in the blink of an eye, became appropriated by the exemplar of the Christian tradition, was indeed a unique and novel historical and theological shift. Although the deity often appeared as the voice in the Hebrew Bible and pre-Christian Jewish pseudepigrapha, such aural manifestation never occurs in the context of early pre-Christian two powers in heaven traditions. In this light, it is not coincidental that in all pre-Christian Jewish two powers accounts God appears with his distinguished *Kavod* attributes, as if continuously attempting to signal that he remains in firm control of the *Kavod* tradition, as his ocular attributes remain superior to those of the second power.

This consequential transition, leading to what is called "*Kavod* Christology," will now be explored in great detail. In what follows we will investigate the various strategies by which ocularcentric attributes of the deity are transferred to Jesus. We begin with an analysis of theophanic currents in the synoptic renderings of the transfiguration. In our investigation of Jesus' ocularcentric profile in the transfiguration account we will draw close attention to the *Kavod* features found in his metamorphosis and their similarities with earlier biblical and extra-biblical Jewish theophanies. Although we will primarily focus on the Markan version of the transfiguration account, we will also take into consideration some unique theophanic features found in Matthew and Luke.

Mark 9:2–10 presents the following rendering of the transfiguration story:

> Six days later, Jesus took with him Peter and James and John, and led them up a high mountain apart, by themselves. And he was transfigured before them, and his clothes became dazzling white, such as no one on earth could bleach them. And there appeared to them Elijah with Moses, who were talking with Jesus. Then Peter said to Jesus, "Rabbi, it is good for us to be here; let us make three dwellings, one for you, one for Moses, and one for Elijah." He did not know what to say, for they were terrified. Then a cloud overshadowed them, and from the cloud there came a voice, "This is my Son, the Beloved; listen to him!" Suddenly when they looked around, they saw no one with them any more, but only Jesus. As they were coming down the mountain, he ordered them to tell no one about what they had seen, until after the Son of Man had risen from the dead. So they kept the matter to themselves, questioning what this rising from the dead could mean.

---

[24] On the possible Christian influences on the *Apocalypse of Abraham*, see A. A. Orlov, "The Messianic Scapegoat in the Apocalypse of Abraham," in: idem, *Divine Scapegoats: Demonic Mimesis in Early Jewish Mysticism* (Albany: SUNY, 2015), 104, 126.

The Gospel of Matthew 17:1–9 provides some additional significant theophanic details, including the motif of Jesus' luminous face:

> Six days later, Jesus took with him Peter and James and his brother John and led them up a high mountain, by themselves. And he was transfigured before them, and his face shone like the sun, and his clothes became dazzling white. Suddenly there appeared to them Moses and Elijah, talking with him. Then Peter said to Jesus, "Lord, it is good for us to be here; if you wish, I will make three dwellings here, one for you, one for Moses, and one for Elijah." While he was still speaking, suddenly a bright cloud overshadowed them, and from the cloud a voice said, "This is my Son, the Beloved; with him I am well pleased; listen to him!" When the disciples heard this, they fell to the ground and were overcome by fear. But Jesus came and touched them, saying, "Get up and do not be afraid." And when they looked up, they saw no one except Jesus himself alone. As they were coming down the mountain, Jesus ordered them, "Tell no one about the vision until after the Son of Man has been raised from the dead."

In the conclusion of Matthew's version Jesus calls the whole ordeal ὅραμα—a "vision," a word missing in Mark. In view of this terminological usage scholars have suggested that Matthew reinforces the tendency of apocalypticizing the transfiguration by calling it a "vision."[25]

The Gospel of Luke shares some theophanic features with Matthew, including the metamorphosis of Jesus' face.[26] Luke also adds some unique "aural" details by stating that the whole endeavor on the mountain was a praying session and that Jesus' transformation took place while he was praying.[27] Jesus' aural plea provides an interesting parallel with the deity's aural response from the cloud.[28] Luke 9:28–37 offers the following rendering of the transfiguration event:

> Now about eight days after these sayings Jesus took with him Peter and John and James, and went up on the mountain to pray. And while he was praying, the appearance of his face changed, and his clothes became dazzling white. Suddenly they saw two men, Moses and Elijah, talking to him. They appeared in glory and

---

[25] Lee, *Jesus' Transfiguration*, 103.

[26] On this, see F. Neirynck, "Minor Agreements: Matthew—Luke in the Transfiguration Story," in: *Orientierung an Jesus: Zur Theologie der Synoptiker: Festschrift Josef Schmid* (ed. P. Hoffmann, N. Brox, and W. Pesch; Freiburg: Herder, 1973), 253–66.

[27] Joseph Fitzmyer notes that "as often elsewhere in this Gospel, the picture of Jesus at prayer precedes an event of importance." J. A. Fitzmyer, *The Gospel According to Luke I-IX* (AB 28; Garden City: Doubleday, 1981), 798.

[28] Commenting on the function of prayer in Luke, John Heil notes that

> although it was while Jesus was praying that the appearance of his face became different in Luke 9:29, this transformation should not be understood as a further description of the prayer itself. It is not part of a mystical-like prayer experience, nor is it an answer to an implicitly voiced petition by Jesus. Rather, it is an external transformation effected by God in response to the praying of Jesus. This accords with the Lukan pattern, in which

were speaking of his departure, which he was about to accomplish at Jerusalem. Now Peter and his companions were weighed down with sleep; but since they had stayed awake, they saw his glory and the two men who stood with him. Just as they were leaving him, Peter said to Jesus, "Master, it is good for us to be here; let us make three dwellings, one for you, one for Moses, and one for Elijah"—not knowing what he said. While he was saying this, a cloud came and overshadowed them; and they were terrified as they entered the cloud. Then from the cloud came a voice that said, "This is my Son, my Chosen; listen to him!" When the voice had spoken, Jesus was found alone. And they kept silent and in those days told no one any of the things they had seen.

Importantly, Luke specifically says the disciples saw his (Jesus') glory (εἶδον τὴν δόξαν αὐτοῦ) and that Moses and Elijah "appeared in glory" (οἳ ὀφθέντες ἐν δόξῃ). The sudden influx of δόξα terminology found in the Lukan version of the transfiguration account is relevant to the main subject of our study. Reflecting on this glory language, Joseph Fitzmyer notes that "the three privileged disciples are said in the Lukan account to have 'seen his glory' (v. 32). Luke has thus made of the scene a special vision of an aspect of Jesus not present in the other Synoptics."[29]

Even a cursory look at the synoptic narratives confirms that they represent joint theophanies, since in all of them a reader encounters two theophanic manifestations, clearly distinguishable by their respective symbolic language.[30] While one of these manifestations is surrounded by peculiar ocularcentric features of the *Kavod* paradigm and tied to the figure of Jesus, the other is fashioned in a strikingly different aural mode, striving not to portray the deity visually. Before proceeding to a close investigation of the two "powers" and their respective theophanic features, it will be helpful to reflect on the order of their appearances in the transfiguration story.

Order of Two Powers Appearances

Thus far we have learned that there are striking differences between the order of the respective powers' appearances in "homogeneous" ocularcentric theophanies (where both powers are fashioned in ocularcentric mode) found in

---

important events occur in the context of and as God's response to the praying of Jesus (Luke 3:21; 5:16; 6:12; 9:18, 28; 11:1; 22:41; 23:46) as an indication of his openness to God's plan.
J. P. Heil, *The Transfiguration of Jesus: Narrative Meaning and Function of Mark 9:2–8, Matt 17:1–8 and Luke 9:28–36* (AnBib 144; Rome: Editrice Pontificio Istituto Biblico, 2000), 77.

[29] Fitzmyer, *The Gospel According to Luke I–IX*, 795.

[30] Commenting on the peculiarities of the theophanic structure in the Gospel of Mark, Adela Yarbro Collins notices that "the first miraculous event has two parts: the transfiguration of Jesus and the appearance of Elijah and Moses (vv. 2c–4). The second miraculous event also has two parts: the appearance of the cloud and the voice from the cloud (v. 7). In between is the human response: Peter's proposal and the fear of the three disciples (vv. 5–6)." A. Yarbro Collins, *Mark: A Commentary* (Hermeneia; Minneapolis: Fortress, 2007), 419–20.

the Book of Daniel, the *Book of the Similitudes*, and the *Exagoge*, and their mixed (ocularcentric/aural) counterparts attested in the *Apocalypse of Abraham* and the *Ladder of Jacob*. In purely ocularcentric accounts, the first power represented by the deity appears first; this is followed by the manifestation of the second power. Yet in the two powers template where the respective powers assume different theophanic modes, the order of appearance is different. In these descriptions, the second power endowed with the ocularcentric attributes is depicted first, followed by the aural epiphany of the first power, which manifests itself as the hypostatic voice. As already noted in our analysis of the *Apocalypse of Abraham* and the *Ladder of Jacob*, the deity's voice plays an important role in these texts, both in the affirmation of the second power in its unique role and in the establishment of its subordination to the first power.

In the ocularcentric/aural two powers template, manifested in the transfiguration and the baptism stories, one encounters a similar procession of the two powers. Thus in all renderings of the transfiguration story, the visible manifestation of the transfigured Jesus is described in the story first, and only after that does the narrative reveal the epiphany of the auricularcentric first power, which appears as a revelation of the divine Voice.[31] As we have already gathered in this study, a similar pattern was influential not only in early Jewish complementary two powers accounts, like the *Apocalypse of Abraham* and the *Ladder of Jacob*, but also in their later rabbinic and Hekhalot counterparts such as *b. Hag.* 15a and *3 Enoch*.

As previously suggested in our study, the order of appearance in joint theophanies is closely tied to the establishment of the hierarchical relationships between the respective powers. In the light of this dynamic it is quite possible that in the purely ocularcentric accounts where both powers assume similar visual qualities, the initial advent of the first power, followed by the procession of the second power, might intend to underline its superior status in the visual hierarchy. Priority of appearance therefore appears to play a significant role in joint ocularcentric theophanies, since, in them, both powers appear in a similar shape, namely, as anthropomorphic beings. In such a potentially confusing situation, the order determines the status. Furthermore, not only does the first power appear first, it also usually carries more exalted ocularcentric attributes, including the attribute of the divine seat. As already noted in our analysis of Metatron developments, the sitting position was an important marker of power and authority that underlined the unique status of the attribute's holder.

Yet in the mixed ocular/aural Jewish and Christian accounts, where the first power appears last, the hierarchical relationships are now constituted differently, namely, through the utterance of the first power at the end of the story. Such a crucial verdict is

---

[31] The similar order of appearances of the first and second powers are detectable also in 2 Peter's account of the transfiguration, the narrative rendered with phrases from Matthew and Luke. 2 Peter 1:16–17 unveils the following tradition:

> For we did not follow cleverly devised myths when we made known to you the power and coming of our Lord Jesus Christ, but we had been eyewitnesses of his majesty. For he received honor and glory from God the Father when that voice was conveyed to him by the Majestic Glory, saying, "This is my Son, my Beloved, with whom I am well pleased."

then able to either deconstruct and subjugate the second power, as in *b. Hag.* 15a and *3 Enoch*, or put it into a complementary hierarchical relationship with the first power through the concept of sonship (Jesus), delegation of the attribute of the divine Name (Yahoel), or possession of the image of God (Adam and Jacob). These complementary dynamics are clearly expressed in God's utterances found at the end of Christian accounts of Jesus' baptism and transfiguration.

Mosaic Settings of the Transfiguration Story

In our analysis of the theophanic features, which the "second power" of the Christian tradition acquires in the synoptic transfiguration accounts, it is important to recognize a possible source of conceptual influences stemming from previous biblical and extra-biblical theophanies. Memory of these influences is reflected not only in the special features of the crucial symbolic nexus of this theophany, the transfigured Jesus, but also in distinctive actions and reactions of the beholders of this crucial vision, not to mention the peculiar spatial and temporal settings of the entire event. In this respect, the reactions of those present at the affair, along with the peculiar depictions of their appearance and behavior, may provide relevant information about the exact nature of the epiphany and its conceptual roots. Even a preliminary glance at the transfiguration account reveals the unmistakable presence of the motifs tied to Moses' encounters with the divine *Kavod* on Mount Sinai.

It is not a coincidence that, in its development of the "*Kavod* Christology," early Christian authors relied on the memory of this paradigmatic theophanic event of the Hebrew Bible.[32] Similar to the baptism account, with its marked Ezekielian allusions, the recollection of the Sinai apparition of the divine Glory and its prominent beholder, the son of Amram, became a theophanic blueprint for this Christological development. Many ancient and modern students of the transfiguration account have previously discerned explicit and implicit influences of the Mosaic theophanic patterns.[33] Ancient

---

[32] Scholars have noticed that the transfiguration account is drawing on a panoply of biblical and extra-biblical theophanic conceptual streams, including Ezekielian, Danielic, and Enochic imagery. On this, see Rowland and Morray-Jones, *The Mystery of God*, 106.

[33] See W. D. Davies and D. C. Allison, Jr., *A Critical and Exegetical Commentary on the Gospel According to Saint Matthew* (ICC; Edinburgh: T&T Clark, 1991), 2.686–7; J. D. G. Dunn, *Christology in the Making: A New Testament Inquiry into the Origins of the Doctrine of the Incarnation* (Philadelphia: Westminster, 1980), 47; C. A. Evans, *Mark 8:27–16:20* (WBC 34B; Nashville: Thomas Nelson, 2001), 34; L. A. Huizenga, *The New Isaac: Tradition and Intertextuality in the Gospel of Matthew* (NovTSup 131; Leiden: Brill, 2009), 211; Lee, *Jesus' Transfiguration*, 17–22; M. D. Litwa, *Iesus Deus: The Early Christian Depiction of Jesus as a Mediterranean God* (Minneapolis: Fortress, 2014), 123; J. Marcus, *The Way of the Lord: Christological Exegesis of the Old Testament in the Gospel of Mark* (Edinburgh: T&T Clark, 1992), 81–83; C. Moss, "The Transfiguration: An Exercise in Markan Accommodation," *BibInt* 12 (2004): 72–73; Yarbro Collins, *Mark*, 416–17; A. Yarbro Collins and J. J. Collins, *King and Messiah as Son of God: Divine, Human, and Angelic Messianic Figures in Biblical and Related Literature* (Grand Rapids: Eerdmans, 2008), 131.

Christian exegetes—Irenaeus,[34] Eusebius of Caesarea,[35] Ephrem the Syrian,[36] and many others entertained such connections.[37] In the context of the modern history of biblical studies, already David Friedrich Strauss has outlined the essential points of similarity between the transfiguration accounts in the synoptic gospels and Moses' ordeals on Sinai in the Old Testament, concentrating mainly on the biblical traditions reflected in Exod 24:1–2, 9–18 and Exod 34:29–35.[38] Since Strauss' pioneering research, these parallels have been routinely reiterated and elaborated by various modern scholars.

The appropriation of the Mosaic theophanic motifs in Mark, Matthew, and Luke is a complex and multifaceted issue, since the evolution of these traditions in the synoptic gospels remains a debated matter. Although some scholars argue that the Mosaic allusions appear to be present in their most articulated form in the Gospel of Matthew,[39]

---

[34] Irenaeus' *Adversus Haereses* 4.20.9 reads:

And the Word spoke to Moses, appearing before him, "just as any one might speak to his friend." But Moses desired to see him openly who was speaking with him, and was thus addressed: "Stand in the deep place of the rock, and with my hand I will cover thee. But when my splendour shall pass by, then thou shalt see my back parts, but my face thou shalt not see: for no man sees my face, and shall live." Two facts are thus signified: that it is impossible for man to see God; and that, through the wisdom of God, man shall see him in the last times, in the depth of a rock, that is, in his coming as a man. And for this reason did he [the Lord] confer with him face to face on the top of a mountain, Elias being also present, as the Gospel relates, he thus making good in the end the ancient promise.

Irenaeus, *Adversus Haereses*, in: *The Ante-Nicene Fathers* (ed. A. Roberts and J. Donaldson; Grand Rapids: Eerdmans, 1980), 5.446.

[35] In his *Proof of the Gospel* 3:2, Eusebius unveils the following tradition:

Again when Moses descended from the Mount, his face was seen full of glory: for it is written: "And Moses descending from the Mount did not know that the appearance of the skin of his face was glorified while he spake to him. And Aaron and all the elders [of the children] of Israel saw Moses, and the appearance of the skin of his face was glorified." In the same way only more grandly our Saviour led his disciples "to a very high mountain, and he was transfigured before them, and his face did shine as the sun, and his garments were white like the light."

W. J. Ferrar, *The Proof of the Gospel: Being the Demonstratio Evangelica of Eusebius of Cæsarea* (2 vols.; London: Society for Promoting Christian Knowledge, 1920), 1.107.

[36] Reflecting on Jesus' transfiguration, Ephrem in his *Hymns on the Church* 36:5–6 recounts: "the brightness which Moses put on was wrapped on him from without, and in that differed from the light of Christ, which shone from within in the womb, at the baptism, and on the mountain top." S. Brock, *The Luminous Eye: The Spiritual World of St. Ephrem* (Kalamazoo: Cistercian Publications, 1992), 71.

[37] D. C. Allison, *The New Moses: A Matthean Typology* (Minneapolis: Fortress, 1993), 243.

[38] Marcus, *The Way of the Lord*, 82; D. F Strauss, *The Life of Jesus Critically Examined* (Philadelphia: Fortress, 1972), 544–45.

[39] Allison notes that

among the Matthean manipulations of Mark's text are the following: Moses has been given the honor of being named before Elijah; "and his face shone like the sun" has been added; the cloud has been made "bright" (*photeine*); "in whom I am well pleased" has been inserted; and the order of *akouete autou* has been reversed. Various suggestions for

already in the Gospel of Mark one can detect the formative influence of the Mosaic blueprint. Mark, however, does not mention several of the Mosaic features found in Matthew and Luke, including the motif of Jesus' luminous face. Some scholars have suggested that Mark could be intentionally silencing Mosaic allusions, battling early "prophetic Christology,"[40] which attempted to envision Jesus as a prophet like Moses.[41] Nevertheless, as William Davies and Dale Allison point out "although Mark... does not appear to have stressed the Mosaic background of the transfiguration, the tradition

> these alterations can and have been made; but simplicity recommends one proposition to account for them all: Matthew rescripted Mark in order to push thoughts towards Moses. Thus the lawgiver now comes first, and no priority of significance is given to Elijah. "Face" and "sun" recall the extra-biblical tradition that Moses' face (cf. Exod 34:29) shone like the sun (Philo, *Vit. Mos.* 2:70; 2 Cor 3:7–18; *LAB* 12:1; *Sipre Num.* §140; *b. B. Bat.* 75a; *Deut. Rab.*11 (207c); this is to be related to the idea that Moses on Sinai went to the place of the sun—*LAB* 12; cf. *2 Bar.* 59:11). *Photeine* alludes to the Shekinah, which accompanied Israel and Moses in the wilderness—and tradition associated Moses' radiance with the glory of the Shekinah. The citation of Isa 42:1 ("in whom I am well pleased") makes Jesus the ʿ*ebed YHWH*, a figure with Mosaic associations (see pp. 68–71, 233–35). Finally, the change to *autou akouete* strengthens the allusion to LXX Deut 18:15 (*autou akousesthe*), which speaks of a prophet like Moses (cf. Tertullian, *Adv. Marc.* 4:22).
>
> Allison, *New Moses*, 244.

[40] One of the proponents of this perspective, John McGuckin, suggests that

> the fact that Mark deliberately omits reference to the Shekinah light on the face of Jesus, and chooses to speak instead of a thoroughgoing metamorphosis (a striking Hellenistic word, very rare in the NT, signifying radical spiritual transformation) argues that he wished to remove any overtly Sinaitic theme in his version of the narrative, and his main reason for doing this, I suggest, is to remove the Moses-Jesus analogy from centre stage, along with its inherently prophetic Christology.
>
> McGuckin, *The Transfiguration of Christ*, 15.

In another part of his study McGuckin proposes that

> by removing reference to the shining face Mark economically removes the Mosaic Christological typology from the narrative. It is his concern to obviate this type of prophetic Christology in the Transfiguration story, and although he retains a Sinai archetype as a structural form, he does not retain the original theological point of using such an archetype in the first place.
>
> McGuckin, *The Transfiguration of Christ*, 66–67.

[41] On this, see O. Cullmann, *The Christology of the New Testament* (Philadelphia: Westminster, 1963), 36–37; M. Goulder, "Elijah with Moses, or a Rift in the Pre-Markan Lute," in: *Christology, Controversy and Community: New Testament Essays in Honour of David R. Catchpole* (ed. D. G. Horrell and C. M. Tuckett; NovTSup 99; Leiden: Brill, 2000), 193–208; T. Hägerland, *Jesus and the Forgiveness of Sins: An Aspect of His Prophetic Mission* (SNTSMS 150; Cambridge: Cambridge University Press, 2011), 217–18; W. Kraus, "Die Bedeutung von Dtn 18,15–18 für das Verständnis Jesu als Prophet," ZNW 90 (1999): 153–76; J. Lierman, *The New Testament Moses: Christian Perceptions of Moses and Israel in the Setting of Jewish Religion* (WUNT 2.173; Tübingen: Mohr Siebeck, 2004), 271–86; Meeks, *The Prophet-King*, 45–46, 87–99; G. Vermes, *Jesus the Jew: A Historian's Reading of the Gospels* (Philadelphia: Fortress, 1981), 97.

he received was largely formulated with Sinai in mind."[42] Therefore, parallels between Mk 9:2–8 and Exod 24 and Exod 34 are rather abundant.[43]

The memory of Mosaic Sinai encounters is even more apparent in the Matthean version of the transfiguration.[44] In fact, the influx of Mosaic allusions caused some

---

[42] Davies and Allison, *Matthew*, 2.686–7. In relation to these developments, Adela Yarbro Collins argues that

> the account of the transfiguration evokes the Old Testament genre of the theophany and especially the Hellenistic and Roman genres of epiphany and metamorphosis. The affinity with biblical theophany is especially apparent in comparison with the account of the theophany on Mount Sinai.... Although it is used differently, both texts have the period of "six days"; both have a cloud on a mountain signifying the presence of God; both have the presence of Moses on the mountain; and both report speech of God on the mountain. In Exodus, the speech of God is reported in 25:1–31:18. This speech concerns the construction of the "tent" or "tabernacle" in the wilderness, including its furniture and rituals.
>
> Yarbro Collins, *Mark*, 416–17.

[43] While reflecting on possible parallels between Exodus and Mark, they notice that

> in both (i) the setting is the same: a high mountain (Exod 24.12, 15–18; 34.3; Mk 9.2); (ii) there is a cloud that descends and overshadows the mountain (Exod 24.15–18; 34.5; Mk 9.7); (iii) a voice comes from the cloud (Exod 24.16; Mk 9.7); (iv) the central figures, Jesus and Moses, become radiant (Exod 34.29–30, 35; Mk 9.2–3); (v) those who see the radiance of the central figure become afraid (Exod 34.30; Mk 9.6); (vi) the event takes place "after six days" (Exod 24.16; Mk 9.2); and (vii) a select group of three people is mentioned (Exod 24.1; Mk 9.2).
>
> Davies and Allison, *Matthew*, 2.686–7.

Further commenting on Elijah and Moses' appearance in the transfiguration story, Davies and Allison note that these two characters both of whom "converse with the transfigured Jesus, are the only OT figures of whom it is related that they spoke with God on Mount Sinai. So their appearance on a mountain in the NT should probably evoke the thought of Mount Sinai." Davies and Allison, *Matthew*, 2.686–7. Some other scholars also registered the overwhelming presence of the Mosaic Sinai motifs by noting that

> there are many features about the transfiguration that have led commentators to conclude that this episode is intended to have some sort of typological connection to Exod 24 and 33–34, passages that describe Moses' ascent up the mountain where he meets God and then descends with a shining face.... The following specific parallels between Mark's account (9:2–8) and Exodus are evident: (1) the reference to "six days" (Mark 9:2; Exod 24:16), (2) the cloud that covers the mountain (Mark 9:7; Exod 24:16), (3) God's voice from the cloud (Mark 9:7; Exod 24:16), (4) three companions (Mark 9:2; Exod 24:1, 9), (5) a transformed appearance (Mark 9:3; Exod 34:30), and (6) the reaction of fear (Mark 9:6; Exod 34:30).
>
> Evans, *Mark 8:27–16:20*, 34.

[44] In his recent study, Leroy Huizenga reflects on these previous scholarly insights by noting that the

> reigning interpretation of the Matthean transfiguration in particular concerns the perceived foregrounding of Sinai motifs and the presentation of Jesus as a new Moses. Commentators point to a multitude of details for support. The phrase "after six days" (Matt 17:1) seems reminiscent of Exod 24:15–18, which relates that the Shekinah covered Sinai for six days (Exod 24:16). Like the Matthean Jesus, Moses is accompanied by three named adherents (Matt 17:1; Exod 24:1, 9). The mountain of Matt 17:1 perhaps recalls Sinai. Like Moses, the Matthean Jesus becomes radiant (Matt 17:2; Exod 34:29–35). Jesus' radiance and Moses' radiance arouse fear (Matt 17:6; Exod 34:29–30). Moses and Elijah appear in Matt 17:3, both of whom conversed with God on Sinai (cf. 1 Kgs 19:8–19). The cloud of Matt 17:5 may concern Moses and Sinai (Exod 19:16; 24:15–18; 34:5), and a cloud was certainly a major feature of wilderness traditions (Exod 13:21–22; 33:7–11; 40:34–38; Num 9:15–23). Both Matt 17:5 and Exod 24:16 share the feature of a voice from

scholars to suggest that Matthew attempted to portray Jesus as a "new Moses." One of the proponents of this idea, Dale Allison, argues that in Matthew "the major theme of the epiphany story would seem to be Jesus' status as a new Moses, and Exod 24 and 34 would seem to be important influences." Reflecting on the motif of Jesus' luminous face found in Matthew, Allison proposes "there is scarcely room for doubt that Matthew has modified Mark for the deliberate purpose of presenting Jesus after the manner of Moses."[45]

However, in the scholarly debates about Jesus as the new Moses, it often remains uncertain which Mosaic developments are under consideration by scholars—traditions of the human Moses found in the biblical theophanic accounts or portrayals of the deified Moses attested in the *Exagoge* of the Ezekiel the Tragedian and the writings of Philo. In these later extra-biblical renderings of Moses' story that precede Christianity, the prophet's visionary ordeals were often reinterpreted in the context of the two powers traditions. Moreover, in the course of these encounters Moses himself often becomes the deified second power.[46]

Scholarly discussions that attempt to envision Jesus as the new Moses often ignore these extra-biblical two powers testimonies, where Moses was portrayed not merely as a seer or a prophet, but as an embodiment of the divine *Kavod*. Instead, contemporary theories about Jesus as the new Moses prefer to rely solely on the memory of biblical Mosaic traditions, while the non-biblical allusions are large ignored. Yet the complex and multifaceted nature of Mosaic influences on the transfiguration accounts should not lead us to the simplified conclusion that the synoptic gospels' intention was merely to portray Jesus as a transformed visionary, similar to the biblical Moses.[47] Scholars have convincingly demonstrated that Jesus' transfiguration clearly supersedes the

a cloud. The word ἐπισκιάζω in Matt 17:5 is found also in Exod 40:35. Finally, the last two words of the heavenly voice in Matt 17:5, ἀκούετε αὐτοῦ, may allude to Deut 18:15, Moses' words concerning the coming eschatological prophet.
    Huizenga, *The New Isaac*, 211.

[45] Davies and Allison, *Matthew*, 2.685–86.

[46] In this respect, Jarl Fossum argues that "although we would be right to see a Moses pattern behind the synoptic account of Jesus' 'transfiguration,' the usual citation of texts from Exodus cannot throw much light on Mark 9:2–8 and its parallels." J. Fossum, "Ascensio, Metamorphosis: The 'Transfiguration' of Jesus in the Synoptic Gospels," in: Fossum, *The Image of the Invisible God*, 76. For Moses' exaltation, see R. Bauckham, "Moses as 'God' in Philo of Alexandria: A Precedent for Christology?" in: *The Spirit and Christ in the New Testament and Christian Theology: Essays in Honor of Max Turner* (ed. I. H. Marshall, V. Rabens, and C. Bennema; Grand Rapids: Eerdmans, 2012), 246–65; G. W. Coats, *Moses: Heroic Man, Man of God* (JSOTSS 57; Sheffield: JSOT Press, 1988), 155–78; D. A. Hagner, "The Vision of God in Philo and John: A Comparative Study," *JETS* 14 (1971): 81–93; W. Helleman, "Philo of Alexandria on Deification and Assimilation to God," *SPhA* 2 (1990): 51–71; C. Holladay, *Theios Aner in Hellenistic Judaism: A Critique of the Use of This Category in New Testament Christology* (Missoula: Scholars, 1977); L. Hurtado, *One Lord, One God: Early Christian Devotion and Ancient Jewish Monotheism* (Philadelphia: Fortress, 1988), 56–59; Lierman, *The New Testament Moses*; Meeks, *The Prophet-King: Moses in Biblical and Extra-Biblical Traditions* (ed. A. Graupner and M. Wolter; BZAW 372; Berlin: Walter de Gruyter, 2007); D. Runia, "God and Man in Philo of Alexandria," *JTS* 39 (1988): 48–75; I. W. Scott, "Is Philo's Moses a Divine Man?" *SPhA* 14 (2002): 87–111; J. W. van Henten, "Moses as Heavenly Messenger in Assumptio Mosis 10:2 and Qumran passages," *JJS* 54 (2003): 216–27.

[47] On Jesus as the new Moses, see Davies and Allison, *Matthew*, 2.696; D. A. Hagner, *Matthew 14–28* (WBC 33B; Dallas: Word Books, 1995), 492–93; Marcus, *The Way of the Lord*, 80–93; F. Refoulé,

biblical patterns of the son of Amram's transformation. Recall that in the Hebrew Bible the luminous face of the great Israelite prophet serves as a mere reflection of God's Glory.[48] However, in the transfiguration account where God assumes the aural aniconic profile, some peculiar features of the missing divine *Kavod* are transferred to the new personalized nexus of the visual theophany—Jesus, now envisioned as an ocularcentric divine manifestation. In this respect one of the significant details underlying the difference between Jesus' luminous metamorphosis and the luminosity of Moses' face is the order of the deity's appearance in the respective visionary traditions. In the biblical accounts, Moses' face becomes luminous only *after* the prophet's encounter with God. The appearance of God's Form thus precedes the transformation of the seer's face, which in these theophanic currents is often understood as a mere mirror of the divine Glory. However, in the transfiguration story, Jesus' luminous metamorphosis occurs *before* the apparition of the Divinity. This manifests a striking contrast to the biblical Exodus theophanies, or even their para-biblical counterparts, like the *Exagoge*, where the initial source of Moses' glorious face, or his glorious apotheosis, the divine Form, appears first.[49] Jesus himself thus became understood as a revelation of the divine Glory and not as its glorious "mirror." In relation to these developments, Adela Yarbro Collins notes that

> the connection with the text from Exodus, however does not explain the statement in v. 2 that Jesus was transfigured. A later passage in Exodus says that, when Moses came down from Mount Sinai, his face "shone" or "had been glorified" because he had been talking with God. One could argue that, analogously, Jesus was transfigured because he was talking with two heavenly beings, the glorified Elijah and Moses. The text, however, seems to imply that Jesus' transfigured state is part of revelation, rather than a result of it.[50]

Furthermore, unlike in Exodus, where the deity is clearly conceived as the divine *Kavod* (and initial theophanic cause for Moses' facial luminosity), in the transfiguration story God is not fashioned as the anthropomorphic divine Glory, but instead as an aniconic aural manifestation. Some of these differences between the two metamorphoses, of Moses and of Jesus, have been discussed by scholars. Criticizing the hypothesis about Jesus as a new Moses, Heil rightly observes that a fatal flaw in such an interpretation is that the transformation involves only the face of Moses and *follows* his speaking with

---

"Jésus, nouveau Moise, ou Pierre, nouveau Grand Prêtre? (Mt 17, 1–9; Mc 9, 2–10)," *RTL* 24 (1993): 145–62.

[48] On the luminosity of Moses' face, see M. Haran, "The Shining of Moses's Face: A Case Study in Biblical and Ancient Near Eastern Iconography [Exod 34:29–35; Ps 69:32; Hab 3:4]," in: *In the Shelter of Elyon* (ed. W. B. Barrick and J. R. Spencer; JSOTSS 31; Sheffield: Sheffield Academic Press, 1984), 159–73; J. Morgenstern, "Moses with the Shining Face," *HUCA* 2 (1925): 1–27; W. Propp, "The Skin of Moses' Face—Transfigured or Disfigured?" *CBQ* 49 (1987): 375–86.

[49] Arthur Michael Ramsey highlights the difference, noting that whereas Moses' glory on Sinai was reflected, Jesus' glory was unborrowed. A. M. Ramsey, *The Glory of God and the Transfiguration of Christ* (London: Longmans, Green & Co., 1949), 120.

[50] Yarbro Collins, *Mark*, 417.

God. Jesus' transfiguration involves not only his face but his clothing and *precedes* his encounter with the deity.[51]

Keeping in mind a rich and multifaceted legacy of the Mosaic developments in the Second Temple Jewish environment, which included not only formative biblical accounts but also their extra-biblical elaborations, we now turn to some of these testimonies, as reflected in the *Exagoge* of Ezekiel the Tragedian, Philo, and the Qumran writings. Within these traditions Moses himself becomes envisioned as the nexus of theophany, often being understood as the second power, endowed with the peculiar ocularcentric attributes of the deity.

The Extra-Biblical Mosaic Developments

Joel Marcus draws attention to three dimensions of Mosaic developments in early Jewish lore that are, for him, significant for understanding Jesus' transfiguration. These include Moses' enthronement, his translation to heaven at his death, and his divinization.[52] With respect to this study, these dimensions are important precisely because in these extra-biblical elaborations Moses is often endowed with the attributes of the divine Glory.

Moses' Enthronement

The conceptual trajectory of Moses' enthronement is already present in the work of the second-century BCE Jewish poet, Ezekiel the Tragedian, where Moses receives tokens of kingship from God on Sinai.[53] As previously noted, Moses' enhanced profile in the *Exagoge* represents one of the most significant advancements, propelling the prophet's story into an entirely new theophanic realm.

Marcus notes similarities between the *Exagoge* and Daniel 7, the conceptual bedrock of the two powers developments, where royal features are now transferred into a distinctive Mosaic context. Marcus points out that in the *Exagoge*, "which has some striking similarities to the vision described in Dan 7:13–14, 16 the ascent of Sinai ... is linked with Moses' reception of a kingly scepter and of a crown, and with his mounting of a throne."[54] Marcus notes that Jethro's interpretation of the dream also contains a reference to Moses' enthronement, since it predicts that "Moses will 'cause a mighty throne to rise ... will rule and govern men' (lines 85–86), thus cementing the royal interpretation of the Sinai ascent."[55]

These developments attested in the *Exagoge* are significant for our further investigation of the Mosaic traditions in the transfiguration story. As previously noted, in this early text Moses' story makes an important symbolic turn by upgrading the exemplar's status from a visionary to an object of vision. It is also instructive that we

---

[51] Heil, *The Transfiguration of Jesus*, 78–79.
[52] Marcus, *The Way of the Lord*, 84.
[53] Marcus, *The Way of the Lord*, 84.
[54] Marcus, *The Way of the Lord*, 85
[55] Marcus, *The Way of the Lord*, 85

can trace this transition in the *Exagoge*, since such a paradigm shift literally unfolds before the eyes of the account's readers. As one remembers, Moses first sees the *Kavod* and then he himself becomes its embodiment. The implicit postulation of the heavenly locale of Moses' ordeal is also significant. Commenting on the *Exagoge*'s portrayal of Moses, Jarl Fossum notes that

> although the author here speaks about ascending Mt. Sinai, it is clear that the locale described is a heavenly one. The throne of the "noble Man" is enormous, reaching to the "corners of heaven." From its place Moses can see everything. The "heavenly bodies," which in Israelite-Jewish religion are identical with the angels, fall down and worship him.[56]

A significant detail of the *Exagoge* account, relevant to our study of the transfiguration story, is a designation of the celestial man, whose place is later taken by Moses as *phōs*. The term φῶς/φώς was often used in the Jewish theophanic traditions to label the glorious manifestations of the deity as well as his anthropomorphic human "icons," who radiate the luminosity of their newly acquired celestial bodies. These traditions often play on the ambiguity of the term, which, depending on the context, can designate either "a man" (φώς) or "light" (φῶς), pointing to both the luminous and anthropomorphic nature of the divine or angelic manifestations.[57]

The *Exagoge*'s identification of the great Israelite prophet with a celestial form is not a unique occurrence. Scholars often point to some Samaritan materials suggestive of Moses' installation into the heavenly realm. Although these traditions survived in the later macroforms, they are similar to some early Jewish pseudepigraphical developments. Jarl Fossum draws attention to a text from the third-century hymn cycle known as the *Defter*, where one finds the following tradition:

> Great God, whose like there is not! Great assembly [that is, the angelic host] without compeer! Great Prophet the like of whom there has never arisen! . . . Verily he was clothed with a garment with which no king can clothe himself. Verily he was covered by the cloud and his face was clothed with a ray of light, so all nations should know that Moses was the Servant of God and his Faithful One.[58]

Looking closely at these Samaritan developments, Fossum concludes that "there can be little doubt that this is a description of the installation of Moses as king in heaven."[59]

---

[56] Fossum, "Ascensio, Metamorphosis," 75.

[57] On the φως traditions, see G. Quispel, "Ezekiel 1:26 in Jewish Mysticism and Gnosis," *VC* 34 (1980): 1–13 at 6–7; Fossum, *The Name of God*, 280; idem, *Image of the Invisible God*, 16–17; Bunta, *Moses, Adam and the Glory*, 92ff.

[58] Fossum, "Ascensio, Metamorphosis," 73–74.

[59] Fossum, "Ascensio, Metamorphosis," 74.

Moses' Glorification at His Death/His Translation to Heaven

Joel Marcus calls attention to another important cluster of para-biblical developments, which unveil a tradition about Moses' translation to heaven. For our study it is important to note that in some renderings of this story, Moses' earthly body undergoes a fiery or glorious transformation. These traditions, moreover, try to connect the metamorphosis of the prophet's face at Sinai with his final full glorification. This correspondence between the seer's proleptic partial and temporary glorification and his future full glorification at the point of his departure from the earthly realm is an important detail for our analysis of the transfiguration story, since Jesus' metamorphosis on the mountain is often understood as a proleptic glimpse into the eschatological role of Christ as the embodiment of the divine Glory. In relation to such an understanding, Marcus observes that "in Mark the transfiguration narrative is not an end in itself; rather, it points beyond itself to an eschatological event, Jesus' resurrection from the dead. The royal Mosaic features of the transfiguration narrative, therefore, foreshadow the enthronement of Jesus that occurs at his resurrection."[60] Marcus further suggests that this association of enthronement with an after-death experience also has a Mosaic precedent.[61]

The traditions of Moses' glorification at his death or his translation to heaven have very early conceptual roots in pre-Christian Jewish lore. The motif of Moses' translation to heaven at the end of his life plays an important role already in Philo. In relation to these developments, Wayne Meeks observes that

> Philo takes for granted that Deuteronomy 34:6, "no man knows his grave," means that Moses was translated. Doubtless this view was traditional in Philo's circle, for he states matter-of-factly that Enoch, "the protoprophet (Moses)," and Elijah all obtained this reward.[62] The end of Moses' life was an "ascent,"[63] an "emigration to heaven," "abandoning the mortal life to be made[64] immortal."[65]

De Vita Mosis 2.288–91 portrays Moses' departure from the earthly realm as follows:

> Afterwards the time came when he had to make his pilgrimage from earth to heaven, and leave this mortal life for immortality, summoned thither by the Father

---

[60] Marcus, *The Way of the Lord*, 87.

[61] Marcus, *The Way of the Lord*, 87. Marcus further notes that

> the linkage of the transfiguration narrative with the resurrection is established redactionally by its juxtaposition with 9:9–10 and is underlined in an intriguing manner by the larger context of the Old Testament passage cited in 9:7. In 9:9, which is a redactional verse, the Markan Jesus establishes a link between the transfiguration narrative and the resurrection by ordering the disciples not to tell anyone what they have seen on the mountain until the Son of Man is raised from the dead.
>
> Marcus, *The Way of the Lord*, 87–88.

[62] QG 1.86.

[63] QG 1.86.

[64] *Mos.* 2.288–92; *Virt.* 53, 72–79.

[65] Meeks, *The Prophet-King*, 124.

who resolved his twofold nature of soul and body into a single unity, transforming his whole being into mind, pure as the sunlight ... for when he was already being exalted and stood at the very barrier, ready at the signal to direct his upward flight to heaven, the divine spirit fell upon him and he prophesied with discernment while still alive the story of his own death.[66]

In the analysis of this passage scholars often see within the statement that God transformed Moses' "whole being into mind, pure as the sunlight" an implicit reference to his glorification.[67] Similarly, Josephus also describes Moses in the same paradigm of otherworldly translation,[68] which vividly recalls the departures of Enoch and Elijah. *Ant.* 4.326[69] unveils the following tradition:

And, while he [Moses] bade farewell to Eleazar and Joshua and was yet communing with them, a cloud all of a sudden descended upon him and he disappeared in a ravine. But he has written of himself in the sacred books that he died, for fear lest they should venture to say that by reason of his surpassing virtue he had gone back to the Deity.[70]

While Philo and Josephus only implicitly intimate Moses' glorification at the point of his transition to the upper realm, some testimonies found in Pseudo-Philo's *Liber Antiquitatum Biblicarum* explicitly express this possibility. Kristine Ruffatto argues that "Pseudo-Philo goes beyond the traditional narrative to ascribe luminosity to Moses multiple times: on his first ascent of Sinai as well as his second, and just prior to his death on Nebo."[71] The assignment of luminosity to Moses before his death is crucial for our study of the Christian developments, in which the luminosity of Jesus' face is put in conspicuous parallel with the glory of his resurrection.

In *LAB*, Ruffatto notes that just prior to his death, when Moses ascends Abarim/Nebo, his "appearance became glorious; and he died in glory according to the word of

---

[66] Philo (ed. F. H. Colson and G. H. Whitaker; 10 vols.; LCL; Cambridge: Harvard University Press, 1929–1964), 6.593–95.

[67] Lierman, *The New Testament Moses*, 201.

[68] J. D. Tabor, "'Returning to the Divinity': Josephus's Portrayal of the Disappearances of Enoch, Elijah, and Moses," *JBL* 108 (1989): 225–38; C. Begg, "Josephus's Portrayal of the Disappearances of Enoch, Elijah, and Moses," *JBL* 109 (1990): 691–93.

[69] The motif of Moses' translation is also attested in *Ant.* 3.96–7:

There was a conflict of opinions: some said that he [Moses] had fallen a victim to wild beasts—it was principally those who were ill disposed towards him who voted for that view—others that he had been taken back to the divinity. But the sober-minded, who found no private satisfaction in either statement—who held that to die under the fangs of beasts was a human accident, and that he should be translated by God to himself by reason of his inherent virtue was likely enough—were moved by these reflections to retain their composure.

H. S. J. Thackeray, *Josephus, Jewish Antiquities* (LCL; Cambridge: Harvard University Press; London: Heinemann, 1967), 3.363.

[70] Thackeray, *Josephus, Jewish Antiquities*, 4.633.

[71] K. J. Ruffatto, *Visionary Ascents of Moses in Pseudo-Philo's Liber Antiquitatum Biblicarum: Apocalyptic Motifs and the Growth of Visionary Moses Tradition* (PhD diss., Marquette University, 2010), 152.

the Lord" (*et mutata est effigies eius in gloria, et mortuus est in gloria secundum os Domini*—19:16)."[72] Ruffatto points out that "this assertion of Moses' pre-death luminosity is not present in Deut 34."[73] She further suggests that the author of *LAB* evidently "saw Moses' radiance as an experience of actual transmutation into transcendent form."[74]

The lore about Moses' translation to heaven and his bodily metamorphosis during this transition receives further development in later midrashic materials. These accounts often speak about the glorious or fiery form of the prophet's body during his final translation. For example, *Deut. Rab.* 11:10 contains the following:

> When Moses saw that no creature could save him from the path of death … He took a scroll and wrote down upon it the Ineffable Name, nor had the Book of Song been completely written down when the moment of Moses' death arrived. At that hour God said to Gabriel: "Gabriel, go forth and bring Moses' soul." He, however, replied: "Master of the Universe, how can I witness the death of him who is equal to sixty myriads, and how can I behave harshly to one who possesses such qualities?" Then [God] said to Michael: "Go forth and bring Moses' soul." He, however, replied: "Master of the Universe, I was his teacher, and he my pupil, and I cannot therefore witness his death." [God] then said to Sammael the wicked: "Go forth and bring Moses' soul." Immediately he clothed himself with anger and girded on his sword and wrapped himself with ruthlessness and went forth to meet Moses. When Sammael saw Moses sitting and writing down the Ineffable Name, and how the radiance of his appearance was like unto the sun and he was like unto an angel of the Lord of hosts, he became afraid of Moses.

In *Midrash Gedullat Moshe*[75] the motif of Moses' translation to heaven coincides with the fiery transformation of his earthly form. In this text God commands the angel Metatron to bring Moses up to heaven. Metatron warns the deity that the prophet would not be able to withstand the vision of angels, "since the angels are princes of fire, while Moses is made from flesh and blood." God then commands Metatron to change the prophet's flesh into torches of fire.

While thoroughly considering the aforementioned traditions and their relevance for the transfiguration accounts, Joel Marcus notes that the parallelism between Sinai and Moses' translation often found in the extra-biblical interpretations "provides a

---

[72] Ruffatto, *Visionary Ascents of Moses*, 168. Other scholars have also noticed these developments. Thus, John Lierman points out that
> Pseudo-Philo writes that Moses at the very end of his life "was filled with understanding and his appearance was changed to a state of glory; and he died in glory (*et mutata est effigies eius in gloria et mortuus est in gloria; LAB* 19:16)," words that recall Philo's description of the physical transformation and endowment with special insight that came upon Moses at his final prophecy.
>
> Lierman, *The New Testament Moses*, 204.

[73] Ruffatto, *Visionary Ascents of Moses*, 168.
[74] Ruffatto, *Visionary Ascents of Moses*, 170.
[75] Wertheimer, *Batei Midrashot*, 1.27.

plausible background for the redactional linkage made in Mark 9:2–10 between the events on the mountain and the reference to resurrection, since resurrection and ascension to heaven are related concepts, although admittedly they have different history-of-religions backgrounds."[76]

Moses' Angelification and Divinization

Another important aspect in the development of the para-biblical Mosaic lore are traditions of Moses' angelification and divinization. Moses' endowment with a unique celestial status and form often coincides in the extra-biblical Jewish materials with assigning to him attributes of the heavenly beings. For example, the *Animal Apocalypse*, an Enochic writing usually dated to the second century BCE,[77] hints at an angelic status and form of the son of Amram in its enigmatic rendering of the Sinai encounter. *1 Enoch* 89:36 depicts Moses as the one who was transformed from a sheep into a man at Sinai. In the metaphorical language of the *Animal Apocalypse*, where angels are portrayed as anthropomorphic and humans as zoomorphic creatures, the transition from sheep to a man clearly indicates that the character has acquired an angelic form and status.

Crispin Fletcher-Louis draws attention to already mentioned developments in Pseudo-Philo that also seem to hint at Moses' angelic status. He notes that in *LAB* 12:1,

> Moses ascends Mount Sinai where he is "bathed with light that could not be gazed upon," surpassing in splendor the light of the sun, moon and stars. Because of his glory the Israelites could not recognize him on his descent. The failure of others to recognize the transformed mortal also appears in some Latin texts for the parallel episode in *Biblical Antiquities* 27:10, where Kenaz is assisted by an angel.[78]

---

[76] Marcus, *The Way of the Lord*, 88.

[77] In relation to the date of the text Daniel Olson notes that

> fragments of the *An. Apoc.* from Qumran provide a *terminus ad quem* before 100 BCE, but greater precision is possible since the allegory appears to describe the ascendancy of Judas Maccabee (90:9), but says nothing about his death (90:12). Based on this, most scholars agree that the *An. Apoc.* was written between 165–160 BCE, and they further agree that the author was probably a member of or a sympathizer with the reform group described in 90:6–9 and a supporter of the Maccabean revolt when it broke out, expecting it to evolve into earth's final battle, God's direct intervention in history, and the inauguration of the eschatological age (90:9–20). If this is correct, one may suppose that one reason the *An. Apoc.* was published was to encourage readers to back the Maccabean revolt.
>
> D. Olson, *A New Reading of the Animal Apocalypse of 1 Enoch: "All Nations Shall be Blessed"* (SVTP 24; Leiden: Brill, 2013), 85–86.

See also D. Assefa, *L'Apocalypse des animaux (1 Hen 85–90): une propagande militaire? Approches narrative, historico-critique, perspectives théologiques* (JSJSS 120; Leiden: Brill, 2007), 220–32.

[78] C. Fletcher-Louis, *All the Glory of Adam: Liturgical Anthropology in the Dead Sea Scrolls* (STDJ 42; Leiden: Brill, 2002), 416–17.

According to Fletcher-Louis, "the visual transformation of the mortal and, sometimes, their consequent unrecognizability, is a frequent motif in angelomorphic transformation texts with a close parallel in the deification of Moses in 4Q374."[79]

Fletcher-Louis' reference to 4Q374 brings us to the Qumran materials, which often feature Moses as an angelomorphic being. Fletcher-Louis suggests that in the Dead Sea Scrolls Moses' divine or angelomorphic identity is often associated with his ascent of Sinai and in the giving of the Torah.[80] To quote his words:

> 4Q374 frag. 2 and 4Q377 specifically locate events at Sinai, although it is true that they do not exclude some earlier angelomorphic identity for Moses, and, of course, 4Q374 uses the statement that Moses became God to Pharaoh in Egypt (Exod 7:1).[81]

Furthermore, it is possible that the Dead Sea Scrolls entertain not only the possibility of Moses' angelification but also his divinization at Sinai. For example, 4Q374 alludes to the deification of the great prophet by saying: "he made him [Moses] like a god[82] over the powerful ones, and a cause of reel[ing] (?) for Pharaoh . . . and then he let his face shine for them for healing, they strengthened [their] hearts again."[83] Another feature of this Qumran passage significant for our future analysis is that the radiance of the glorified Moses' face, similar to the divine luminosity, appears to be able to transform human nature.

Yet, another important cluster of Mosaic traditions that attests to the son of Amram's possession of angelic attributes are the stories regarding his miraculous features revealed at birth. Although these stories are preserved in their full scope only in later rabbinic materials,[84] these narrative currents appear to have early pre-Christian conceptual roots, since they parallel stories of Noah's miraculous birth found in Jewish pseudepigrapha and Qumran materials.[85] Some have persuasively argued that the

---

[79] Fletcher-Louis, *All the Glory of Adam*, 416–17.

[80] Fletcher-Louis, *All the Glory of Adam*, 149.

[81] Fletcher-Louis, *All the Glory of Adam*, 149. See also C. Fletcher-Louis, "4Q374: A Discourse on the Sinai Tradition: The Deification of Moses and Early Christology," *DSD* 3 (1996): 236–52.

[82] The Mosaic title "god" is already attested in Exod 7:1: "See, I have made you a god to Pharaoh." See also Philo's *Life of Moses* 1.155–58: "for he [Moses] was named god and king of the whole nation."

[83] 4Q374 2:6–8. *The Dead Sea Scrolls Study Edition* (ed. F. García Martínez and E. J. C. Tigchelaar; 2 vols.; Leiden; New York; Cologne: Brill, 1997), 2.740–41.

[84] Fletcher-Louis points out that there is "no parallel to the birth of Noah for Moses among the Dead Sea Scrolls." Fletcher-Louis, *All the Glory of Adam*, 149.

[85] The traditions are discernible, for example, in Pseudo-Philo. Kristine Ruffatto notes that

> *LAB* 9 contains a colorful introduction to Moses' birth and life, the vast majority of which is not present in the Hebrew Bible. Pseudo-Philo's considerable embellishment of the traditional canonical text of Exod 1–2 includes the proclamation by God to Amram that Moses will see God's "house"/heavenly temple (9:8) and the statement that Moses was born circumcised (he was "born in the covenant of God and the covenant of the flesh"—9:13). The text goes on to proclaim that Moses was nursed "and became glorious above all other men" (*et gloriosus factus est super omnes homines*), a declaration of Moses' singularity among humans and a likely reference to Moses' future luminosity.
> Ruffatto, *Visionary Ascents of Moses*, 154–55.

stories of Moses' birth influenced the Mosaic typology of Jesus' nativity stories found in the synoptic gospels, especially in Matthew. Later rabbinic stories reminiscent of the Noahic lore reflected in *1 Enoch* and the *Genesis Apocryphon* provide interesting details about the miraculous birth of the great prophet. According to *Pirke de Rabbi Eliezer* 48, at birth Moses' body was like an angel of God. *b. Sotah* 12a recounts that at his birth the house was filled with light. According to *Deut. Rab.* 11:10, the young prophet was able to speak at only a day old, and to prophesy at four months.[86] These later rabbinic traditions echo previously discussed traditions within Qumran literature in which Moses is envisioned as a celestial being.

Another cluster of conceptual developments related to the angelification and divinization of Moses is found in the works of Philo of Alexandria. Scholars who have engaged with these traditions are often perplexed by the motif of Moses' divinization, as it relates to prevailing concepts of Jewish monotheism. Although the Philonic corpus has not featured in our discussion regarding the early Jewish two powers in heaven traditions, Philo's speculations about the Logos and other mediatorial figures are often seen as closely related to these developments. As in these early two powers traditions, the motif of the second power's enthronement is a pivotal point in the construction of its unique identity. Joel Marcus notes that, in the *Life of Moses* 1.158,[87] "Philo implies that the enthronement of Moses on Sinai involved his becoming a god."[88] David Litwa

---

Looking at *LAB*'s tradition that Moses was born circumcised, Ruffatto says that

> the commentators note that this is, surprisingly, the only reference to circumcision in all of *LAB*. One may ask why only Moses is singled out as circumcised in the text, and why the author has stressed that the covenant mediator was born that way. It may well be a statement about Moses' unique angel-like identity as one who, like the angels, was born in this holy state. *LAB* knows *Jubilees*, and *Jub.* 15:27 links circumcision to the angels, who were born circumcised ("the nature of all the angels of the presence and all of the angels of sanctification was thus from the day of their creation").

Ruffatto, *Visionary Ascents of Moses*, 155.

[86] See also *Exod. Rab.* 1:20 and *Zohar* II.11b.

[87] *De Vita Mosis* I.156–58 reads:

> For if, as the proverb says, what belongs to friends is common, and the prophet is called the friend of God, it would follow that he shares also God's possessions, so far as it is serviceable. For God possesses all things, but needs nothing; while the good man, though he possesses nothing in the proper sense, not even himself, partakes of the precious things of God so far as he is capable. And that is but natural, for he is a world citizen, and therefore not on the roll of any city of men's habitation, rightly so because he has received no mere piece of land but the whole world as his portion. Again, was not the joy of his partnership with the Father and Maker of all magnified also by the honor of being deemed worthy to bear the same title? For he was named god and king of the whole nation, and entered, we are told, into the darkness where God was, that is into the unseen, invisible, incorporeal and archetypal essence of existing things. Thus he beheld what is hidden from the sight of mortal nature, and, in himself and his life displayed for all to see, he has set before us, like some well-wrought picture, a piece of work beautiful and godlike, a model for those who are willing to copy it.

Colson and Whitaker, *Philo*, 6.357–59.

[88] Marcus, *The Way of the Lord*, 90.

recently offered a nuanced and insightful reassessment of Moses' divinization's motifs in Philo. He writes that

> in his *Questions on Exodus*, for instance, Philo says that Moses was "divinized" (2.40), "changed into the divine," and thus became "truly divine" (2.29). Moreover, ten times Philo calls Moses "(a) god" (θεός) in accordance with Exod 7:1: "I [God] have made you a god to Pharaoh." In *On the Sacrifices*, for instance, Philo says that God appointed Moses as god, "placing all the bodily region and the mind which rules it in subjection and slavery to him" (§9).[89]

Comparable to the *Exagoge* and Qumran materials, Philo's reflections on Moses' exaltation are often put in the context of Sinai traditions. According to Litwa, "Philo presents Moses' ascent on Sinai as a proleptic experience of deification."[90] The tendency to view Moses' encounter on the mountain as the proleptic experience that anticipates Moses' permanent deification after his death is important for our analysis of Jesus' transfiguration; like Moses, his acquisition of the divine Glory on the mountain also anticipates his future role as the divine *Kavod* after his death and resurrection. Touching on Moses' final translation Litwa observes that

> Moses's translation was his final pilgrimage to the heavenly realm in which all the transformations he experienced at Sinai became permanent (*Mos.* 2.288). Just as in *Questions on Exodus* 2.29, the departing Moses is resolved "into the nature of unity" and "changed into the divine." His "migration" from this world was an "exaltation," in which he "noticed that he was gradually being disengaged from the [bodily] elements with which he had been mixed" (*Virt.* 76). When Moses shed his mortal encasing, God resolved Moses's body and soul into a single unity, "transforming [him] wholly and entirely into most sun-like νοῦς" (ὅλον δι' ὅλων μεθαρμοζόμενος εἰς νοῦν ἡλιοειδέστατον) (*Mos.* 2.288; cf. *Virt.* 72–79). It is important to note the brilliant light imagery here, since it connects Moses to divine Glory traditions. At Sinai, Moses saw the divine Glory (the Logos), and participated in it. Philo translated these scriptural ideas into philosophical terms. Moses, who once saw God's glorious Logos (or Mind), is now permanently transformed into the brilliant reality of νοῦς.[91]

---

[89] M. D. Litwa, "The Deification of Moses in Philo of Alexandria," *SPhA* 26 (2014): 1–27 at 1. For discussion on the concept of deification in Philo, see R. Cox, *By the Same Word: Creation and Salvation in Hellenistic Judaism and Early Christianity* (BZNW 145; Berlin: Walter de Gruyter, 2007), 87–140; R. Radice, "Philo's Theology and Theory of Creation," in: *The Cambridge Companion to Philo* (ed. A. Kamesar; Cambridge: Cambridge University Press, 2009), 128–29; D. T. Runia, "The Beginnings of the End: Philo of Alexandria and Hellenistic Theology," in: *Traditions of Theology: Studies in Hellenistic Theology, Its Background and Aftermath* (ed. D. Frede and A. Laks; PA 89; Leiden: Brill, 2002), 281–312 at 289–99; D. Winston, "Philo's Conception of the Divine Nature," in: *Neoplatonism and Jewish Thought* (ed. L. E. Goodman; Albany: SUNY, 1992), 21–42 at 21–23.

[90] Litwa, "The Deification of Moses in Philo of Alexandria," 14–15.

[91] Litwa, "The Deification of Moses in Philo of Alexandria," 20–21.

Litwa points out an important connection between Moses' deification and Philo's attention to the visionary traditions, observing that

> perhaps the clearest indication of Moses's deification is his vision of (the second) God and its results. . . . The Existent granted Moses's request. He did not, however, reveal his essence to Moses. Rather, he revealed his Image, the Logos. . . . By gazing at the Logos, the Existent's splendor reached Moses in order that through the secondary splendor, Moses beheld "the more splendid (splendor of the Existent)." . . . In Exodus, Moses descends Mt. Sinai with a radiant face (Exod 34:29–35). Philo interprets this radiance in terms of beauty: Moses was "far more beautiful (πολὺ καλλίων) with respect to his appearance [or face, ὄψιν] than when he had gone up [Mount Sinai]." Beauty was one of the trademarks of divinity. Diotima asks Socrates in Plato's *Symposium*, "Don't you say that all the gods are . . . beautiful (κάλους)?" (202c)? The historian Charax says of Io that she was considered a goddess on account of her beauty (θεός ἐνομίσθη διὰ τὸ κάλλος). Brilliance and beauty, furthermore, are often revealed in a divine epiphany.[92]

Other scholars have also reflected on the value of the Philonic portrayals of Moses' divinization and enthronement for our understanding of the transfiguration story. Commenting on the Philonic rendering of Moses' experience on Sinai, Joel Marcus notes that "Moses' ascent of Mount Sinai (his entry into the darkness where God was; cf. Exod 20:21) is interpreted as an enthronement ('he was named . . . king')."[93] Marcus further suggests that

> the connection between Moses' transfiguring experience on Sinai and his reception of God's kingship is strikingly reminiscent of the fact that the account of Jesus' transfiguration immediately follows 8:38–39:1, in which the coming of the kingdom of God (9:1) is paralleled to Jesus' own coming as Son of Man (8:38) . . . Like Moses, then, Jesus ascends the mount and there is seen to be a king, a sovereign whose kingship partakes of God's own royal authority over the universe.[94]

Marcus further proposes that "in line with this royal context, the transfiguration of Jesus' clothing, like Moses' transfiguration in some Jewish traditions, is probably symbolic of a royal robing. For biblically literate readers, therefore, one of the chief functions of the Mosaic typology in the transfiguration narrative would be to drive home the association between Jesus' kingship and the coming of God's kingdom."[95] Marcus' suggestion that the tradition of Jesus' garment may also have a Mosaic provenance is significant and will be explored later in our study.

---

[92] Litwa, "The Deification of Moses in Philo of Alexandria," 17–18.
[93] Marcus, *The Way of the Lord*, 85.
[94] Marcus, *The Way of the Lord*, 86.
[95] Marcus, *The Way of the Lord*, 87.

The Afterlife of Biblical Mosaic Traditions in Other Second Temple Mediatorial Trends

Earlier we mentioned that many who espouse "Mosaic typology" limit their comparison of Jesus and Moses to the Exodus account. Only a small number of experts dare to extend their reach to the extra-biblical Mosaic elaborations found at Qumran, in Philo, Pseudo-Philo, the *Exagoge*, and other early Jewish accounts. Often, however, even they fail to recognize other dimensions, which are crucial for understanding the transfiguration story, but which are contained not inside the Mosaic lore but outside its symbolic fence. Frequently these expansions do not bear Moses' name and are not explicitly related to his story, but unfold in the accounts of other biblical heroes, such as Enoch, Abraham, or Jacob. Within these mediatorial trends the imagery of Moses' incandescent face often receives its novel and complex afterlife.

One cluster of such traditions that reveals a panoply of distinctive Mosaic motifs is present in *2 Enoch*, an early Jewish apocalypse that we have already examined. Within the narrative of Enoch's metamorphosis into the supreme angel and the second power (which in later Jewish mysticism will be labeled as the Lesser YHWH), one finds familiar Mosaic motifs. Although the main protagonist of this text is not Moses, but instead the seventh antediluvian patriarch, Enoch's exalted profile is built on the foundation of the biblical and extra-biblical Mosaic traditions, similar to Jesus' exaltation in the transfiguration account. Here one can find an interesting specimen of a pre-Christian "Mosaic typology." In the same way as in the synoptic gospels, the story of Moses' elevation is perpetuated through a biography of his conceptual rival, the seventh antediluvian hero, who became regarded as a new Moses. Several features of this novel "Mosaic" account are important for our future analysis of the transfiguration story. One such detail relevant for our study is *2 Enoch*'s tendency to designate God's anthropomorphic extent as his Face. This terminological application, in fact, may provide crucial insights into the symbolism of Jesus' luminous face in some versions of the transfiguration story.

2 Enoch contains two theophanic portrayals involving the motif of the divine Face. The first occurs in *2 Enoch* 22, which portrays Enoch's encounter with the deity in the celestial realm. Later, in chapter 39, the seventh patriarch recounts this theophanic experience to his sons, adding new details. Although both passages demonstrate a number of terminological affinities, the second explicitly connects the divine Face with God's anthropomorphic extent, the divine *Kavod*.

Elsewhere, I have argued that Mosaic traditions played a formative role in shaping the theophanic imagery of the divine *Panim* in *2 Enoch*.[96] It is not a coincidence that both the Bible and *2 Enoch* associate the divine extent with light and fire. In biblical theophanies smoke and fire often serve as a divine envelope, protecting mortals from the sight of the divine form. Thus it is easy to recognize *2 Enoch*'s appropriation of familiar theophanic imagery from the Exodus accounts.[97]

---

[96] See Orlov, *The Enoch-Metatron Tradition*, 254ff.
[97] See Exod 19:9; Exod 19:16–18; Exod 34:5.

In *2 Enoch* 39:3–6, as in the Mosaic account from Exod 33, the Face is closely associated with the divine extent and seems to be understood not simply as a part of the deity's body (his face) but as a radiant *façade* of his anthropomorphic form.[98] This identification between the deity's Face and the deity's form is reinforced by additional parallels in which Enoch's face is identified with Enoch's form:

> You, my children, you see my face, a human being created just like yourselves; but I am one who has seen the face of the Lord, like iron made burning hot by a fire, emitting sparks.... And you see the form of my body, the same as your own: but I have seen the form (extent) of the Lord, without measure and without analogy, who has no end (*2 Enoch* 39:3–6, shorter recension).

This passage alludes to the biblical tradition from Exod 33:18–23. Similar to the biblical text, the divine *Panim* of *2 Enoch* connected to the glorious divine form—God's *Kavod*:

> Then Moses said, "Now show me your glory." And the Lord said, "I will cause all my goodness to pass in front of you, and I will proclaim my name, the Lord, in your presence... but," he said, "you cannot see my face, for no one may see me and live."

Here the impossibility of seeing the Lord's Face is understood not simply as the impossibility of seeing a particular part of the Lord but rather as the impossibility of seeing the full range of his glorious body. The logic of the whole passage, which employs such terms as God's "face" and God's "back," suggests that the word *Panim* refers here to the forefront of the divine form. The imagery of the divine Face found in the Psalms[99] also favors this motif of the identity between the face and the anthropomorphic form of the Lord. For example, in Ps 17:15 the Lord's Face is closely tied to his form or likeness: "As for me, I shall behold your face in righteousness; when I awake, I shall be satisfied with beholding your form."

The early Enochic accounts appear to follow these biblical parallels. Thus, the identification between the Face and the divine form also seems to be hinted at in the *Book of the Watchers*, where the enthroned Glory is designated as the Face (*gaṣṣ*). *1 Enoch* 14:20–21 reads: "And no angel could enter, and at the appearance of the face (*gaṣṣ*) of him who is honored and praised no (creature of) flesh could look."[100]

---

[98] The Face terminology as relating to the entire extent of the deity was already known to the authors of the *Book of the Watchers*. It seems to apply also to the body of the transformed visionary, not only in *2 Enoch*, but in *Ascension of Isaiah* 7:25 as well, where the seer, describing his journey through the seven heavens, attests that his "face" was being transformed.

[99] On the face of God in the Psalms, see S. Balentine, *The Hidden God: The Hiding of the Face of God in the Old Testament* (Oxford: Oxford University Press, 1983), 49–65; W. Eichrodt, *Theology of the Old Testament* (2 vols.; Philadelphia: The Westminster Press, 1967), 2.35–39; M. Fishbane, "Form and Reformulation of the Biblical Priestly Blessing," *JAOS* 103 (1983): 115–21; J. Reindl, *Das Angesicht Gottes im Sprachgebrauch des Alten Testaments* (ETS 25; Leipzig: St. Benno, 1970), 236–37; M. Smith, "'Seeing God' in the Psalms: The Background to the Beatific Vision in the Hebrew Bible," *CBQ* 50 (1988): 171–83.

[100] Knibb, *The Ethiopic Book of Enoch*, 2.99.

It is possible that Exodus 33:18–23, Psalm 17:15, *1 Enoch* 14, and *2 Enoch* 39:3–6 represent a single conceptual stream in which the divine Face serves as the *terminus technicus* for the designation of the deity's anthropomorphic form. It is also clear that all these accounts deal with the specific anthropomorphic manifestation known as God's *Kavod*.[101] The possibility of such identification is already hinted at in Exod 33; Moses, upon asking the Lord to show him his *Kavod*, hears that it is impossible for him to see the deity's Face.

Moreover, the anthropomorphic extent of the second power in the form of the patriarch Enoch is also labeled in *2 Enoch* as the "face." According to *2 Enoch*, beholding the divine Face has dramatic consequences for Enoch's appearance: his body endures radical changes and is covered by divine light. Describing the patriarch's metamorphosis, *2 Enoch* 39 underlines peculiar parallels between the deity's face and the face of the transformed patriarch.[102] The description of Enoch's transformation provides a series of analogies in which the earthly Enoch likens his face and parts of his body to the attributes of the Lord's Face and body. These comparisons manifest the connection between the divine corporeality and its prominent replica, the body of the seventh antediluvian hero. In the light of this evidence, it is possible that the luminous face of Jesus in some versions of the transfiguration story serves more than just an allusion to biblical motif of Moses' luminous visage, but instead serves as a reference to the entirety of the second power's anthropomorphic extent, now envisioned as the divine *Kavod*. We will explore such a possibility later in our study.

Furthermore, an important detail can be found in Enoch's radiant metamorphosis before the divine Countenance, which further links Enoch's transformation with the Mosaic accounts. *2 Enoch* 37 includes information about an unusual procedure performed on Enoch's "face," at the final stage of his encounter with the deity. According to the text, the Lord called one of his senior angels to chill the face of Enoch. The angel was "terrifying and frightful," and appeared frozen; he was as white as snow, and his hands were as cold as ice. With these cold hands he then chilled the patriarch's face. Immediately following this chilling procedure, God informs Enoch that if his face had

---

[101] *Contra* Walther Eichrodt, who insists that the *Panim* had no connection with the *Kavod*; he argues that the two concepts derived from different roots and were never linked with one another. Eichrodt, *Theology of the Old Testament*, 2.38.

[102] *2 Enoch* 39:3–6 reads

> And now, my children it is not from my lips that I am reporting to you today, but from the lips of the Lord who has sent me to you. As for you, you hear my words, out of my lips, a human being created equal to yourselves; but I have heard the words from the fiery lips of the Lord. For the lips of the Lord are a furnace of fire, and his words are the fiery flames which come out. You, my children, you see my face, a human being created just like yourselves; I am one who has seen the face of the Lord, like iron made burning hot by a fire, emitting sparks. For you gaze into (my) eyes, a human being created just like yourselves; but I have gazed into the eyes of the Lord, like the rays of the shining sun and terrifying the eyes of a human being. You, (my) children, you see my right hand beckoning you, a human being created identical to yourselves; but I have seen the right hand of the Lord, beckoning me, who fills heaven. You see the extent of my body, the same as your own; but I have seen the extent of the Lord, without measure and without analogy, who has no end.
>
> Andersen, "2 Enoch," 1.163.

not been chilled, no human being would have been able to look at him.[103] The dangerous radiance of Enoch's face parallels the incandescent countenance of Moses after the Sinai experience (Exod 34).

The appropriation of the Mosaic motif of the seer's radiant face is not confined, in *2 Enoch*, to the encounter with the "frozen" angel, but is also reflected in other sections of the book. According to the Slavonic apocalypse, despite the chilling procedure performed in heaven, Enoch's face retains its transformative power and is even capable of glorifying other human subjects. Thus, in *2 Enoch* 64:2, people ask the transformed Enoch for blessings so they can be glorified in front of his face.[104] This theme of the transforming power of the patriarch's visage may here be polemical; it recalls the Mosaic passage[105] preserved in the Dead Sea Scrolls in which Moses' face is able to transform the hearts of the Israelites.

The aforementioned developments that gather familiar biblical Mosaic motifs into their novel conceptual existence are important for our investigation as they provide unique spectacles that enable us to discern additional facets of Mosaic imagery in the synoptic transfiguration accounts.

Mosaic Features of the Transfiguration Story

Keeping in mind the preceding biblical and extra-biblical testimonies, we now turn to analyze certain Mosaic features of the transfiguration accounts.

Timing of the Story

The transfiguration story in Mark begins by mentioning that Jesus took his disciples up the mountain after six days.[106] Scholars have noted that no other temporal statement in Mark outside the Passion Narrative is so precise.[107] Among several other possibilities,[108] this chronological marker has often been interpreted as an allusion

---

[103] Andersen, "2 Enoch," 1.160.

[104] See *2 Enoch* 64:4 (the longer recension): "And now bless your [sons], and all the people, so that we may be glorified in front of your face today." Andersen, "2 Enoch," 1.190.

[105] 4Q374 2:6–8: "and he made him like a God over the powerful ones, and a cause of reel[ing] (?) for Pharaoh... and then he let his face shine for them for healing, they strengthened [their] hearts again." García Martínez and Tigchelaar, *The Dead Sea Scrolls Study Edition*, 2.740–41.

[106] Yarbro Collins notes that "although the epiphany of the Markan Jesus is depicted as real, rather than faked, it is staged in the sense that Jesus chooses the time and place. It thus may be seen as a device for authorizing Jesus and instructing the disciples." Yarbro Collins, *Mark*, 419.

[107] Joel Marcus claims that "Mark's readers would have been immediately alerted to this Mosaic typology by the first four words of his account, 'and after six days,' which correspond to the six days mentioned in Exod 24:16; the similarity is particularly impressive because time indications outside the passion narrative are rare and tend to be vague." J. Marcus, *Mark 8–16: A New Translation with Introduction and Commentary* (AB 27; New Haven: Yale University Press, 2009), 1114.

[108] Analyzing scholarly hypotheses regarding the transfiguration story, Yarbro Collins notes that
> in keeping with his theory that the transfiguration was originally a resurrection story, Wellhausen suggested that the six days refer to the period between Jesus' death and his appearance in Galilee. Others have argued that they allude to the six days between the appearance of the cloud on Mount Sinai and God's calling Moses. Yet others that "after

to Mosaic encounters at Sinai.[109] Reflecting on Mark 9:2 ("and after six days Jesus takes along Peter and James and John"), Craig Evans suggests that "the chronological notation 'after six days' recalls Exod 24:16."[110] In an attempt to elucidate the conceptual background of this numerical symbolism, Evans reminds us that "it was after six days that God spoke out of the cloud to Moses. No other event in Jewish salvation history was remembered with greater reverence."[111]

Chosen Companions

Another possible Mosaic feature also situated in the initial verse of the transfiguration account is the recognition that Jesus took with him *three* disciples. Scholars often see in this peculiar number of chosen companions an allusion to Moses' story. Clarifying connections with the Exodus encounter, A. D. A. Moses notes that "both accounts have the idea of chosen companions: in Exodus 24 Moses separates himself first from the people, taking with him the seventy elders and Aaron, Nadab and Abihu (Exod 24:1, 9)[112] and later, further up the mountain, takes only Joshua (Exod 24:13). This parallels (not in every detail) Mark 9:2–3 . . . where Jesus takes with him the three disciples."[113] Morna Hooker also believes the peculiar number of Jesus' companions represents a Mosaic allusion, observing that "Moses was accompanied by Joshua, who later succeeded him; Jesus takes three of his disciples with him—those who, in Mark's account, are closest to him—and goes up a 'high mountain.'"[114]

A notable difference, however, is that while Moses and his companions are regarded as a group of seers, in the transfiguration account Jesus is not a part of the visionary cohort, but rather the vision's center. Because of this, Charles Cranfield concludes "it seems clear that what is related, whether visionary or factual, was directed toward the three disciples rather than toward Jesus. . . . If it was a vision and audition, then it was apparently shared by the three disciples."[115]

---

six days" is equivalent to "on the seventh day" and that therefore the allusion is to the Sabbath. Foster McCurley argued that "after six days" is a Semitic idiom in which decisive action is then described on the seventh day.

Yarbro Collins, *Mark*, 420.

[109] For criticism of this hypothesis, see McGuckin, *The Transfiguration of Christ*, 53.

[110] Evans, *Mark 8:27–16:20*, 35. Exod 24:16 reads: "The glory of the Lord settled on Mount Sinai, and the cloud covered it for six days; on the seventh day he called to Moses out of the cloud."

[111] Evans, *Mark 8:27–16:20*, 35. Similarly, A. D. A. Moses draws his attention to the unusually precise time reference in Mark 9:2 and Mt 17:1 which recall Exod 24:16–17, where for six days the cloud covered Mount Sinai, and on the seventh day Yahweh called Moses out of the midst of the cloud. A. D. A. Moses, *Matthew's Transfiguration Story and Jewish-Christian Controversy* (JSNTSS 122; Sheffield: Academic Press, 1996), 43–44.

[112] Exod 24:1: "then he said to Moses, 'Come up to the Lord, you and Aaron, Nadab, and Abihu, and seventy of the elders of Israel, and worship at a distance.'"

[113] Moses, *Matthew's Transfiguration Story*, 43–44.

[114] M. D. Hooker, "'What Doest Thou Here, Elijah?' A Look at St Mark's Account of the Transfiguration," in: *The Glory of Christ in the New Testament: Studies in Christology in Memory of George Bradford Caird* (ed. L. D. Hurst and N. T. Wright; Oxford: Clarendon Press, 1987), 59–70 at 60.

[115] C. E. B. Cranfield, *The Gospel According to St. Mark* (Cambridge: Cambridge University Press, 1983), 294.

Motif of the Mountain

Another important feature of the initial verses of each of the transfiguration stories is the reference to a mountain. This motif again brings to mind Moses' theophany. Thus, in Exod 24:12 the deity summons the prophet to the mountain by issuing the following command: "Come up to me on the mountain, and wait there; and I will give you the tablets of stone, with the law and the commandment, which I have written for their instruction." Several verses later in Exod 24:15–18 the motif of the mountain appears again:

> Then Moses went up on the mountain, and the cloud covered the mountain. The glory of the Lord settled on Mount Sinai, and the cloud covered it for six days; on the seventh day he called to Moses out of the cloud. Now the appearance of the glory of the Lord was like a devouring fire on the top of the mountain in the sight of the people of Israel. Moses entered the cloud, and went up on the mountain. Moses was on the mountain for forty days and forty nights.

The same theme is found in Exod 34:3: "No one shall come up with you, and do not let anyone be seen throughout all the mountain; and do not let flocks or herds graze in front of that mountain."

Scholars have suggested a connection between the mountain of Jesus' metamorphosis and Mount Sinai. According to Morna Hooker, "the traditional site of the transfiguration is Mount Tabor, which is hardly a high mountain, but the exact location is unimportant, for the mountain is the place of worship, the place of revelation, perhaps also the new Sinai of the messianic era."[116] Several other scholars also affirm this connection with the famous Mosaic locale by noting that in both stories (Exod 24:16 and Mk 9:2–8 and par.) the setting is a mountain.[117] For our study it is also important that the high place in the transfiguration story can be understood not simply as a geographical space, but also as a mythological one, with the latter referring to the mountain of *Kavod*. In her reflection on the mountain of the transfiguration, Adela Yarbro Collins entertains its broader mythological significance, noting that

> if the account is pre-Markan, the mountain was apparently unspecified at that stage of the tradition. Even though it is unlikely to have been Mount Sinai itself, the generic character of the mountain would allow that association to be made. Furthermore, "a high mountain" would, in Mark's cultural context, call to mind the mythic notion of the cosmic mountain or the mountain as the dwelling place of a god or of the gods.[118]

It has also been suggested that the mountain can be understood as a heavenly or para-heavenly location. Considering this option, Simon Gathercole observes that "a number

---

[116] Hooker, "What Doest Thou Here, Elijah?" 60.
[117] Moses, *Matthew's Transfiguration Story*, 43–44.
[118] Yarbro Collins, *Mark*, 421.

of commentators interpret the mountain as something of a 'suburb of heaven,' or a 'half-way house between earth and heaven.'"[119]

Mountain as the Throne of the Divine Glory

Separating the transfiguration story from previously explored Jewish two powers in heaven traditions is a lack of explicit reference to the second power's possession of the divine throne—the theme that features prominently in the *Book of the Similitudes* and the *Exagoge*, and is possibly hinted at in the Book of Daniel. Yet such an enthronement motif can still be implied by the reference to the mountain on which Jesus' transfiguration takes place. In this respect, it is instructive that in some pre-Christian Jewish accounts the mountain itself is envisioned as the throne of the deity.

Recall that Exod 24:16–18, a formative passage with regard to the transfiguration account, describes the theophany of the divine *Kavod* on the mountain. Similar to the transfiguration story, Exod 24 does not provide any reference to the attribute of the divine seat, a crucial feature of the *Kavod* symbolic complex. This leaves the impression that the mountain may itself fulfill this function, being conceptualized as the divine throne.[120]

Although in the Exodus account the role of the mountain as the divine seat remains hidden, in the *Book of the Watchers* this possibility becomes explicit. In this early Enochic composition, the mountain of God's presence is repeatedly labeled as the deity's throne. From *1 Enoch* 18:6–8 we learn the following: "And I went towards the south—and it was burning day and night—where (there were) seven mountains of precious stones.... And the middle one reached to heaven, like the throne of the Lord, of stibium, and the top of the throne (was) of sapphire."[121] In this passage an enigmatic mountain is compared with God's throne and described as being fashioned from the material (sapphire) often mentioned in the prophetic and apocalyptic depiction of the *Kavod*.[122] Analyzing the mountain motif present in this text, George

---

[119] S. J. Gathercole, *The Preexistent Son: Recovering the Christologies of Matthew, Mark, and Luke* (Grand Rapids: Eerdmans, 2006), 48.

[120] On the mountain as a throne of a deity, see R. E. Clements, *God and Temple: The Idea of the Divine Presence in Ancient Israel* (Philadelphia: Fortress, 1965), 52–54; R. J. Clifford, *The Cosmic Mountain in Canaan and the Old Testament* (Cambridge: Harvard University Press, 1972), 57–79; K. Coblentz Bautch, *A Study of the Geography of 1 Enoch 17–19: "No One Has Seen What I Have Seen"* (JSJSS 81; Leiden: Brill, 2003), 120–25; R. L. Cohn, "The Mountains and Mount Zion," *Judaism* 26 (1977): 97–115 at 98; T. L. Donaldson, *Jesus on the Mountain: A Study in Matthean Theology* (JSNTSS 8; Sheffield: JSOT, 1985); T. Eskola, *Messiah and the Throne: Jewish Merkabah Mysticism and Early Christian Exaltation Discourse* (WUNT 142; Tübingen: Mohr Siebeck, 2001), 74–75; F. T. Fallon, *The Enthronement of Sabaoth* (Leiden: Brill, 1978); Gallusz, *The Throne Motif*, 29, 245; A. M. Rodriguez, "Sanctuary Theology in the Hebrew Cultus and in Cultic-Related Texts," *AUSS* 24 (1986): 127–45.

[121] Knibb, *The Ethiopic Book of Enoch*, 2.104.

[122] Reflecting on these connections, Kelley Coblentz-Bautch notes that

> the reference to sapphire/lapis lazuli and the suggestion that this mountain is in some way like a seat for God call to mind several of the theophanies in the Hebrew Bible.... Exod 24:9-10 suggests that the bottom surface of God's realm is made of lapis lazuli. Ezek 1:26-28 and 10:1 also know of a throne of God that is in the appearance of lapis lazuli. The description of a mountaintop throne recalls the setting of Isaiah's vision in the

Nickelsburg notes that "its apex, to the northwest, is the throne of God, and its two sides, comprising three mountains each, lie on west-east and north-south axes."[123] Experts, furthermore, have argued for similarities between the mountain throne in *1 Enoch* 18 and the Sinai imagery. According to Kelley Coblentz Bautch, "it appears quite plausible that *1 Enoch* 18:8 might well have in mind Mount Sinai itself as the mountain throne of the Lord."[124]

In *1 Enoch* 24:3 the motif of the throne-mountain appears again: "And (there was) a seventh mountain in the middle of these, and in their height they were all like the seat of a throne, and fragrant trees surrounded it."[125] Yet, from the preceding passages, it remains unclear if these descriptions of the mountainous seats are directly related to the actual Throne of YHWH. Such an affirmation, however, is made explicitly in *1 Enoch* 25:3, where we learn from an *angelus interpres* that the mountain indeed serves as the throne of God during the deity's visit to the earth: "And he answered me, saying: 'This high mountain which you saw, whose summit is like the throne of the Lord, is the throne where the Holy and Great One, the Lord of Glory, the Eternal King, will sit when he comes down to visit the earth for good.'"[126]

Due to the antediluvian perspective of the Enochic narration, it is possible that, besides the eschatological allusions, the text's authors also had in mind the future Sinai ordeal, an event that occurs many generations after the revelation given to Enoch.[127]

---

temple, where he sees the Lord seated on a high and lofty throne (Isa 6:1). The references to lapis lazuli and to a summit like the throne of the Lord in *1 Enoch* 18:8 indicate that the mountain will be the site of a theophany, a place where God would appear and could be seen on earth.

Coblentz Bautch, *A Study of Geography*, 120–21.

[123] G. W. F. Nickelsburg, *1 Enoch 1: Chapters 1–36; 81–108* (Hermeneia; Minneapolis: Fortress, 2001), 285. In relation to this imagery, Coblentz Bautch notes that

one fascinating hypothesis regarding the purpose of the mountains is suggested by Nickelsburg: since the middle mountain represents the throne of God (*1 Enoch* 18:8; 25:3), perhaps the six mountains to the east and west are thrones of his divine entourage. A similar phenomenon may be attested in a later Zoroastrian work. A. V. Williams Jackson, reflecting upon the seats of the archangels around the throne of God in *Num. Rab.* 2, calls attention to a passage from the Zoroastrian Great Bundahishn.

Coblentz Bautch, *A Study of Geography*, 114–15.

[124] Coblentz Bautch, *A Study of Geography*, 121.

[125] Knibb, *The Ethiopic Book of Enoch*, 2.113.

[126] Knibb, *The Ethiopic Book of Enoch*, 2.113.

[127] Coblentz Bautch points to this possibility, noting that "perhaps the presence of Michael, the archangel in charge of the people of Israel (*1 Enoch* 20:5) who provides Enoch a tour of the mountain throne of God (*1 Enoch* 24–25), also hints that this mountain is Sinai." Coblentz-Bautch, *A Study of Geography*, 124. She further states that,

given the significance of Sinai in *1 Enoch* 1:4 (along with Hermon, it is one of the few locales to be referred to by name!) and the important role the south plays as the site where the Most High will descend (*1 Enoch* 77:1), connecting the mountain of *1 Enoch* 18:8 that reaches to heaven (a mountain with a lapis lazuli summit that is a veritable throne of God) with Sinai appears a most plausible reading. This interpretation is confirmed as well by the parallel tradition in *1 Enoch* 24–25 which provides more information about the coming theophany and the tree of life to be replanted in the north near the temple.

Coblentz Bautch, *A Study of Geography*, 124–25.

In the light of the aforementioned traditions it is possible that the understanding of the mountain as the throne of the divine *Kavod* may also feature in the synoptic renderings of the transfiguration. Scholars have suggested that such a motif of enthronement may be hinted in the account of Jesus' transfiguration. In previous studies, however, such enthronement is often connected with Jesus' messianic or royal role,[128] while the theophanic dimension, tied to Jesus' role as the divine *Kavod*, has often escaped scholarly attention.[129] However, the insights coming from proponents of the messianic or royal enthronement view are valuable, since they allow us to see additional biblical allusions present in the transfiguration account. One of these important facets is God's utterance "This is my Son," which some scholars argue represents a typical enthronement formula reminiscent of 2 Sam 7:14[130] and Ps 2:7[131] in

---

On parallels between mountain-throne in *1 Enoch* 18 and *1 Enoch* 24–25 and the mountain-throne in Exodus 24, see also A. Dillmann, *Das Buch Henoch. Übersetzt und erklärt* (Leipzig: Wilhelm Vogel, 1853), 129; A. Lods, *Le livre d'Hénoch: fragments grecs découverts à Akhmîm (Haute-Egypte): publiés avec les variantes du texte éthiopien* (Paris: Ernest Leroux, 1892), 185; P. Grelot, "La géographie mythique d'Hénoch et ses sources orientales," *RB* 65 (1958): 33–69 at 38–41.

[128] One of the recent proponents of this hypothesis, Terence Donaldson, argues that "the possibility presents itself that the mountain setting of the Transfiguration Narrative functions as a mountain of enthronement." Donaldson, *Jesus on the Mountain*, 147. He further notes that in the Hebrew Bible,

the mountain is referred to as the site for the throne of Yahweh (e.g. Ps 48:2; cf. Ps 99:1–5; 146:10; Jer 8:19), or for his anointed king (e.g. Ps 2:6; cf. Ps 110:2; 132:11–18). And this theme was carried over into Zion eschatology as well: on that day Yahweh (Isa 24:23; 52:7; Ezek 20:33, 40; Mic 4:6f.; Zech 14:8–11) or the messianic king (Ezek 17:22–24; 34:23–31; Mic 5:2–4) will reign on Mount Zion.

Donaldson, *Jesus on the Mountain*, 147.

Donaldson further recalls that "in Second Temple Judaism, the mountain was also seen as the seat of God's throne (*Jub.* 1:17–29; *1 Enoch* 18:8, 24:2–25:6; *Tob.* 13:11; *Sib. Or.* 3:716–20) and the place where the Messiah will exercise his rulership over the nations (*4 Ezra* 13; *2 Bar.* 40:1–4; cf. *Ps. Sol.* 17:23–51)." Donaldson, *Jesus on the Mountain*, 147.

[129] On the transfiguration as a messianic or royal enthronement see J. Daniélou, "Le symbolisme eschatologique de la Fête des Tabernacles," *Irénikon* 31 (1958): 19–40; Donaldson, *Jesus on the Mountain*, 146–49; M. Horstmann, *Studien zur Markinischen Christologie: Mk 8.27–9.13 als Zugang zum Christusbild des zweiten Evangeliums* (NTAbh 6; Münster: Aschendorff, 1969), 80–103; H. Riesenfeld, *Jésus transfiguré: L'arrière-plan du récit évangélique de la transfiguration de Notre-Seigneur* (Copenhagen: Ejnar Munksgaard, 1947), 292–99; M. Sabbe, "La rédaction du récit de la Transfiguration," in: *La venue du Messie* (ed. E. Massaux; RechBib 6; Paris: Desclée de Brouwer, 1962), 65–100. For criticism of these hypotheses, see R. de Vaux, *Ancient Israel: Its Life and Institutions* (Grand Rapids: Eerdmans, 1997), 495–502; Moses, *Matthew's Transfiguration Story*, 202ff.

[130] "I will be a father to him, and he shall be a son to me. When he commits iniquity, I will punish him with a rod such as mortals use, with blows inflicted by human beings."

[131] "I will tell of the decree of the Lord: He said to me, 'You are my son; today I have begotten you.'" Looking at the use Ps 2:7, Ulrich Luz notes that

the transfiguration story is reminiscent of an inthronization.... We are on safer ground if we think of Ps 2:7, which stands behind the heavenly voice of v. 5. It is a psalm that comes from the enthronement ritual of the Jerusalem kings and that was a major influence on the New Testament Son of God Christology. In the early confession of Rom 1:3–4 Jesus' "inthronization" as Son of God was connected with the resurrection (cf. Acts 13:33–34). It meant at the same time Jesus' exaltation and his association with divine spirit and power.

Luz, *Matthew 8–20*, 396.

which the king's ascension to the throne coincides with his adoption as Son by the deity.[132]

Additionally, some features of the previously explored Mosaic two powers in heaven accounts also hint at the possibility that the mountain was understood as both the divine seat and the seat of the second power. Thus, as we recall in the *Exagoge*—the motif of Mount Sinai was juxtaposed with the theme of the divine throne and the seat of the second power.

An objection to the motif of Jesus' enthronement is the absence of any references to his sitting position. Yet, already in the biblical Mosaic theophanies God is described as standing on the mountain. This position of the deity is later emphasized in Philonic and Samaritan sources. Charles Gieschen argues that the Philonic and the Samaritan understanding of God as "the Standing One" "probably originates from Deut 5:31, where God invites Moses to 'stand' by him as he delivers the Law."[133] The concept of the standing position of the second power as an enthronement is also discernible in some previously explored Jewish two powers in heaven traditions. For example, in *2 Enoch*, the second power in the form of the seventh antediluvian hero is promised a place to stand in front of the Lord's Face for eternity and takes a seat next to the deity. Such a conceptual constellation of standing/sitting may also be present in the *Exagoge*, where Moses is described as standing (ἐστάθην) and then sitting on the throne.[134]

Secrecy

The singling out of three trusted disciples brings us to another important element of the transfiguration story connected with the Mosaic visionary ordeals, namely, an emphasis on secrecy and concealment. Yarbro Collins brings attention to the distinctive language used to convey this conceptual dimension in Mark, noting that the narrowing of the group, which heightens the awesome and secret character of the transformation, is supported in Mark 9:2 by the phrase "alone by themselves" (κατ' ἰδίαν μόνοι).[135]

The motif of secrecy appears again, even more forcefully, in the conclusion of the story, where Jesus asks his disciples[136] not to share the memory of their visionary experience with anyone.[137] The repeated occurrences of these peculiar indicators of

---

[132] Donaldson, *Jesus on the Mountain*, 146.

[133] C. A. Gieschen, *Angelomorphic Christology: Antecedents and Early Evidence* (AGJU 42; Leiden: Brill, 1998), 31.

[134] Jacobson, *The Exagoge of Ezekiel*, 54.

[135] Yarbro Collins, *Mark*, 421. Further in her study, Yarbro Collins notes that "in keeping with the theme of the section 8:27–10:45, the identity of Jesus is revealed in a special way to three selected disciples. That only three disciples see the transfiguration indicates that Jesus' identity is still to some degree a secret. That the identity of Jesus is concealed here as much as it is revealed is supported by the ambiguity in the statement of the divine voice." Yarbro Collins, *Mark*, 426.

[136] Regarding this tradition, Ulrich Luz notes that "while coming down from the mountain he commands them to be silent about their mountain experience until his resurrection. As in 16:20, the command to silence serves to define the boundaries against outsiders. The revelation on the mountain is granted only to the disciples, who as a special group are contrasted with the people." Luz, *Matthew 8–20*, 399.

[137] See Mark 9:9: "As they were coming down the mountain, he ordered them to tell no one about what they had seen, until after the Son of Man had risen from the dead." This tradition is attested also in

secrecy and concealment placed at the beginning and end of the transfiguration story are noteworthy, since similar constellations often occur in Jewish apocalyptic and mystical accounts dealing with the construction of the theophanic profiles of various second powers, including the previously discussed *Apocalypse of Abraham* and *Sefer Hekhalot*.

Scholars often connect the motif of concealment with the revelation of the glory. In relation to this theme, Mark Morna Hooker observes that

> the theme of suffering (8:31) is taken up again immediately after the story of the transfiguration, when Jesus warns his disciples to tell no one what they have seen, until the Son of Man has risen from the dead (9:9). This particular demand for secrecy suggests that the vision which the disciples have shared is of the glory which belongs to Jesus after the resurrection; this would mean that Mark intends us to see the transfiguration as a confirmation not only of Jesus' messianic status, but of the necessity of the way of suffering, death, and resurrection which lie before him. The story itself is often interpreted as a fulfilment (or a foretaste) of the promise in 9:1 about the coming Kingdom of God; but it seems more likely that Mark sees it as a prefigurement of 8:38, which speaks of the future glory of the Son of Man.[138]

Such an aura of secrecy and concealment, which accompany the revelation of the divine *Kavod*, is typical for Jewish apocalyptic and mystical lore. There the apprehension of the divine Glory enthroned on the Chariot is often listed among the utmost secrets, which were prohibited from being revealed to the wider public.[139] For our study it is important that the aesthetics of concealment pertaining to the revelation of the divine Glory are already discernible in the formative depiction of the Sinai encounter found in Exod 33, where Moses is told that it is impossible for him to see God's Face and live. Here we find reference to the deity's glorious *Panim*, itself synonymous with the divine *Kavod*.

Jesus' Metamorphosis

The theophanic proclivities of the transfiguration story reach their symbolic threshold in Jesus' metamorphosis. The conceptual roots of this enigmatic transformation remain a contended issue among scholars.[140] Some argue for a Greco-Roman background,

---

Matthew and Luke: Matt 17:9: "As they were coming down the mountain, Jesus ordered them, 'Tell no one about the vision until after the Son of Man has been raised from the dead.'" Luke 9:36: "And they kept silent and in those days told no one any of the things they had seen."

[138] Hooker, "What Doest Thou Here, Elijah?" 59–60.

[139] *m. Hag.* 2:1 unveils the following tradition: "The forbidden degrees may not be expounded before three persons, nor the Story of Creation before two, nor [the chapter of] the Chariot before one alone, unless he is a Sage that understands of his own knowledge." H. Danby, *The Mishnah* (Oxford: Oxford University Press, 1992), 212–13.

[140] Andrew Chester observes that in the transfiguration accounts

> the disciples have a vision of Jesus taking on heavenly form. Thus Jesus here assumes, apparently, the form of an angelic figure: or better, perhaps, the form of a being who

while others see the formative influences of the Jewish theophanic traditions in relation to putative Greco-Roman influences. According to Adela Yarbro Collins, "the author of Mark, or his predecessor(s), appears to have drawn upon the Hellenistic and Roman genres of epiphany and metamorphosis, but in a way that adapts them to the biblical tradition, especially to that of the theophany on Sinai."[141] Besides allusions to Sinai traditions, many scholars find in the metamorphosis of Jesus traces of other Jewish theophanies, including the vision of the Ancient of Days from Daniel 7.

The exact nature and extent of Jesus' transformation also remains a debated issue. Ramsey points out that "the word μετεμορφώθη tells of a profound change of the form (in contrast with mere appearances), without describing its character."[142] In the light of these peculiarities, some scholars argue that the terminology suggests a change of Jesus' "form." Jarl Fossum, for example, argues that "Mark's verb implies that Jesus' form or body was changed."[143] Heil notes that

> the verb μεταμορφόω, employed by Mark and Matthew to describe the "transfiguration" of Jesus, refers in a very general sense to a "transformation" or "change in form" of some kind. What it means more specifically must be determined by the context. Thus, Jesus' transfiguration is further defined as his clothing as becoming extremely white in Mark 9:3 and as both his face shining and clothes becoming white in Matt 17:2.[144]

Moreover, with regard to Mark's unique word choice, some scholars see a connection with the glory traditions.[145] As Morna Hooker observes, the same term is used in 2 Cor 3:18, where Paul speaks about the glorified believers. She writes: "the verb μεταμορφοῦν itself is an interesting one, used in the New Testament only in this story (by Mark and Matthew), in Rom 12:2 and in 2 Cor 3:18."[146] According to her, 2 Cor 3:18 "is of particular interest . . . since it refers to Christians who with unveiled faces see (or reflect)

> belongs in the heavenly world. The point also needs to be made that the designation of this vision as a "Transfiguration" is misleading; it should in fact be called "Transformation."
> Chester, *Messiah and Exaltation*, 98.

[141] Yarbro Collins, *Mark*, 419. Joel Marcus also points to the Mosaic connections by noting that "Philo, for example, uses *metaballein* ('to change') and *metamorphousthai* ('to be transformed'), the word employed by Mark in 9:2, to describe the prophetic exaltation that gripped Moses (*Life of Moses* 1.57, 2.280)." Marcus, *Mark 8–16*, 1114.

[142] Ramsey, *The Glory of God*, 114.

[143] Fossum, "Ascensio, Metamorphosis," 82.

[144] Heil, *The Transfiguration of Jesus*, 76. George Henry Boobyer suggests that, despite Mark, where only the garments are explicitly said to assume this glistening appearance, μετεμορφώθη in his opinion "without doubt implies a similar change in Christ's whole figure. Matthew and Luke make that plainer by adding that his face was involved in the transformation." Boobyer, *St. Mark and the Transfiguration Story*, 65.

[145] Thus, Boobyer suggests that "Jesus was changed into a body of radiant δόξα which shone with exceeding brightness, although only Luke uses the word δόξα in describing the vision." Boobyer, *St. Mark and the Transfiguration Story*, 65.

[146] Hooker, "What Doest Thou Here, Elijah?" 60.

the glory of the Lord, and are transformed into the same image, from glory to glory."[147] Yet, unlike 2 Cor 3, which hints at the believer's changed anthropology via reference to the image, the synoptic accounts do not explicitly delve into such elaboration. Instead, only "visible" things appear to be revealed; so for the recipients of the transfiguration vision, especially in its Markan version, metamorphosis is manifested largely through the external features of the adept, including Jesus' attire. Compared to other synoptic authors, these external features in Mark are rather subdued. Reflecting on Markan peculiarities, Morna Hooker further observes,

> the statement that Jesus "was transfigured before them" reminds us of the gulf between him and his disciples: he is revealed as sharing in God's glory, while they are the witnesses to his glory. Unlike Matthew, who refers to Jesus' face shining like the sun (Matt 17:2), Mark does not explain in what way Jesus himself was transfigured: he refers only to the transformation of his clothes, which became whiter than any earthly whiteness.[148]

Scholars have noted that the transfiguration account appears to be underlining the *external* nature of Jesus' transformation, visible to the beholders of this event, represented by the disciples. As Heil notes,

> since it is seen by the disciples, the transfiguration of Jesus refers to an external transformation outwardly visible rather than an internal transformation invisible to the physical eye.... The aorist passive form (μετεμορφώθη) indicates that this external transformation of the physical appearance of Jesus was effected objectively, from outside, by God (divine passive) rather than subjectively or interiorly by Jesus himself.[149]

Heil also sees the external aspect of the transfiguration in the Lukan rendering of the transformation of Jesus' face, noting that the phrase "the appearance (τὸ εἶδος) of his face," rather than just in his "face," underscores the external rather than the internal nature of transformation.[150] Heil concludes by arguing that

> the depiction of Jesus' transfiguration in all three versions as an external change, a transformation from outside of Jesus effected by God, does not support those interpretations that speak in terms of a "revelation," or "disclosure," or "unveiling" of an inner, permanent glory or heavenly status which Jesus already possesses. Although the transfiguration of Jesus takes place on a mountain that he ascends together with three of his disciples, it does not represent an "ascension" into

---

[147] Hooker, "What Doest Thou Here, Elijah?" 61.
[148] Hooker, "What Doest Thou Here, Elijah?" 60.
[149] Heil, *The Transfiguration of Jesus*, 76–77.
[150] Heil, *The Transfiguration of Jesus*, 77.

heaven. Rather, he has been temporarily transfigured into a heavenly being while on a mountain still on the earth.[151]

As mentioned above, the verb μεταμορφόω, employed by Mark and Matthew, also occurs in several Pauline passages, including 2 Cor 3:18, where Paul anticipates the believer's metamorphosis: "all of us, with unveiled faces, seeing the glory of the Lord as though reflected in a mirror, are *being transformed* (μεταμορφούμεθα) into the same image *from one degree of glory to another* (ἀπὸ δόξης εἰς δόξαν); for this comes from the Lord, the Spirit." This rare terminology of transformation coincides here with the *Kavod* imagery. Scholars also note connections with Phil 2:6–11 where once again the transformation of believers is surrounded by *Kavod* symbolism. In the light of this link, Yarbro Collins notes:

> the narrator's statement that "he was transfigured in their presence" evokes the ancient genre of the epiphany or metamorphosis. This statement may be understood in either of two ways. One is that Jesus walked the earth as a divine being, whose true nature is momentarily revealed in the transfiguration (cf. Phil 2:6–11). The other is that the transfiguration is a temporary change that Jesus undergoes here as an anticipation of his glorification after death (cf. 1 Cor 15:43, 49, 51–53). The motif of a temporary transformation, anticipating the final one, is typical of a group of apocalypses, but there it is associated with a heavenly journey.[152]

These connections point to the fact that the term "metamorphosis," as found in Mark and Matthew represents the concept found elsewhere in the New Testament materials, which are, in turn, closely associated with the ocularcentric theophanic imagery.

Jesus' Garment

The account of Jesus' transformation in Mark is accompanied by the reference to his dazzlingly white garment. Scholars have linked this particular attribute of Jesus with the multifaceted legacy of the Jewish biblical theophanies. Commenting on Jesus' attire, Davies and Allison note that "the supernatural brightness of the clothes of divine or heavenly beings or of the resurrected just is a common motif in the biblical tradition. . . . Like God, who 'covers himself with light as with a garment' (Ps 104:2), those who belong to him are also destined to shine like the sun."[153]

---

[151] Heil, *The Transfiguration of Jesus*, 78.

[152] Yarbro Collins, *Mark*, 421.

[153] Davies and Allison, *Matthew*, 2.697. Lee notes that these connections are present not only in Mark but also in other synoptic accounts by arguing that

> in the transfiguration story, the radiant face of Jesus and his white garments also serve Matthew in his understanding of the story as an apocalyptic "vision" (17:9). In Jewish apocalyptic writings, a facial radiance and white garments are general characteristics of belonging to the heavenly world. For example, angelic beings are often portrayed with radiant faces and white garments (Dan 12:3; *1 Enoch* 62:15–16; *4 Ezra* 7:97; *2 Bar.* 51:3).
> Lee, *Jesus' Transfiguration*, 95.

The symbolism of Jesus' garment also evokes imagery contained in the Jewish pseudepigrapha.[154] John Paul Heil calls attention to *1 Enoch* 14:20, where the following description of the deity's attire is found: "And he who is great in glory sat on it, and his raiment was brighter than the sun, and whiter than any snow."[155] Reflecting on this clothing metaphor, Heil notes that

> when Enoch had a heavenly vision (*1 Enoch* 14:8) of the "Great Glory," God himself, sitting on a throne, he described God's clothing: "as for his gown, which was shining more brightly than the sun, it was whiter than any snow" (14:20). Enoch goes on to mention the "face" of God: "None of the angels was able to come in and see the face of the Excellent and the Glorious One" (14:21). The vocabulary of *1 Enoch* 14:20–21 recalls especially the Matthean description of the transfigured Jesus: "his face shone as the sun, while his clothes became white as the light" (Matt 17:2). In *1 Enoch* 14:20 we have another example, in addition to Dan 7:9, of the white clothing of God himself indicating that white is the color of divine, heavenly clothing.[156]

Scholars have indicated that Jesus' white garment also evokes the memory of the attire of the Ancient of Days in Daniel 7. Some see in this clothing metaphor a transfer of the deity's attribute to a new scion of the theophanic tradition. According to Craig Evans, "Mark's depiction of Jesus is also reminiscent of Daniel's vision of the 'Ancient

---

[154] In relation to this Andrew Chester observes that

> in Jewish transformation traditions . . . a change into glorious (angelic) clothing symbolizes transformation into angelic form (or into a form, at least, that belongs fully within the heavenly world); that is so, for example, at *1 En.* 62:15; *2 En.* 22:8; *Apoc. Zeph.* 8:3. In other texts (for example, *1 En.* 39:14), it is the face itself that is specifically said to be transformed; in 4Q491 it would certainly seem that the figure who is speaking has been transformed, and it plausible (but not provable) that in this text both face and clothes have undergone transformation. In any case, in those texts where the focus is on the clothing, the implication obviously is that the face and whole appearance are transformed into angelic or heavenly mode (as at *2 En.* 22:10).
> Chester, *Messiah and Exaltation*, 96–97.

[155] Knibb, *The Ethiopic Book of Enoch*, 2.99.

[156] Heil, *The Transfiguration of Jesus*, 86–87. These parallels were earlier noted by Christopher Rowland in his seminal study *The Open Heaven*. Rowland observes that

> in *1 Enoch* 14:20f. two aspects of the divinity are mentioned, his clothing ("his raiment was like the sun, brighter and whiter than any snow") and his face. Precisely these two elements are mentioned in Matthew 17:2 and Luke 9:29, though no mention is made of Jesus' face in Mark. The presence of a man with shining raiment is thus remarkably like the two passages just quoted, both of which are intimately linked with the vision of the throne-chariot. No less than five words are used in both the Greek of *1 Enoch* 14:20f. and the synoptic accounts of the transfiguration, namely, sun, face, white, snow (in some manuscripts) and the clothing (which involves a different Greek word, *himatia* in the Gospels and *peribolaion* in *1 Enoch*). What is more, the word translated "dazzling" (*exastrapton*) in Luke 9:29 is reminiscent of the use of the word *astrape* (lightning) on two occasions in *1 Enoch* 14 (vv. 11 and 17, cf. Ezek 1:4). Indeed, in the description of the angel in Dan 10:6, the appearance of that being is said to resemble lightning.
> Rowland, *The Open Heaven*, 367.

of Days,' whose 'clothing was white as snow, and the hair of his head like pure wool.'"[157] He further suggests that

> perhaps in his transformation we should understand that Jesus... has taken on some of God's characteristics (much as Moses' face began to shine with God's glory). If this is correct, then the transfiguration should be understood as a visual verification of Jesus' claim to be the "Son of Man" who will come in the glory of his Father with the holy angels (see Mark 8:38; Dan 7:10).[158]

Similarly, John Paul Heil underlines the connection with the Danielic account, noting that

> in Dan 7:9, as part of his dream visions (cf. 7:1–2), Daniel watched God himself, as the "Ancient One," take his throne for judgment. God's clothing was "like snow, white" (ὡσεὶ χιὼν λευκόν in the Theodotion recension) and the hair of his head like pure wool. Here, in a vision, God himself is dressed in white clothing indicative of his divine heavenly glory and splendor.[159]

These particular connections to the attributes associated with the Ancient of Days are important, since they recall the peculiar features of the Son of Man in the *Book of the Similitudes* as well as the portrayals of Yahoel and Metatron in the *Apocalypse of Abraham* and *3 Enoch*, where the ocularcentric profile of the second power is similarly constructed through the transference of divine features associated with the Ancient of Days.[160] In this respect, the transference of the garment does not appear coincidental, since it underlines the ocularcentric nature of the celestial manifestation.[161] To an even greater degree, the Gospel of Matthew highlights the ocular aspect of the garment's symbolism by saying that Jesus' garments became white as the light (τὰ δὲ ἱμάτια αὐτοῦ ἐγένετο λευκὰ ὡς τὸ φῶς).[162]

---

[157] Evans, *Mark 8:27–16:20*, 36.

[158] Evans, *Mark 8:27–16:20*, 36.

[159] Heil, *The Transfiguration of Jesus*, 86. Likewise, Morna Hooker also attempts to interpret Jesus' white garments in the light of the symbolism surrounding the deity's attire in Dan 7:9. She says: "the whiteness of garments often features in apocalyptic writings which attempt to describe heavenly scenes, e.g. Dan 7:9, and Mark himself describes the young man in the tomb on Easter Day as wearing white—a hint, perhaps, that he is a heavenly being." Hooker, "What Doest Thou Here, Elijah?," 60.

[160] On this see Orlov, *Yahoel and Metatron*, 83–85, 200.

[161] Simon Gathercole notes that "Jesus' clothes... are whiter than any launderer on earth could wash them, hence they reflect a heavenly whiteness." Gathercole, *The Preexistent Son*, 48.

[162] Exploring this motif of shining garments, Richard Bauckham notes that

> a standard set of descriptives that could be used to describe any heavenly being, including quite ordinary as well as quite exalted heavenly beings. The basic idea behind all these descriptions is that heaven and its inhabitants are shining and bright. Hence the descriptions employ a stock series of images of brightness: heavenly beings or their dress are typically shining like the sun or the stars, gleaming like bronze or precious stones, fiery bright like torches or lightning, dazzling white like snow or pure wool.
> Bauckham, "The Throne of God and the Worship of Jesus," 51.

Some supporters of the "Mosaic typology" hypothesis, who have previously attempted to explain all the details of Jesus' transfiguration solely through comparison with the biblical Mosaic traditions, often have encountered problems with the interpretation of Jesus' celestial garment. Although the tradition of Jesus' supernatural attire plays a prominent role in the transfiguration account, the biblical accounts are silent about the reception of a garment by the son of Amram. In relation to this situation, Jarl Fossum notes that "the Pentateuchal books have nothing to say about Moses' garments being changed on Mt. Sinai. We should consider the possibility that Matthew and Luke have filled out Mark's story about Jesus' ascent and transformation with traditional elements."[163] Nevertheless, in some extra-biblical accounts, Moses is often depicted as being "clothed" with glory, light, or the divine Name.

The theme of the prophet's clothing with the divine Name received its most extensive elaboration in the Samaritan materials, including the compilation known to us as *Memar Marqah*.[164] In the very first chapter of this document, the deity himself announces to the great prophet that he will be vested with the divine Name.[165] Several other passages of *Memar Marqah* affirm this striking clothing metaphor.[166] Linda Belleville points out that in the Samaritan *Memar Marqah* "Moses' ascent of Mt Sinai is described as an *investiture* with light: he was 'crowned with light' (*Memar Marqah* 2.12) and 'vested with glory' (*Memar Marqah* 4.1): as he descended Mt Sinai according to *Memar Marqah* 4.4) he 'wore the light on his face.'"[167] Fossum draws attention to

---

[163] Fossum, "Ascensio, Metamorphosis," 78.

[164] The motif of the investiture with the divine Name can be found also in the *Defter*, the Samarian liturgical materials in which praise is given to the great prophet who clad himself in the Name of the deity.

[165] *Memar Marqah* 1.1 reads: "He said *Moses, Moses*, revealing to him that he would be vested with prophethood and the divine Name." J. Macdonald, *Memar Marqah: The Teaching of Marqah* (2 vols.; BZAW 84; Berlin: Töpelmann, 1963), 2.4.

[166] *Memar Marqah* 1.9 iterates a similar tradition: "I have vested you with my Name." Macdonald, *Memar Marqah*, 2.32; *Memar Marqah* 2.12:

> Exalted is the great prophet Moses whom his Lord vested with his Name. . . . The Four Names led him to waters of life, in order that he might be exalted and honoured in every place: the name with which God vested him, the name which God revealed to him, the name by which God glorified him, the name by which God magnified him. . . . The first name, with which Genesis opens, was that which he was vested with and by which he was made strong.
>
> Macdonald, *Memar Marqah*, 2.80–81;
> *Memar Marqah* 4.7:

> O Thou who hast crowned me with Thy light and magnified me with wonders and honoured me with Thy glory and hid me in Thy palm and brought me into the Sanctuary of the Unseen and vested me with Thy name, by which Thou didst create the world, and revealed to me Thy great name and taught me Thy secrets.
>
> Macdonald, *Memar Marqah*, 2.158.

[167] L. L. Belleville, *Reflections of Glory: Paul's Polemical Use of the Moses-Doxa Tradition in 2 Corinthians 3.1–18* (JSNTSS 52; Sheffield: Sheffield Academic Press, 1991), 49–50. Joel Marcus also notes that "Markan Jesus' shining garments are in line with some postbiblical Mosaic traditions, since Samaritan texts, *Memar Marqah* 4:6 and passages from *Defter*, describe Moses as being clothed with light or with a garment superior to any king's." Marcus, *Mark 8–16*, 1115. Marcus further notices that "one of the *Defter* texts . . . depicts Moses on Sinai as being covered with a cloud (A. E. Cowley, *The Samaritan Liturgy* (2 vols.; Oxford: Clarendon Press, 1908, 1.40–41), and this is reminiscent of

another Samaritan text where "Moses upon his ascension was clothed in a super-royal robe."[168]

A significant feature of this tradition within the Samaritan materials is that the investiture with the Tetragrammaton entails a ritual of "crowning" with the divine Name.[169] Thus, *Memar Marqah* 1:9 unveils the following actions of the deity:

> On the first day I created heaven and earth; on the second day I spread out the firmament on high; on the third day I prepared a dish and gathered into it all kinds of good things; on the fourth day I established signs, fixing times, completing my greatness; on the fifth day I revealed many marvels from the waters; on the sixth day I caused to come up out of the ground various living creatures; on the seventh day I perfected holiness. I rested in it in my own glory. I made it my special portion. I was glorious in it. I established your name then also—my name and yours therein as one, for I established it and you are crowned with it.[170]

In this passage the endowment of Moses with a crown is given a creational significance when the letters on both headdresses are depicted as demiurgic tools, tools through which heaven and earth came into being. In the light of this imagery, it is possible that the motif of the investiture with the divine Name is also present in another Mosaic account—the *Exagoge* of Ezekiel the Tragedian. As we recall from the *Exagoge*, Moses receives a mysterious crown and immediately thereafter is able to permeate the secrets of creation and to control the created order. *Exagoge* 75–80 relates: "Then he gave me a royal crown and got up from the throne. I beheld the whole earth all around and saw beneath the earth and above the heavens. A multitude of stars fell before my knees and I counted them all."[171] Here, crowned, Moses suddenly has immediate access to all created realms, "beneath the earth and above the heaven," and the stars are now kneeling before the newly initiated demiurgic agent.

In some Samaritan sources, Moses' clothing with the Name is set in parallel to Adam's endowment with the image. Fossum suggests[172] that in *Memar Marqah*, Moses' investiture with the Name also appears to be understood as vestment with the image.[173]

Mark 9:7 ('And there came a cloud, overshadowing them') and different from the Exodus account, in which the cloud covers the mountain rather than the person on it." Marcus, *Mark 8–16*, 1115.

[168] Fossum, "Ascensio, Metamorphosis," 83.

[169] On crowning with the divine Name in later Jewish mysticism, see A. Green, *Keter: The Crown of God in Early Jewish Mysticism* (Princeton: Princeton University Press, 1997), 42ff.

[170] Macdonald, *Memar Marqah*, 2.31.

[171] Jacobson, *The Exagoge of Ezekiel*, 54.

[172] Fossum argues that "Moses' investiture and coronation, which usually were connected with his ascension of Mt. Sinai, were seen not only as a heavenly enthronement, but also as a restoration of the glory lost by Adam. The possession of this Glory was conceived of as a sharing of God's own Name, i.e., the divine nature." Fossum, *The Name of God*, 94.

[173] *Memar Marqah* 6.3 reads: "He [Moses] drew near to the holy deep darkness where the Divine One was, and he saw the wonders of the unseen—a sight no one else could see. His image dwelt on him. How terrifying to anyone who beholds and no one is able to stand before it!" Macdonald, *Memar Marqah*, 2.223.

Jesus' Luminous Face

Memories of the Mosaic Sinai encounters receive a more pronounced expression in Matthew and Luke's accounts of the transfiguration,[174] in particular, through the symbolism of Jesus' luminous face.[175] As previously mentioned, Jesus' luminous face was often interpreted through the lens of the biblical "Mosaic typology," which resulted in a portrayal of Jesus as the new Moses. Be that as it may, this link has often been criticized by scholars. For example, Simon Lee points out that the luminous face represents more than a mere replication of a Mosaic feature found in the Hebrew Bible. He argues that

> while Jesus' radiant face at the transfiguration clearly reminds readers of Moses' experience at the Sinai Theophany, it is questionable whether Matthew, by mentioning his radiant face, intends to legitimize Jesus as the new Moses or affirm his teaching authority. For Jesus was already appointed as God's divine Son in the infancy narrative and at the baptism (3:1–17), and his teaching authority became manifest to the public (7:28).[176]

Lee further points out the limitations of the biblical Mosaic typology by noting that "Mosaic typology cannot be the single dominant hermeneutical key for the entire Matthean Christological project, including the transfiguration. Against Dale Allison's new Moses Christology, I argue that Matthew reads the scriptural stories, including Moses, on the basis of his understanding of Jesus."[177] Yet it should be noted that Allison's own position might not be as straightforward as Lee envisions, since he is well aware that the face imagery far transcends the limited scope of biblical Mosaic traditions.[178] Furthermore, a plethora of possible interpretations of the face imagery points not only to various possessors of this attribute but also to the ambiguity of the designation itself. This imagery can be interpreted in a variety of ways, namely, as a part of the human

---

[174] The absence of this tradition in Mark remains a debated issue. Cranfield proposes that

> in view of the parallels it is surprising that Mark does not mention Jesus' face. That a reference to it has dropped out of the text by mistake at a very early stage, as Streeter suggested, is conceivable; but perhaps it is more likely that Mt. and Lk. have both introduced the reference independently under the influence of Exod. xxxiv. 29 ff.

Cranfield, *The Gospel According to St. Mark*, 290.

[175] The same theophanic constellations where the features of the Ancient of Days coincide with the symbolism of the shining face will appear in Rev 1. In relation to these developments, Yarbro Collins notes that "Jesus is not depicted as luminous or as wearing white garments in the resurrection-appearance stories. He is so depicted, however, in epiphany stories, including Rev 1:16, which speaks about Christ's face shining like the sun." Yarbro Collins, *Mark*, 422.

[176] Lee, *Jesus' Transfiguration*, 95.

[177] Lee, *Jesus' Transfiguration*, 95.

[178] Allison points to the ubiquity of such imagery by noting that "seemingly the most cogent objection to the Mosaic interpretation of the transfiguration is this: many stories from antiquity attribute radiance to others besides Moses, so why should the motif be especially associated with him? ... in view of all the evidence, it must be conceded that the motif of radiance was far from being exclusively associated with Moses." Allison, *The New Moses: A Matthean Typology*, 246.

or divine body, as a glorious body itself, or as one of its cognates, such as an image or an *iqonin*.

Although scholars have attempted to interpret the symbolism of Jesus' luminous face through the biblical imagery of Moses' incandescent visage,[179] another important theophanic trend, which speaks about the deity's *Panim*, remains neglected. This tradition, in which the deity's *Panim* becomes a technical term for the Glory of God, is rooted in the biblical theophanic accounts, where, in response to Moses' plea to behold the deity's *Glory*, God tells the seer it is impossible for him to see his *Face*. The tradition of the *panim* as a designation for the luminous divine body receives further development in the Enochic literature. In one of the earliest Enochic booklets, the *Book of the Watchers*, the notion of the deity's *Panim* plays an important role in theophanic descriptions. For our study it is significant that within these early extra-biblical accounts, the imagery of the deity's face often coincides (as in the transfiguration account) with the symbolism of its dazzlingly white/glorious garment. Regarding these developments, Christopher Rowland observes that "in *1 Enoch* 14:20 two aspects of the divinity are mentioned, his clothing ('his raiment was like the sun, brighter and whiter than any snow') and his face. Precisely these two elements are mentioned in Matthew 17:2 and Luke 9:29."[180]

The symbolism of God's Face receives further elaboration in *2 Enoch* where God's *Panim* is understood not as a part of God's body, but as his entire extent. Moreover, the *panim* became a terminological correlative for another concept prominent in many early Jewish two powers accounts, namely, the image of God or his *iqonin*. We have previously seen this correlation in early Mosaic, Enochic, and Jacobite two powers in heaven traditions, where *tselem* is often used interchangeably with *panim*. If, in Matthew's and Luke's transfiguration account, Jesus' luminous face was indeed understood as his *iqonin*, it provides an important connection with other early Jewish two powers theophanic accounts. In the transfiguration account, Jesus' luminous face may also be envisioned not merely as a part of the second power's body but as a reference to his glorious *tselem* or *iqonin*. An important feature—indicating that Jesus' face relates not to Moses' but to God's countenance—is the fact that the reference to "face" occurs in the account before the advent of the first power, rather than after such a theophany as is the case with Moses.

Another distinctive aspect of the transfiguration account that hints that it does not operate with the concept of Moses' face as understood in the Hebrew Bible is that, unlike the biblical account where the prophet's face is understood as the mirror of divine Glory, a material testimony that the seer then carries to the lower realm as a

---

[179] Exod 34:29–30 unveils the following tradition:

> Moses came down from Mount Sinai. As he came down from the mountain with the two tablets of the covenant in his hand, Moses did not know that the skin of his face shone because he had been talking with God. When Aaron and all the Israelites saw Moses, the skin of his face was shining, and they were afraid to come near him.

Exod 34:35 affirms a similar tradition: "the Israelites would see the face of Moses, that the skin of his face was shining; and Moses would put the veil on his face again, until he went in to speak with him."

[180] Rowland, *The Open Heaven*, 367.

witness of the divine encounter, here the glowing effects of Jesus' face are not retained in further narration.[181] Furthermore, in Exodus and at Jesus' transfiguration the glorious face is manifested in two different realms: the upper realm in the case of Jesus and the lower realm in the case of biblical Moses. One can see in this topological situation a curious theophanic reversal: the face of the great prophet, not luminous on the mountain, started emitting light upon his descent from the high place; while Jesus' face, shining on the mountain, does not remain incandescent in the lower realm at his descent.[182]

Also important in the transfiguration story is an attempt to connect the face with the imagery of the sun. Once again, this juxtaposition recalls extra-biblical Mosaic testimonies, especially ones reflected in Pseudo-Philo's *Biblical Antiquities*. There we learn that the light of Moses' face surpassed the splendor of the sun and the moon.[183] *LAB* 12:1 unveils the following tradition: "Moses came down. Having been bathed with light that could not be gazed upon, he had gone down to the place where the light of the sun and the moon are. The light of his face surpassed the splendor of the sun and the moon, but he was unaware of this."[184] The same comparison between the face of the great prophet and sun is then perpetuated in rabbinic literature. For example, according to *b. Bava Batra* 75a, "the face of Moses was like that of the sun but the face of Joshua was like that of the moon."[185]

Earlier we suggested that the symbolism of Jesus' face is connected with the notion of image or *iqonin*. Why is this important? Because in early Jewish materials, the second power is often conceived as the image or the *iqonin* of God. This is evident, for example, in the Adamic lore, where the protoplast is understood as the divine image.

---

[181] Jarl Fossum underlines this discrepancy with Moses' situation by noting that the luminosity of Jesus' face, unlike in Moses' story, was not retained after the descent from the mountain of the transfiguration. He notes that

> Matt 17:2 says that Jesus' "face shone like the sun," while Luke 9:29 states that "the appearance of his countenance was altered." In Exod 34:29–35 it is related that Moses' face shone while he descended from Mt. Sinai. It is tempting to see a connection here, but it should be borne in mind that neither Matthew nor Luke relates that Jesus came down from the mountain with a luminous face.
>
> Fossum, "Ascensio, Metamorphosis," 77.

[182] Ulrich Luz also notes this difference by arguing that "the transformation of Moses in Exodus 34 is also something different. It became visible after God had spoken with him, and it did not immediately end, while Jesus' transformation took place before God spoke and was only temporary." Luz, *Matthew 8–20*, 396.

[183] Reflecting on these traditions in *LAB*, Kristine Ruffatto notes that

> *LAB* 12:1 declares that when Moses descended from his heavenly ascent on Sinai, his radiant face "surpassed the splendor of the sun and moon" (*vicit lumen faciei sue splendorem solis et lune*). Jacobson writes that comparisons to the sun and moon are fairly commonplace in classical Greek and Latin texts, and that a nearly exact parallel is found at *Pal. Hist.* p. 242 where Moses' face is said to shine ὑπὲρ τὸν ἥλιον. The idea that Moses' shining face surpassed the brilliance of the sun is also found in *Lev. Rab.* 20:2.
>
> Ruffatto, *Visionary Ascents of Moses*, 160.

[184] H. Jacobson, *A Commentary on Pseudo-Philo's Liber Antiquitatum Biblicarum, with Latin Text and English Translation* (2 vols.; AGAJU 31; Leiden: Brill, 1996), 110. For the discussion of this tradition see Belleville, *Reflections of Glory*, 41.

[185] Epstein, *The Babylonian Talmud. Bava Batra*, 75a.

The same understanding is implied in the Mosaic and Jacobite two powers in heaven accounts through the motif of angelic veneration and hostility. Furthermore, we learned that the role of the second power as the image of God is closely intertwined in early Jewish accounts with the symbolism of the *panim* or the face. This is especially noticeable in the *Ladder of Jacob*, where the conceptual bridge between the notions of image and face are openly expressed in the symbolism of Jacob's *iqonin*.[186]

If the concept of the *iqonin* is indeed present in the symbolism of Jesus' luminous face, it is possible that such imagery does not originate in the traditions about the patriarch Jacob, but rather from the Mosaic currents, currents that, in turn, exercised an unmatched influence on this Christian theophany. In this regard, it is noteworthy that in extra-biblical Jewish lore Moses' luminous face was often reinterpreted as his *iqonin*.

For instance, *Targum Pseudo-Jonathan* of Exod 34:29, while rendering the account of Moses' shining visage, adds to it the *iqonin* terminology:

> At the time that Moses came down from Mount Sinai, with the two tables of the testimony in Moses' hand as he came down from the mountain, Moses did not know that the splendor of the *iqonin* of his face shone because of the splendor of the Glory of the Shekinah of the Lord at the time that he spoke with him.[187]

The next verse (34:30) of the same targumic account also uses the *iqonin* formulae: "Aaron and all the children of Israel saw Moses, and behold, the *iqonin* of his face shone; and they were afraid to go near him."[188] Finally, verses 33–35 speak about Moses' veil again demonstrating the appropriation of the image symbolism:

> When Moses ceased speaking with them, he put a veil on the *iqonin* of his face. Whenever Moses went in before the Lord to speak with him, he would remove the veil that was on the *iqonin* of his face until he came out. And he would come out and tell the children of Israel what he had been commanded. The children of Israel would see Moses' *iqonin* that the splendor of the *iqonin* of Moses' face shone. Then Moses would put the veil back on his face until he went in to speak with him.[189]

In these targumic renderings one detects the creative interchange between *panim* and *tselem* symbolism. The application of "image" terminology to Moses' story here has profound anthropological significance—since Moses' luminosity becomes envisioned as a restoration of Adam's original *tselem*, which, according to some traditions, was itself a luminous entity. The Adamic connection is often articulated in various non-biblical accounts describing Moses' face. The Samaritan *Memar Marqah*, for instance,

---

[186] The correlation between *panim* and *iqonin* is also discernible in *Joseph and Aseneth*. On this see Orlov, *The Greatest Mirror*, 141–48.

[187] M. J. McNamara, R. Hayward, and M. Maher, eds., *Targum Neofiti 1 and Pseudo-Jonathan: Exodus* (ArBib 2; Collegeville: Liturgical Press, 1994), 260.

[188] McNamara et al., *Targum Neofiti 1 and Pseudo-Jonathan: Exodus*, 261.

[189] McNamara et al., *Targum Neofiti 1 and Pseudo-Jonathan: Exodus*, 261.

makes this connection between the shining face of Moses and the luminosity of Adam's image. According to Linda Belleville, several passages of this Samaritan collection link Moses' luminosity to the primordial glory Adam had prior to the Fall.[190]

The understanding of Moses' face restoring the original luminous *tselem* is also expressed in later rabbinic midrashim where the protoplast's glorious image is put in conspicuous parallel with the radiant *panim* of the great prophet.[191] We find this correspondence divulged in *Deut. Rab.* 11:3:

> Adam said to Moses: "I am greater than you because I have been created in the image of God." Whence this? For it is said, And God created man in his own image (Gen 1:27). Moses replied to him: "I am far superior to you, for the honour which was given to you has been taken away from you, as it is said, But man (Adam) abideth not in honour (Ps 49:13); but as for me, the radiant countenance which God gave me still remains with me."[192]

Another specimen of this tradition is found in *Midrash Tadshe* 4 where the creation of the protoplast in God's image is compared with the bestowal of luminosity on Moses' face: "In the beginning: 'and God created man in his image,' and in the desert: 'and Moshe knew not that the skin of his face shone.'"[193] It is also noteworthy that later rabbinic materials often speak of the luminosity of Adam's face,[194] a feature most likely pointing to an Adam-Moses connection. Take, for example, *Leviticus Rabbah* 20.2, which runs as follows:

> Resh Lakish, in the name of R. Simeon the son of Menasya, said: The apple of Adam's heel outshone the globe of the sun; how much more so the brightness of his face! Nor need you wonder. In the ordinary way if a person makes salvers, one for himself and one for his household, whose will he make more beautiful? Not his own? Similarly, Adam was created for the service of the Holy One, blessed be He, and the globe of the sun for the service of mankind.[195]

---

[190] See Belleville, *Reflections of Glory*, 50.

[191] See Davies and Allison, *Matthew*, 2.705.

[192] Freedman and Simon, *Midrash Rabbah*, 7.173. I have argued that already in 4Q504 the glory of Adam and the glory of Moses' face were creatively juxtaposed. The luminous face of the prophet serves in this text as an alternative to the lost luminosity of Adam and as a new symbol of God's glory once again manifested in the human body. On this, see A. A. Orlov, "Vested with Adam's Glory: Moses as the Luminous Counterpart of Adam in the Dead Sea Scrolls and the Macarian Homilies," *Christian Orient* 4.10 (2006): 498–513.

[193] A. Goshen Gottstein, "The Body as Image of God in Rabbinic Literature," *HTR* 87 (1994): 183. Going over this passage, Linda Belleville observes that "*Midrash Tadshe* 4 associates Moses' glory with being created in the image of God, stating that God created man in his own image, first in the beginning and then in the wilderness." Belleville, *Reflections of Glory*, 65.

[194] According to Jewish sources, the image of God was especially reflected in the radiance of Adam's face. On this, see Fossum, *The Name of God*, 94.

[195] Freedman and Simon, *Midrash Rabbah*, 4.252.

In a similar tradition, *Genesis Rabbah* 11 focuses not on Adam's luminous garments, but on his glorious face:

> Adam's glory did not abide the night with him. What is the proof? But Adam passeth not the night in glory (Ps. XLIX, 13). The Rabbis maintain: His glory abode with him, but at the termination of the Sabbath he deprived him of his splendor and expelled him from the Garden of Eden, as it is written, Thou changest his countenance, and sendest him away (Job XIV, 20).[196]

The roots of the preceding rabbinic trajectories can be traced to documents of the Second Temple period. For example, the theme of the superiority of Moses over Adam is already present in Philo. Wayne Meeks draws attention to a tradition from *Quaestiones et solutiones in Exodum* 2.46, which identifies the ascendant Moses as the heavenly man[197] created in God's image on the seventh day:[198]

> But the calling above of the prophet is a second birth better than the first. . . . For he is called on the seventh day, in this (respect) differing from the earth-born first molded man, for the latter came into being from the earth and with body, while the former (came) from the ether and without body. Wherefore the most appropriate number, six, was assigned to the earth-born man, while to the one differently born (was assigned) the higher nature of the hebdomad.[199]

It is possible that such an interpretation of Moses' shining visage, not merely as the luminous face but also functioning as the luminous image, could stand behind the symbolism of Jesus' luminous face in the transfiguration accounts. In the peculiar theophanic context of the transfiguration, with its postulation of God's invisibility, the famous Pauline phrase—"Christ as the image of the invisible God"—can be seen in an entirely new light.

Elijah and Moses

One of the important features of the transfiguration account is the presence of Elijah—another prominent seer of the Hebrew Bible associated with aural apparitions of the deity.[200] The appearance of two paradigmatic participants in the Old Testament theophanies at the transfiguration event is not coincidental. Morna Hooker suggests

---

[196] Freedman and Simon, *Midrash Rabbah*, 1.81.

[197] Meeks observes that in the early Mosaic accounts "Moses' elevation at Sinai was treated not only as a heavenly enthronement, but also as a restoration of the glory lost by Adam. Moses, crowned with both God's name and his image, became in some sense a 'second Adam,' the prototype of a new humanity." Meeks, "Moses as God and King," 365.

[198] Meeks, "Moses as God and King," 364–65.

[199] Philo, *Questions and Answers on Exodus* (tr. R. Marcus; LCL; Cambridge: Harvard University Press; London: Heinemann, 1949), 91–92.

[200] The Lukan version of the transfiguration story appears to further strengthen Elijah's and Moses' connections with the theophanic traditions by mentioning that both "appeared in glory." On this terminology see Fitzmyer, *The Gospel According to Luke I–IX*, 794–95.

that the "link between Elijah and Moses, and one that is clearly relevant to the transfiguration, is the fact that both of them experienced theophanies on mountains."[201] Both characters, it appears, were strategically placed in the story to bear witness to the novel divine manifestation in the form of Jesus. As in the Hebrew Bible, where both adepts are linked with the respective *Kavod* and *Shem* developments with their corresponding ocular and aural symbolism, the transfiguration account curiously unfolds both theophanic paradigms with their peculiar expressions at the same time: the second power appearing as a glorious form while the first power appears as a formless voice.

As previously discussed, the biblical materials underline the role of Moses and Elijah as the respective exemplars of two rival theophanic trends: biblical encounters of Moses are permeated with ocularcentric motifs, while the story of Elijah is expressly linked to the aural ideology. Therefore, it may not be coincidental that Mark inverts the historical sequence by listing Elijah first, possibly attempting to underline the priority of the first power associated in the transfiguration story with the aural paradigm to which Elijah serves as the primary biblical exemplar. Ramsey suggests that "the order is peculiar to Mark, and it may be dictated by the greater prominence of Elijah in his gospel."[202] The Gospel of Luke appears to further highlight Moses' and Elijah's connections with the theophanic traditions by mentioning that they both appeared in glory (Μωϋσῆς καὶ Ἡλίας, οἳ ὀφθέντες ἐν δόξῃ).

Three Dwellings

Peter's statement about building three dwellings for Jesus, Moses, and Elijah has often puzzled scholars. Countless hypotheses attempting to contextualize this statement have been offered. Jesus' silence appears to underline the problematic nature of Peter's suggestion, as he places his teacher alongside the two prominent seers of the Hebrew Bible. Scholars have proposed that the essence of the statement could refer to Jesus' unique status in comparison with Moses and Elijah. Exploring the tradition of the three dwellings, John McGuckin suggests:

> there is a presupposition of equality of status here . . . that Mark is concerned to reject . . . which is designed to correct Peter's faulty theology by emphasizing the unique and special status of Jesus . . . a uniqueness that has replaced and outstripped all prophetic predecessors and hence the meaning of the phrase: "and looking around they saw no-one only Jesus."[203]

---

[201] Hooker, "What Doest Thou Here, Elijah?" 61. Joel Marcus also suggests that "the key to the symbolism of the appearance of 'Elijah with Moses' on the mountain probably lies in their common association with Mt. Sinai = Horeb, where they both encountered God (Exod 19–24, 34; 1 Kgs 19)." Marcus, *Mark 8–16*, 632.

[202] Ramsey, *The Glory of God*, 114.

[203] McGuckin, *The Transfiguration of Christ*, 17. Other scholars note that Matthew's phrase, that upon raising their faces the disciples saw "no one except Jesus himself, alone" (οὐδένα εἶδον εἰ μὴ αὐτὸν Ἰησοῦν μόνον) suggests that Jesus "alone remains on center stage" in order to reinforce for the disciples his uniqueness vis-à-vis Moses and Elijah. M. Kibbe, *Godly Fear or Ungodly Failure? Hebrews 12:18–29 and the Sinai Theophanies* (Berlin: Walter de Gruyter, 2016), 104. On this see also

Considering the peculiar choice of the characters, including two major participants in the Hebrew Bible's theophanies, it is not merely their abstract statuses that remain under consideration, but their position in relation to the theophanic situation of the story. In these settings Jesus is clearly envisioned as the center of the theophanic event, while Moses and Elijah are predetermined to constitute its periphery. The three booths tradition therefore may underline the unique status of Jesus as the symbolic nexus of the transfiguration theophany and clearly distinguish him from Moses and Elijah, who are mere recipients of theophanic encounters. Peter's way of addressing Jesus as "rabbi"[204] in Mark might further underline Peter's faulty "human" perception of the unique status of the second power who became conceived in the transfiguration story as the divine *Kavod*.

The three dwellings tradition, with its tendency to underline the unique place of the main protagonist of the vision, helps to discern a peculiar multitiered hierarchy of various characters in the story, including crowds and chosen disciples, Elijah and Moses, the transfigured Jesus, and the divine Voice. If in our story Elijah and Moses are indeed envisioned as heavenly beings, as some scholars have suggested,[205] then their separation from Jesus in the episode of the three dwellings takes on another important function often found in two powers in heaven accounts. This role involves a peculiar distancing of the second power from the rest of the heavenly citizens and the simultaneous affirmation of his unique proximity to the deity. Such a role is often reaffirmed in various two powers in heaven traditions through the routines of angelic obeisance and disdain. Although in the transfiguration story Elijah and Moses are not bowing down before the transfigured second power, the prostration of the disciples may allude to angelic obeisance.

The Fear Motif

All three synoptic renderings of the transfiguration story speak about the disciples' fear. These references are important, since fear often accompanies a divine encounter in early

---

Davies and Allison, *Matthew*, 2.268; Huizenga, *New Isaac*, 233; L. Morris, *The Gospel According to Matthew* (PNTC; Grand Rapids: Eerdmans, 1992), 441; J. Nolland, *The Gospel According to Matthew* (NIGTC 1; Grand Rapids: Eerdmans, 2005), 705; G. R. Osborne, *Matthew* (ZECNT; Grand Rapids: Zondervan, 2010), 648.

[204] In relation to this term Joel Marcus notes that

> in Jewish sources, "Rabbi" and "Rab" ("great one") eventually became technical terms for ordained teachers and/or jurists and are still used so today. Scholars of Judaism, however, debate how far the development toward "Rabbi" as a technical term had gone in NT times. Some think that it was not yet a title but only a vague honorific, roughly equivalent to "sir." In support of this interpretation are Matt 20:33, which translates *rabbouni* from Mark 10:51 with *kyrie* ("sir"), and early inscriptions from Palestine and the Diaspora that use *rab*, *rabbi*, and related words as general terms of respect for influential men who were not necessarily teachers.... As Cohen sums up the situation, in the first several centuries of the Christian era the term was "a popular designation for anyone of high position, notably—but not exclusively—a teacher."
>
> Marcus, *Mark 8–16*, 633.

[205] Luz, *Matthew 8–20*, 396.

Jewish accounts.[206] Early Pentateuchal stories of the primordial humans encountering divine manifestations contain references to the fear that otherworldly realities instill in humans. For example, immediately after the protoplast's transgression, Genesis 3 reports Adam's fear regarding God's visitation to the Garden. This biblical book also recounts the fear of Abraham, Isaac, and Jacob during their encounters with divine and angelic manifestations. The fear of the visionary becomes a prominent motif in prophetic and apocalyptic accounts of the Hebrew Bible, including the Book of Ezekiel and the Book of Daniel.[207]

The fear motif was not forgotten in extra-biblical Jewish literature, including early Enochic lore, a body of materials that represents one of the most extensive early compilations of Jewish visionary traditions. Already in one of the earliest Enochic booklets, the *Book of the Watchers*, we learn about the fear of the seventh antediluvian patriarch as he approaches the divine presence. Chapter 14 of this early Enochic work portrays the seer's entrance into what seems to be regarded as the heavenly temple, the sacred abode of the deity, a very special *topos* that is terrifying not only to human beings but also to the celestial creatures. *1 Enoch* 14:9–14 offers the following report of the seer's progress into the celestial sanctuary:

> And I proceeded until I came near to a wall which was built of hailstones, and a tongue of fire surrounded it, and it began to make me afraid. And I went into the tongue of fire and came near to a large house which was built of hailstones, and the wall of that house (was) like a mosaic (made) of hailstones, and its floor (was) snow. Its roof (was) like the path of the stars and flashes of lightning, and among them (were) fiery Cherubim, and their heaven (was like) water. And (there was) a fire burning around its wall, and its door was ablaze with fire. And I went into that house, and (it was) hot as fire and cold as snow, and there was neither pleasure nor life in it. Fear covered me and trembling took hold of me. And as I was shaking and trembling, I fell on my face.[208]

It is significant that Enoch is not simply frightened by his otherworldly experience, he is literally "covered with fear." Scholars have pointed out the unusual strength of

---

[206] On fear as the human response to theophany, see J. C. VanderKam, *From Revelation to Canon: Studies in Hebrew Bible and Second Temple Literature* (Leiden: Brill, 2000), 343; J. Becker, *Gottesfurcht im Alten Testament* (AnBib 25; Rome: St. Martin's Press, 1965), 22.

[207] For example, see:

> So he came near where I stood; and when he came, I became frightened and fell prostrate. But he said to me, "Understand, O mortal, that the vision is for the time of the end." As he was speaking to me, I fell into a trance, face to the ground; then he touched me and set me on my feet.
>
> (Dan 8:17–18)
>
> I, Daniel, alone saw the vision; the people who were with me did not see the vision, though a great trembling fell upon them, and they fled and hid themselves. So I was left alone to see this great vision. My strength left me, and my complexion grew deathly pale, and I retained no strength. Then I heard the sound of his words; and when I heard the sound of his words, I fell into a trance, face to the ground.
>
> (Dan 10:7–9)

[208] Knibb, *The Ethiopic Book of Enoch*, 2.98.

these formulae of fear. For example, John Collins notes the text's "careful observation of Enoch's terrified reaction."[209] Another scholar, Martha Himmelfarb, notes the power of the visionary's reaction to the divine presence, which, in her opinion, supersedes some formative biblical visionary accounts, including Ezekiel's visions. She points out that "Ezekiel's prostrations are never attributed to fear; they are reported each time in the same words, without any mention of emotion, as almost ritual acknowledgments of the majesty of God. The *Book of the Watchers*, on the other hand, emphasizes the intensity of the visionary's reaction to the manifestation of the divine."[210]

For purposes of our investigation of the Mosaic influences, it is also significant that the fear motif plays a crucial role in biblical and extra-biblical renderings of Moses' story. In the light of these traditions, scholars frequently connect the disciples' fear with the fear of the Israelites when they encountered Moses' luminous face. Thus, from Exod 34:29–30 we learn that "when Aaron and all the Israelites saw Moses, the skin of his face was shining, and they were afraid to come near him." Exod 34:35 then repeats this motif: "the Israelites would see the face of Moses, that the skin of his face was shining; and Moses would put the veil on his face again, until he went in to speak with him."

Returning to the transfiguration story it is important to note that the fearful reaction of the disciples occurs at different places in each of the synoptic gospels. In Luke the disciples are terrified as they entered the cloud from which they will later hear the deity's voice.[211] In Matthew it occurs even later than in Luke, appearing after the divine utterance about Jesus' unique role in relation to the deity. Scholars argue that "in the Matthean version of the transfiguration it is actually the divine voice, and not Jesus' radiance, which provokes fear."[212]

In Mark, however, the fearful reaction of the disciples happens before the aural theophany. Although it is not entirely clear what provokes the fear in this case, the sudden apparition of Elijah and Moses, or Jesus' metamorphosis,[213] scholars often see it as related to the transfigured Jesus.[214] For example, Davies and Allison note that "Mark places the awe felt by the disciples early in the narrative, immediately after the transfiguration and the vision of Moses and Elijah: not the fact that Jesus commands

---

[209] J. Collins, *The Apocalyptic Imagination: An Introduction to Jewish Apocalyptic Literature* (2nd ed.; Grand Rapids: Eerdmans, 1998), 55.

[210] M. Himmelfarb, *Ascent to Heaven in Jewish and Christian Apocalypses* (New York, Oxford: Oxford University Press, 1993), 16.

[211] Davies and Allison note that "Luke makes the descent of the cloud the occasion for fear (Lk 9:34)." Davies and Allison, *Matthew*, 2.703. Huizenga comments further that "in Luke 9:34 the three disciples become afraid as they enter the cloud." Huizenga, *New Isaac*, 218.

[212] Huizenga, *New Isaac*, 211. Davies and Allison also note that Matthew "reserves the experience of awe on the part of the disciples until immediately after the words, 'Hear ye him.' It is the divine word which is awesome." Davies and Allison, *Matthew*, 2.703.

[213] Some scholars argue that the three disciples in Mark had become terrified at the appearance of Moses and Elijah in conversation with the transfigured Jesus. On this see Heil, *The Transfiguration of Jesus*, 30.

[214] Leroy Huizenga suggests "in Mark 9:6, Jesus' radiance and the appearance of Moses and Elijah precipitate the disciples' fear." Huizenga, *New Isaac*, 218.

but his transfiguration itself is emphasized."²¹⁵ A similar correspondence—between fear and the ocularcentric manifestation—may also be reflected in Luke, since it is not entirely clear if the cloud's imagery in that gospel is related to Jesus' theophany, or pertains to the revelation of the divine Voice, or both. Luke's attribution of the theophanic fear, therefore, remains rather ambiguous.

In Mark, at least, the symbolism of theophanic fear can be compared to the aforementioned ocularcentric theophany found in biblical and extra-biblical accounts. An additional detail emphasizing the disciples' role as the visionaries of Jesus' glory is highlighted in unique fashion in Luke 9:32, underscoring the progress of the disciples' visionary abilities, since they were first depicted as "heavy with sleep" and then fully awake.²¹⁶ In the same verse, Luke also points out that they "saw his glory" (εἶδον τὴν δόξαν αὐτοῦ).

Although scholars connect the disciples' fear in Matthew with the revelation of the divine voice, they often forget that the essence of this divine utterance is closely tied to the previous ocularcentric theophanic ordeal of the transfigured Jesus. In fact, it provides an interpretation of this theophany by telling the seers they are privileged to behold the divine Son. In this light, it is possible that even in Matthew the theophanic fear is related to Jesus' epiphany, since it coincides with God's revelation about the true status of the ocularcentric second power. Given this, it is noteworthy that some scholars choose to read the fear motif in Matthew as indeed related to the ocularcentric theophany. For instance, Christopher Rowland observes that "Matthew 17:6 has the disciples falling on their faces, a typical reaction to a theophany or angelophany (cf. Ezek 2:1; Dan 10:9)."²¹⁷

Veneration Motif?

Among the synoptic gospels, only Matthew relates the tradition in which the disciples, upon hearing the divine utterance, fall to the ground in fear. Jesus then raises them up, encouraging them not to be afraid. For some, these additions are the most important Matthean contributions. Along these lines, Ulrich Luz argues that "the most important Matthean change in the transfiguration story is the addition of vv. 6–7, telling of the disciples' fear and how Jesus raises them up."²¹⁸

The disciples' reactions of fear and obeisance in Matthew are often seen as related solely to the aural manifestation of God, namely, his Voice.²¹⁹ Yet Jesus' peculiar affirmations to "get up" and "don't be afraid," can lead to a different interpretation. It is significant that in Jewish and Christian theophanic accounts similar exhortations to visionaries to not fear or to get up usually come from the very objects of such visions:

---

[215] Davies and Allison, *Matthew*, 2.703.

[216] Luke 9:32: "ὁ δὲ Πέτρος καὶ οἱ σὺν αὐτῷ ἦσαν βεβαρημένοι ὕπνῳ· διαγρηγορήσαντες δὲ εἶδον τὴν δόξαν αὐτοῦ καὶ τοὺς δύο ἄνδρας τοὺς συνεστῶτας αὐτῷ."

[217] Rowland, *The Open Heaven*, 367.

[218] Luz, *Matthew 8–20*, 395.

[219] Thus, Huizenga argues that "in the Matthean version, however, it is the divine voice which declares that Jesus is the beloved Son and commands Peter to remember the prior passion prediction which precipitates the fear." Huizenga, *New Isaac*, 218.

that is, angelic or divine figures whose sudden appearance provokes feelings of fear and reverence.[220] This is the case, for example, in Dan 10:9–12, where we can find a celestial visitor touching a prostrated seer filled with fear and telling him not to be afraid:

> then I heard the sound of his words; and when I heard the sound of his words, I fell into a trance, face to the ground. But then a hand touched me and roused me to my hands and knees. He said to me, "Daniel, greatly beloved, pay attention to the words that I am going to speak to you. Stand on your feet, for I have now been sent to you." So while he was speaking this word to me, I stood up trembling. He said to me, "Do not fear, Daniel, for from the first day that you set your mind to gain understanding and to humble yourself before your God, your words have been heard, and I have come because of your words."

In Dan 10:18–19 a similar cluster of motifs is repeated again: "again one in human form touched me and strengthened me. He said, 'Do not fear, greatly beloved, you are safe. Be strong and courageous!' When he spoke to me, I was strengthened and said, 'Let my lord speak, for you have strengthened me.'"

A similar arrangement of motifs can be found in the Jewish pseudepigrapha.[221] The shorter and longer recensions of *2 Enoch* 1:6–8 portray angels appearing before Enoch. The text recounts that, as he was overwhelmed with fear, the patriarch prostrates himself before them. The angels then tell the seer not to be afraid: "Then I awoke from my sleep, and saw those men, standing in front of me, in actuality. Then I bowed down to them; and I was terrified; and the appearance of my face was changed because of fear. Then those men said to me, 'Be brave, Enoch! In truth, do not fear!'"[222]

In *2 Enoch* 22 a similar motif appears during the patriarch's encounter with the deity's glorious form, labeled there as God's "face": "I saw the view of the face of the Lord, like iron made burning hot in a fire and brought out, and it emits sparks and is incandescent.... And I fell down flat and did obeisance to the Lord. And the Lord, with his own mouth, said to me, 'Be brave, Enoch! Don't be frightened! Stand up, and stand in front of my face forever.'"[223] Here again the phrase "do not fear" (or "be brave") coincides with the motif of bringing the adept into a standing position ("stand up").

Importantly, in the Gospel of Matthew the disciples' obeisance occurs immediately after the divine affirmation regarding the exalted status of the second power, and therefore it is possible that the content of the utterance and not the voice itself is what

---

[220] Loren Stuckenbruck notes that "the expression 'Do not fear' was frequently used in biblical and Ancient Near Eastern literature to communicate a message of divine comfort." Stuckenbruck, *Angel Veneration and Christology*, 88.

[221] See also *3 Enoch* 15B:5: "At once Metatron, Prince of the Divine Presence, said to Moses, 'Son of Amram, fear not! for already God favors you. Ask what you will with confidence and boldness, for light shines from the skin of your face from one end of the world to the other.'" Alexander, "3 Enoch," 1.304.

[222] Andersen "2 Enoch," 1.106–8.

[223] Andersen, "2 Enoch," 1.136–38.

provokes the disciples' sudden reaction.²²⁴ Davies and Allison noted a certain correspondence between the disciples' bowed faces and the face of the transfigured Jesus, noting that "the motif of falling on one's face in fear is a standard part of any heavenly ascent or revelation story. But here there is more, for there is a contrast between Jesus' face, which is shining, and the faces of the disciples, which are hidden."²²⁵ This motif of the covering/uncovering of faces has ancient roots in the biblical prophetic tradition. In Isaiah's vision, for example, the seraphim avoid looking God in the face. The same motif plays a prominent role in the Hekhalot literature, about which James Davila observes: "the attending angels ... must cover their faces to protect themselves from the divine radiance. Only then is it safe for God to uncover his face in this cosmic game of peekaboo."²²⁶

Unlike Mark, the Gospel of Matthew applies the symbolism of luminous *panim*/face to Jesus, which, as in other Jewish two powers traditions, may signify the divine image. If so, the disciples' obeisance provides additional evidence that, in some versions of the transfiguration story, Jesus' face is envisioned as the *iqonin*. This links the transfiguration account to Jewish two powers accounts, which depict the second power as the image of God, an office requiring angelic veneration.

Another important similarity with Jewish two powers accounts is that the disciples' prostration occurs after the deity's affirmation about the status of the second power. This recalls a tradition found in *3 Enoch* 4, where angelic obeisance to the second power is given after the deity's assurance that Enoch-Metatron, who just underwent a celestial transformation, represents the "chosen one."

As previously noted, early specimens of this tradition are present in *2 Enoch*²²⁷ and the *Primary Adam Books*,²²⁸ where angelic obeisance coincides with affirmations of the second power's unique status.

---

²²⁴ The motif of the disciples' veneration is reminiscent of the one performed by the magi earlier in the gospel. According to Allison and Davies, "the magi do not simply bend their knees (cf. 17.14; 18.29). They fall down on their faces. This is noteworthy because there was a tendency in Judaism to think prostration proper only in the worship of God (cf. Philo, *Leg. Gai.* 116; *Decal.* 64; Mt 4.9–10; Acts 10.25–26; Rev 19.10; 22.8–9)." Davies and Allison, *Matthew*, 1.248. Robert Gundry notes that "they (the magi) knelt down before him with heads to the ground." R. H. Gundry, *Matthew: A Commentary on His Handbook for a Mixed Church under Persecution* (Grand Rapids: Eerdmans, 1994), 31.

²²⁵ Davies and Allison, *Matthew*, 2.703.

²²⁶ J. Davila, *Descenders to the Chariot: The People behind the Hekhalot Literature* (Leiden: Brill, 2001), 139.

²²⁷ Cf. *2 Enoch* 22:5: "And the Lord, with his own mouth, said to me, 'Be brave, Enoch! Don't be frightened! Stand up, and stand in front of my face forever.'" Andersen, "2 Enoch," 1.136–38.

²²⁸ In the Georgian version of the *Primary Adam Books* the affirmation mentions Adam's unique role as the divine image: "Bow down before the likeness and the image of the divinity." The Latin version also speaks about the divine image: "Worship the image of the Lord God, just as the Lord God has commanded." In the Armenian version, too, Adam's name is not mentioned and the new created "second power" seems to be understood now as the divine manifestation: "Then Michael summoned all the angels, and God said to them, 'Come, bow down to god whom I made.'" Anderson and Stone, *A Synopsis of the Books of Adam and Eve*, 16E.

To conclude our analysis of the disciples' obeisance, we should note that in Matthew this motif fits nicely in the chain of previous veneration occurrences, evoking the memory of the prostrating magi and Satan's quest for worship.[229]

Imagery of the Cloud

All three synoptic accounts mention the cloud overshadowing the protagonists of the story. Scholars often see in this imagery a connection with the theophanic symbolism found in Exodus, where the cloud overshadows the mountain and the Israelite prophet.[230] From Exod 24:15–18 one learns the following:

> Then Moses went up on the mountain, and the cloud covered the mountain. The glory of the Lord settled on Mount Sinai, and the cloud covered it for six days; on the seventh day he called to Moses out of the cloud. Now the appearance of the glory of the Lord was like a devouring fire on the top of the mountain in the sight of the people of Israel. Moses entered the cloud, and went up on the mountain. Moses was on the mountain for forty days and forty nights.

In this passage the cloud serves as the screen that conceals both the divine Voice and the divine Form—the *Kavod*. This double function of the theophanic cloud, able to conceal both aural manifestation of the deity and its ocularcentric counterpart, may also be present in the transfiguration accounts.

Although the cloud is traditionally understood as a part of the aural epiphany of the divine Voice, it is also possible that such overshadowing pertains to Jesus' glory, since he is described as enveloped in it.[231] With regard to the cloud symbolism, Ramsey notes that Luke "infers that the cloud enveloped all, including the disciples who 'feared as they entered into the cloud.' Saint Mark leaves the point obscure."[232] He further suggests that "the νεφέλη ἐπισκιάζουσα is the sign of the presence of the glory; and the promise is being fulfilled that in the messianic age 'the glory of the Lord shall be seen and the cloud' (2 Macc 2:7)."[233]

---

[229] Another unique Matthean occurrence of this motif is found in Matt 18:26 where we find a familiar constellation of "πεσών" and "προσεκύνει." Gundry observes that, besides the magi story, "Matthew inserts the same combination of falling down and worshiping in 4:9 and uses it in unique material at 18:26." He further notes that, "[I]n particular, πεσόντες sharpens Matthew's point, for in 4:9 falling down will accompany worship in the alternatives of worshiping God and worshiping Satan, and without parallel it describes the response of the disciples who witnessed the transfiguration (17:6)." Gundry, *Matthew: A Commentary on His Handbook for a Mixed Church under Persecution*, 31–32.

[230] McGuckin notes that "both Matthew and Luke recount the awe of the disciples as a result of the cloud theophany. This is a common and typical theophany-form based upon the Sinai archetype." McGuckin, *The Transfiguration of Christ*, 11.

[231] As in many others Jewish visionary accounts, the cloud here serves as a paradoxical theophanic device that simultaneously reveals and conceals the deity. In this respect, Charles Cranfield rightly observes that "the cloud is at the same time the sign both of God's self-revelation and of his self-veiling." Cranfield, *The Gospel According to St. Mark*, 295.

[232] Ramsey, *The Glory of God*, 115.

[233] Ramsey, *The Glory of God*, 115.

Additionally, Matt 17:5 appears to highlight the "visual" dimension of the cloud symbolism by mentioning a "bright" cloud (νεφέλη φωτεινή). Such a reference (once again) may connect the cloud with the visual, rather than the audial, theophany.

Another important conceptual facet is that the bright cloud may be understood here as a kind of a garment of the aural deity, a counterpart to the second power's dazzling attire in the form of the transfigured Jesus. Indeed, scholars have entertained the possibility of interpreting the bright cloud as the "garment" of the aural power, a vestment corresponding to the glorious clothes of the ocular power. Jarl Fossum, for example, suggests that "the brilliant garment and the cloud ... are variants of the same theme. Matthew actually says the cloud was 'bright' (φωτεινή), which suggests that he took it to be 'the glory of the Shekinah,' as is the phrase in *b. Shab.* 88b."[234]

The Divine Voice Traditions

Although all versions of the transfiguration story mention the apparition of the divine Voice, they fashion the context of the aural manifestation of the deity differently. Experts have suggested that in the Gospel of Matthew the voice of God plays a more central role than in other versions of the transfiguration story. Ulrich Luz proposes that for Matthew, it is "in substance the most important element, as the detailed reaction of the disciples demonstrates. Thus in contrast to the other synoptics, he has clearly made the audition (and not the vision of the transfigured one!) the center of his story."[235] A. D. A. Moses concurs, arguing that "the 'voice from the cloud' ... undoubtedly is the climax of Matthew's τὸ ὅραμα (Matt 17:9)."[236]

Often the centrality of the audial revelation in the Gospel of Matthew is postulated on the basis of the disciples' reaction, or, one might say, overreaction to the divine utterance. Yet, as I have suggested above, it is difficult to determine if the reaction is related to the aural manifestation itself or to the peculiar content of this audial message in which the status of the second power/person is suddenly revealed. In other words, it remains unclear if the disciples' fear and reverence were provoked by the revelation *of* the first power or the revelation *about* the second power.

As in certain two powers accounts, for example, the *Apocalypse of Abraham*,[237] *b. Hag.* 15a and *3 Enoch*, in the transfiguration story the ocularcentric apparition of the second power is followed by an epiphany of the divine voice. However, unlike in *b. Hag.* 15a and *3 Enoch*, this voice does not intend to expose or demote the second power's controversial stand, but is rather determined to affirm and elevate the extraordinary

---

[234] Fossum, "Ascensio, Metamorphosis," 93.

[235] Luz, *Matthew 8–20*, 394.

[236] Moses, *Matthew's Transfiguration Story*, 138. A similar suggestion also comes from Donaldson. While exploring Matthew's version of the transfiguration, he observes that "there can be no doubt that the key and climax to the transfiguration account is to be found in the content of the heavenly proclamation.... It is the divine proclamation, with its identification of Jesus as the Son, that overshadows and clarifies all other elements in the narrative." Donaldson, *Jesus on the Mountain*, 148.

[237] Scholars sometimes compare the manifestation of the divine voice in the baptism and the transfiguration accounts with the personified voice in the *Apocalypse of Abraham*. Thus, in relation to these parallels, Allison notes that "the voice itself (personified? cf. Rev 1.12; *Ladder of Jacob* 3; *Apoc. Abr.* 9) speaks." Davies and Allison, *Matthew*, 1.336.

status of this new custodian of the ocularcentric trend. Scholars rightly make a connection between this aural manifestation of the deity and its earlier counterpart found in the scene of Jesus' baptism, an account we explore in detail later.

As with other details of the transfiguration story, the symbolism of the divine Voice again evokes the memory of the theophanic imagery found in the Book of Exodus.[238] From Exod 24:16 one learns that "the glory of the Lord settled on Mount Sinai, and the cloud covered it for six days; on the seventh day he called to Moses out of the cloud."[239] The crucial difference here is that while in the Exodus account the manifestations of the *Kavod* and the divine Voice belong to the single divine "power," in the transfiguration account these two manifestations are now divided between separate theophanic agents.

Many commentators have attempted to elucidate the symbolism of the divine voice in the transfiguration story through the Jewish traditions about the *bat qol* imagery.[240] These comparisons are important, since they provide an important parallel with rabbinic and Hekhalot two powers in heaven accounts; here the aural reprimand of Aher and Metatron is clearly rendered as the *bat qol*.[241]

We can see an almost identical withdrawal of the deity into an aural mode in the account of Jesus' baptism. For now we mention in passing that the parallelism between the epiphany of the divine Voice at the baptism (3:17) and the transfiguration (17:5) is especially lucid in Matthew, where the message is repeated verbatim.

Another important aspect of the divine Voice imagery in the synoptic gospels is its marked distance from the *Kavod* symbolism, representing a striking departure from the Jewish accounts. As we recall in the *Apocalypse of Abraham* and the *Ladder of Jacob*, the deity's Voice remained closely associated with the *Kavod* imagery. Thus, in chapter 18 of the *Apocalypse of Abraham*, when the seer encounters the divine Voice in heaven, the divine utterance appears to be situated in close proximity to, if not enthroned upon, the Seat of Glory. *Apoc. Ab.* 18:2–3 reads:

> And I heard a voice like the roaring of the sea, and it did not cease because of the fire. And as the fire rose up, soaring higher, I saw under the fire a throne [made] of fire and the many-eyed Wheels, and they are reciting the song. And under the throne [I saw] four singing fiery Living Creatures.[242]

---

[238] A. D. A. Moses notes that both in Exod 24:16 and Mark 9:7, the divine voice speaks out of the cloud. Moses, *Matthew's Transfiguration Story*, 43–44.

[239] A. D. A. Moses suggests that "the 'voice' in Exodus 24–31; 33–34 is addressed to Moses, while at the transfiguration it is directed at the disciples (not Jesus)." Moses, *Matthew's Transfiguration Story*, 45.

[240] Reflecting on the divine Voice traditions in the baptism and the transfiguration accounts, Davies and Allison note that it is natural to link the voice from the heavens with the rabbinic *bat qol* ("daughter of a voice"). This vehicle of revelation is sometimes quoted in Scripture, often to declare God's favorable estimation of a righteous individual or to settle disputes, it was often spoken of as being from the heavens, and could be thought of as the voice of God himself. Davies and Allison, *Matthew*, 1.335–36.

[241] Although the *bat qol* has often been interpreted as an inferior revelation, scholars argue that in the transfiguration account, given its theophanic context, "the voice from the cloud is clearly a divine voice." Yarbro Collins, *Mark*, 425.

[242] Kulik, *Retroverting Slavonic Pseudepigrapha*, 24.

In the *Ladder of Jacob* the associations between the divine Voice and the *Kavod* are made clearer, since the symbolic link is found present in the midst of the two powers theophany. As one recalls from the *Ladder*, the divine Voice is portrayed as the apex of the *Kavod* complex, situated above the "upper face":[243]

> And God was standing above its highest face, and he called to me from there, saying, "Jacob, Jacob!" And I said, "Here I am, Lord!" And he said to me, "The land on which you are sleeping, to you will I give it, and to your seed after you. And I will multiply your seed."[244]

Yet, in the synoptic transfiguration accounts and elsewhere in the synoptic gospels the divine Voice is never associated with the *Kavod*. Such a dissociation of the aural manifestation of the first power solidifies Jesus' role as the unique custodian of features attributed to the divine *Kavod*. The same tendency is observed in the rabbinic and Hekhalot two powers traditions, which refrain from linking the *bat qol* and *Kavod* symbolism.

"Listen to Him"

In all three renderings of the transfiguration story the message of the divine voice climaxes with the command "listen to him." Scholars often see this as a clear allusion to the Sinai encounters. For example, Joel Marcus suggests that "the concluding words of the heavenly voice, 'Listen to him!' (ἀκούετε αὐτοῦ) are so close to the exhortation of Deut 18:15, 'To him you shall listen,' (αὐτοῦ ἀκούσεσθε) that we may speak of a virtual citation."[245] He further notes that

> in its Old Testament context, the exhortation "to him you shall listen" is part of Moses' instructions to the children of Israel to obey the prophet who will arise after his death: "Yahweh your God will raise up for you a prophet like me from among you, from your brethren—to him you shall listen.... And Yahweh said to me... 'I will raise up for them a prophet like you from among their brethren; and I will put my words in his mouth, and he shall speak to them all that I command him" (Deut 18:15–18).[246]

Marcus concludes by suggesting that "if the larger context of this passage is in view in the words 'listen to him!' in Mark 9:7, then the Markan transfiguration narrative

---

[243] I have argued that the upper fiery face in the *Ladder of Jacob* bears similarities with the *Kavod* complex. It brings to mind *2 Enoch*'s depiction of the *Kavod* as the fiery Face in *2 Enoch* 22. The salient detail that connects both texts is that the Face in *2 Enoch* is similarly defined as "fiery" and "terrifying." This tendency to equate the *Panim* with the *Kavod* is already present in some biblical accounts, including Exod 33:18–20, where in response to Moses' plea to God to show him his Glory, God answers that it is impossible for a human being to see God's Face.

[244] Lunt, "Ladder of Jacob," 2.407.

[245] Marcus, *The Way of the Lord*, 80–81.

[246] Marcus, *The Way of the Lord*, 80–81.

identifies Jesus as this prophet-like-Moses; who became an important figure in the eschatological expectation of postbiblical Judaism."[247]

Adela Yarbro Collins also entertains the Mosaic connection, noting that

> the command "listen to him" (ἀκούετε αὐτοῦ) was probably taken by some members of the audience as a general expression of the authority of Jesus and the attitude that his followers should take toward him. For those knowledgeable about scripture, it probably recalled the statement in Deut 18:15 LXX, "to him you shall listen" (αὐτοῦ ἀκούσεσθε). Those familiar with the expectation of an eschatological prophet like Moses were especially likely to make this connection.[248]

While Mosaic connections have been acknowledged in previous studies, parallels with another mediatorial trend, the Angel of the Lord traditions, have consistently escaped scholarly attention. These associations with the chief angelic mediator of the Hebrew Bible are crucial for our study. The Angel of the Lord figure played a pivotal role in the conceptual framework of the Deuteronomic aural ideology,[249] often functioning as a replacement for the divine presence. Comparable to the synoptic transfiguration accounts, where Jesus becomes the embodiment of the invisible deity, it is possible to discern early traces of a similar concept already in the biblical traditions regarding the Angel of the Lord. As in the transfiguration account, the deity in the Hebrew Bible also orders the people to listen to his mediator. From Exod 23:20–22 we learn the following:

> I am going to send an angel in front of you, to guard you on the way and to bring you to the place that I have prepared. Be attentive to him and listen to his voice; do not rebel against him, for he will not pardon your transgression; for my name is in

---

[247] Marcus, *The Way of the Lord*, 81. Jarl Fossum also argues that

> the continuation, ἀκούετε αὐτοῦ, undoubtedly refers to LXX Deut 18.15, where Moses says: "A prophet from the midst of your brothers, like me, the Lord your God shall raise up for you; him shall you listen to (αὐτοῦ ἀκούσεσθε)." Jesus is thus designated as the Prophet like Moses. Like his prototype, he has to descend from heaven in order to proclaim God's will.
>
> Fossum, "Ascensio, Metamorphosis," 93–94. See also McGuckin, *The Transfiguration of Christ*, 79.

[248] Yarbro Collins, *Mark*, 426. See also Cranfield who argues that "the last two words ἀκούετε αὐτοῦ, attest Jesus as the one in whom the prophecy of Deut. xviii. 15, 18 is fulfilled and underline his unique position." Cranfield, *The Gospel According to St. Mark*, 295–96.

[249] There are various opinions about the possible conceptual roots of Exod 23:20–22. Some scholars suggest that it represents the Deuteronom(ist)ic redaction of Exodus. On this, see W. Johnstone, "Reactivating the Chronicles Analogy in Pentateuchal Studies, with Special Reference to the Sinai Pericope in Exodus," *ZAW* 99 (1987): 16–37 at 26; L. Schwienhorst-Schönberger, *Das Bundesbuch (Ex 20, 22–23, 33). Studien zu seiner Entstehung und Theologie* (BZAW 188; Berlin: Walter de Gruyter, 1990), 406–14; J. Blenkinsopp, "Deuteronomic Contribution to the Narrative in Genesis-Numbers: A Test-Case," in: *Those Elusive Deuteronomists. The Phenomenon of Pan-Deuteronomism* (ed. L. S. Schearing and S. L. McKenzie; JSOTSS 268; Sheffield: Sheffield Academic Press, 1999), 84–115 at 94–97.

him. But if you listen attentively to his voice and do all that I say, then I will be an enemy to your enemies and a foe to your foes.

The first important detail of this address is the phrase "listen to him," found in Exod 23:21, which the Septuagint renders "εἰσάκουε αὐτοῦ." This command is then repeated in Exod 23:22, as the deity again instructs the Israelites to listen attentively to the angel's voice (ἀκοῇ ἀκούσητε τῆς ἐμῆς φωνῆς). The deity's utterances thus parallel the tradition found in the synoptic transfiguration accounts, in which God's instructions about listening to his envoy take on the form of a command.[250]

The parallels with the Angel of the Lord traditions are important for our study since Jesus' novel theophanic identity, as with the Exodus angel, is constructed through the ocularcentric absence of the deity, now withdrawn in the aniconic aural dimension. Scholars have argued that a similar situation can be detected in the mediatorial profile of the Angel of the Lord. According to Darrell Hannah, "the Exodus angel . . . becomes to some extent an expression of the divine absence in that he is a substitute for Yahweh (Exod 33:1–3). As a replacement for the divine presence, it would appear that the angel of the Exodus is beginning to have a quasi-individual existence."[251]

Scholars have argued about the formative role of the Angel of the Name within the conceptual framework of the Deuteronomic and Deuteronomistic *Shem* ideologies.[252] According to one hypothesis, the figure of the Angel of the Lord constitutes one of the

---

[250] On the commanding language in the transfiguration story, see Marcus, *The Way of the Lord*, 81, footnote 1.

[251] D. D. Hannah, *Michael and Christ: Michael Traditions and Angel Christology in Early Christianity* (WUNT 2.109; Tübingen: Mohr Siebeck, 1999), 21. On this see also Boyarin, *Border Lines: The Partition of Judaeo-Christianity*, 134. Charles Gieschen argues that the figure of the Angel of the Lord exhibits "a delicate distinction between YHWH and his visible form. . . . This text testifies that a figure that has some independence from YHWH can still share in his being through the possession of the divine Name (i.e., a divine hypostasis)." C. Gieschen, "The Divine Name in the Ante-Nicene Christology," *VC* 57 (2003): 115–58 at 122–23. Camilla von Heijne, in her recent study, points out that

> the relationship between God and this angel is far from clear and the identity of YHWH and his angel is merged in many texts, e.g., Gen 16:7–14; 21:17–20; 22:1–19; 31:10–13; 48:15–16; Exod 3:1–6; Josh 5:13–15; 6:2, and Judges chapters 6 and 13. In these pericopes, "the angel of YHWH" seems to be completely interchangeable with YHWH himself. According to Exod 23:20–21, the angel possesses the name of God, it is "in him," and it appears to be implied that this "divine Name angel" has the power to forgive sins, an ability that elsewhere in the Bible is reserved for God. This angel is always anonymous and speaks with divine authority in the first person singular as if he is God himself, thus there is no clear distinction between the sender and the messenger. Unlike other biblical angels, the "angel of the Lord" accepts being worshiped by men and seems to be acknowledged as divine; e.g., Gen 16:13; 48:15–16; Josh 5:13–15, and Judg 13:17–23.
>
> von Heijne, *The Messenger of the Lord*, 1.

[252] Von Heijne discerns that in Exod 23, "the angel is apparently distinct from God and yet not completely separate from him. By possessing the divine Name, he also shares the divine power and authority. Compare this to the Deuteronomistic theology, in which the concept of the name of God is used to describe the way in which YHWH is present in the Temple of Jerusalem." von Heijne, *The Messenger of the Lord*, 97–98.

conceptual roots of *Shem* theology. Thus, Mettinger observes: "it appears that when the Deuteronomistic theologians choose *shem*, they seized on a term that was already connected with the idea of God's presence. Exod 23:21 tells us how God warned Israel during her wanderings in the desert to respect his angel and obey his voice, 'for my name is in him.'"[253]

Some aspects of the aural ideology are already notably present in Exod 23 through the repeated references to the voice of the angelic mediator. Thus, in Exod 23:21-22 Moses is advised to listen to the Angel of the Name's voice. In the light of such affirmations, it is possible that the celestial messenger mediates not only the divine Name but also the deity's Voice. Deliberating on the imagery of the voice in Exod 23, Moshe Idel notes that

> this angel is not just a visual yet silent apparition, a sort of pillar that guides the tribes day and night; rather it has a voice that is its own, though at the same time it is God who is speaking. The ambiguity here is quintessential: though God is the speaker, it is the angel's voice that is heard. Thus it seems the angel serves as a form of loud speaker for the divine act of speech.[254]

The Angel of the Lord's abilities in mediating not only the deity's visible presence, but also functioning as its aural counterpart are intriguing. These features evoke the Christological developments found in the first chapter of the Book of Revelation where Christ assimilates both the divine Form and the divine Voice.

Not only does Exod 23:20-22 contain a command to listen to the mediator now embodying the deity; the passage also affirms his possession of the divine Name. The deity instructs the Israelites not to rebel against the Exodus angel, "for my name is in him." Here the call for obedience to the mediator and the divine command to listen to his voice is justified by his role as the embodiment of the Tetragrammaton.[255] In the light of this onomatological tradition, it is possible that God's aural address in the transfiguration story also contains an allusion to Jesus' possession of the divine Name. In this regard Jesus' designation as the "Son" is especially noteworthy. Already in the Gospel of John "Son" can be interpreted as the divine Name.[256] This interpretation, in fact, was perpetuated in later Christian texts. Thus, for example, from the *Gospel of Truth* 38:6-7 we learn that "the name of the Father is the Son."[257] The *Gospel of Truth*

---

[253] Mettinger, *The Dethronement of Sabaoth*, 124-25.

[254] M. Idel, *Ben: Sonship and Jewish Mysticism* (London: Continuum, 2007), 17.

[255] On the language of abiding and its connection with the divine Name traditions see J. J. F. Coutts, *The Divine Name in the Gospel of John: Significance and Impetus* (WUNT 2.447; Tübingen: Mohr Siebeck, 2017), 132ff.

[256] On these traditions, see J. McPolin, *The Name of the Father and of the Son in the Johannine Writings* (PhD diss.; Pontifical Biblical Institute, 1971), 71; Fossum, *The Name of God*, 106, 122-23; Coutts, *The Divine Name in the Gospel of John*, 16; 206.

[257] H. W. Attridge, ed., *Nag Hammadi Codex I (The Jung Codex): Introductions, Texts, Translations, Indices* (NHS 22; Leiden: Brill, 1985), 111.

39:19–27 contains the same tradition: "It is the Father. The Son is his name.... The name, therefore, is that of the Father, as the name of the Father is the Son."[258] With regard to these passages Jarl Fossum argues that "the *Gospel of Truth* . . . teaches that the Son, being born from the Father . . . is the proper Name of God."[259]

Conclusion

To conclude our analysis of the transfiguration account and Jesus' association with the features of the divine Glory or *Kavod*, the question raised earlier must now be addressed: why are Jesus' exalted attributes, including his luminous face and garment, not retained after his descent from the mountain? Such absence might serve as a key for better understanding the significance of Jesus' transfiguration and its relation to his role as the Glory of the invisible God. Previous interpreters have rightly pointed to the proleptic nature of the transfiguration account, which attempts to provide a glimpse into Jesus' role as the divine *Kavod*, the theophanic office fully revealed only after his death and resurrection. Cranfield suggests that the transfiguration

> was a revelation for a few moments of the glory which even then, before his Passion, belonged to Jesus. It was a temporary exhibition of his glory . . . which would enable the disciples after the Resurrection to realize for certain that even during the time that he emptied himself (Phil 2:7), he continued to retain his divinity entire, though it was concealed under the veil of the flesh.[260]

The proleptic nature of the transfiguration story again evokes the memory of Mosaic accounts where the prophet's luminous face serves as a preliminary glimpse into his final glorification at the time of his translation to heaven.

Several scholars pointed to a possibility that, at least in the Gospel of Mark, the key to understanding the transfiguration is situated in chapter 8, which precedes the transfiguration account in this gospel. From that chapter we learn that the Son will come in the glory of his Father with the holy angels, thus intimating the transference of the *Kavod* symbolism to Jesus.[261] Touching on this, Joel Marcus observes: "in 8:38 the

---

[258] Attridge, *Nag Hammadi Codex I*, 113.

[259] Fossum, *The Name of God*, 107.

[260] Cranfield, *The Gospel According to St. Mark*, 295. Moving along the same lines, Boobyer also suggests that the transfiguration might represent a momentary breaking through of the body of Christ's pre-existent glory, which throughout his life on earth was concealed beneath the outward human form. Boobyer, *St. Mark and the Transfiguration Story*, 66. He further add that "no doubt the evangelist could have conceived Christ's δόξα appearance as the fashion of his pre-existent state. Christ had had such a form in heaven, according to the view of the early Church, just as God himself was thought to possess a similar appearance." Boobyer, *St. Mark and the Transfiguration Story*, 66.

[261] Mark 8:38 unveils the following tradition: "Those who are ashamed of me and of my words in this adulterous and sinful generation, of them the Son of Man will also be ashamed when he comes in the glory of his Father with the holy angels."

Son of Man is more precisely designated as one who will come 'in the glory of his Father with the holy angels.' Although the title 'Son of God' does not explicitly appear here, it is certainly implied ('in his Father's glory')."[262] Marcus further notes that, according to this Markan passage, "this Son of Man/Son of God . . . will bear his father's δόξα ('glory') when he comes, and the latter term, which goes back to the Old Testament, denotes 'the divine mode of being.'"[263] This situation reveals that the objectives of the transfiguration account include not only a proleptic depiction of Jesus' glory, but also his construal as the "Lord of the Glory," thus making him a new custodian of this exclusive theophanic attribute. This is underlined by the withdrawal of the deity into the aural mode. As Marcus states, the

> decisive step taken in some New Testament passages, including Mark 8:38, of using in relation to Christ a word that was used almost exclusively in relation to God in the Old Testament and Jewish sources. The association of the Son of Man with the divine δόξα in 8:38, thus, implies Christ's exalted status and links 8:38 with the picture of the glorified Jesus in 9:2–8. The high Christology of 8:38 is further evidenced by the fact that this glorified Son of Man will come with the angels.[264]

The reference to the angels may be connected with the apparition of the divine Glory, usually tied in Jewish theophanic accounts with the angelic retinue that accompanies the theophany.[265]

The transfiguration account thus prefigures Jesus as the divine *Kavod* and provides a glimpse into his reception of the theophanic attributes in this role. Ramsey sums up this idea by stating, "the transfiguration prefigures a glory that lies in the future."[266] Although we do not yet witness a permanent ocularcentric manifestation of the deity, the stage is certainly set for such a transition.

---

[262] Marcus, *The Way of the Lord*, 91.

[263] Marcus, *The Way of the Lord*, 91.

[264] Marcus, *The Way of the Lord*, 91.

[265] Thus, Simon Lee argues that

> in Mk 8:38, Mark claims that the Son of Man will return at the *parousia* with his "Father's glory." When Jesus makes these promises, he is claiming his participation in the same glory as God's and thereby, in the divine mode of being. In the following transfiguration story, Jesus' transfigured appearance with glory visually demonstrates his sharing with God's divine mode and God's voice audibly witnesses Jesus' divine sonship. This idea of Jesus' participation in God's divine mode of being has been explained by Mark in many ways: Jesus is called the Lord (1:2–3), shares the same prerogative of forgiving sins as God, belongs to the heavenly hierarchy with angels and is recognized by demonic powers. . . . The idea of Jesus' glory as the paradigm of glory in Mark is almost identical to Paul's understanding of Christ as God's glory and the image after which believers are being transformed "from glory to glory" (2 Cor 3:18).
>
> Lee, *Jesus' Transfiguration*, 44–45.

[266] Ramsey, *The Glory of God*, 117.

Kavod on the River: The Baptism Account

Theophanic Settings of the Account

After our in-depth examination of the transfiguration story, we now advance to another conceptual nexus of the two powers traditions in the synoptic gospels—the account of Jesus' baptism. Like in the case of the transfiguration story, we must establish reasonable boundaries for our study of Jesus' baptism as well; our analysis is limited to investigating theophanic imagery within synoptic portrayals of Jesus' baptism, along with their possible connections to the two powers traditions.

Before we proceed with a careful analysis of Jesus' baptismal vision we must highlight the topological settings of the encounter, which takes place on a river. Comparable to the mountain imagery in the transfiguration account, which points to the Sinai traditions, the river symbolism here serves to recall the Ezekielian theophany on the river Chebar.

Ancient and modern interpreters of the gospels' baptismal accounts have acknowledged symbolic ties to Ezekiel's vision of the divine Glory.[267] Early in the third century, Origen saw Ezekiel's vision as the typological precedent[268] for Jesus' baptism, and offered a detailed comparison of their similarities.[269] In his presentation, Origen specifically directed his attention to Ezekiel 1:1, "in the thirtieth year, in the fourth month, on the fifth day of the month, as I was among the exiles by the river Chebar, the heavens were opened." Origen construes the "thirtieth year" as a reference to the prophet's age, connecting it at the same time to the age of Jesus at his baptism.[270] Origen's *Hom. Ezech.* 1.4.5–9 relates the following tradition: "So then, by the river

---

[267] For influences of Ezekiel 1 on the baptismal narratives, especially in the Gospel of Matthew, see D. B. Capes, "Intertextual Echoes in the Matthean Baptismal Narrative," *BBR* 9 (1999): 42; Davies and Allison, *Matthew*, 1.329; R. T. France, *The Gospel of Matthew* (NICNT; Grand Rapids: Eerdmans, 2007), 121; J. Gnilka, *Das Matthäusevangelium* (2 vols.; HTKNT; Freiburg: Herder, 1986), 1.78; R. H. Gundry, *Matthew: A Commentary on His Literary and Theological Art* (2nd ed.; Grand Rapids: Eerdmans, 1994), 52; D. Hagner, *Matthew 1–13* (WBC 33a; Dallas: Word, 1993), 57; F. Lentzen-Deis, *Die Taufe Jesu nach den Synoptikern: Literarkritische und gattungsgeschichtliche Untersuchungen* (FTS 4; Frankfurt: Knecht, 1970), 108; U. Luz, *Matthew 1–7* (Hermeneia; Minneapolis: Fortress, 1989), 179; D. Mathewson, "The Apocalyptic Vision of Jesus According to the Gospel of Matthew: Reading Matthew 3:16–4:11 Intertextually," *Tyndale Bulletin* 62 (2011): 89–108; J. P. Meier, *A Marginal Jew: Rethinking the Historical Jesus 2: Mentor, Message, and Miracles* (New York: Doubleday, 1994), 107; Nolland, *The Gospel According to Matthew*, 155; Rowland, *The Open Heaven*, 359; L. Sabourin, *The Gospel According to St. Matthew* (Bombay: St. Paul, 1982), 281; D. L. Turner, *Matthew* (BECNT; Grand Rapids: Baker, 2008), 119–20; B. Witherington, *The Christology of Jesus* (Minneapolis: Fortress, 1990), 148–52.

[268] "Now if you are willing to hear Ezekiel, the 'son of man' preaching in the captivity, he too was a type of Christ." Origen. *Homilies 1–14 on Ezekiel* (tr. T. P. Scheck; ACW 62; New York: Paulist Press, 2010), 32.

[269] "By the river Chebar" (Ezek 1:1). This refers to that very heavy river of the world. "And the heavens were opened" (Ezek 1:1). The heavens had been closed and they are opened for the advent of Christ, so that when they are unbolted the Holy Spirit may come upon him in the form of a dove. For he could not pass to us unless he first came down to one who shares in his own nature. Jesus ascended on high, he led captivity captive, he received gifts among men. The one who descended is also the very one who ascended above all the heavens, that he might fulfill all things. Scheck, *Origen. Homilies 1–14 on Ezekiel*, 36.

[270] On this tradition, see A. R. Christman, *"What Did Ezekiel See?" Christian Exegesis of Ezekiel's Vision of the Chariot from Irenaeus to Gregory the Great* (BAC 4; Boston: Brill, 2005), 25.

Chebar Ezekiel saw the heavens opened when he was thirty years old. And the Lord Jesus Christ, 'when he began he was about thirty years old' [Luke 3:23], by the Jordan River [cf. Matt 3:13], and 'the heavens were opened' [Luke 3:21]."[271] Origen also establishes a link between the Ezekielian "fourth month" and the time of Jesus' baptism, arguing that "in the fourth month on the fifth day of the month" refers to the fourth month of the Jewish year, the time when Jesus was baptized.[272]

An acknowledgment of these parallels is also found in Jerome's *Commentary on Ezekiel*. Drawing attention to Ezekiel's phrase about the opening heavens on the river Chebar, Jerome compares this imagery to the symbolism of the torn heavens at Jesus' baptism, noting "this is also why at the baptism of the Savior, when the Holy Spirit came down upon him in the form of a dove, we read that the heavens were opened."[273] In *Comm. Ezech.* 1.3a Jerome draws attention to the topological similarities of both revelatory encounters—both taking place on the rivers—and informs his readers that "to both Daniel and Ezekiel, who were by rivers in Babylon, the mysteries of the future are disclosed upon waters, or rather, in the purest of waters, so that the power of baptism could be shown."[274]

Jerome also unveils his familiarity with traditions we have already seen in Origen with regard to Ezek 1:1, "in the thirtieth year, in the fourth month, on the fifth day of the month." In *Comm. Ezech.* 1.3a he offers his reflections on the similarity of Ezekiel's and Jesus' ages, pointing out calendrical parallels between both revelatory encounters.[275] The same tradition about the identical ages of both

---

[271] Scheck, *Origen. Homilies 1–14 on Ezekiel*, 32–33.

[272] *Hom. Ezech.* 1.4.53–68 reads:

> When, in accordance with the capacity of my understanding, I investigate what is also said: "In the fourth month, on the fifth day of the month" [Ezek 1:1], I pray to God that I may be able to understand what is in agreement with the intention of the Scriptures. A new year is now imminent for the Jews, and among them the first month is numbered from the commencement of the new year. (But another new year is counted from Passover: "Among the months of the year it will be to you as the beginning of the months" [Exod 12:2].). From this year count with me the fourth month and understand that Jesus was baptized in the fourth month of the new year. For in that month, which is called January among the Romans, we know that the baptism of the Lord was carried out.
>
> Scheck, *Origen. Homilies 1–14 on Ezekiel*, 34. For the discussion of this passage see Christman, "What Did Ezekiel See?" 25.

[273] T. S. Scheck, *St. Jerome: Commentary on Ezekiel* (ACW 71; New York: The Newman Press, 2017), 17.

[274] Scheck, *St. Jerome: Commentary on Ezekiel*, 17. For a discussion of this tradition, see Christman, "What Did Ezekiel See?" 27.

[275] *Comm. Ezech.* 1.3a reads:

> One should also understand the following, that the Lord was baptized in the thirtieth year of his life [cf. Luke 3:23]; in the fourth month, which among us is called January, and is the first, as the commencement of the year, besides Nisan, the month of new things, in which the Passover is celebrated for among the eastern peoples, October was the first month after the ingathering of the crops and the winepresses, when tithes were brought in to the temple, and January was the fourth. But he adds the fifth day of the month and signifies baptism in which the heavens were opened for Christ. And up until today, the day of Epiphany is revered, not as some think, as his birth in the flesh, for at that time he was hidden and was not manifest. For it corresponded to this time when it was said, "This is my beloved Son, in whom I am well-pleased" [Matt 3:16].
>
> Scheck, *St. Jerome: Commentary on Ezekiel*, 17–18.

seers at the time of their revelations on the rivers is present in Gregory the Great's *Homilies on Ezekiel* I.2.5.[276]

Like their ancient counterparts, modern interpreters have also acknowledged the connections between Ezekiel's vision and Jesus' baptism, noticing that already in the earliest version of the baptismal narrative, as it is attested in the Gospel of Mark, the presence of the Ezekielian traditions is substantial. Other evangelists, most notably Matthew, attempted to further strengthen these connections with Ezekiel's theophany. Scholars often argue that Matthew has modeled Jesus' experience on Ezekiel as "the Old Testament's exemplar of a visionary experience."[277] Thus, some claim that Matthew deliberately alters Mark's statement σχιζομένους τοὺς οὐρανούς ("the heavens were split") to ἠνεῴχθησαν οἱ οὐρανοί ("the heavens were opened") in order to make a more explicit link with the Ezekielian theophany.[278] Additionally, some experts point to another important similarity mentioned above, namely, that both revelations take place on rivers—in Ezekiel's case on the river Chebar, and in the synoptic accounts on the river Jordan.[279] Another possible parallel is that both stories take place against the backdrop of occupation of the Holy Land: by the Babylonians in Ezekiel and by the Romans in the synoptic accounts.[280] Both narratives, moreover, mention that the Spirit came upon the visionaries.[281] Scholars have also observed some ocularcentric tendencies in the terminology of "seeing" found in both accounts (Ezek 1:1, 3; Matt 3:16).[282] In thinking about these ocularcentric connections, David Capes notes that "utilizing a recognized vision formula, the evangelist portrays Jesus as the end-time, apocalyptic prophet according to the order of Ezekiel."[283]

Some similarities and differences in the depiction of the revealed "objects" also warrant attention. According to David Mathewson, "the reference to the visionary object as coming down, the visionary object depicted symbolically (as [ὡσεί] a dove), the inclusion of ἰδού to introduce the visionary elements ... establish this account of Jesus' post-baptism experience semantically as an apocalyptic visionary experience."[284]

---

[276] *Hom. Ez.* I.2.5 reads:

> But if indeed the intention is to define some mystery in the actual expression of his age, it is not absurd that the Prophet shows forth the Lord, Whom he proclaims in words, also in the very time of his age. For in the thirtieth year of the Prophet Ezekiel the heavens were opened and he saw visions of God beside the river Chobar, because also in the thirtieth year of his age the Lord came to the River Jordan. Thus there the heavens were opened, because the Spirit descended in the form of a dove; and a voice resounded from heaven, saying: "This is my beloved Son, in whom I am well pleased" (Mt 3:17).
>
> T. Gray, *The Homilies of Saint Gregory the Great "On the Book of the Prophet Ezekiel"* (Etna: Center for Traditionalist Orthodox Studies, 1990), 23.

[277] Mathewson, "The Apocalyptic Vision of Jesus," 94.

[278] Capes, "Intertextual Echoes," 42; Mathewson, "The Apocalyptic Vision of Jesus," 98.

[279] Capes, "Intertextual Echoes," 42; Mathewson, "The Apocalyptic Vision of Jesus," 98.

[280] Capes, "Intertextual Echoes," 42. Origen stresses the motif of captivity, which in his opinion is present in both accounts by noting that "if you wish to hear Ezekiel, the son of man, preaching in captivity, understand him as a type of Christ." Origen, *Hom. in Ezech.*, 1.5.1–8. On this tradition, see Christman, *"What Did Ezekiel See?"* 24.

[281] Capes, "Intertextual Echoes," 43; Mathewson, "The Apocalyptic Vision of Jesus," 98.

[282] Capes, "Intertextual Echoes," 49; Mathewson, "The Apocalyptic Vision of Jesus," 98.

[283] Capes, "Intertextual Echoes," 49.

[284] Mathewson, "The Apocalyptic Vision of Jesus," 98.

Although scholars have acknowledged parallels with the Ezekielian theophany, they often fail to give attention to the reasons why the synoptics strive to link Jesus' baptism to Ezekiel's vision of the divine *Kavod* through an elaborate array of allusions. A close analysis of these parallels also reveals that the bulk of them pertain to a very specific part of the prophetic book, namely, to its first chapter, which deals with the revelation of the divine Glory. Therefore, it is natural to assume that, in the minds of the synoptic authors, Jesus' baptism was somehow associated with the revelation of the divine *Kavod*. At first glance it may appear strange, since in the synoptic baptismal narratives God is not manifested in his ocularcentric form but remains visibly hidden, conveying his revelation via aural address. These theophanic peculiarities open the possibility that other characters of the baptismal accounts, including the mysterious dove-spirit or Jesus himself, might be envisioned as the manifestation of the divine Glory.

Jesus as a Visionary

As mentioned earlier, the synoptic accounts of Jesus' baptism exhibit a plethora of similarities with the transfiguration story. One of the most obvious features is the deity's utterance that concludes both accounts. In this speech Jesus is addressed as "my beloved Son" (ὁ υἱός μου ὁ ἀγαπητός). Also important is that, in both the baptism and transfiguration accounts, Jesus appears along with the invisible deity, whose revelations are conveyed through aural discourse. It is significant that in Jesus' baptism account, as in the transfiguration story, the "two powers" appear together. Likewise, in both accounts the ocularcentric theophanic profile of the second power appears juxtaposed and contrasted with the aural manifestation of the deity. Furthermore, as in the transfiguration account, in some synoptic renderings of the baptism story the construction of Jesus' upper identity as the second power/person coincides with his visionary experience. Yet, unlike the transfiguration story, where Jesus' role as an ocularcentric seer remained rather hidden, in the baptismal vision he is openly portrayed as a visionary.[285] Jesus' role as a seer,[286] however, does not diminish his unique mediatorial

---

[285] Robert Guelich notes that

> in Mark's account, Jesus' actual identity comes neither from John nor his baptism as such but from the event, couched in the language of visionary experiences, that immediately followed the baptism (1:10-11). As Jesus came out of the water, he saw the heavens splitting and the Spirit like a dove descending and heard a heavenly voice that set the Spirit's coming in perspective.
> R. A. Guelich, *Mark 1-8:36* (WBC 34A; Dallas: Word, 1989), 32.

Guelich also notes that

> "He saw" can only refer to Jesus, the subject of 1:9 and the one addressed in 1:11 (so Matt 3:16; cf. John 1:32, 33). "Seeing" in the context of heaven opening often connotes a visionary experience (e.g., Acts 7:56; 10:11; Rev 19:11; *T. Levi* 2.6; *T. Jud.* 24.2; *2 Apoc. Bar.* 22.1). Luke 3:22 drops the verb and Matt 3:16 changes the formula and has Jesus simply seeing the descending Spirit.
> Guelich, *Mark 1-8:26*, 32.

[286] Joel Marcus points out that "it does seem probable that Jesus' baptism was a formative experience in his life, and this may suggest that it had a visionary element.... If Jesus did have such an experience, either it occurred at his baptism or it left no record in the tradition, for the tradition provides no other plausible setting for it." J. Marcus, "Jesus' Baptismal Vision," *NTS* 41 (1995): 512-21 at 513.

position as the second power and heir of the glorious attributes of the deity.²⁸⁷ As we already noted in our investigation of various Jewish two powers in heaven accounts, in these materials the second powers often begin their initiations as beholders of the divine theophanies, in order that later they themselves might become the very centers of these theophanic events. This dynamic constitutes an important element of the two powers in heaven traditions. Within this conceptual framework, the initiate first sees what he will later become. We have already witnessed such metamorphoses in several early Jewish two powers in heaven traditions, including the *Book of the Similitudes* and the *Exagoge* of Ezekiel the Tragedian. This conceptual tendency was further perpetuated in the Christian two powers in heaven accounts. In the baptism narratives Jesus appears to be portrayed not only as the recipient of the vision, but also as the theophanic manifestation, thus undergoing in the course of his vision a momentous transition from a beholder of a theophany to the embodiment of the theophany himself.²⁸⁸

The baptismal accounts of both the Gospel of Mark and the Gospel of Matthew affirm Jesus' role as the visionary, but through different terminology. While in Mark's version²⁸⁹ Jesus sees "the heavens torn apart and the Spirit descending like a dove on him," (εἶδεν σχιζομένους τοὺς οὐρανοὺς καὶ τὸ πνεῦμα ὡς περιστερὰν καταβαῖνον

---

[287] It does not appear coincidental that Jesus is portrayed as a visionary in Mark and other synoptic accounts. In the ocularcentric currents, in order to mediate the divine you must "see" its form. The vision of the divine form transforms the form of the visionary, as we have already witnessed in various ocularcentric mediatorial currents. Surveying the Johannine developments, where Jesus' is portrayed as the seer of the Father, Marianne Meye Thompson notes that

> many of the qualifications found in both the OT and later Jewish traditions apply to the Johannine understanding of seeing God. In the Gospel of John, one sees the glory of God manifested in the person of Jesus; but no human being directly sees God. In fact, the gospel makes it clear that "no one has ever seen God" (1:18; 5:37; 6:46). Even the vision of the Father in the Son remains a mediated vision. But the Son has seen the Father. These Johannine assertions single Jesus out as the one who knows God uniquely, because he has been with God and seen God and, indeed, because he himself is the incarnate Word of God. To be sure, he also hears the Father, but he has not only heard; he has seen. Jesus is the unique eyewitness to God, whose testimony is, therefore, trustworthy.
> M. Meye Thompson, "Jesus. 'The One Who Sees God,'" in: *Israel's God and Rebecca's Children: Christology and Community in Early Judaism and Christianity: Essays in Honor of Larry W. Hurtado and Alan F. Segal* (ed. D. Capes et al.; Waco: Baylor University Press, 2007), 226.

[288] Analyzing Jesus' role as a visionary in the baptism story, Andrew Chester suggests that

> Jesus not only has (and helps bring about) a vision of the world and human society being transformed by God. He also has visions of himself and his human status being transformed as well. Thus the accounts of his baptism by John the Baptist, found at the very start of the narrative, before he sets in motion his activity and proclamation, and the distinctive movement he brings into being, show Jesus having a dramatic vision of the heavenly world opened up, and the Spirit descending on him, like a dove. Indeed, the vision consists not only of the Spirit descending on him from heaven, but also of the divine voice from heaven proclaiming him as "the Son of God." It is difficult, certainly, to understand at least some aspects of this vision, or to be sure about the precise form the vision took; but it is entirely plausible that Jesus did indeed have such a vision, and that it was crucially important for the activity that he then embarked on.
> Chester, *Messiah and Exaltation*, 95.

[289] Many scholars believe that Mark's gospel contains the earliest version of the baptismal tradition, which other evangelists used with slight redactions.

εἰς αὐτόν), Matthew's gospel[290] renders the visionary ordeal slightly differently, saying, "suddenly the heavens were opened to him and he saw the Spirit of God descending like a dove and alighting on him" (καὶ ἰδοὺ ἠνεῴχθησαν [αὐτῷ] οἱ οὐρανοί, καὶ εἶδεν [τὸ] πνεῦμα [τοῦ] θεοῦ καταβαῖνον ὡσεὶ περιστερὰν [καὶ] ἐρχόμενον ἐπ' αὐτόν).[291] In contrast to the Markan and Matthean narratives, the Gospel of Luke does not emphasize Jesus' role as seer, instead depicting him in prayer.[292] Luke also puts an emphasis on the corporeal form of the Spirit by mentioning that it descended in "bodily form."[293]

Comparable to the transfiguration story, in which the first part is permeated by theophanic features related to the ocularcentric ideology, and the second part of the story exhibits the presence of aural currents, in all synoptic versions of the baptismal account the first part of the narration reveals several important visual markers. As in the transfiguration account, the procession of the respective powers also remains similar; we first witness the appearance of the ocularcentric power, and only after that

---

[290] In relation to the Matthean baptismal account, Capes notes that

> while Matthew's and Mark's version agree significantly, there are a few differences worthy of notation including (1) Matthew adds ἰδού ("Behold!") to the visionary aspects of the story; (2) he changes Mark's σχιζομένους τοὺς οὐρανούς ("the heavens were split") to ἠνεῴχθησαν οἱ οὐρανοί ("the heavens were opened"); (3) he writes that Jesus saw the "Spirit of God" while Mark simply has the "Spirit"; (4) he alters Mark's phrase, the Spirit comes down "into him" (εἰς αὐτόν), to say that the Spirit comes upon him (ἐπ' αὐτόν); and (5) he changes the heavenly voice to say, "This is my Son, the beloved, in whom I am well pleased" from Mark's more personal "You are my Son, the beloved, in you I am well pleased." This latter change, probably the most well-known, functions within the story to direct the voice to spectators in attendance at Jesus' baptism. In effect, God declares to them that Jesus is his beloved Son. But for Matthew's readers and hearers in the first century and beyond, it functions as a declaration of the ongoing significance of Jesus as Immanuel, "God with us," the one who promised to be "with you always, even to the end of the age."
>
> Capes, "Intertextual Echoes," 41.

[291] In Matthew's gospel one can detect a shift from Jesus as seer to Jesus' role as an object of vision. In relation to this transition, Davies and Allison observe that

> Matthew has displaced εἶδεν so that it now comes after the opening of the heavens. This makes the event more public because the occurrence in the sky is no longer qualified by "he saw" but instead narrated as a straightforward fact: "and behold! the heavens opened".... Similarly, the alteration in 3:17 of Mark's "You are my Son" to "This is my Son" serves the same purpose: the voice is not speaking to Jesus alone.... Mark's account, by way of contrast, is readily understood as relating the experience of one individual, a θεωρία νοητή (Origen, Comm. in Jn. on 1.31; cf. C. Cels. 2.71).
>
> Davies and Allison, Matthew, 1.330.

In the Gospel of John, Jesus is further removed from his role as visionary; it is now John the Baptist who beholds the vision in which Jesus assumes the role of the theophany. In relation to this tradition, Davies and Allison observe that "In John 1:29–34 it is evidently John alone who sees the Spirit rest upon Jesus. In Luke matters are ambiguous. While the opening of the heavens is recounted as an objective event, and while 'in bodily form' has been added, the voice is addressed to Jesus alone ('You are my Son'; cf. Acts 22.9?)." Davies and Allison, Matthew, 1.330.

[292] Luke 3:21b: "καὶ Ἰησοῦ βαπτισθέντος καὶ προσευχομένου ἀνεῳχθῆναι τὸν οὐρανόν."

[293] Luke 3:22: "τὸ πνεῦμα τὸ ἅγιον σωματικῷ εἴδει ὡς περιστεράν." Markus Bockmuehl suggests that "Luke . . . seeks to stress the facticity of revelation and therefore presents the Spirit's descent as in some sense physical ('in bodily form') rather than merely visionary." M. Bockmuehl, "The Baptism of Jesus as 'Super-Sacrament' of Redemption," Theology 115 (2012): 88.

the aural one. We turn now to consider the theophanic details found in the initial verses of the baptismal vision.

The Motif of Water

The first significant theophanic detail is the association of revelation with a body of water.[294] Although in the formative biblical vision of Ezekiel water is not explicitly regarded as the medium of the prophet's revelation, in later Jewish interpretations it is often conceptualized as a mirror in which the divine *Kavod* appeared to the son of Buzi. In the light of these extra-biblical traditions, it is possible that Jesus' baptism could also be understood as an apparition of the divine Glory in the watery mirror. As we shall see, the earliest Christian interpretations of the baptism account could provide a clear witness to this understanding. Our study, therefore, should pay close attention not only to the details of Ezekiel's vision, but also to later Jewish interpretations of this prophetic account. Like our analysis of Jesus' theophany in the transfiguration story with its appropriation of biblical *and* extra-biblical renderings of the Sinai encounter, here in the baptismal story we likely see the influences not only of the biblical version of Ezekiel's vision, but also of its later reinterpretations, which point to the apparition of the divine *Kavod* in the Chebar river.

Scholars have discussed the importance of water symbolism in Jewish apocalypticism and mysticism.[295] In Jewish apocalypticism and the Hekhalot literature, "water not only appears as a ritual precondition for divine revelation, but also as the site where revelation takes place, and, most notably, as a medium for inducing the altered state of consciousness."[296] Moreover, in the Hekhalot accounts the vision of water, or rather, its "likeness," often becomes a test for a visionary when the adept enters the sixth celestial palace.[297]

---

[294] Exploring the river imagery in the Matthean baptismal narrative, Mathewson notes that
> Jesus is at the Jordan river for the express purpose of being baptized (v. 13). Yet a river was also a common setting for apocalyptic-type visions. Thus Ezekiel has the seer at the river Chebar (1:3) when the heavens are opened. Likewise, the seer in Daniel is at the river Tigris in preparation for his vision in 10:4. Extra-canonical examples include *1 Enoch* 13:7 (the river Dan) and *3 Bar.* 2 (the river Kidron). So it is not incidental that Jesus' vision takes place alongside the Jordan river, an ideal setting for an apocalyptic vision like that of Ezekiel, Daniel or Enoch.
> Mathewson, "The Apocalyptic Vision of Jesus," 97–98. On this see also Davies and Allison, *Matthew*, 327–28.

[295] G. W. Dennis, "The Use of Water as a Medium for Altered States of Consciousness in Early Jewish Mysticism: A Cross-Disciplinary Analysis," *AC* 19 (2008): 84–106. Rebecca Lesses draws attention to one such mystical ritual: "You will observe through the bowl—divination on whatever day or night you want, in whatever place you want, beholding the god in the water and hearing a voice from the god which speaks in verses in answer to whatever you want." R. M. Lesses, *Ritual Practices to Gain Power: Angels, Incantations, and Revelation in Early Jewish Mysticism* (Harrisburg: Trinity Press International, 1998), 329.

[296] M. Nissinen, "Sacred Springs and Liminal Rivers: Water and Prophecy in the Ancient Eastern Mediterranean," in: *Thinking of Water in the Early Second Temple Period* (ed. E. Ben Zvi and C. Levin; BZAW 461; Berlin, Boston: Walter de Gruyter, 2014), 35.

[297] On this motif, see Morray-Jones, *A Transparent Illusion*.

Such symbolism may be implicit in the earliest formative source of Jewish apocalypticism and mysticism—the first chapter of the Book of Ezekiel. Later Jewish visionary accounts often make such imagery more explicit by attempting to explain Ezekiel's revelation as a vision received in the mirror of waters, namely, the waters of the river Chebar.[298] In later Jewish interpretations of Ezekiel's vision, the river Chebar often serves as a medium of the theophany, envisaged as the mirror in which the son of Buzi received his revelation. In one such mystical interpretation, contained in *Visions of Ezekiel*, the following striking explanation is found:

> While Ezekiel was watching, God opened to him seven firmaments, and he saw the Power. They coined a parable. To what may the matter be likened? To a man who went to a barber shop, got a haircut, and was given a mirror to look into. While he was looking into the mirror, the king passed by. He saw the king and his forces through the doorway. The barber turned and said to him, "Turn around and see the king." He said, "I have already seen the mirror." So Ezekiel stood by the river Chebar and looked into the water, and the seven firmaments were opened to him and he saw God's glory, and the *hayyot*, angels, troops, seraphim, and sparkling-winged ones joined to the merkavah. They passed by in the heavens and Ezekiel saw them in the water. So it is written: At the river Chebar (Ezek 1:1).[299]

Closely scrutinizing this enigmatic passage, David Halperin suggests that "looking into the river Chebar, Ezekiel sees the primordial waters, and the *Hayyot* and other merkavah beings in them (understood to mean, reflected in them)."[300] Some scholars argue that the practice of seeing the *Kavod* in bodies of water itself became a mystical

---

[298] In relation to the tradition of Ezekiel's vision as in a mirror, Seyoon Kim observes:
> Now, in light of the descriptions of epiphanic visions that we have examined, especially Ezek 1, we know that its primary sense is to "behold as in a mirror."... To see God in such a surrounding is like seeing him reflected in a mirror, that is seeing his mirror image. In Ezek 1.5 we are given a picture of a mirror in the midst of fire.... So Ezekiel saw God "as in a mirror."
>
> S. Kim, *The Origin of Paul's Gospel* (WUNT 2.4; Tübingen: Mohr Siebeck, 1981), 232.

[299] Halperin, *The Faces of the Chariot*, 265. Later midrashic accounts also underline the provenance of water revelations received by another great Jewish seer—Daniel. Thus, from *Mekhilta de Rabbi Ishmael* one learns the following:
> Some say: Even though he did speak with them outside of the land, and because of the merit of the fathers, he did so only at a pure spot, near water, as it is said: "And I was by the stream Ulai" (Dan 8:2). Again it says: "As I was by the side of the great river, which is Tigris" (Dan 10:4); "The word of the Lord came expressly unto Ezekiel the priest the son of Buzi, in the land of the Chaldeans by the river Chebar" (Ezek 1:3).
>
> J. Z. Lauterbach, ed., *Mekhilta de-Rabbi Ishmael: A Critical Edition on the Basis of the Manuscripts and Early Editions with an English Translation, Introduction and Notes* (2 vols.; Philadelphia: The Jewish Publication Society, 2004), 1.4–5.

[300] Halperin, *The Faces of the Chariot*, 230. Halperin also points to a haggadah in *Exodus Rabbah* 23:14, in which the celestial heights appear to the Egyptian horses in the Red Sea. *Exodus Rabbah* 23:14 reads: "*Ramah bayam* (he hath thrown into the sea) should be read *re'eh mah bayam*, 'Behold what is in the sea!' I behold in the sea the height (*rumo*) of the world." Freedman and Simon, *Midrash Rabbah*, 3.292.

ritual, known to Jewish apocalypticists and mystics. As Halperin argues, the passage from the *Visions of Ezekiel* represents

> a reflection of the actual practice of early Jewish visionaries, who used natural bodies of water as mirrors in which they could see supernatural beings appear in the sky. Water-divination of this sort, using a vessel filled with water (often with oil added) as a mirror in which the medium can see divine images, seems to have been common enough in the ancient world.[301]

Halperin further proposes that this ritual allowed a mystic to bridge realms, since "when the merkavah appears in the waters, the upper realms are merged into the lower."[302] The tradition of beholding the divine *Kavod* in a "mirror" becomes a prominent *topos* in later Jewish rabbinical and mystical lore. For example, both *Leviticus Rabbah* 1:14[303] and *Zohar* II.82b[304] make a connection between the revelation at the river Chebar and Moses' vision of the *Kavod*, speaking about both visionary ordeals as revelations in the mirror.

In the light of these developments it is possible that the story of Jesus' baptism also depicts reflective interplay of the upper and lower realms by revealing a peculiar parallelism between the opening of the waters during Jesus' baptism and the tearing of the heavens. In this peculiar spatial arrangement, not only the opening of the upper heaven and the dove's descent, but also Jesus' ascent from the Jordan's waters during his

---

[301] Halperin, *The Faces of the Chariot*, 231.

[302] Halperin, *The Faces of the Chariot*, 237.

[303] *Lev. Rab.* 1:14 reads:

> What difference is there between Moses and all other prophets? R. Judah b. Il'ai and the Rabbis [gave different explanations]. R. Judah said: Through nine mirrors did the prophets behold [prophetic visions]. This is indicated by what is said, And the appearance of the vision which I saw, was like the vision that I saw when I came to destroy the city; and the visions were like the vision that I saw by the River Chebar.
>
> Freedman and Simon, *Midrash Rabbah*, 4.17.

[304] *Zohar* II.82b relates the following tradition:

> R. Hiya also expounded, in accordance with the esoteric teaching, Ezekiel's vision: "Out of the midst thereof came the likeness of four living creatures, and this was their appearance, they had the likeness of a man," saying that there is a sacred Hall in which dwell four living Creatures, which are the most ancient celestial beings ministering to the Holy Ancient, and which constitute the essence of the Supernal Name; and that Ezekiel saw only the likeness of the supernal Chariots, because his beholding was from a region which was not very bright. He furthermore said that there are lower beings corresponding to these upper ones, and so throughout, and they are all linked one with another. Our teachers have laid down that Moses derived his prophetic vision from a bright mirror, whereas the other prophets derived their vision from a dull mirror. So it is written concerning Ezekiel: "I saw visions of God," whereas in connection with the difference between Moses and all other prophets it says: "If there is a prophet among you, I the Lord will make Myself known to him in a vision.... My servant Moses is not so, who is faithful in all my house: and with him I will speak mouth to mouth" (Num 12:7–8). R. Jose remarked that all the prophets are in comparison with Moses like females in comparison with males.
>
> Sperling and Simon, *The Zohar*, 3.248.

baptism, can be conceived as a theophanic event, similar to later Jewish renderings of the Ezekielian vision, with their portrayals of the divine *Kavod* in the water.

The parallelism of the opening heaven and the opening of the watery surface of the river during Jesus' baptism has often been neglected by scholars. Yet in the light of the aforementioned traditions, it appears that here the water itself may serve as a medium of revelation, envisioned as the mirror reflecting a theophany.

Furthermore, if Jesus' baptism was indeed conceptualized as a manifestation of the divine Glory reflected in the waters of the Jordan, it is intriguing that the earliest Christian exegetes already attempted to describe peculiar theophanic features, usually associated with apparitions of the divine *Kavod*, in their retelling of Jesus' baptism. These interpretations therefore provide an important testimony to early Christian understanding of Jesus' baptism as the theophany of the divine Glory. We turn now to consider these witnesses.

Fire and Light in Water

Several early Christian authors speak about the appearance of fire and light during Jesus' baptism.[305] Justin Martyr in his *Dialogue with Trypho* 88.3, while describing the event at the Jordan, mentions a fire that ignites the waters of Jesus' immersion.[306] A similar motif can be found in the *Sibylline Oracles* 7.81–84 where the theme of the baptismal waters again coincides with the symbolism of fire: "You shall pour a libation of water on pure fire, crying out as follows: 'As the father begot you, the Word, so I have dispatched a bird, a word which is swift reporter of words, sprinkling with holy waters your baptism, through which you were revealed out of fire.'"[307] Another Christian account, the *Preaching of Paul*, cited in Pseudo-Cyprian, also recounts that when Jesus "was baptized, fire was seen to be upon the water."[308] Comparable to the biblical and

---

[305] On this tradition see also D. Vigne, *Christ au Jourdain: Le Baptême de Jésus dans la tradition judéo-chrétienne* (Paris: Gabalda, 1992), 270–72; E. Ferguson, *Baptism in the Early Church: History, Theology, and Liturgy in the First Five Centuries* (Grand Rapids: Eerdmans 2009), 110–12.

[306] "And when Jesus came to the river Jordan, where John was baptizing, he stepped down into the water and a fire ignited the waters of the Jordan." M. Slusser, ed., *St. Justin Martyr: Dialogue with Trypho* (tr. T. F. Falls and T. P. Halton; Washington: Catholic University of America Press, 2003), 137. Some Syrian authors, like Jacob of Sarugh and Narsai, envision the baptismal waters as a furnace. On this see K. McDonnell, *The Baptism of Jesus in the Jordan: The Trinitarian and Cosmic Order of Salvation* (Collegeville: Liturgical Press, 1996), 107–18.

[307] J. J. Collins, "Sibylline Oracles," in: *The Old Testament Pseudepigrapha* (ed. J. H. Charlesworth; 2 vols.; New York: Doubleday, 1983–1985), 1.412. Another passage from *Sibylline Oracles* 6.1–7 appears to attest to the same tradition:

> I speak from my heart of the great famous son of the Immortal, to whom the Most High, his begetter, gave a throne to possess before he was born, since he was raised up the second time according to the flesh, when he had washed in the streams of the river Jordan, which moves with gleaming foot, sweeping the waves. He will escape the fire and be the first to see delightful God coming in the spirit on the white wings of a dove.
>
> Collins, "Sibylline Oracles," 1.407.

[308] A. Roberts and J. Donaldson, eds., "A Treatise on Re-Baptism by an Anonymous Writer," in: *The Ante-Nicene Fathers* (Grand Rapids: Eerdmans, 1980), 5.677.

extra-biblical portrayals of the divine *Kavod*, with its paradoxical conflation of the elements incapable of existing together, here too fire dwells upon the water.

Another significant development that may stem from the same conceptual roots[309] is the motif of light present at the baptism, the tradition that is usually traced by scholars to Tatian's *Diatessaron*.[310] The heterodox *Gospel of Ebionites*, a writing possibly influenced by Tatian, reports that during Jesus' baptism "a great light shone round about the place."[311] The motif of light at Jesus' baptism also appears in the *Gospel of the Hebrews* known to Epiphanius. A tradition preserved in the *Panarion* 30.13.7 conveys that during Jesus' baptism "a great light shone round about the place."[312] Similarly, several manuscripts of the Old Latin version of the gospels expand the details of the baptismal narrative found in Matthew with already familiar theophanic details. William Petersen points out that two Vetus Latina manuscripts, the witnesses that reflect the text of the gospels prior to Jerome's Vulgate revision in the late fourth century, interpolate the motif of light in the water into the Matthean baptismal account.[313] The oldest Vetus Latina manuscript, namely, fourth-century MS *a* (Codex Vercellensis), inserts the following phrase: "a great light shone about from the water" (*lumen ingens circumfulsit de aqua*). Another Old Latin manuscript, the sixth-century MS g¹ (Codex Sangermanensis I), also injects the theme of light: "a big light shone from the water" (*lumen magnum fulgebat de aqua*).[314] Reflecting on this evidence, Petersen suggests that

> in order to have found its way into the canonical Matthew of MS *a*, the reading must have originated earlier than the fourth century. Since Epiphanius states that the reading stood in the "Hebrew gospel," and since a similarly named document is cited in the second century by Clement of Alexandria and in the third century by Origen, circulation of the reading in the second century seems likely.[315]

---

[309] William Petersen suggested the possibility that "the bifurcation of the tradition might have arisen in Aramaic, from confusion between two homophones which are also orthographically almost identical: *nuhra*—'light' and *nura*—'fire.'" W. L. Petersen, *Tatian's Diatessaron: Its Creation, Dissemination, Significance and History in Scholarship* (VCS 25; Leiden: Brill, 1994), 16.

[310] See Petersen, *Tatian's Diatessaron*, 18–20; H. J. W. Drijvers und G. J. Reinink, "Taufe und Licht. Tatian, Ebionäerevangelium und Thomasakten," in: *Text and Testimony: Essays on New Testament and Apocryphal Literature in Honour of A. F. J. Klijn* (ed. T. Baarda et al.; Kampen: J. H. Kok, 1988), 91–110; L. Leloir, *Le témoignage d'Éphrem sur le Diatessaron* (CSCO 227; Subsidia 19; Louvain: Secretariat du Corpus SCO, 1962), 106; Vigne, *Christ au Jourdain*, 76.

[311] W. Schneemelcher, *New Testament Apocrypha* (ed. R. McL. Wilson; 2 vols.; Cambridge: James Clarke & Co.; Louisville: Westminster/John Knox Press, 1991), 1.169.

[312] F. Williams, *The Panarion of Epiphanius of Salamis* (2 vols.; NHS 35–36; Leiden: Brill, 1987, 1994), 1.142. On this see also S. E. Myers, *Spirit Epicleses in the Acts of Thomas* (WUNT 2.281; Tübingen: Mohr Siebeck, 2010), 127.

[313] Petersen, *Tatian's Diatessaron*, 15.

[314] A. Jülicher, *Itala: Das neue Testament in altlateinischer Überlieferung* (4 vols.; Berlin: Walter de Gruyter, 1938–1963), 1.14.

[315] Petersen, *Tatian's Diatessaron*, 15.

Petersen further proposes the possibility that the motif about fire and light in the Jordan might even represent "a proto-synoptic tradition."³¹⁶ Reflecting on the presence of such motifs in Justin and the Vetus Latina manuscripts, he argues that

> the fact that two Vetus Latina manuscripts of Matthew also contain this variant reinforces the conclusion that Justin's source was a synoptic or proto-synoptic tradition. The oldest canonical account of the baptism from a synoptic gospel is in P^{75}, dated to about 200; it contains Luke 3:18–4:2. But Justin's reading antedates P^{75} by at least half a century; in fact, if one compares Justin's absolute date with that of the papyrus, then it is Justin who offers the earliest "synoptic" account of Jesus' baptism. And its description includes a "fire" in the Jordan.³¹⁷

The preceding theophanic developments received further elaboration in various Christian milieus. Everett Ferguson points out that "the light of fire at the Jordan accompanying Jesus' baptism was particularly preserved in Syriac sources."³¹⁸ It appears, then, that these interpretations were not inventions of the Syrian authors, but instead perpetuations of the ancient traditions and sources similar to Justin and Tatian. In this regard, it is not coincidental that such motifs appear in later commentaries on these ancient authors. Ephrem the Syrian in his *Commentary on the Diatessaron*, while describing Jesus' baptism, speaks about "the splendor of the light which appeared on the water."³¹⁹

Very similar theophanic markers also play a prominent role in Jacob of Serugh's renderings of the baptismal event. Susan Myers points out that

> in the description of Christ's baptism in the Jordan in Jacob of Serugh, the sanctification of the water (and thereby all waters of the earth) is also described in terms of fire: "The Holy One came to the water to go down to be baptized; his fire kindled amongst the waves and set them alight."³²⁰

The already familiar motif of fire at Jesus' baptism appears also in the *Hymn on Epiphany* 14, attributed to Ephrem. There Jesus himself is portrayed as the flaming fire who ignites the waters of the Jordan. *Hymn on Epiphany* 14.32 unveils the following imagery: "the waters in My Baptism are sanctified,—and fire and the Spirit from Me shall they receive;—and if I be not baptized they are not made perfect—to be fruitful

---

³¹⁶ As one option, Petersen suggests that Justin might have had "access to a Hebrew or Aramaic gospel, the same early Hebrew or Aramaic traditions which are the *Vorlage* from which our Greek Matthew was later translated and given a specific redaction. In this case, Justin's text would be valuable as a witness to the pre-canonical form of Matthew traditions." Petersen, *Tatian's Diatessaron*, 17–18.

³¹⁷ Petersen, *Tatian's Diatessaron*, 16.

³¹⁸ Ferguson, *Baptism in the Early Church*, 112.

³¹⁹ C. McCarthy, *Saint Ephrem's Commentary on the Diatessaron* (Oxford: Oxford University Press, 1993), 85. On this tradition see also S. Brock, "St Ephrem on Christ as Light in Mary and in the Jordan: Hymni de Ecclesia 36," *ECR* 7 (1975): 79–88.

³²⁰ Myers, *Spirit Epicleses in the Acts of Thomas*, 127.

of children that shall not die."³²¹ This conceptual development is significant since Jesus himself is now understood as the fiery center of the theophany.

It is important for our study that the symbolism of fire and light, with which early Christian exegetes surround Jesus' baptism, is reminiscent of the theophanic imagery wherein the divine *Kavod* is portrayed in biblical and extra-biblical Jewish accounts.³²² Everett Ferguson rightly discerns the theophanic significance of such motifs, noting that "light was a common element of a theophany, and its accompaniment of Jesus' baptism would be theologically significant in association with the heavenly voice and the descent of the Spirit as testimonies to Jesus' unique status."³²³ The reception history of the baptism story demonstrates that it was often understood by the earliest Christian interpreters as a theophanic event reminiscent of the manifestation of the divine Glory in the water. Such proclivities already appear to be manifested in the earliest source of this tradition: Justin Martyr. According to Ferguson,

> Justin's reference to "fire" is not only the earliest reference to the phenomenon that can be dated with some confidence but is also distinct from the light tradition, for he puts the appearance of the fire at the time when Jesus entered water, whereas the reports of light put the phenomenon either at the baptism or after it as with the other divine acknowledgements.³²⁴

Robe of Glory in the Jordan

Another important aspect of Christian interpretations of Jesus' baptism that may also be related to the understanding of this event as a manifestation of the divine Glory in the river is the tradition about the presence of the glorious robe in the Jordan. Although the synoptic baptismal accounts do not speak explicitly about Jesus' endowment with any garment at the baptism event, implicit allusions to the clothing symbols may be present in the text. This possibility that the baptismal clothing metaphors could be implicitly present, even in the synoptic accounts, receives additional support in the light of the Pauline passage attested in Gal 3:27, where the apostle conveys to early Christians that many of them who were baptized into Christ were clothed themselves with Christ (Χριστὸν ἐνεδύσασθε). This passage hints at the early Christian understanding of baptism as an endowment with an eschatological garment. Importantly, later Christian exegetes often interpret both the descent of the spirit on Jesus and his immersion into the water as respective clothing metaphors; the heavenly garments that later generations of Christian adepts receive during their own baptisms.

---

[321] E. Johnston, "Ephraim Syrus: Fifteen Hymns for the Feast of Epiphany," in: *A Select Library of Nicene and Post-Nicene Fathers of the Christian Church. Second Series* (ed. P. Schaff and H. Wace; New York: The Christian Literature Company, 1898), 13.265–89 at 13.285.

[322] Vigne, *Christ au Jourdain*, 263.

[323] Ferguson, *Baptism in the Early Church*, 111.

[324] Ferguson, *Baptism in the Early Church*, 111.

We first need to give our attention to the tradition associating clothing with water. Sebastian Brock notes that in the Syrian authors "the Word not only 'puts on a body,' but he also 'put on the waters of baptism.'"[325] In one of the *Hymns on Epiphany*, attributed by tradition to Ephrem the Syrian, baptism is interpreted as being clothed with the water of glory: "in baptism Adam found again that glory that was among the trees of Eden. He went down, and received it out of the water; he put it on, and went up and was adorned therein. Blessed be he that has mercy on all" (*Hymn on Epiphany* 12.1).[326] The endowment with the eschatological garment of glory in this hymn is contrasted with the protological, ominous garments of fig leaves that the protoplasts received after their fall:

> Man fell in the midst of Paradise, and in baptism compassion restored him: he lost his comeliness through Satan's envy, and found it again by God's grace. Blessed be he that has mercy on all! The wedded pair were adorned in Eden; but the serpent stole their crowns: yet mercy crushed down the accursed one, and made the wedded pair goodly in their raiment. Blessed be he that has mercy on all! They clothed themselves with leaves of necessity; but the Merciful had pity on their beauty, and instead of leaves of trees, he clothed them with glory in the water (*Hymn on Epiphany* 12.2–4).[327]

Also important is the tradition of Jesus' vestment with the spirit at his baptism. Sebastian Brock points to such imagery in one of Ephrem's *Hymns on Nativity*,[328] from which we learn that "our body was Your garment; Your spirit became our robe" (*Nativity* 22.39).[329] A similar motif is present in the *Hymns on Epiphany*: "Descend, my brethren, put on from the waters of baptism the Holy Spirit."[330] According to Kilian McDonnell, the same imagery can be found in Aphrahat's *Demonstrations* 6.14. Aphrahat similarly reassures baptismal candidates to take the robe of the Spirit from the water and reinvest themselves in the original attire that Adam had before the Fall.[331]

It is important that although the previously examined passages often discuss the glorious baptismal robes of the Christian adepts, they often disclose that this robe of

---

[325] Brock, *The Luminous Eye*, 90.

[326] Johnston, "Ephraim Syrus: Fifteen Hymns for the Feast of Epiphany," 13.282.

[327] Johnston, "Ephraim Syrus: Fifteen Hymns for the Feast of Epiphany," 13.282.

[328] Brock, *The Luminous Eye*, 93.

[329] K. E. McVey, *Ephrem the Syrian: Hymns* (Classics of Western Spirituality; New York: Paulist Press, 1989), 185.

[330] *Hymn on Epiphany* 5.1. Johnston, "Ephraim Syrus: Fifteen Hymns for the Feast of Epiphany," 13.272.

[331] Aphrahat's *Demonstrations* 6.14 relates the following tradition:

> Now it is from baptism that we receive the Spirit of Christ: for at that moment when the priests invoke the Spirit, (the Spirit) opens up the heavens, descends and hovers over the water (Gen 1:2), while those who are being baptised clothe themselves in her. The Spirit remains distant from all who are of bodily birth until they come to the birth (that belongs to the baptismal) water: only then do they receive the Holy Spirit. For at (their) first birth they are born with an animate spirit which is created inside a person, which is furthermore immortal, as it is said "Adam became a living soul" (Gen 27; 1 Cor 15:45).

glory[332] was placed in the baptismal water by Jesus himself.[333] For example, Jacob of Serugh informs his readers that "Christ came to baptism, he went down and placed in the baptismal water the robe of glory, to be there for Adam, who had lost it."[334] Brock, reflecting on this passage, suggests that "Christ's baptism, and the sanctification of the Jordan waters provide the occasion for the recovery of the lost robe of glory in Christian baptism."[335] Kilian McDonnell adds that for Jacob of Serugh "all who come to baptism receive a garment, wholly of light ... woven with fire and Spirit, a garment of living fire."[336]

Note also that the Syrian traditions regarding the glorious robe of the baptism are permeated with protological overtones that envision this attire as the garment of prelapsarian humanity. Brock notes that, in the *Hymns on Epiphany* attributed to Ephrem, the recovery of the robe of glory, once lost by Adam, is specifically connected with baptism.[337] As mentioned above, according to *Hymn on Epiphany* 12.1, "in baptism Adam found again—that glory that was among the trees of Eden. He went down, and received it out of the water; he put it on, and went up and was adorned therein."[338] McDonnell suggests that in such a conceptual framework the adept "goes down into the waters to take up the robe of glory which Adam had lost, and which Christ had recovered and deposited in the Jordan."[339]

These baptismal motifs are vital for our present study, since in many Jewish accounts the second powers are endowed with supernatural garments in the process of their initiations. As we have shown, this is the case in the *Exagoge* of Ezekiel the Tragedian, *2 Enoch*, and in the *Primary Adam Books*.

And at the second birth, which occurs at baptism, they receive the Holy Spirit, from a portion of divinity and this too is immortal.
K. Valavanolickal, *Aphrahat: Demonstrations* (2 vols.; CTSI 3–4; Kerala: HIRS, 1999), 1.152.

[332] Brock notes that in the baptismal traditions "when he or she is baptized, the Christian is himself going down into the Jordan waters and from them he picks up and puts on the 'robe of glory' which Christ left there. The 'robe of glory' which Adam and Eve lost in Paradise at the Fall is thus recovered by the Christian at Baptism in the font." S. Brock, "Clothing Metaphors as a Means of Theological Expression in Syriac Tradition," in: *Typus, Symbol, Allegorie bei den ostlichen Vatern und ihren Parallelen im Mittelalter* (ed. M. Schmidt; Regensburg: Verlag Friedrich Pustet, 1982), 11–38 at 12–13.

[333] Brock, *The Luminous Eye*, 93. According to this understanding Jesus "places his glory in the womb of the Jordan waters when the Holy Spirit descends on him." A. M. Aagaard "'My Eyes Have Seen Your Salvation.' On Likeness to God and Deification in Patristic Theology," *Religion & Theology* 17 (2010): 302–28 at 320.

[334] Brock, *The Luminous Eye*, 93.

[335] Brock, *The Luminous Eye*, 93.

[336] McDonnell, *The Baptism of Jesus in the Jordan*, 142.

[337] Brock, *The Luminous Eye*, 94.

[338] Johnston, "Ephraim Syrus: Fifteen Hymns for the Feast of Epiphany," 13.282.

[339] McDonnell, *The Baptism of Jesus in the Jordan*, 143.

The Glorification of Jesus at the Jordan

One of the most significant aspects of the later Christian interpretations of the baptism story relevant for our study is the tradition of Jesus' glorification at the Jordan. One early testimony that attests to such an understanding can be found in Origen's *Homilies on Joshua*. *Homily on Joshua* 4.2 unveils the following tradition:

> What great things were manifested before! The Red Sea was crossed on foot, manna was given from heaven, springs were burst open in the wilderness, the Law was given through Moses. Many signs and marvels were performed in the wilderness, but nowhere is it said that Jesus was "exalted." But where the Jordan is crossed, there it is said to Jesus, "In this day I am beginning to exalt you in the sight of the people." Indeed, Jesus is not exalted before the mystery of baptism. But his exaltation, even his exaltation in the sight of the people, assumes a beginning from then on. If "all who are baptized [into Christ Jesus] are baptized into his death," and the death of Jesus is made complete by the exaltation of the cross, deservedly then, Jesus is first exalted for each of the faithful when that person arrives at the mystery of baptism. Because thus it is written that "God exalted him, and gave him a name that is above every name, that at the name of Jesus every knee should bend, in heaven and on earth, and below the earth."[340]

Scholars have suggested that this text traces "the beginning of Jesus' glorification to the Jordan."[341] It is not coincidental that the tradition of Jesus' glorification is found in the same author who, as was noted above, was particularly attentive to the Ezekielian background of the baptismal story.

Another possible reference to Jesus' glorification at the Jordan can be found in the *Testament of Levi* 18:6–7, a passage that relates the following tradition:

> The heavens will be opened (οἱ οὐρανοὶ ἀνοιγήσονται), and from the temple of glory sanctification will come upon him, with a fatherly voice, as from Abraham to Isaac. And the glory of the Most High shall burst forth upon him. And the spirit of understanding and sanctification shall rest upon him [in the water].[342]

Many have noted that this passage brings to memory some details of Jesus' baptism. Considering the similarities between Jesus' baptism in Mark and Levi's initiation, Joel Marcus says, "in the latter the heavens are opened, the Glory of God burst forth on the eschatological high priest 'with a fatherly voice, as from Abraham to Isaac,' the Spirit

---

[340] C. White, ed., *Origen: Homilies on Joshua* (Washington: Catholic University of America Press, 2002), 53–54.

[341] McDonnell, *The Baptism of Jesus in the Jordan*, 82.

[342] H. C. Kee, "Testaments of the Twelve Patriarchs," in: *The Old Testament Pseudepigrapha* (ed. J. H. Charlesworth; 2 vols.; New York: Doubleday, 1983–1985), 1.795; M. de Jonge et al., *The Testaments of the Twelve Patriarchs: A Critical Edition of the Greek Text* (PVTG 12; Leiden: Brill, 1978), 48–49.

rests upon him in the water, and Beliar (= Satan) is bound (cf. Mark 1:12–13; 3:27)."[343] Marcus also points out some terminological similarities, noting that, like Matthew and Luke, the *Testament of Levi* uses the verb *anoigein* in its description of the heavenly opening (οἱ οὐρανοὶ ἀνοιγήσονται).[344]

Researchers have suggested that the passage from the *Testament of Levi* appears to address the glorification of Jesus at his baptism. Entertaining this possibility, Kilian McDonnell points out that, in the *Testament of Levi* 18, "the glory, tied to the theology of rest, will be fully manifested in his resurrection, but it begins already here at the Jordan."[345]

McDonnell also draws attention to another example of this interpretive tradition found in Ephrem the Syrian's *Hymn on the Church* 36.3, a text that also places the initial glorification of Jesus at his baptism.[346] According to Ephrem, "the river in which he was baptized conceived him again symbolically; the moist womb of the water conceived him in purity, bore him in chastity, made him ascend in glory."[347]

The tradition of Jesus' glorification at baptism is also attested in the *Teaching of St. Gregory*, which contains the Armenian baptismal catechesis and possibly stems from the end of the fifth century.[348] Through the prism of the Johannine language of glorification, the *Teaching of St. Gregory* 425 interprets Jesus' baptism as follows:

> And he himself said to the Father: "The hour has come, Father; glorify your Son." And there came a voice from heaven: "I have glorified, and I shall glorify again." This was not to seek a refuge, or because he is lacking at all of the Father's glory, but in order that the creatures might hear and be confirmed in the Son. In the same way the Son, standing in our midst, shows the Father and the Holy Spirit to the world, as the Father cried concerning the Only begotten: "This is my only begotten Son; he is pleasing to myself. I shall set my Spirit over him," who was revealed at his descending and resting on him; just as he himself said of the Holy Spirit: "He glorifies me."[349]

Although McDonnell argues that the tradition of the glorification of Jesus is preserved here in its most explicit form,[350] exegetical effort is required to untangle the complexity

---

[343] J. Marcus, *Mark 1–8: A New Translation with Introduction and Commentary* (AB 27; New York: Doubleday, 2000), 159.

[344] Marcus, *Mark 1–8*, 159.

[345] K. McDonnell, "Jesus' Baptism in the Jordan," *TS* 56 (1995): 209–36 at 226.

[346] McDonnell, "Jesus' Baptism in the Jordan," 226.

[347] S. P. Brock and G. A. Kiraz, *Ephrem the Syrian: Select Poems* (Provo: Brigham Young University Press, 2006), 71.

[348] McDonnell finds a similar tradition, which traces the beginning of Jesus' glorification to the Jordan in another Armenian text, the so-called *The Key of Truth*: "[first at his baptism] he was glorified, then [first] he was praised ... then [first] he shone forth." McDonnell, *The Baptism of Jesus in the Jordan*, 83.

[349] R. W. Thomson, ed., *The Teaching of St. Gregory: An Early Armenian Catechism* (Cambridge: Harvard University Press, 1970), 93.

[350] McDonnell, "Jesus' Baptism in the Jordan," 226.

of various biblical allusions. McDonnell suggests that in this passage God's promise about the hour of glorification, reflected in John 12:28; "I have glorified it, and I will glorify again," is anticipated at the baptism.[351]

Some Christian interpretations, moreover, attempt to link Jesus' transfiguration on the mountain with his glorious metamorphosis in the waters of the Jordan, thus making the link between the two theophanic encounters.[352] Ephrem in his *Hymn on the Church* 36 unveils such a connection between the baptism and the transfiguration by uniting both events to the memory of Moses' Sinai encounter. *Hymn on the Church* 36.5–9 reads:

> As the Daystar in his river, the Bright One in his tomb, he shone forth on the mountain top and gave brightness too in the womb; he dazzled as he went up [from the river], gave illumination at his ascension. The brightness which Moses put on was wrapped on him from without, the river in which Christ was baptized put on Light from within, [Mary's] body, in which he resided, was made gleaming from within. Just as Moses gleamed with the [divine] glory because he saw the splendor briefly, how much more should the body wherein [Christ] resided gleam, and the river in which he was baptized? The brightness that the stammering Moses put on in the wilderness did not allow the darkness to darken the inside of his dwelling, for the light from his face served as a sun that went before his feet, like the supernal beings whose eyes need no other light, since their pupils flow with light, and they are clothed in rays of glory.[353]

Deliberating on this passage, Serafim Seppälä calls attention to the striking contrast between Moses' illumination, which came from outside, and Christ's baptism in the Jordan, where light is put on from within.[354] As in the previously explored transfiguration story, unlike Moses, Jesus himself is the source of the divine light.

In the *Hymn on Epiphany* 9.12, attributed to Ephrem, one again sees symbolic ties between the transfiguration and the baptism epiphanies: "his worshippers are made white like his garments, the garments in Tabor and the body in the water. Instead of the garments, the peoples are made white, and have become for him a clothing of glory."[355] Here, Jesus' glorification on the mount and his glorification in the river are linked by common theophanic features, some borrowed from synoptic accounts of the transfiguration.[356]

---

[351] McDonnell, *The Baptism of Jesus in the Jordan*, 83.

[352] Vigne, *Christ au Jourdain*, 263.

[353] Brock and Kiraz, *Ephrem the Syrian: Select Poems*, 73–75.

[354] S. Seppälä, "Baptismal Mystery in St. Ephrem the Syrian and Hymnen de Epiphania," in: *Ablution, Initiation, and Baptism: Late Antiquity, Early Judaism, and Early Christianity* (ed. D. Hellholm; BZNW 176; Berlin: Walter de Gruyter, 2011), 1148.

[355] Johnston, "Ephraim Syrus: Fifteen Hymns for the Feast of Epiphany," 13.280.

[356] On the interconnections between the baptism and the transfiguration in this passage, see Seppälä, "Baptismal Mystery in St. Ephrem the Syrian and Hymnen de Epiphania," 1140.

The Motif of the Torn Heaven

After our brief excursus into the reception history of the baptism story, we should return to the theophanic details of Jesus' vision at the Jordan. Another conceptual nexus of the synoptic versions of Jesus' baptism is the motif of the "opened" or "torn" heaven.[357] The synoptic accounts use different terminology in their renderings of this event. Mark uses σχίζω (to rent)[358] while Matthew and Luke use ἀνοίγω (to open). The verb forms, however, are not identical in Matthew and Luke: Matthew uses the aorist passive indicative (ἠνεῴχθησαν),[359] while Luke employs the aorist passive infinitive (ἀνεῳχθῆναι).[360]

As previously mentioned, ancient and modern interpreters often read this motif in the light of the Ezekielian imagery, in particular, its portrayal of the open heavens on the river Chebar. Scholars also point out that the opening of the heavens represents a principal element of early Jewish and Christian apocalyptic visionary accounts, understood as a prelude to a vision.[361]

Indeed, the theme of the upper realm's opening in the synoptics appears to rely on a rich theophanic legacy. Thus, Richard Thomas France notes: "the opening of heaven is a recurrent theme in biblical and other literature (Jewish and pagan) to indicate a vision which reaches beyond the earthly dimension (Ezek 1:1; John 1:51; Acts 7:56; 10:11; Rev 4:1; 19:11)."[362] Christopher Rowland and Christopher Morray-Jones further narrow the possible conceptual background of the heavens opening motif, noting that the heavens were opened just as they were to Ezekiel by the river Chebar, thus fulfilling the prophetic longing that God would rend the heavens and fulfil the divine purposes.[363]

---

[357] Matthew (ἠνεῴχθησαν οἱ οὐρανοί) and Luke (ἀνεῳχθῆναι τὸν οὐρανόν) use the same verb while Mark employs the participle σχιζομένους.

[358] Mark 1:10: "σχιζομένους τοὺς οὐρανοὺς." Scholars have suggested that Mark's terminological choice appears to imply an irreversible cosmic change with his picture of the torn heavens. This is in contrast to the tamer Matthean/Lukan scenario, in which they are merely "opened," since what is opened may be closed but what is torn apart cannot easily return to its former state. Marcus, *Mark 1–8*, 165; D. H. Juel, *Mark* (Augsburg Commentary on the New Testament; Minneapolis: Augsburg, 1990), 33.

[359] Matt 3:16: "ἠνεῴχθησαν οἱ οὐρανοί."

[360] Luke 3:21: "ἀνεῳχθῆναι τὸν οὐρανὸν." On this terminology see Fitzmyer, *The Gospel According to Luke I–IX*, 480.

[361] Mathewson, "The Apocalyptic Vision of Jesus," 92. Joel Marcus notes that "the Markan account of the baptism of Jesus should probably be viewed as a description of an eschatological theophany, like the pertinent passages from Isaiah. As E. Lohmeyer points out, the violent tearing of the heavens, emphasized by the Markan verb σχίζειν points to a background in apocalyptic dualism: [The tearing of the heavens] is rooted in the view that heaven and earth are shut up against each other, so that God can no longer associate with his people in an unmediated manner, or they with him, as once happened. It is therefore a sign of unusual grace when the heaven opens. This occurs in a miracle that embraces the entirety of the people or of the world; not accidentally, the motif is found almost solely in apocalypses." Marcus, *The Way of the Lord*, 56. See also W. Lane, *The Gospel According to Mark* (NICNT; Grand Rapids: Eerdmans, 1974), 55.

[362] R. T. France, *The Gospel of Mark: A Commentary on the Greek Text* (NIGTC 2; Grand Rapids: Eerdmans, 2002), 77. In his other commentary France notes that "the phrase 'the heavens were opened' echoes Ezekiel's inaugural vision (Ezek 1:1)." R. T. France, *Matthew* (TNTC 1; Grand Rapids: Eerdmans, 1985), 95.

[363] Rowland and Morray-Jones, *Mystery of God*, 104–5.

The process of gradual assimilation to the Ezekielian traditions can be discerned through a comparative analysis of the synoptic baptismal accounts. On the subject of the different renderings of the torn heaven theme in the gospels, Davies and Allison point out that "Matthew differs from Mark in putting 'heavens'—the plural ... and by changing the verb to the passive of ἀνοίγω,"[364] suggesting that "both modifications probably signal assimilation to Ezek 1:1: ἠνοίχθησαν οἱ οὐρανοί, καὶ εἶδον ὁράσεις θεοῦ."[365]

In the gospels, furthermore, the theme of the torn heaven appears to be related not only to the apparition of the heavenly *Kavod*, as described in Ezekiel 1 and other early Jewish accounts. The motif also appears to relate to a different, this time earthly, theophany of the divine Glory, which was only accessible once a year to the high priest in the Holy of Holies of the Jerusalem Temple. This connection is likely referred to in the Gospel of Mark and other synoptic accounts through a set of corresponding metaphors of tearing, present not only in the baptismal account, but also in the portrayal of Jesus' death on the cross where the motif of tearing appears again. In Mark 15:38–39,[366] a passage describing events immediately following Jesus' crucifixion, an extraordinary incident occurs:

> And the curtain of the temple was torn in two, from top to bottom (Καὶ τὸ καταπέτασμα τοῦ ναοῦ ἐσχίσθη εἰς δύο ἀπ' ἄνωθεν ἕως κάτω). Now when the centurion, who stood facing him, saw that in this way he breathed his last, he said, "Truly this man was God's Son!"

Here, like the heavens during Jesus' baptism, the curtain of the earthly temple is described to be torn. The tearing of the sacred fabric from the top, rather than from the bottom to the top, might suggest it was torn not by a human agent but by an unnamed heavenly force.

According to David Ulansey, the two ripping events in Mark do not occur at random points in the narrative, but were intentionally placed at two pivotal moments in the story, where they provide an ideal counterpoint for each other. These moments in Ulansey's view represent the precise beginning (the baptism) and the precise end (the death) of the spiritual career of Jesus.[367] Ulansey proposes that such placement of the two instances of the tearing motif form a symbolic "inclusio"—a narrative device

---

[364] Davies and Allison, *Matthew*, 1.329.

[365] Davies and Allison, *Matthew*, 1.329. The motif of splitting heaven associated with the appearance of the otherworldly being recalls another important Jewish account where the visionary currents reach their conceptual apex, namely, *Joseph and Aseneth*. In relation to this connection, Adela Yarbro Collins notices that the unusual Markan expression "the heavens split" (σχιζομένους τοὺς οὐρανοὺς) does not occur in the LXX or anywhere else in the New Testament. However, it does occur in *Joseph and Aseneth* where the heaven was split (ἐσχίσθη ὁ οὐρανός) near the morning star revealing a "man," that is, an angel, who came down to Aseneth from heaven (*Jos. Asen.* 14:1–3). Yarbro Collins, *Mark*, 148. In the baptism account, however, the open heaven does not reveal the descent of the anthropomorphic being, but rather a pteromorphic creature, which may suggest that in the baptismal narrative Jesus himself remains the main theophanic focus of the vision.

[366] See also Matt 27:51 and Luke 23:45.

[367] D. Ulansey, "The Heavenly Veil Torn: Mark's Cosmic 'Inclusio,'" *JBL* 110 (1991): 123–25 at 123.

well known in biblical and other ancient texts in which a detail repeated at the beginning and end of a narrative unit provides a sense of closure and structural integrity.[368] Ulansey concludes by suggesting that "seen in this context, the presence at both moments of the motif of something being torn is unlikely to be coincidental."[369] Ulansey, however, was not the first scholar to draw attention to this correspondence. Joel Marcus reminds us that already Ernst Lohmeyer's apocalyptic interpretation of the Markan baptismal account was based on a comparison with Mark 15:38–39, a passage whose vocabulary and context are strikingly similar to 1:10–11.[370] In turn, Marcus also reflects on several common features of the two Markan "tearing" episodes, which both include an appropriation of the verbs σχίζειν (in the passive voice) and ἰδεῖν ("to see"), a reference to spirit (ἐξέπνευσεν/πνεῦμα), and the use of an identification formula ("this man was"/"you are") that points to Jesus' divine sonship.[371] Both passages, furthermore, reflect a descending divine action (the descent of the Spirit, the tearing of the Temple veil from top to bottom).[372]

The parallelism between the tearing of the sacerdotal fabric and the opening of the heavenly realm evokes some early Jewish testimonies in which the veil of the earthly temple was likened to the heavens. Ulansey reminds us about an oft neglected witness—Josephus's *Jewish War* in which the sanctuary's veil was portrayed as a panorama of the heavens.[373] Analyzing this tradition, Ulansey proposes that the outer veil of the Jerusalem temple was actually one huge image of the starry sky.[374] He further suggests that Markan readers "who had ever seen the temple or heard it described would instantly have seen in their mind's eye an image of the heavens being torn, and would immediately have been reminded of Mark's earlier description of the heavens being torn at the baptism."[375]

Notably, recognition of the connections between Mark 1:10 and Mark 15:38 have been gaining steady support in recent scholarship.[376] Adela Yarbro Collins affirms this scholarly consensus in her Hermeneia commentary on Mark. Like Ulansey, she notes that, for members of the Markan community who heard about the torn curtain, "the announcement of the rending of the curtain would evoke an image of 'the heavens

---

[368] Ulansey, "Heavenly Veil Torn," 123.
[369] Ulansey, "Heavenly Veil Torn," 123–24.
[370] Marcus, *The Way of the Lord*, 57.
[371] Marcus, *The Way of the Lord*, 57.
[372] Marcus, *The Way of the Lord*, 57.
[373] Ulansey, "Heavenly Veil Torn," 124–25.
[374] Ulansey, "Heavenly Veil Torn," 124.
[375] Ulansey, "Heavenly Veil Torn," 124–25.
[376] E. Malbon, *Narrative Space and Mythic Meaning in Mark* (San Francisco: Harper & Row, 1986), 187, n. 93; S. Motyer, "The Rending of the Veil: A Markan Pentecost," *NTS* 33 (1987): 155–57; H. M. Jackson, "The Death of Jesus in Mark and the Miracle from the Cross," *NTS* 33 (1987): 23–31; J. Heidler, "Die Verwendung von Psalm 22 im Kreuzigungsbericht des Markus: ein Beitrag zur Frage nach der Christologie des Markus," in: *Christi Leidenspsalm: Arbeiten zum 22. Psalm; Festschrift zum 50. Jahr des Bestehens des Theologischen Seminars "Paulinum" Berlin* (ed. H. Genest; Neukirchen-Vluyn: Neukirchener Verlag, 1996), 26–34; D. M. Gurtner, *The Torn Veil: Matthew's Exposition of the Death of Jesus* (Cambridge: Cambridge University Press, 2007), 172–74.

being torn and they would immediately have been reminded' of the account of Jesus' baptism."[377]

The parallelism between the torn heaven at Jesus' baptism and the rending of the sacerdotal fabric that once concealed the Glory of God in the earthly temple is significant for our study; it provides additional support for the possibility of *Kavod* symbolism in the synoptic baptismal accounts. Also important is that in both Mark 1:10 and Mark 15:38, Jesus is not in the Temple or in heaven, typical places for the divine *Kavod*; he is rather placed outside of these conventional sacerdotal *topoi*. This may underline Jesus' role as a new custodian, and possibly even the center, of the *Kavod* ideology, predestined to replace old theophanic realities.

Topological Peculiarities

At this point we must draw attention to a parallelism between the opening of heaven and the opening of the waters that now also become "torn" during the event of Jesus' baptism.[378]

Although the ripping of the heavens has been adequately explored by various interpreters, little or no attention has been given to the ripped watery substance below. Yet, both Mark and Matthew specifically mention Jesus' ascent from the waters of the Jordan.[379] In the light of this ascending progression, which rips apart the surface of the waters, it is possible that the baptismal story may hint here at a tradition of two cosmological curtains—lower and upper, represented accordingly by the heavenly and the watery realms. If so, this may reveal not one but two visual theophanic dimensions, subsequently connected not only with the epiphany of the spirit/dove's descent from the torn heaven, but also with the theophany of Jesus' ascent from the ripped waters of the Jordan. Such theophanic processions, accompanied in the synoptic accounts by the corresponding ἀναβαίνω/καταβαίνω terminology, reaffirm Jesus' role not only as a seer of the upper theophany but also as a symbolic center of the lower watery theophany. The descent of the one theophanic entity, represented by the spirit/dove, thus inversely mirrors the ascent of the other theophanic actor, who emerges from the curtain of the primordial waters. Such ascent/descent dynamics are typical for Jewish two powers in heaven accounts, in which the ascent of the new beloved of the deity often coincides with the descent of the former favorite; the latter either becomes accommodated by a new second power or demoted and sent to the lower realm in the process of such an inauguration. These dynamics—of exaltation and demotion—may also be present in the synoptic renderings of Jesus' baptism, as some scholars have suggested.[380] This theme also unfolds in the temptation story,

---

[377] Yarbro Collins, *Mark*, 762.

[378] Reflecting on the spatial peculiarities in the baptismal account, David Capes notes that "it portrays the above-below spatial dichotomy via the descent of the Spirit and the voice from above." Capes, "Intertextual Echoes," 40.

[379] Mark 1:10: "ἀναβαίνων ἐκ τοῦ ὕδατος"; Matt 3:16: "ἀνέβη ἀπὸ τοῦ ὕδατος."

[380] Marcus, "Jesus' Baptismal Vision."

which follows the baptism accounts in the synoptic gospels. We will explore these traditions later in our study.

Cosmological Ramifications

The preceding parallelism between the heavenly and watery realms alludes to the potential cosmological significance of the waters of Jesus' baptism. Ancient and modern interpreters often speak about a cosmological framework that might stand behind Jesus' baptism account with its symbolism of water, heavens, and dove/spirit by tracing the symbolic background of these realities to the creational imagery found in Genesis 1. Indeed, the cosmological meaning of Jesus' baptism can be illuminated by later Jewish interpretations of this creational symbolism.[381] One example, which appears to be useful for the elucidation of the possible cosmological overtones in the story of Jesus' baptism, is a rabbinic tradition preserved in *b. Hag.* 15a. The passage depicts Rabbi Ben Zoma, a famous rabbinic seer who, as we have already learned, was often associated with the two powers in heaven debates. In *b. Hag.* 15a, as in the famous Story of the Four in Pardes, he is depicted as a visionary who beholds the upper and lower waters, and the spirit of God as a dove hovering between them. *B. Hag.* 15a brings to mind some cosmological themes from Gen 1:2 and 1:6:

> Our rabbis taught ... a story concerning R. Yoshua b. Hananya who was sitting on top of the Temple mount and Ben Zoma saw him but did not stand up before him. Yoshua said to him, Whence and whither, Ben Zoma? Ben Zoma said to him, I was looking at the space between the upper and lower waters and there is only three fingers breadth between them as it is said, The spirit of God was hovering on the face of the waters like a dove which hovers over its young without any touching. R. Yoshua said to his disciples, Ben Zoma is still outside.[382]

One finds here a constellation of already familiar motifs, including the themes of the water, the parallelism between upper and lower realms, and a visionary who is

---

[381] Summarizing these scholarly insights, Joel Marcus argues that

> the most plausible is the theory that dove is meant to echo Gen 1:2, where the Spirit soars, birdlike, over the waters. This theory is supported by *b. Hag.* 15a, in which the Spirit's hovering over the primeval waters is compared with a dove's brooding over its young, and by 4Q521 1:6, which reapplies the vocabulary of Gen 1:2 to an eschatological empowerment of human beings ("over the poor his Spirit will hover").
>
> Marcus, *Mark 1–8*, 159–60.

For cosmological allusions in the baptismal account, especially in relation to the dove imagery, see also I. Abrahams, *Studies in Pharisaism and the Gospels* (2 vols.; Library of Biblical Studies; New York: Ktav, 1967), 1.49–50; C. K. Barrett, *The Holy Spirit and the Gospel Tradition* (London: SPCK, 1947), 38–39; Cranfield, *The Gospel According to St. Mark*, 54; Davies and Allison, *Matthew*, 1.334; Keck, "Spirit and the Dove," 41–67; V. Taylor, *The Gospel According to St Mark: The Greek Text with Introduction, Notes, and Indexes* (New York: St. Martin's Press, 1966), 161.

[382] Epstein, *The Babylonian Talmud. Hagiga*, 15a. On this tradition, see also *t. Hag.* 2:5 and parallels in *y. Hag.* 2, 77b and *Gen. Rab.* 2, 4.

gazing on the spirit of God hovering like a dove. Many distinguished students of early Christian traditions[383] have drawn attention to this unique passage, in which a rabbinic seer, like Jesus in the synoptic gospels, beholds the spirit of God in the form of a dove.[384] Joy Palachuvattil's research highlights what he sees as the two most important parallels with the synoptic baptismal traditions,[385] that is, a comparison of the spirit to the dove and the spirit's appearance "on the face of the waters," which in his opinion fits well with the baptismal scene at the Jordan.[386]

Despite its relatively late date, Ben Zoma's vision may still be useful for our investigation; it serves as a reminder about the possible cosmological significance of the waters of Jesus' baptism.[387] It is noteworthy that, already in the earliest Christian interpretations of Jesus' baptism, we find an attempt to connect this event, as with the Ben Zoma episode, to the cosmological imagery found in the first chapter of Genesis. Shulamit Laderman notes that the *Odes of Solomon*, an early Christian liturgical collection of hymns dated to the late first or early second century CE, echoes the

---

[383] See also D. Allison, "The Baptism of Jesus and a New Dead Sea Scroll," *BAR* 18 (1992): 58–60; Capes, "Intertextual Echoes," 46; Rowland, *The Open Heaven*, 361.

[384] Adela Yarbro Collins draws attention to another important tradition from *Targ. on Cant.* 2:12, noting that it interprets the voice of the turtledove as the voice of the Holy Spirit. Yarbro Collins, *Mark*, 148. In relation to this tradition Davies and Allison point out that

> the *bat qol* is said in rabbinic sources to be like the cooing of a dove (b. Ber. 3a); and in *Trg. Cant.* on 2:12, the voice of the turtle dove "becomes the voice of the Spirit of salvation." This is interesting because in the gospels the dove precedes a heavenly voice. Yet, the relevant rabbinic sources are of rather late date, and in the gospels the Spirit and the voice are two different motifs.
>
> Davies and Allison, *Matthew*, 1.332.

[385] Rowland and Morray-Jones also note that

> in the story of Ben Zoma the meditation is a detached piece of cosmological speculation, however, whereas in the story in the synoptic gospels the creative spirit hovers over the head of the Son of God, and Jesus is depicted not as a detached observer of matters of mystical interest, like Ben Zoma, who penetrated the secrets of a particular part of the cosmos by his interest in *maʿase bereshit*. Rather, Jesus is represented as seeing the Spirit coming towards him with the commission of himself as the anointed agent of God (cf. Luke 4:18 and Acts 2:17).
>
> Rowland and Morray-Jones, *Mystery of God*, 105.

[386] J. Palachuvattil, *"He Saw": The Significance of Jesus' Seeing Denoted by the Verb Eiden in the Gospel of Mark* (TG 84; Rome: Editrice Pontificia Università Gregoriana, 2002), 74. Palachuvattil also draws attention to some similarities with the Gospel of John, noting that

> in John 1:51 Jesus tells Nathanael, "you will see the heavens opened, and the angels of God ascending and descending upon the Son of Man." There are common elements with the narrative of Mark 1:10ff: there is a seeing, an opening of the heavens, and the descent of the divine beings. The only thing that is lacking is heavenly voice.
>
> Palachuvattil, *"He Saw,"* 76.

[387] McDonnel notices that early Christian interpreters often construe Jesus' baptism as a cosmological event. He notes, for example, that the *Teaching of St Gregory*

> places the Jordan event in the context of the Genesis account of the creation of the world. In the beginning the Spirit transformed chaos into cosmos, "moving over the waters, and thence set out the order of the creatures," including the ornamenting of the heavens where the angels dwell. The Spirit transforms chaos into cosmos. But there is a larger, cosmic role of the Spirit at creation. "He came down to the waters and sanctified the lower waters of the earth." What happened at creation is echoed at baptism.
>
> McDonnell, *The Baptism of Jesus in the Jordan*, 217.

possible link between Jesus' baptism and the biblical account of creation.[388] Laderman points out that in *Ode* 24, Jesus' baptism[389] appears to be linked to the primordial state of the created order.[390] Another scholar, Stephen Gero, also suggests that *Ode* 24 "depicts the baptism as an epiphany which perturbs all creation."[391] *Ode* 24:1-9 unveils the following tradition:

> The dove flew onto the head of our Lord Messiah, because he was her Head. And she cooed on/over him, and her voice was heard. And the inhabitants were afraid, and the sojourners were disturbed. The birds gave up their wing [beat], and all creeping things died in their hole. And the primal deeps were opened and covered. And they sought the Lord like those who are about to give birth, and/but he was not given to them for food, because he was not their own. But the primal deeps were submerged in the submersion of the Lord and perished in that though in which they had been from before. For they were destructive from the beginning, and the end/completion/goal of their destruction was life. And all that was lacking perished through/was destroyed by them, because they could not give the [pass] word, that they might abide.[392]

Here Jesus' baptism appears to be understood as a cosmological event, as his immersion is compared with God's taming the primordial waters at the moment of creation. Laderman argues that the memory of these cosmological allusions are reflected in the symbolism of early Christian baptismal fonts.[393] She notes that

> the separation of the waters marked the end of the chaos and the parting from the deep that represented the underworld. The dome above the baptismal font, which symbolized the firmament and the separation, was designed to give the individual undergoing the sacrament a sense of taking part in a cosmic act—separating himself from the underworld and from impurity, the place where the dead dwell, and being born again in a new, pure world of life.[394]

---

[388] S. Laderman, *Images of Cosmology in Jewish and Byzantine Art: God's Blueprint of Creation* (JCPS 25; Leiden: Brill, 2013), 16.

[389] Reflecting on the conceptual background of *Ode* 24, Stephen Gero suggests that "the setting with most likelihood is indeed the baptism of Jesus." S. Gero, "The Spirit as Dove at the Baptism of Jesus," *NovT* 18 (1976): 17–35 at 18.

[390] Laderman, *Images of Cosmology in Jewish and Byzantine Art*, 16.

[391] Gero, "Spirit as Dove," 18.

[392] M. Lattke, *Odes of Solomon* (Hermeneia; Minneapolis, Fortress, 2009), 340.

[393] Jean Daniélou observes that "the sacramental rite of baptism, immersion in the font, recalls the symbolism of water in the Bible; it is a going down into the deep waters of death, where Christ went down before us, to accomplish the baptism he had to be baptized with." J. Daniélou, *The Lord of History: Reflections on the Inner Meaning of History* (London: Longmans, 1958), 131.

[394] Laderman, *Images of Cosmology in Jewish and Byzantine Art*, 17.

The cosmological understanding of Jesus' baptism is also attested in a text already discussed previously in our study, the *Teaching of St. Gregory*. The *Teaching of St. Gregory* 412 reads:

> And because he made the first earth emerge from the waters by his command, and by water were fattened all plants and reptiles and wild animals and beasts and birds, and by the freshness of the waters they sprang from the earth; in the same way by baptism. He made verdant the womb of generation of the waters, purifying by the waters and renewing the old deteriorated earthy matter, which sin had weakened and enfeebled and deprived of the grace of the Spirit. Then the invisible Spirit opened again the womb by visible water, preparing the newly born fledglings for the regeneration of the font, to clothe all with robes of light who would be born once more.[395]

The *Teaching of St. Gregory* 413 continues the theme of the primordial waters of Jesus' baptism:

> For in the beginning of the creation of time, the Spirit of the Deity moved over the waters, and thence set out the order of the creatures, and commanded the coming into being and establishing of the creatures. He also ordered to be established the firmament of heaven, the dwelling of the fiery angels, which appears to us as water. In the same way he came and completed the covenant which he made with our fathers. He came down to the waters and sanctified the lower waters of this earth, which had been fouled by the sins of mankind.[396]

Reflecting on these passages, Kilian McDonnell suggests that

> the *Teaching of St. Gregory* places the Jordan event in the context of the Genesis account of the creation of the world. In the beginning the Spirit transformed chaos into cosmos, "moving over the waters, and thence set out the order of the creatures," including the ornamenting of the heavens where the angels dwell.[397] The Spirit

---

[395] Thomson, *The Teaching of St. Gregory*, 89.

[396] Thomson, *The Teaching of St. Gregory*, 89. The theme of the cosmological waters of the baptism is further developed in the *Teaching of St. Gregory* 414:
> Treading the waters with his own footsteps, he sanctified them and made them purifying. And just as formerly the Spirit moved over the waters, in the same way he will dwell in the waters and will receive all who are born by it. And the waters massed together above are the dwelling of the angels. But he made these waters just as those, because he himself came down to the waters that all might be renewed through the Spirit by the waters and become angels, and the same Spirit might bring all to adoption by the waters for ever. For he opened the gates of the waters below, that the gates of the upper waters of heaven might be opened, and that he might elevate all men in glory to adoption.
> Thomson, *The Teaching of St. Gregory*, 89–90.

[397] McDonnell notes that in the *Teaching of St. Gregory*
> at creation the Spirit moved over the waters, and from this act "set out the order of the creatures." The Spirit changes disorder to order. Sin "had weakened and enfeebled and

transforms chaos into cosmos. But there is a larger, cosmic role of the Spirit at creation. "He came down to the waters and sanctified the lower waters of the earth." What happened at creation is echoed at baptism.[398]

If the Jordan's waters were indeed understood in the synoptic baptismal accounts as the cosmological waters, it is significant that in early Jewish and Christian accounts the portrayals of the divine *Kavod* are accompanied by the symbolism of the cosmological waters. Both the Hebrew Bible and the Jewish pseudepigrapha often depict the *Kavod* in the midst of the primordial waters. Already Ezekiel's portrayal of the eschatological temple unveils this symbolic constellation, linking the abode of the divine *Kavod* to the imagery of living water, which there serves as a designation of the primordial or paradisal waters. Avigdor Hurowitz notes that "Ezekiel's temple of the future has a river flowing from under the threshold (Ezek 47:1). . . . The river envisioned by Ezekiel seems to replace the basins in Solomon's temple—basins that may have symbolized the rivers of a divine garden."[399] Ezekiel 47:1–8 offers the following description of the sacred waters:

> Then he brought me back to the entrance of the temple; there, water was flowing from below the threshold of the temple toward the east (for the temple faced east); and the water was flowing down from below the south end of the threshold of the temple, south of the altar. Then he brought me out by way of the north gate, and led me around on the outside to the outer gate that faces toward the east; and the water was coming out on the south side. Going on eastward with a cord in his hand, the man measured one thousand cubits, and then led me through the water; and it was ankle-deep. Again he measured one thousand, and led me through the water; and it was knee-deep. Again he measured one thousand, and led me through the water; and it was up to the waist. Again he measured one thousand, and it was a river that I could not cross, for the water had risen; it was deep enough to swim in, a river that could not be crossed. He said to me, "Mortal, have you seen this?" Then he led me back along the bank of the river. As I came back, I saw on the bank of the river a great many trees on the one side and on the other. He said to me, "This water flows toward the eastern region and goes down into the Arabah; and when it enters the sea, the sea of stagnant waters, the water will become fresh."

---

deprived of the grace of the Spirit" the waters and "the old deteriorated earthy matter." The Spirit touches created matter in first creation, but when Adam sinned, the Spirit left Adam, but departed also from the whole of the creation, including the firmament of the heaven. However Christ stepped down into the Jordan and "by treading the waters with his own footstep, he sanctified them and made them purifying," restoring both the lower and the upper waters, a reference to Semitic cosmology.
McDonnell, "Jesus Baptism in Jordan," 217.

[398] McDonnell, "Jesus Baptism in Jordan," 217.
[399] V. Hurowitz, "Inside Solomon's Temple," *Bible Review* 10.2 (1994): 24–36.

Gregory Beale notes[400] that similar sacerdotal imagery of primordial "waters" is present in the description of Israel's temple in Ps 36:8–9.[401] The same motif of sacred waters also occurs in various Jewish extra-biblical accounts, including the *Letter of Aristeas* 89–91[402] and *Joseph and Aseneth* 2.[403] Christian materials also demonstrate an acquaintance with the sacerdotal tradition of flowing waters associated with the divine *Kavod*. Thus, Rev 22:1–2 describes a river of the water of life flowing from the throne of God.[404]

The imagery of the divine *Kavod*, located in the midst of the cosmological waters, is also reflected in the setting and architecture of the earthly temple, with its symbolism of the molten sea. Well known in Jewish sacerdotal reinterpretations of creational imagery, the sea often symbolizes the courtyard of the sanctuary of the world. According to *Numbers Rabbah* 13:19, the court encompasses the sanctuary just as the sea surrounds the world.[405] *B. Sukkah* 51b likewise tells how the white and blue marble of the temple walls were reminiscent of the waves of the sea.[406] The association between the sacred chamber and the sea may also be suggested by the symbolism of the bronze

---

[400] G. K. Beale, *The Temple and the Church's Mission: A Biblical Theology of the Dwelling Place of God* (NSBT 17; Downers Grove: Apollos, 2004), 72.

[401] "They feast on the abundance of your house, and you give them drink from the river of your delights. For with you is the fountain of life; in your light we see light."

[402] There is an uninterrupted supply not only of water, just as if there were a plentiful spring rising naturally from within, but also of indescribably wonderful underground reservoirs, which within a radius of five stades from the foundation of the Temple revealed innumerable channels for each of them, the streams joining together on each side. All these were covered with lead down to the foundation of the wall; on top of them a thick layer of pitch, all done very effectively. There were many mouths at the base, which were completely invisible except for those responsible for the ministry, so that the large amounts of blood which collected from the sacrifices were all cleansed by the downward pressure and momentum. Being personally convinced, I will describe the building plan of the reservoirs just as I understood it. They conducted me more than four stades outside the city, and told me to bend down at a certain spot and listen to the noise at the meeting of the waters. The result was that the size of the conduits became clear to me, as has been demonstrated.
R. J. H. Shutt, "Letter of Aristeas," *The Old Testament Pseudepigrapha* (ed. J. H. Charlesworth; 2 vols.; New York: Doubleday, 1983–1985), 2.7–34 at 2.18–19.

[403] A similar image of the overflowing water surrounding the Temple courtyard is found in *Joseph and Aseneth* 2:17–20: "And there was in the court, on the right hand, a spring of abundant living water." Scholars have noted that the "detailed description of [Aseneth's] garden clearly echoes Ezekiel's account of what he saw in his celebrated temple-vision (Ezek 40:8)." G. Bohak, *Joseph and Aseneth and the Jewish Temple in Heliopolis* (EJL 10; Atlanta: Scholars, 1996), 68.

[404] "Then the angel showed me the river of the water of life, bright as crystal, flowing from the throne of God and of the Lamb through the middle of the street of the city."

[405] "His offering was one silver dish, etc. The dish was in allusion to the court which encompassed the Tabernacle as the sea encompasses the world." Freedman and Simon, *Midrash Rabbah*, 6.546. Concerning a similar tradition in *Midrash Tadshe*, see G. MacRae, *Some Elements of Jewish Apocalyptic and Mystical Tradition and Their Relation to Gnostic Literature* (2 vols.; PhD diss.; University of Cambridge, 1966), 55.

[406] "The reference is to the building of Herod. Of what did he build it?—Rabba replied, Of yellow and white marble. Some there are who say, With yellow, blue and white marble. The building rose in tiers in order to provide a hold for the plaster. He intended at first to overlay it with gold, but the Rabbis told him, Leave it alone for it is more beautiful as it is, since it has the appearance of the waves of the sea." Epstein, *The Babylonian Talmud. Sukkah*, 51b.

tank in the courtyard of Israel's temple, designated in some texts as the "molten sea."[407] It has been suggested that

> the great size of the tank ... in conjunction with the fact that no practical application is offered for the "sea" during the time of Solomon, supports the supposition that the tank served symbolic purpose.[408] Either the "cosmic waters" or the "waters of life," which emanated from below the garden of Eden, or the "great deep" of chaos is most often cited as the underlying symbolism of the molten sea.[409]

These conceptual developments indicate that in early Jewish lore the domains of the divine Glory, *Kavod*, represented respectfully by the heavenly and earthly sanctuaries, were consistently associated with the primordial waters. These traditions are important for our study of the possible presence of the *Kavod* symbolism in the synoptic baptismal accounts.

Likeness Language

Another important theophanic detail of the baptismal narrative is the terminology of likeness applied to the object of vision. All three of the synoptics report that the object of the disclosure was descending like (ὡς/ὡσεί) a dove.[410] Experts argue that this terminology again evokes Ezekiel's vision of the divine *Kavod*. Indeed, the peculiar usage the ὡς/ὡσεί language ("as a dove") vividly brings to memory the Ezekielian descriptions. According to Mathewson, "the particle ὡς or ὡσεί to introduce a visionary symbol is common in apocalyptic discourse, not least of all in the book of Ezekiel."[411] He points out, further, that the LXX version of Ezekiel 1 contains several instances of ὡς used in this manner,[412] and suggests that the terminological choice underlines the

---

[407] 1 Kgs 7:23–25 relates the following tradition:
> Then he made the molten sea; it was round, ten cubits from brim to brim, and five cubits high, and a line of thirty cubits measured its circumference. Under its brim were gourds, for thirty cubits, compassing the sea round about; the gourds were in two rows, cast with it when it was cast. It stood upon twelve oxen, three facing north, three facing west, three facing south, and three facing east; the sea was set upon them, and all their hinder parts were inward.

See also 2 Kgs 16:17; 2 Kgs 25:13; 1 Chr 18:8; 2 Chr 4:2; Jer 52:17.

[408] Elizabeth Bloch-Smith observes that "the exaggerated size of the structures of the Solomonic Temple courtyard would suggest that they were not intended for human use, but belonged to the realm of the divine." E. Bloch-Smith "'Who Is the King of Glory?' Solomon's Temple and Its Symbolism," in: *Scripture and Other Artifacts. Essays on the Bible and Archeology in Honor of Philip J. King* (ed. M. Coogan et al.; Louisville: Westminster, 1994), 19–31 at 21.

[409] Bloch-Smith "'Who Is the King of Glory?' Solomon's Temple and Its Symbolism," 20. See also C. L. Meyers, "Sea, Molten," in: *Anchor Bible Dictionary* (ed. D. N. Freedman; 6 vols.; New York: Doubleday, 1992), 5.1061–62.

[410] Mark 1:10: "ὡς περιστεράν"; Matt 3:16 "ὡσεὶ περιστεράν;" Luke 3:22: "ὡς περιστεράν."

[411] Mathewson, "The Apocalyptic Vision of Jesus," 96.

[412] Mathewson, "The Apocalyptic Vision of Jesus," 96.

visionary character of the baptismal account, further supporting the view that the dove is the object-symbol of Jesus' vision.[413]

Acquisition of the Spirit as the Restoration of the Image of God

Reflecting on the Ezekielian allusions in the Matthean baptismal narrative, Mathewson notes another verbal parallel with Ezekiel, namely, Matt 3:16, where the spirit comes "upon" Jesus (ἐπ' αὐτόν); this enhances the connection with the Ezekielian visionary experience, where the Spirit also came upon (Ezek 2:2 LXX: ἐπ' ἐμέ) the prophetic seer.[414] Acquisition of the spirit by the protagonist may have profound anthropological significance; several ancient interpreters regarded the spirit's descent on Jesus as the restoration of the original image of God, which, according to some traditions, was lost by the protoplast after his fall in the garden of Eden.

Kilian McDonnell, for example, noted the presence of this idea in Cyril of Alexandria, who believed that Adam lost the image of God because he lost the Spirit. In Cyril's Adam Christology, the Spirit was returned by the New Adam (Jesus) at the Jordan, thus "restoring human nature to its ancient state . . . its unshaken state."[415] The identification between the divine image and the spirit is also found in Pseudo-Macarius,[416] who explicitly links Adam's possession of the image of God with the

---

[413] Mathewson, "The Apocalyptic Vision of Jesus," 96.
[414] Mathewson, "The Apocalyptic Vision of Jesus," 96.
[415] McDonnell, *The Baptism of Jesus in the Jordan*, 221. Elsewhere McDonnell notes that
> Cyril believes Adam lost the image of God because he lost the Spirit: "Our father Adam . . . did not preserve the grace of the Spirit, and thus in him the whole nature lost at last [gradually] the God-given goods." If the loss of the image is tied to the loss of the Spirit, then the restoration of the image can only be linked to the return of the Spirit. The loss of the Spirit was universal in Adam; its restoration is universal in the New Adam.
>
> McDonnell, "Jesus' Baptism in the Jordan," 221.

[416] In relation to these pneumatological developments, Roelof van der Broek notes that the *Macarian Homilies* offer acute speculations about the relationship between the Holy Spirit and the spirit of man. These reflections are also overlaid with the peculiar symbolism of the "image." He observes that
> in *Homily* 30.3, Macarius expounds his theory that the soul without the Spirit is dead. It has to be born out of the Spirit and in that way become Spirit itself: "All angels and holy powers rejoice in the soul which has been born out of the Spirit and has become Spirit itself." The soul is the image of the Holy Spirit. Christ, the heavenly painter, paints after his own image "a heavenly man" in the believer who constantly looks at him: "Out of his own Spirit, out of his substance, the ineffable light, he paints a heavenly image and presents that to the soul as its noble and good bridegroom" (*Hom.* 30.4). . . . this "image of the heavenly Spirit," as it is called, is identified with Christ and with the Holy Spirit. The soul that does not possess "the heavenly image of the divine light, which is the life of the soul," is useless and completely reprehensible: "Just as in this world the soul is the life of the body, so in the eternal, heavenly world it is the Spirit of Divinity which is the life of the soul" (*Hom.* 30.5).
>
> R. van den Broek, "The Cathars: Medieval Gnostics?" in: *Gnosis and Hermeticism from Antiquity to Modern Times* (ed. R. van den Broek and W. J. Hanegraaff; SUNY Series in Western Esoteric Traditions; Albany: SUNY, 1997), 100.

For the author of the *Macarian Homilies*, therefore,
> it is absolutely necessary to obtain this life of the soul, the Spirit, in this earthly existence, for otherwise the soul will be unable to enter the Kingdom of Heaven and will end in hell

Holy Spirit.[417] Reflecting on the conceptual link between the image and the Spirit in the *Macarian Homilies*, Gilles Quispel claims that Pseudo-Macarius, who reflected views of the Syrian church, implied in several passages that the Spirit and the Image are identical.[418] The same view, he argues, is found in the *Hymn of the Pearl* in the *Acts of Thomas* 112. With respect to this passage, Quispel thinks that the Self, which comes to encounter the prince, is on the one hand the garment left in heaven, the Holy Spirit; on the other hand, the Image (*eikōn*) of the King of Kings, God, was woven into it.[419]

This tradition of the restoration of the divine Image in Jesus during his baptism is relevant for our discussion of his identity as the second power, since in many early Jewish two powers in heaven accounts, the second power becomes closely associated with the symbolism of the divine image and even personifies this anthropological entity.

The Divine Voice Traditions

The dynamics of descent and ascent, articulated in the synoptic accounts through ἀναβαίνω/καταβαίνω terminology, reflect not only the movements of the story's embodied protagonists, who appear in the form of Jesus and dove, but also the processions of two powers, one of which is depicted as ascending, and the other as descending.

> (*Hom.* 30.6). Before the Fall, Adam possessed this heavenly image, which meant that he was in possession of the Holy Spirit; he lost it when he fell (*Hom.* 12.6). Christ, "who had formed body and soul," comes to bring the works of the Evil One to an end: "[H]e renews and gives shape to the heavenly image and makes a new soul, so that Adam [i.e., man] can become king of death and lord of the creatures again" (*Hom.* 11.6) . . . "the heavenly man unites with your [earthly] man, resulting in one communion" (*Hom.* 12.18).
>
> van den Broek, "The Cathars: Medieval Gnostics?" 100.

[417] Thus, Homily II.12.6 reads: "Since Adam lost his own image and also that heavenly image, therefore, if he shared in the heavenly image, did he have the Holy Spirit (πνεῦμα ἅγιον)? As he was instructed, so he named them." Pseudo-Macarius, *The Fifty Spiritual Homilies and the Great Letter* (tr. G. A. Maloney; New York: Paulist Press, 1992), 97. H. Dörries et al., *Die 50 Geistlichen Homilien des Makarios* (PTS 4; Berlin: Walter de Gruyter, 1964), 110. The confluence of the spirit and the image is also attested in Jewish mystical lore. *Zohar* III.43a-b:

> And the Holy One, blessed be He, directs an emissary who is in charge of human embryos, and assigns to him this particular spirit, and indicates to him the place to which it should be entrusted. This is the meaning of "The night said, a man-child has been conceived" (Job 3:3). "The night said" to this particular emissary, "a man-child has been conceived" by so and so. And the Holy One, blessed be He, then gives this spirit all the commands that he wishes to give, and they have already explained this. Then the spirit descends together with the image, the one in whose likeness [the spirit] existed above. With this image [man] grows; with this image he moves through the world. This is the meaning of "Surely man walks with an image" (Ps 39:7).
>
> I. Tishby, *The Wisdom of the Zohar* (3 vols.; London: The Littman Library of Jewish Civilization, 1994), 2.787–89.

[418] G. Quispel, "Genius and Spirit," in: *Gnostica, Judaica, Catholica. Collected Essays of Gilles Quispel* (ed. J. van Oort; NHMS 55; Leiden: Brill, 2008), 103–18 at 108.

[419] Quispel, "Genius and Spirit," 108.

These spatial dynamics, where the ocularcentric manifestation (in the form of Jesus) is portrayed as ascending from water, and the aural manifestation as descending from heaven, recall the processions of the respective powers in the transfiguration story, explored earlier. There too, the second power in the form of Jesus is portrayed as ascending the mountain, while the first power, in the form of the divine voice, is depicted as descending from heaven. In the synoptic baptismal accounts the descent of the divine voice is further accentuated by the descent of the pteromorphic mediator—the dove,[420] which makes the rabbinic parallels between the *bat qol* and the dove especially significant. From *b. Ber.* 3a we learn about another such parallel: "R. Jose says . . . 'I heard a divine voice, cooing like a dove, and saying: Woe to the children, on account of whose sins I destroyed My house and burnt My temple and exiled them among the nations of the world!'"[421] Reflecting on this text, Jarl Fossum suggests that "the cooing of doves in the temple could be seen as a reminiscence of the *bat qol*, 'daughter of the voice,' a substitute for the prophetic Spirit."[422] Fossum notes, moreover, that in another passage, reflected in the *Targum to the Song of Songs* 2:12,[423] the voice of the turtledove is said to be the "voice of the Spirit of deliverance," or in other interpretations, the voice of the Messiah or Moses.[424]

In the light of these rabbinic developments, scholars often interpret God's aural address in the baptismal story as an equivalent to the rabbinic *bat qol*[425]—an aural

---

[420] Joy Palachuvattil underlines the interrelationship between the descent of the dove and the descent of the divine voice, noting that "the heavenly voice cannot also be interpreted without reference to the vision. In explaining Jesus' seeing the Spirit descending upon him we have established that its importance lies in proclaiming the mystery of Jesus." Palachuvattil, *"He Saw,"* 83.

[421] Epstein, *The Babylonian Talmud. Berachot*, 3a.

[422] J. Fossum, "Dove," in: *Dictionary of Deities and Demons in the Bible* (ed. K. van der Toorn, B. Becking, and P. W. van der Horst; 2nd ed.; Leiden: Brill, 1999), 264.

[423] A passage from the Song of Songs 2:12, "the flowers appear on the earth; the time of singing has come, and the voice of the turtledove is heard in our land," is rendered in the *Targum of Canticles* in the following way:

> And Moses and Aaron, who are compared to palm branches, have appeared in order to work miracles in the land of Egypt. The time for cutting off the firstborn has arrived, and the voice of the holy spirit, [proclaiming] the redemption of which I spoke to Abraham, your forefather, you have already heard—how I said to him: "Moreover, the people whom they shall serve will I judge, and after that they will depart with much possessions." Now I want to perform what I promised to him through My Word.
> P. S. Alexander, *The Targum of Canticles, Translated, with a Critical Introduction, Apparatus, and Notes* (ArBib 17a; Collegeville: Liturgical Press, 2003), 108.

Reflecting on this targumic tradition, Philip Alexander notes that the *Targum of Canticles* "takes 'the voice of the turtledove' as referring to the proclamation of the redemption uttered by the holy spirit in fulfillment of the promise to Abraham 'between the pieces' (Gen 15:14)—an event that happened in the Land of Israel ('our Land')." Alexander, *The Targum of Canticles*, 108.

[424] Fossum, "Dove," 264.

[425] Analyzing the divine Voice tradition in Mark Joel Marcus observes that "the *bat qol* here at the baptism . . . is very similar to that at the transfiguration (Mark 9:7 pars.)." Marcus, "Jesus' Baptismal Vision," 513.

manifestation, prominent in various two powers in heaven accounts, including b. Hag. 15a and 3 Enoch 16, the texts that openly render the divine utterance as the *bat qol*.[426]

Many scholars affirm the presence of the *bat qol* tradition in the baptism and the transfiguration stories, the aural expressions still maintaining their close ties with the biblical lore. Thus, Markus Bockmuehl says that "for all three Synoptics, the *bat qol* speaks in biblical terms (Isa 42:1; Ps 2:7) of the Father's love from whom the Spirit proceeds upon the Son of God, who will in due course bestow him on his people (Luke 24:49; Acts 2:17–18, 33)."[427]

Other scholars are reluctant to embrace the concept of the *bat qol*, often interpreting it as an "echo" of the divine voice, rather than the direct speech of God. Robert Guelich points out that while some scholars have identified the divine voice at the baptism with the *bat qol* of rabbinic writings, the relative inferiority of this sound, if compared to God's word as spoken through the prophets, makes this connection unlikely.[428] Joy Palachuvattil also suggests that the voice from heaven is the voice of God and not a "daughter of the voice" (*bat qol*) by arguing that in the synoptic scenes of Jesus' baptism and the transfiguration God's voice is much greater than in the call-narratives of the Hebrew Bible.[429]

Joel Marcus, while acknowledging that the *bat qol* is not the unmediated voice of God, but its echo, and that traditions such as *t. Sota* 13:2 explicitly contrast it with the Holy Spirit, posits that some rabbinic devaluations of the *bat qol* may represent a polemic against Christian claims of extraordinary audial revelations, including those reflected in the synoptic baptism and transfiguration accounts.[430]

Scholars point out that the revelation of the divine voice dominates the revelatory framework of the narrative, positioned here, as in the transfiguration account, strategically at the end of the story. According to Marcus,

> the vision consists of two things seen by Jesus (torn heavens, Spirit descending) and one thing heard by him (heavenly voice). Of these components, the final one, the voice, is climactic because of its position at the end, the change from sight to sound, the greater number of words devoted to it, and its role in interpreting the visual elements.[431]

The Dove Symbolism

The pteromorphic imagery found in the synoptic baptismal accounts has baffled readers, remaining a stumbling block for generations of ancient and modern

---

[426] On the *bat qol*, see Barrett, *The Holy Spirit and the Gospel Tradition*, 39–41; B. Chilton, *Rabbi Paul: An Intellectual Biography* (New York: Doubleday, 2004), 126–27; J. Jeremias, *New Testament Theology* (New York: Charles Scribner's Sons, 1971), 81.

[427] Bockmuehl, "The Baptism of Jesus as 'Super-Sacrament' of Redemption," 88.

[428] Guelich, *Mark 1–8:26*, 33.

[429] Palachuvattil, *"He Saw,"* 84.

[430] Marcus, *Mark 1–8*, 160–61. On this, see also Davies and Allison, *Matthew*, 1.335–36.

[431] Marcus, *Mark 1–8*, 164.

interpreters. Traditionally, scholars see in the dove's descent an element of the apocalyptic worldview, a conceptual dimension underlined in the narrative by the dove's peculiar movement. In respect to this procession scholars note that "the object of Jesus' vision (the dove) is depicted as 'coming down' (καταβαῖνον), a conception that conveys the heavenly origin of various visionary entities in apocalyptic texts."[432]

Another important detail is the way in which the pteromorphic entity becomes "united" with the protagonist during its descent, which is described differently in each of the synoptic accounts. Mark recounts that the dove/spirit descended *into* Jesus (εἰς αὐτόν),[433] while Matthew and Luke suggest that the dove descended *upon* Jesus (ἐπ' αὐτόν). Marcus notes that since in classical Greek εἰς means "into," some scholars[434] have suggested that Mark attempts to depict the Spirit as uniting itself with Jesus in a way that may reflect Hellenistic conceptions.[435] Marcus points out, however, that "in Koine Greek, including Mark, *eis* + accusative can be equivalent to *epi* + accusative, which means 'upon.'"[436] Yet the protagonist's interaction with the dove/spirit and its nature remain unclear. The possibility of Jesus' transformation during the encounter is rarely discussed by scholars, although it may represent an ocularcentric conceptual counterpart to Jesus' metamorphosis in the transfiguration account.[437]

A third detail pertinent to our discussion of the theophanic molds in the gospels is the tradition about the Spirit's descent in *bodily form*, a reading attested in the Lukan version of the baptismal narrative.[438] Here, again a reference to the corporeal form of the celestial being may underline a connection with the ocularcentric conceptual streams, in which depictions of celestial beings are often enveloped with distinctive

---

[432] Mathewson, "The Apocalyptic Vision of Jesus," 95.

[433] Hans Dieter Betz notes that "εἰς αὐτόν can mean different things: 'toward him,' 'pointing to him,' 'settling down on him,' or 'entering into him.'" H. D. Betz, "Jesus' Baptism and the Origins of the Christian Ritual," in: *Ablution, Initiation, and Baptism* (ed. D. Hellholm et al.; BZNW 176; Berlin: Walter de Gruyter, 2011), 377–96 at 386.

[434] F. Hahn, *Christologische Hoheitstitel. Ihre Geschichte im frühen Christentum* (3rd ed., FRLANT 83; Göttingen: Vandenhoeck & Ruprecht, 1966), 342–43.

[435] Marcus, *Mark 1–8*, 160.

[436] Marcus, *Mark 1–8*, 160.

[437] The most common interpretation understands the text to be speaking of an induction into the messianic office. Joel Marcus suggests that

> the descent of the Spirit at Jesus' baptism might be taken to imply that it was at this point that he became the Messiah and Son of God. . . . The descent of the Spirit upon Jesus, therefore, could be understood as his induction into messianic office; such a view would cohere with an interpretation of the divine pronouncement in 1:11, "You are my son," that sees it as performative, i.e. accomplishing what it proclaims.
>
> Marcus, *Mark 1–8*, 160.

[438] With respect to this imagery, Guelich observes that

> although the dove has subsequently become a popular symbol for the Holy Spirit, the occurrence of the imagery in 1:10 appears to stand without previous parallel, a fact that should discourage any attempt at finding a symbolic meaning behind this reference. The importance of the event lies in the Spirit's coming. It corresponds to the OT hope integral to the age of salvation (e.g., esp. Isa 11:2; 42:1; 61:1; cf. 63:10–64:1), a motif fundamental to John's comparison between his baptism and that of the Greater One (1:8). The Spirit comes, therefore, as God's enabling presence to equip Jesus for his ministry.
>
> Guelich, *Mark 1–8:26*, 35.

corporeal imagery. Scholars have reflected on the Spirit's curious appearance in bodily form and its ties to the bodily transformation of Jesus in the transfiguration accounts.[439]

In the light of these connections it is possible that the Spirit's descent in "the bodily form" on Jesus is intended to highlight the corporeality of the second power. Such emphasis may indicate that the symbolism of the spirit-dove is somehow associated with the tradition of the divine form—the *Kavod*. According to Fossum, already in Ezekiel 8[440] the divine Glory appears to be identified with the spirit.[441]

The emphasis on the pteromorphic shape of the celestial visitor, who in the baptism story descends on the human protagonist, may be closely related to the aforementioned process that associated Jesus with the ocularcentric *Kavod* ideology. In this respect the pteromorphic shape of the celestial mediator, present in the narrative with Jesus, poses no threat to the new guardian of the ocularcentric *Kavod* paradigm, who in his anthropomorphic shape remains the only viable candidate for the visible representation of the divine *Kavod*. Note also that the stripping of anthropomorphic attributes from the potential celestial contender may represent a polemical strategy found in other apocalyptic accounts.[442]

Pteromorphic Glory

In an attempt to clarify the conceptual background of the pteromorphic imagery found in the baptismal accounts, various witnesses, including later rabbinic traditions, have relentlessly been ushered into discussion. However, one important source has been neglected. This neglected evidence can be found in the *Apocalypse of Abraham*, where

---

[439] See Heil, *The Transfiguration of Jesus*, 77, footnote 5.

[440] Ezek 8:2–4 relates the following tradition:

> I looked, and there was a figure that looked like a human being; below what appeared to be its loins it was fire, and above the loins it was like the appearance of brightness, like gleaming amber. It stretched out the form of a hand, and took me by a lock of my head; and *the spirit* lifted me up between earth and heaven, and brought me in visions of God to Jerusalem, to the entrance of the gateway of the inner court that faces north, to the seat of the image of jealousy, which provokes to jealousy. And the glory of the God of Israel was there, like the vision that I had seen in the valley.

[441] In relation to these conceptual currents Fossum observes that

> there is some evidence from later times that the Spirit of God could be seen as the Glory, but biblical foundations for this view are weak. In Ezek 8:3, the glory, whose body is described in the preceding verse, is referred to as the "Spirit." A Jewish amulet, which appears to allude to Ezekiel's description of the retreat and return of the Glory, calls the Glory *pneuma hagiōsynēs*, the "Spirit of Holiness." T. Levi 18:6 says: "And the Glory of the Most High shall burst forth upon him, and the Spirit of Understanding and Sanctification shall rest upon him." This refers to the possession of the Spirit by the Messiah in Isa 11:2. The Glory might here be equated with the Spirit. In Rom 1:4, it is said that Jesus was designated as the Son of God "*kata* the Spirit of Holiness by resurrection from the dead." The resurrection of Jesus may here be understood as being effected by the Spirit. In Rom 6:1, it is stated plainly that Jesus was resurrected by the Glory of God.
>
> J. Fossum, "Glory," in: *Dictionary of Deities and Demons in the Bible* (ed. K. van der Toorn, B. Becking, and P. W. van der Horst; 2nd ed.; Leiden: Brill, 1999), 352.

[442] On this polemical strategy, see A. A. Orlov, "The Pteromorphic Angelology in the *Apocalypse of Abraham*," *CBQ* 71 (2009): 830–42.

the second power in the form of the angel Yahoel appears both as the pteromorphic manifestation and as an embodiment of the divine *Kavod*.[443]

As we have already learned from the first part of our study, the portrayal of Yahoel in the *Apocalypse of Abraham* represents an amalgam of various depictions of the divine Glory, ranging from Ezek 1:27 to the *Shiʿur Qomah* accounts.[444] This description is especially reminiscent of various portrayals of the *Kavod* in later Jewish mysticism, where one frequently finds references to "chrysolite" in descriptions of the divine Form: "His body is like chrysolite. His light breaks tremendously from the darkness."[445] Scholars have also noted a close similarity between Yahoel and the Ezekielian *Kavod*, since both entities are portrayed with rainbow-like attributes.[446] In fact, the features of the divine Glory became so accentuated in Yahoel's appearance that several distinguished students of Jewish apocalyptic and mystical traditions, for example, Christopher Rowland and Jarl Fossum, even suggest that Yahoel is conceived in the *Apocalypse of Abraham* as the missed rider of the divine Chariot.

Such transference of the *Kavod* imagery to the second power in and of itself is not uncommon in early Jewish apocalyptic and mystical accounts where the principal angels or the exalted patriarchs and prophets are often portrayed as representations or even measures (*Shiʿur Qomah*) of the glorious anthropomorphic extent of God. However, what is unusual in the second power's depiction found in the *Apocalypse of Abraham* is that the work's authors, like the authors of the synoptic baptismal accounts, depart from the standard anthropomorphic descriptions of the celestial mediators by seeking to portray Yahoel as a pteromorphic creature. The combination of *Kavod* and bird features is relevant for our study of Jesus' baptism, where the appearance of the enigmatic celestial visitor in the form of a dove is associated with the peculiar details of Ezekiel's account of the divine *Kavod*. We must therefore closely consider these developments. *Apoc. Ab.* 11:2-3 unveils details regarding Yahoel's pteromorphic physique that became closely intertwined in this passage with peculiar features of the *Kavod*:

> The appearance of the griffin's (ноryero)[447] body was like sapphire, and the likeness of his face like chrysolite, and the hair of his head like snow, and a turban on his

---

[443] Edward Dixon's study of the dove symbolism in Mark 1:10 serves as an apt illustration of this consistent neglect of the *Apocalypse of Abraham*'s evidence where the angel Yahoel appears in the pteromorphic form. Thus, Dixon states that to his knowledge,

> no ancient Jewish text depicts a "descent" of any heavenly being in the form of a bird. The OT tells of many descents—of angels, of the Lord, of the Spirit from the Lord (once, in Isa 63:14 LXX), and so on—but the idea that these figures should descend as birds is completely foreign to the OT and other pre-Markan Jewish literature.

E. P. Dixon, "Descending Spirit and Descending Gods: A 'Greek' Interpretation of the Spirit's 'Descent as a Dove' in Mark 1:10," *JBL* 128 (2009): 759–80 at 764.

[444] Fossum, *The Name of God*, 319–20.

[445] Fossum, *The Name of God*, 319–20.

[446] Fossum, *The Name of God*, 319–20; Rowland, *The Open Heaven*, 102–3.

[447] The reading is supported by mss A, C, D, I, H, and K. It is omitted in mss B, S, and U. For the sigla of the known manuscripts of the *Apocalypse of Abraham*, see Kulik, *Retroverting Slavonic Pseudepigrapha*, 97.

head like the appearance of the bow in the clouds, and the closing of his garments [like] purple, and a golden staff [was] in his right hand.[448]

The Slavonic word "ноүеro" used here in the description of Yahoel's body, has long puzzled scholars. This term can be translated as "his leg" (ноүеro), but this rendering does not fit the larger context of Yahoel's description. Previous translators preferred to drop the puzzling word and translate the first sentence of Yahoel's description as "the appearance of his body was like sapphire."[449] Alexander Kulik, however, recently offered a hypothesis that the Slavonic term "ноүеro" might derive from the Slavonic "ногъ" or "ногуи"—"a griffin." He proposed that the whole phrase can be translated as "the appearance of the griffin's (ногуева) body" and thus refers to the bird-like body of Yahoel. Additionally, Yahoel may even be a composite creature, a man-bird, since he is depicted in *Apoc. Ab.* 10:4 as the angel who is sent to Abraham in "the likeness of a man." Kulik argues this because Yahoel has "hair on his head," as well as his hands, since he is able to hold a golden staff, and it appears that "only the torso of Yahoel must be of griffin-like appearance, while his head is like that of a man."[450]

The *Apocalypse of Abraham*'s tendency to depict the second power in the form of a bird-like *Kavod* looks quite unusual. Elsewhere I have suggested that in Yahoel's composite bird-human body, one can possibly detect a polemical interaction with the anthropomorphic traditions of the divine Glory.[451] Yet the amalgam of the attributes of a bird and the divine *Kavod* provides an important parallel to the synoptic baptism accounts, with their enigmatic merger of two beings—one pteromorphic and the other anthropomorphic, the corporeal amalgam associated in the synoptic gospels with the memory of the Ezekielian *Kavod* traditions.

In this respect, it is noteworthy that some scholars have entertained the possibility that the dove imagery may also be connected with the *Kavod* traditions. According to John Moorhead, the descent of the Spirit as a dove recalls the Sinai encounter in the LXX, where the same word καταβαίνω describes the deity's descent on the mountain (Exod 19:11ff.).[452]

---

[448] Kulik, *Retroverting Slavonic Pseudepigrapha*, 19.

[449] Kulik, Retroverting Slavonic Pseudepigrapha, 83.

[450] Kulik's hypothesis about the pteromorphic features of Yahoel has been supported by Basil Lourié, "Review of A. Kulik's *Retroverting Slavonic Pseudepigrapha*," *JSP* 15.3 (2006): 229–37 at 233.

[451] Orlov, "Pteromorphic Angelology in the *Apocalypse of Abraham*," 830–42.

[452] J. Moorhead, "The Spirit and the World," *GOTR* 26 (1981): 113–17 at 114. Weighing in on the apocalyptic significance of καταβαίνον in the Matthean account Mathewson notes that

> the object of Jesus' vision (the dove) is depicted as "coming down" (καταβαῖνον), a conception which conveys the heavenly origin of various visionary entities in apocalyptic texts (cf. Acts 10:11). Thus John's Apocalypse contains numerous instances of the seer witnessing objects descending (καταβαίνω) from heaven, using the participle form (Rev 3:12; 10:1; 12:12; 13:13; 16:21; 18:1; 20:1, 9; 21:2, 10). In the *Testament of Abraham* 7:3 the seer envisions a figure coming down out of heaven (also v. 5). Further, an important feature of records of apocalyptic visionary experiences is communication through the medium of symbol. Thus in apocalyptic fashion the descending object in Matthew's vision report is depicted in symbolic language. While it is not necessary at this point to decide on the precise derivation of the dove (περιστεράν) imagery in v. 16, the point to be made is that it is likely that the dove constitutes the object of Jesus' vision. It is

Another important similarity between the *Apocalypse of Abraham* and the synoptic accounts of Jesus' baptism involves not only the descent of the pteromorphic mediator, but also the revelation of the divine Voice following the mediator's *katabasis*, an aural revelation that affirms Yahoel's mission and identity. Importantly, Yahoel makes his first appearance in the *Apocalypse of Abraham* in the course of the two powers traditions, manifested in the dual theophany. As we have learned previously in this study, like the synoptic baptismal stories, both the first and the second powers in the *Apocalypse of Abraham* also appear in two separate and distinctive theophanic modes: one as the ocularcentric, visible manifestation, and the other as the aniconic voice.

There are, however, some important differences between the two accounts. While in the *Apocalypse of Abraham* the pteromorphic mediator is described in detail, in the baptism accounts his depiction is strikingly terse and subdued. Second, in the Abrahamic pseudepigraphon, the pteromorphic mediator is clearly separated from the human protagonist during the whole course of the narration, while in the baptismal accounts his individuality appears to be absorbed by the seer through his descending procession upon the protagonist.

Yet the aftermaths of the initial encounters between the pteromorphic and human protagonists still reveal some striking similarities. Recall, for instance, how in the *Apocalypse of Abraham* the pteromorphic mediator takes Abraham to the wilderness of Sinai. Such guidance in a peculiar procession is comparable to the consequences of the baptism account, where the pteromorphic spirit takes Jesus into the desert. According to Guelich, "the context conveys the impression of the Spirit's coming (1:10) and taking control of Jesus (cf. Luke 4:1), illustrated by his impelling Jesus to go into the wilderness."[453] Here, like the pteromorphic Yahoel who serves as the guide for the human adept in the *Apocalypse of Abraham*, the spirit (who was earlier described as a dove) also leads the seer into the wilderness. These spatial transitions present in both accounts now bring us to the temptation narrative—an account that is closely linked to Jesus' baptism in the synoptic gospels.

The Image of God Traditions and the Temptation Story

As previously noted, in many early Jewish accounts the second powers were often envisioned as the image of God or the *iqonin*. We suggested that the second power's role as the image could feature implicitly in the transfiguration story via the symbolism of Jesus' luminous face, which often appears as the conceptual cognate of the *iqonin* in the Jewish pseudepigrapha and targumic materials. Could it be possible that the hidden presence of the second power as the image of God is also found in the baptism

---

commonly asserted that ὡσεὶ περιστεράν functions adverbially to modify καταβαῖνον, purportedly indicating the manner in which the spirit descends owing to its syntactical position following καταβαῖνον. However, since Matthew claims that Jesus saw (εἶδεν) it, the ὡσεὶ περιστεράν probably describes the visible form of the spirit (πνεῦμα), indicating the content of εἶδεν. As R. T. France correctly observes, "some visible form must have been required to make the descent of the invisible Spirit visible."
      Mathewson, "The Apocalyptic Vision of Jesus," 95–96.

[453] Guelich, *Mark 1–8:26*, 38.

account? According to scholars, later Christian interpreters often construed Jesus' endowment with the spirit in the form of the descending dove as the reinstallation of the divine image, the entity lost after the first couple's transgression in Eden. Syrian traditions regarding Christ's deposition of the glorious robe in the Jordan also appear to be tied to the concept of the image of God. Despite these later interpretations, the synoptic baptismal narratives lack explicit references to the symbolism of the divine image.

Nevertheless, the tradition about the second power's identity as the *imago Dei* may still be present in the story of Jesus' temptation, which immediately follows the baptismal narrative in all three synoptic gospels.[454] In the light of such an option, we turn to consider the synoptic renderings of the temptation story.

Possible conceptual links connecting Jesus' baptism and Jesus' temptation in the wilderness have been acknowledged by scholars. Kristian Bendoraitis, for example, reminds us that one of the defining characteristics of the temptation narrative in all three synoptics is its placement following Jesus' baptism.[455] It is more than merely the sequential order of the accounts that suggest these two narratives should be read together. According to Bendoraitis, the Spirit descending as Jesus rises out of the water is likely the same Spirit that leads Jesus out into the desert (Mt 3:16; Mk 1:10; Lk 3:22; cf. Jn 1:32).[456] The author also reminds us of another significant link, namely that, in Matthew and Luke, Jesus is recognized as the "Son of God" at his baptism and temptation. While Luke separates the baptism from the temptation with his genealogy, culminating with Jesus as the Son of God (Lk 3:38), Matthew tightly draws the two narratives together, seating the temptation narrative right against the final words of the baptism, the voice from heaven announcing, "This is my beloved Son, in whom I am very pleased" (Mt 3:17).[457] Joel Marcus points out to another link that ties the two narratives together, that is, their common Adamic typology. He notes that echoes of baptismal theology are especially likely in the temptation story, because in early Christianity, as noted previously, the newly baptized person was often associated with Adam.[458]

If the temptation story is indeed, as scholars have suggested, narratively and ideologically linked with the baptism account, it is intriguing that in the descriptions of Jesus' ordeal in the wilderness one finds several details that recall constructions of the second power as God's image in early Jewish two powers in heaven traditions.

---

[454] On this, see A. A. Orlov, "The Veneration Motif in the Temptation Narrative of the Gospel of Matthew: Lessons from the Enochic Tradition," in: idem, *Divine Scapegoats: Demonic Mimesis in Early Jewish Mysticism* (Albany: SUNY, 2015), 153–66.

[455] K. A. Bendoraitis, *"Behold, the Angels Came and Served Him": A Compositional Analysis of Angels in Matthew* (London, New York: Bloomsbury, 2015), 55. See also S. Hultgren, *Narrative Elements in the Double Tradition: A Study of Their Place within the Framework of the Gospel Narrative* (BZNW 113; Berlin, New York: Walter de Gruyter, 2002), 119ff; G. H. P. Thompson, "Called—Proved—Obedient: A Study in the Baptism and Temptation Narratives of Matthew and Luke," *JTS* 11 (1960): 1–12 at 9.

[456] Bendoraitis, *"Behold, the Angels Came and Served Him,"* 55.

[457] Bendoraitis, *"Behold, the Angels Came and Served Him,"* 55.

[458] Marcus, *Mark 1–8*, 170.

Especially notable are the motifs of angelic opposition and angelic veneration. As mentioned earlier several two powers in heaven accounts, including the *Primary Adam Books*, *2 Enoch*, the *Ladder of Jacob*, and, possibly, the *Exagoge*, contain references to angelic opposition and veneration,[459] which are understood in these texts as crucial narrative markers connected with the second power's role as God's image.[460] Such dynamics of exaltation and demotion, often intertwined in Jewish apocalyptic and mystical lore, are closely related to the process of the protagonist's initiation into the office of the second power, thus paradoxically reaffirming his unique standing in the celestial community. As we have already witnessed in our analysis of the Adamic lore, such angelic opposition often comes from former favorites of the deity who are reluctant to surrender their former office of the second power to the deity's new appointee. In the *Primary Adam Books* the role of the new power's opponent is openly assigned to Satan and his angels. Recall how in this compilation of early Adamic legends the antagonist himself recounts his demotion from his former place of dominion and glory, revealing that his demise was caused by his rejection to prostrate himself before the new favorite of the deity—the protoplast.

Even a cursory look at the temptation story reflected in the synoptic gospels reveals a striking panoply of allusions to the previously discussed Adamic traditions. As with the *Primary Adam Books*, which attempt to portray Satan as a celestial power endowed with ocularcentric attributes of the deity, the temptation story too associates its enigmatic antagonist with a plethora of exalted attributes, placing him on the high mountain of his theophany, reminiscent of the summit of the divine glory as depicted in some biblical and pseudepigraphical accounts. The choice of the mountain for the antagonist's apotheosis is not happenstance; in the Enochic and Mosaic traditions, such a place is often envisioned as the seat of the divine Glory.

If the Gospel of Matthew is indeed has in mind the mountain of the *Kavod*, Satan's ability to show Jesus all the kingdoms of the world and their splendor (καὶ δείκνυσιν αὐτῷ πάσας τὰς βασιλείας τοῦ κόσμου καὶ τὴν δόξαν αὐτῶν) may refer to the celestial curtain *Pargod*, the sacred veil of the divine Face, which in *3 Enoch* 45 is described as an entity that literally shows all generations and all kingdoms simultaneously at the same time.[461]

---

[459] Fletcher-Louis also detects the memory of such motifs in Philo's treatise *On the Creation of the World* and 4Q381 frag. 1, lines 10–11. On this, see Fletcher-Louis, *Jesus Monotheism*, 262–63.

[460] Reflecting on the story of the angelic veneration of Adam in the various versions of the *Primary Adam Books*, Fletcher-Louis notes that in these accounts "Adam was created to bear divine presence as God's physical and visual image." Fletcher-Louis, *Jesus Monotheism*, 272–73. On this see also C. Fletcher-Louis, "The Worship of Divine Humanity as God's Image and the Worship of Jesus," in *The Jewish Roots of Christological Monotheism. Papers from the St. Andrews Conference on the Historical Origins of the Worship of Jesus* (ed. C. Newman et al.; JSJSS 63; Leiden: Brill, 1999), 112–28; idem, *All the Glory of Adam*, 101–2.

[461] In *3 Enoch* 45:1–4 we find the following tradition about the *Pargod*:

> R. Ishmael said: Metatron said to me: Come and I will show you the curtain of the Omnipresent One which is spread before the Holy One, blessed be he, and on which are printed all the generations of the world and their deeds, whether done or to be done, till the last generation . . . the kings of Judah and their generations, their deeds and their

Associating the antagonist with the familiar symbolism usually linked in Jewish apocalyptic and mystical accounts with the *Kavod* imagery is noteworthy. Furthermore, in the temptation story, Satan fulfills the roles of Jesus' psychopomp and *angelus interpres*. Here we may find again an allusion to Satan's role as a celestial power. Scholars have noted terminological similarities between the temptation narrative and Deut 34:1-4,[462] in which God serves as an *angelus interpres* during Moses' vision on Mount Nebo, showing the prophet the Promised Land and giving him an explanation.[463]

As we remember, in the *Primary Adam Books* Satan serves as a negative mirror of the positive second power, often revealing and reaffirming the protagonist's exalted status by comparing the new appointee's glory with his previous exalted state. In the *Primary Adam Books*, therefore, much information about the second power's exalted attributes is conveyed through Satan's laments. The *Primary Adam Books* also contain the tradition of the conflict between two second powers when a former holder of this exalted office retaliates, attempting to seduce and corrupt the deity's new appointee. To do this, the antagonist often assumes an apparition of the first power attempting to mislead and corrupt the new beloved of the deity. It appears that this tradition of the negative second power that serves as an inverse mirror and contender with the protagonist can also be found in the longer versions of the temptation story reflected in Matthew and Luke.

Furthermore, in the temptation story one may find an attempt to reverse the transferal of the power from Satan to the human protagonist—Satan, who fell because he once refused to venerate the First Adam, now attempts to take revenge by asking the Last Adam to bow down before him.[464]

Such Adamic typology has often been recognized as a conceptual backbone of the temptation story. Some studies suggest that the chain of pivotal Adamic themes, known from biblical and extra-biblical accounts, is already introduced in the terse narration of Jesus' temptation in the Gospel of Mark.[465] For example, Joachim Jeremias draws

---

acts; the kings of Israel and their generations, their deeds and their acts; the kings of the gentiles and their generations, their deeds and their acts.
Alexander, "3 Enoch," 1.295-98.

[462] Then Moses went up from the plains of Moab to Mount Nebo, to the top of Pisgah, which is opposite Jericho, and the Lord showed him the whole land: Gilead as far as Dan, all Naphtali, the land of Ephraim and Manasseh, all the land of Judah as far as the Western Sea, the Negeb, and the Plain—that is, the valley of Jericho, the city of palm trees—as far as Zoar. The Lord said to him, "This is the land of which I swore to Abraham, to Isaac, and to Jacob, saying, I will give it to your descendants; I have let you see it with your eyes, but you shall not cross over there."

[463] J. Dupont, "L'arrière-fond biblique du récit des tentations de Jésus," *NTS* 3 (1957): 287-304 at 297.

[464] Already the earliest Christian interpreters including Justin (*Dial.* 103) and Irenaeus (*Adv. Haer.* 5.21.2) saw the temptation of Jesus as the reversal of Adam's sin. On this, see D. C. Allison, "Behind the Temptations of Jesus: Q 4:1-13 and Mark 1:12-13," in: *Authenticating the Activities of Jesus* (ed. B. D. Chilton and C. Evans; NTTS 28.2; Leiden: Brill, 2002), 196.

[465] W. A. Schultze, "Der Heilige und die wilden Tiere. Zur Exegese von Mc 1,13b," *ZNW* 46 (1955): 280-83; A. Feuillet, "L'épisode de la tentation d'après l'Évangile selon Saint Marc (I, 12-13)," *EstBib* 19 (1960): 49-73; J. Jeremias, "Nachwort zum Artikel von H.-G. Leder," *ZNW* 54 (1963): 278-79; idem, "Adam," in: *Theological Dictionary of the New Testament* (ed. G. Kittel; tr. G. W. Bromiley; 10 vols.; Grand Rapids: Eerdmans, 1964), 1.141-43; A. Vargas-Machuca, "La tentación de Jesús según Mc. 1, 12-13 ¿Hecho real o relato de tipo haggádico?" *EE* 48 (1973): 163-90; P. Pokorný, "The Temptation Stories and Their Intention," *NTS* 20 (1973-1974): 115-27; J. Gnilka, *Das Evangelium*

attention to the phrase in Mark 1:12 that Jesus "was with the wild beasts" (ἦν μετὰ τῶν θηρίων). In his opinion, this phrase is reminiscent of the protoplast who lived among the wild animals in paradise according to Gen 2:19. Jeremias suggests that Jesus may be foreseen in the Gospel of Mark as an eschatological Adam who restores peace between humans and animals.[466] He proposes that Mark's account sets forth a belief that "paradise is restored, the time of salvation is dawning; that is what ἦν μετὰ τῶν θηρίων means. Because the temptation has been overcome and Satan has been vanquished, the gate to paradise is again opened."[467] Jeremias' insights are important; they point to the possibility that already in the Markan version of the temptation, Jesus is understood as the image of God. In this respect, it is noteworthy that the *Primary Adam Books* construe the possession/absence of the image of God in humanity through motifs of obedience or hostility of the wild beast.

Jeremias also discerns the Adamic typology in the saying that the angels gave Jesus "table service" (διηκόνουν αὐτῷ). In his view, "this feature, too, is part of the idea of paradise and can only be understood in that light. Just as, according to the Midrash, Adam lived on angels' food in paradise, so the angels give Jesus nourishment. The table-service of angels is a symbol of the restored communion between man and God."[468] Like Jeremias, Richard Bauckham sees a cluster of Adamic motifs in Mark's version of the temptation story and argues that it envisions Jesus "as the eschatological Adam who, having resisted Satan, instead of succumbing to temptation as Adam did, then restores paradise: he is at peace with the animals and the angels serve him."[469] From this perspective, Jesus' temptation by Satan plays a pivotal role in the unfolding of the Adamic typological appropriations.[470] Dale Allison draws attention to another possible connection with the protoplast story, wondering whether Mark's "forty days" is also part of his Adamic typology. He notes that, according to *Jubilees* 3:9, Adam was placed

---

nach Markus (2 vols.; EKKNT 2.1-2; Zürich: Benziger; Neukirchen-Vluyn: Neukirchener Verlag, 1978-1979), 1.58; Guelich, *Mark 1-8:26*, 38-39; R. Bauckham, "Jesus and the Wild Animals (Mark 1:13): A Christological Image for an Ecological Age," in: *Jesus of Nazareth: Lord and Christ: Essays on the Historical Jesus and New Testament Christology* (ed. J. B. Green and M. Turner; Grand Rapids: Eerdmans, 1994), 3-21; J. Gibson, *Temptations of Jesus in Early Christianity* (JSNTSS 112; Sheffield: Sheffield Academic Press, 1995), 65-66; Allison, "Behind the Temptations of Jesus: Q 4:1-13 and Mark 1:12-13," 196-99.

[466] Jeremias, *New Testament Theology*, 69. The theme of alienation between humanity and animals already looms large in the *Book of Jubilees*. This theme receives further development in the *Primary Adam Books* in which Eve and Seth are predestined to encounter a hostile beast.

[467] Jeremias, *New Testament Theology*, 69-70.

[468] Jeremias, *New Testament Theology*, 70.

[469] Bauckham, "Jesus and the Wild Animals," 6.

[470] Davies and Allison suggest that

> in Mark 1:12-13 Jesus is probably the last Adam (cf. Rom 5.12-21; 1 Cor 15.42-50; Justin, *Dial.* 103; *Gospel of Philip* 71.16-21; Irenaeus. *Adv. haer.* 5.21.2). He, like the first Adam, is tempted by Satan. But unlike his anti-type, he does not succumb, and the result is the recovery of paradise (cf. *Testament of Levi* 18.10) the wild beasts are tamed and once again a man dwells with angels and is served by them.
>
> Davies and Allison, *Matthew*, 1.356.

in Eden forty days after he was created, and in the *Primary Adam Books*, Adam does penance for forty days.[471]

In Matthew and Luke, the Adamic typology hinted at in Mark receives further conceptual development, being closely tied to the familiar details of the two powers in heaven traditions. Thus, in Matthew's gospel, the tempter asks Jesus to prostrate himself, suggesting literally that he will "fall down" (πεσών) before Satan. Matthew seems here to adhere more closely to the Adamic blueprint than Luke, since in Luke πεσών is missing.

One can see that the theme of the veneration of the second power is introduced in the temptation story by Satan himself. This motif of obeisance is paradoxically reformulated in the novel Christian framework of the synoptic gospels. Instead of giving obeisance to the new second power, who has just been inaugurated in his office at the Jordan theophany, the antagonist seeks to reverse this process by asking Jesus to venerate him. It again demonstrates the essential nature of angelic obeisance in the formation of the identity and authority of the second power. As noted earlier, such veneration usually comes at the final stage of the second power's initiation, signifying the acceptance of the adept into his role as the leader of the celestial community.

The motif of the rejection of veneration, explicitly narrated in the *Primary Adam Books* and suggested in *2 Enoch*, plays its own unique role here, too, in the temptation story in the construction of the Christian second power, since by refusing to venerate Satan, Jesus offers revenge for Satan's protological refusal.

Additionally, it is not coincidental that the protagonist's installation into the office of the second power, which unfolds in the baptism and temptation narratives, does not result in mockery but ends with actual angelic veneration.[472] We learn from Mark and Matthew that the angels ministered to him (διηκόνουν αὐτῷ). As in the *Primary Adam Books* and *Sefer Hekhalot*, where the angelic opposition precedes the angelic veneration,[473] here, too, in the temptation story, Jesus' opposition to the veneration of Satan is narrated prior to the angelic obeisance at the end of the story. One can see that the temptation story curiously deconstructs the protological scenario of the second power's inauguration found in the *Primary Adam Books* and *2 Enoch* by refashioning it into a new eschatological ordeal that still preserves memories of the old encounter.[474] In this

---

[471] Allison, "Behind the Temptations of Jesus: Q 4:1–13 and Mark 1:12–13," 198.

[472] In relation to this motif, Crispin Fletcher-Louis suggests that

> given the ways in which Jesus undoes the disobedience of Adam in the Gospel temptation story, it is also possible that the reference to the angels serving him in Mark 1:13 and Matt 4:11 is an allusion to the story of the angelic worship of Adam that is meant to alert the reader to the fact that the angels already recognize his true identity as the one who inaugurates a new humanity, and in rendering him worshipful service they anticipate the future worship of him by his human followers.
>
> Fletcher-Louis, *Jesus Monotheism*, 263.

Commenting on Mark 1:13, Joel Marcus notes that "*diakonein* can also, like Heb. ʿbd, mean 'worship' (see e.g. Josephus *Ant.* 7.365), and this may be a secondary nuance in our passage, in view of the legend in which Adam is worshiped by angels." Marcus, *Mark*, 1.168–71.

[473] The similar order is also intimated in *2 Enoch*.

[474] The angelic veneration can be seen as an essential step of the second power's initiation into his role as the custodian of the ocularcentric trend. Since the routine of obeisance and worship is often

respect it does not appear coincidental that in the inauguration of the Christian second power into the office of the image of God, as in the case of the Jewish second power in the form of Adam, the old antagonist of the story, Satan, must remain present.

Concluding this section of our study, we can see that if the baptism and temptation narratives were indeed interconnected in the minds of the synoptic authors, the temptation story may be seen as an important subsequent development in the construction of the second power that began earlier in the baptism story. In this narrative sequel, the second power is now envisioned as the image of God. The role of the *imago Dei*, encompassed in the temptation story via the distinctive motifs of veneration and rejection, prominent in early Jewish accounts, further affirms the possibility that in the baptism-temptation conceptual nexus we indeed encounter an elaborate construction of the Christian second power.

Conclusion

Our analysis of the synoptic baptismal accounts points to the possibility that these conceptual developments attempt to enhance Jesus' profile as the embodiment of the divine *Kavod*. Several details of the baptismal narratives support this possibility.

First, the synoptic accounts reveal the tendency to connect Jesus' baptism with the imagery and terminology present in the first chapter of Ezekiel, a distinctive portion of the prophetic book where the *Kavod* imagery reaches its most developed symbolic expression in the entire Hebrew Bible.

Second, the Gospel of Mark, as well as the other synoptic gospels, unveils the connection between the imagery of the torn heaven in the baptismal story and the symbolism of the torn veil of the Jerusalem temple in the story of Jesus' crucifixion. Two depictions, unified by similar terminology, point to the possibility that the ripped curtain that concealed the *Kavod* in the earthly sanctuary is associated in the minds of the synoptic authors with the opening of the cosmological curtain of the *Kavod* represented by the heavens.

Third, in the light of the aforementioned connections with the Book of Ezekiel and its later interpretations, in which the divine Glory is said to be manifested to the great prophet in the watery mirror of the river Chebar, it is likely that, in the synoptic accounts, Jesus' baptism was also understood as a revelation of the divine *Kavod* in the Jordan river.

Fourth, the positioning of the protagonist in the midst of the primordial waters is reminiscent of some depictions of the divine Glory in early Jewish biblical and extra-biblical materials, where the *Kavod* is portrayed in the midst of the cosmological waters.

Fifth, possible similarities are demonstrated between the motif of the second power in the form of the pteromorphic *Kavod* in the *Apocalypse of Abraham* and the conceptual synthesis found in the synoptic accounts where the human protagonist is

---

interpreted by scholars as a sign of Jesus' divinity, it raises an important question: does the transference the ocularcentric attributes and practices associated with the *Kavod* complex from the deity to the second power makes these qualities less "divine"? This issue has not received any attention from scholars who see Jesus' worship as a sign of his divinity.

unified with the heavenly mediator in the form of a bird in the midst of the Ezekielian allusions to the *Kavod* imagery.

Sixth, Jesus' role as the image of God is indicated in the temptation story, a narrative in the synoptic gospels closely tied to the baptism account, which also points to the possibility of Jesus' role as the divine *Kavod*. Already within the Pauline corpus, Jesus' role as εἰκών was closely linked with the notions of μορφή and δόξα.[475]

Finally, the reception history of the synoptic baptismal accounts in later Christian interpretation suggests that Jesus' baptism was the first step to his glorification; in these materials the process is inundated with the peculiar ocularcentric markers of the *Kavod* ideology.

Taken together, these features point to the possibility that the synoptic accounts attempted to closely connect Jesus' baptism with the *Kavod* traditions, thus envisioning him as the representation of the divine Glory.

---

[475] Several scholars have argued that Paul's usage of μορφή, δόξα, and εἰκών are closely related to each other, if not synonymous. On this see F.-W. Eltester, *Eikon im Neuen Testament* (BZNW 23; Berlin: Töpelmann, 1958), 23–24, 133; J. Fossum, "Jewish-Christian Christology and Jewish Mysticism," *VC* 37 (1983): 263–69; idem, *The Name of God and the Angel of the Lord*, 283–84; idem, "Glory," 351–52; idem, *The Image of the Invisible God*, 29; J. Héring, *Le Royaume de Dieu et sa venue. Étude sur l'espérance de Jésus et de l'apôtre Paul* (Paris: Alcan, 1937), 159 ff.; Jervell, *Imago Dei*, 195–98; R. Martin, *Carmen Christi: Philippians ii, 5–11 in Recent Interpretation and in the Setting of Early Christian Worship* (SNTSMS 4; Cambridge: Cambridge University Press, 1967), 106–16; G. Stroumsa, "Forms of God: Some Notes on Metatron and Christ," *HTR* 76 (1983): 269–88 at 284. Yet some scholars argue against such conceptual parallels. Thus, Markus Bockmuehl notes that "it has therefore become commonplace to argue that the theological context of Phil 2:6 effectively makes it the equivalent of the terms εἰκών and δόξα. Despite the widespread claims to this effect, however, the evidence for actual synonymy is very weak indeed.... Their conceptual proximity does not make them synonyms." Bockmuehl, "The Form of God," 8.

Conclusion

Our analysis of the earliest Christological developments reflected in the baptism and transfiguration stories of the synoptic gospels demonstrates that Jesus' divine identity gradually developed, in part, through his endowment with the attributes and functions of the ocularcentric deity. The synoptic gospels provide important details of this transference by elaborating the ocular and anthropomorphic settings of this transition. This transition is clearly demonstrated in the account of Jesus' transfiguration, where Jesus' metamorphosis is enveloped in the features of the ocularcentric theophanic paradigm as well as the details of its conceptual counterpart—the aural trend applied in the depiction of the divine Voice. Earliest Christology thus emerges from this creative tension of the ocularcentric and aural theophanic molds in which the deity steadily abandons its corporeal profile in order to relieve the symbolic space for the new guardian, who from then on becomes the image and the glory of the invisible God. At the conclusion of our study we must now reiterate some important similarities and differences between the two powers traditions reflected in the story of Jesus' baptism and transfiguration.

First, in both accounts the respective powers are portrayed in two different theophanic modes. While the audial expression of the first power is almost identical in both accounts, the presentations of the ocularcentric features of the second power are different in the baptism and transfiguration stories.

Second, in both accounts the processions of the respective powers are identical; the ocularcentric second power in the form of Jesus appears first, and is followed by the manifestation of the first power in the form of the *bat qol*.

Third, the directions of the respective powers' movements also appear to be identical. The second powers are portrayed as ascending (in the baptism story from the water and in the transfiguration story to the mountain), while the first powers are portrayed as descending from heaven in the form of the *bat qol*. The dynamics reflecting the ascent and descent of the respective powers were present in the previously explored Jewish two powers in heaven accounts. As we recall in the *Exagoge* of Ezekiel the Tragedian, Moses ascends to the throne that was vacated by the "noble man," who descends from his divine seat.

Fourth, in both the baptism-temptation narrative and the transfiguration story, the second powers are understood as the restorers and embodiments of the *imago Dei*.

Fifth, both accounts attest to the metamorphoses of the second powers: in the transfiguration account it is expressed through the terminological description of Jesus' ontological passage (the word μετεμορφώθη) as well as through alteration of the adept's clothing and face. In the baptism account, the transformation of the second power is intimated through the descent of the dove/spirit in/upon the protagonist and his passage through water.

Sixth, both accounts rely on the Hebrew Bible's pivotal theophanies in their endowment of the Christian second power with the ocularcentric attributes. The transfiguration story uses the story of Moses' vision of the divine Glory on Mount Sinai. The baptism narratives employ another crucial theophanic nexus of the Hebrew Bible, namely, the revelation of the divine *Kavod* to the son of Buzi on the river Chebar, in its construction of Jesus' novel theophanic profile.

Seventh, in both accounts the hierarchy between the respective powers is established through a set of similar narrative devices, namely, through resembling processions and addresses in which we find a declaration of the second power's sonship. The hierarchical relationships between the respective powers, in which the second power is labeled as the "Son," are evocative of several previously explored two powers in heaven accounts (Dan 7, the *Book of the Similitudes*) where the second power's designations are also tied to the concept of sonship (the Son of Man). This strategy is also detected in later Jewish two powers in heaven developments. As one can recall, in *Hagiga Bavli* the *bat qol*'s address includes the phrase "backsliding children," again hinting at the first power's fatherly role.[1]

Eighth, in both accounts the initiations of the second powers are invested with the *Kavod* symbolism. In the baptism story such imagery is subdued and mainly implied through parallels with the Ezekielian traditions. In contrast, the transfiguration openly assigns several prominent ocularcentric attributes to Jesus while placing him on the high mountain, a transition which likely suggests the enthronement of the second power.

Ninth, the ocularcentric details—only hinted in the baptism story—reach their fully expressed form in the transfiguration account. The baptism and transfiguration episodes can therefore be seen as unfolding conceptual steps in which Jesus' ocularcentric profile receives its steady expansion.

Tenth, although the gradual transference of the *Kavod*'s attributes and functions have often been noted in previous studies, these investigations rarely take into account another important dynamic present in the New Testament materials, namely, the gradual withdrawal of the deity into the invisible aural mode. The accentuation of these two inverse theophanic developments and their significance for early Christology represent the main contribution of this study.

---

[1] *b. Hag.* 15a reads that "a *bat qol* went forth and said: Return, ye backsliding children—except Aher. [Thereupon] he said: Since I have been driven forth from yonder world, let me go forth and enjoy this world. So Aher went forth into evil courses." Epstein, *The Babylonian Talmud. Hagiga* 15a.

Bibliography

Texts and Translations

Alexander, Philip. "3 (Hebrew Apocalypse of) Enoch." In *The Old Testament Pseudepigrapha*. Edited by J. H. Charlesworth, 1.223–315. 2 vols. New York: Doubleday, 1983–1985.

———. *The Targum of Canticles. Translated, with a Critical Introduction, Apparatus, and Notes*. The Aramaic Bible 17a. Collegeville, MN: The Liturgical Press, 2003.

Andersen, Francis. "2 (Slavonic Apocalypse of) Enoch." In *The Old Testament Pseudepigrapha*. Edited by J. H. Charlesworth, 1.91–221. 2 vols. New York: Doubleday, 1983–1985.

Anderson, Gary and Stone, Michael. *A Synopsis of the Books of Adam and Eve. Second Revised Edition*. EJL 17. Atlanta, GA: Scholars Press, 1999.

Attridge, Harold. *Nag Hammadi Codex I (The Jung Codex): Introductions, Texts, Translations, Indices*. NHS 22. Leiden: Brill, 1985.

Blanc, Cécile. *Origène, Commentaire sur Saint Jean. Tome I (Livres I-V)*. SC 120. Paris: Cerf, 1966.

Böttrich, Christfried. *Das slavische Henochbuch*. JSHRZ 5. Gütersloh: Gütersloher Verlagshaus, 1995.

Braude, William. *The Midrash on Psalms*. 2 vols. YJS 13. New Haven, CT: Yale University Press, 1959.

Braude, William and Kapstein, Israel. *Pesikta de-Rab Kahana. R. Kahana's Compilation of Discourses for Sabbaths and Festal Days*. Philadelphia, PA: Jewish Publication Society of America, 1975.

Brock, Sebastian and Kiraz, George. *Ephrem the Syrian. Select Poems*. Provo, UT: Brigham Young University Press, 2006.

Charles, Robert Henry and Forbes, Nevill. "The Book of the Secrets of Enoch." In *The Apocrypha and Pseudepigrapha of the Old Testament*. Edited by R. H. Charles, 2.425–269. 2 vols. Oxford: Clarendon Press, 1913.

Charles, Robert Henry and Morfill, William Richard. *The Book of the Secrets of Enoch*. Oxford: Clarendon Press, 1896.

Clements, Ronald. *Deuteronomy*. Old Testament Guides. Sheffield: JSOT, 1989.

Collins, John. "Sibylline Oracles." In *The Old Testament Pseudepigrapha*. Edited by J. H. Charlesworth, 1.317–472. 2 vols. New York: Doubleday, 1983–1985.

———. *Daniel*. Hermeneia. Minneapolis, MN: Fortress, 1993.

Colson, Francis Henry and Whitaker, George Herbert. *Philo*. 10 vols. LCL. Cambridge, MA: Harvard University Press, 1929–1964.

Cowley, Arthur Ernest. *The Samaritan Liturgy*. 2 vols. Oxford: Clarendon Press, 1908.

Cranfield, Charles. *The Gospel According to St. Mark*. Cambridge: Cambridge University Press, 1983.

Danby, Herbert. *The Mishnah*. Oxford: Oxford University Press, 1992.

Davies, William David and Allison, Dale. *A Critical and Exegetical Commentary on the Gospel According to Saint Matthew*. ICC. Edinburgh: T&T Clark, 1991.

Davila, James. *Hekhalot Literature in Translation: Major Texts of Merkavah Mysticism*. SJJTP 20. Leiden: Brill, 2013.

De Jonge, Marinus, Harm Wouter Hollander, Henk Jan De Jonge, and Theo Korteweg, *The Testaments of the Twelve Patriarchs. A Critical Edition of the Greek Text*. PVTG 12. Leiden: Brill, 1978.

Denis, Albert-Marie. *Fragmenta pseudepigraphorum quae supersunt Graeca*. PVTG 3. Leiden: Brill, 1970.

Dillmann, August. *Das Buch Henoch. Übersetzt und erklärt*. Leipzig: Wilhelm Vogel, 1853.

Dörries, Hermann, Erich Klostermann, and Matthias Kroeger, *Die 50 geistlichen Homilien des Makarios*. PTS 4. Berlin: Walter de Gruyter, 1964.

Epstein, Isidore. *The Babylonian Talmud*. London: Soncino, 1935-1952.

Evans, Craig. *Mark 8:27—16:20*. WBC 34B. Nashville, TN: Thomas Nelson, 2001.

Falls, Thomas, Michael Slusser, and Thomas Patrick Halton, *St. Justin Martyr. Dialogue with Trypho*. Washington, DC: Catholic University of America Press, 2003.

Ferrar, William John. *The Proof of the Gospel: Being the Demonstratio Evangelica of Eusebius of Cæsarea*. 2 vols. London: Society for Promoting Christian Knowledge, 1920.

Fitzmyer, Joseph. *The Gospel According to Luke I–IX*. AB 28. Garden City, NY: Doubleday, 1981.

France, Richard Thomas. *Matthew*. TNTC 1. Grand Rapids, MI: Eerdmans, 1985.

———. *The Gospel of Mark. A Commentary on the Greek Text*. NIGTC 2. Grand Rapids, MI: Eerdmans, 2002.

———. *The Gospel of Matthew*. NICNT. Grand Rapids, MI: Eerdmans, 2007.

Freedman, Harry and Simon, Maurice. *Midrash Rabbah*. 10 vols. London: Soncino, 1961.

Friedlander, Gerald. *Pirke de Rabbi Eliezer*. 2nd ed. New York: Hermon Press, 1965.

García Martínez, Florentino and Tigchelaar, Eibert. *The Dead Sea Scrolls Study Edition*. 2 vols. Leiden; New York; Köln: Brill, 1997.

Gnilka, Joachim. *Das Evangelium nach Markus*. 2 vols. EKKNT 2.1-2. Zürich; Benziger; Neukirchen-Vluyn: Neukirchener Verlag, 1978-1979.

———. *Das Matthäusevangelium*. 2 vols. HTKNT. Freiburg: Herder, 1986-1988.

Gray, Theodosia. *The Homilies of Saint Gregory the Great "On the Book of the Prophet Ezekiel."* Etna, CA: Center for Traditionalist Orthodox Studies, 1990.

Guelich, Robert. *Mark 1–8:36*. WBC 34A. Dallas, TX: Word, 1989.

Guggenheimer, Heinrich. *The Jerusalem Talmud. Tractates Taʿaniot, Megillah, Hagigah and Moʿed Qatan. Edition, Translation and Commentary*. SJ 85. Berlin: Walter de Gruyter, 2015.

Gundry, Robert. *Matthew: A Commentary on His Handbook for a Mixed Church under Persecution*. Grand Rapids, MI: Eerdmans, 1994.

———. *Matthew: A Commentary on His Literary and Theological Art*. 2nd ed. Grand Rapids, MI: Eerdmans, 1994.

Hagner, Donald. *Matthew 1–13*. WBC 33A. Dallas, TX: Word, 1993.

———. *Matthew 14–28*. WBC 33B. Dallas, TX: Word Books, 1995.

Holladay, Carl. *Fragments from Hellenistic Jewish Authors*. 3 vols. SBLTT 30. Pseudepigrapha Series 12. Atlanta, GA: Scholars, 1989.

Jacobson, Howard. *The Exagoge of Ezekiel*. Cambridge: Cambridge University Press, 1983.

———. *A Commentary on Pseudo-Philo's Liber Antiquitatum Biblicarum, with Latin Text and English Translation*. 2 vols. AGAJU 31. Leiden: Brill, 1996.

Johnston, Edward. "Ephraim Syrus. Fifteen Hymns for the Feast of Epiphany." In *A Select Library of Nicene and Post-Nicene Fathers of the Christian Church. Second Series*. Edited by P. Schaff and H. Wace, 13.265–89. New York: The Christian Literature Company, 1898.

Juel, Donald. *Mark*. Augsburg Commentary on the New Testament. Minneapolis, MN: Augsburg, 1990.

Jülicher, Adolf. *Itala: Das neue Testament in altlateinischer Überlieferung*. 4 vols. Berlin: Walter de Gruyter, 1938–1963.

Kee, Howard. "Testaments of the Twelve Patriarchs." In *The Old Testament Pseudepigrapha*. Edited by J. H. Charlesworth, 1.775–828. 2 vols. New York: Doubleday, 1983–1985.

Knibb, Michael. *The Ethiopic Book of Enoch: A New Edition in the Light of the Aramaic Dead Sea Fragments*. 2 vols. Oxford: Clarendon Press, 1978.

Kulik, Alexander. *Retroverting Slavonic Pseudepigrapha: Toward the Original of the Apocalypse of Abraham*. TCS 3. Atlanta, GA: Scholars, 2004.

Kulik, Alexander and Minov, Sergey. *Biblical Pseudepigrapha in Slavonic Tradition*. Oxford: Oxford University Press, 2016.

Lane, William. *The Gospel According to Mark*. NICNT 2. Grand Rapids, MI: Eerdmans, 1974.

Lattke, Michael. *Odes of Solomon: A Commentary*. Hermeneia. Minneapolis, MN: Fortress, 2009.

Lauterbach, Jacob. *Mekhilta de-Rabbi Ishmael: A Critical Edition on the Basis of the Manuscripts and Early Editions with an English Translation, Introduction and Notes*. 2 vols. Philadelphia, PA: The Jewish Publication Society, 2004.

Lods, Adolphe. *Le livre d'Hénoch: fragments grecs découverts à Akhmîm (Haute-Egypte): publiés avec les variantes du texte éthiopien*. Paris: Ernest Leroux, 1892.

Lunt, Horace. "Ladder of Jacob." In *The Old Testament Pseudepigrapha*. Edited by J. H. Charlesworth, 2.401–11. 2 vols. New York: Doubleday, 1983–1985.

Luz, Ulrich. *Matthew 1–7*. Hermeneia. Minneapolis, MN: Fortress, 1989.

———. *Matthew 8–20*. Hermeneia. Minneapolis, MN: Fortress, 2001.

Macdonald, John. *Memar Marqah. The Teaching of Marqah*. 2 vols. BZAW 84. Berlin: Walter de Gruyter, 1963.

Maloney, George. *Pseudo-Macarius. The Fifty Spiritual Homilies and the Great Letter*. New York: Paulist Press, 1992.

Marcus, Joel. *Mark 1–8: A New Translation with Introduction and Commentary*. AB 27. New York: Doubleday, 2000.

———. *Mark 8–16: A New Translation with Introduction and Commentary*. AB 27A. New Haven, CT: Yale University Press, 2009.

Marcus, Ralph. *Philo. Questions and Answers on Genesis*. LCL. Cambridge, MA/London: Harvard University Press/Heinemann, 1949.

McCarthy, Carmel. *Saint Ephrem's Commentary on the Diatessaron*. Oxford: Oxford University Press, 1993.

McNamara, Martin, Robert Hayward, and Michael Maher, *Targum Neofiti 1 and Pseudo-Jonathan: Exodus*. ArBib 2. Collegeville, MN: Liturgical Press, 1994.

McVey, Kathleen. *Ephrem the Syrian: Hymns*. Classics of Western Spirituality. New York: Paulist Press, 1989.

Milik, Józef Tadeusz. *The Books of Enoch: Aramaic Fragments of Qumrân Cave 4*. Oxford: Clarendon Press, 1976.

Morris, Leon. *The Gospel According to Matthew*. PNTC. Grand Rapids, MI: Eerdmans, 1992.

Mras, Karl. *Eusebius, Praeparatio Evangelica.* 2 vols. GCS 43.1–2. Leipzig: J. C. Hinrichs, 1954–1956.
Neusner, Jacob. *Pesiqta de Rab Kahana.* 2 vols. BJS 122–23. Atlanta, GA: Scholars, 1987.
———. *The Tosefta. Translated from the Hebrew with a New Introduction.* 2 vols. Peabody, MA: Hendrickson, 2002.
Nickelsburg, George. *1 Enoch 1: A Commentary on the Book of 1 Enoch: Chapters 1–36; 81–108.* Hermeneia. Minneapolis, MN: Fortress, 2001.
Nickelsburg, George and VanderKam, James. *1 Enoch 2: A Commentary on the Book of 1 Enoch: Chapters 37–82.* Hermeneia. Minneapolis, MN: Fortress, 2012.
Nolland, John. *The Gospel According to Matthew.* NIGTC 1. Grand Rapids, MI: Eerdmans, 2005.
Odeberg, Hugo. *3 Enoch or the Hebrew Book of Enoch.* New York: KTAV, 1973.
Osborne, Grant. *Matthew.* ZECNT. Grand Rapids, MI: Zondervan, 2010.
Philonenko-Sayar, Belkis and Philonenko, Marc. *L'Apocalypse d'Abraham. Introduction, texte slave, traduction et notes.* Semitica 31. Paris: Librairie Adrien-Maisonneuve, 1981.
Resch, Alfred. *Agrapha: Aussercanonische Schriftfragmente.* Leipzig: J. C. Hinrichs, 1906.
Roberts, Alexander and Donaldson, James. *The Ante-Nicene Fathers. Translations of the Writings of the Fathers down to A.D. 325.* 10 vols. Grand Rapids, MI: Eerdmans, 1980.
Robinson, Joseph Armitage. *Origen, Philocalia.* Cambridge: Cambridge University Press, 1893.
Sabourin, Leopold. *The Gospel According to St. Matthew.* Bombay: St. Paul, 1982.
Schäfer, Peter, Schlüter, Margaret and von Mutius, Hans George. *Synopse zur Hekhalot-Literatur.* TSAJ 2. Tübingen: Mohr Siebeck, 1981.
Scheck, Thomas. *Origen. Homilies 1—14 on Ezekiel.* ACW 62. New York: Paulist Press, 2010.
———. *St. Jerome. Commentary on Ezekiel.* ACW 71. New York: The Newman Press, 2017.
Schneemelcher, Wilhelm. *New Testament Apocrypha.* 2 vols. Cambridge/ Louisville, KY: James Clarke & Co./Westminster/John Knox Press, 1991.
Shutt, Robert. "Letter of Aristeas." In *The Old Testament Pseudepigrapha.* Edited by J. H. Charlesworth, 2.7–34. 2 vols. New York: Doubleday, 1983–1985.
Smith, Jonathan. "Prayer of Joseph." In *The Old Testament Pseudepigrapha.* Edited by J. H. Charlesworth, 2.699–714. 2 vols. New York: Doubleday, 1983–1985.
Snell, Bruno. *Tragicorum Graecorum fragmenta I.* Göttingen: Vandenhoeck & Ruprecht, 1971.
Sperling, Harry and Simon, Maurice. *The Zohar.* 5 vols. London/New York: Soncino, 1933.
Taylor, Vincent. *The Gospel According to St Mark: The Greek Text with Introduction, Notes, and Indexes.* New York: St. Martin's Press, 1966.
Thackeray, Henry and Marcus, Ralph. *Josephus.* 10 vols. LCL. Cambridge, MA: Harvard University Press, 1926–1965.
Thomson, Robert. *The Teaching of St. Gregory: An Early Armenian Catechism.* Cambridge, MA: Harvard University Press, 1970.
Tishby, Isaiah. *The Wisdom of the Zohar.* 3 vols. London: The Littman Library of Jewish Civilization, 1994.
Turner, David. *Matthew.* BECNT. Grand Rapids, MI: Baker, 2008.
Valavanolickal, Kuriakose. *Aphrahat, Demonstrations.* CTSI 3-4. Kerala: HIRS, 1999.
Van der Horst, Pieter and Newman, Judith. *Early Jewish Prayers in Greek.* CEJL. Berlin: Walter de Gruyter, 2008.
Weinfeld, Moshe. *Deuteronomy 1–11.* AB 5. New York: Doubleday, 1991.
Wertheimer, Solomon. *Batei Midrashot.* 2 vols. Jerusalem: Mossad Harav Kook, 1950–1953.

White, Cynthia. *Origen. Homilies on Joshua*. Washington, DC: Catholic University of America Press, 2002.
Williams, Frank. *The Panarion of Epiphanius of Salamis*. 2 vols. NHS 35–36. Leiden: Brill, 1987, 1994.
Yarbro Collins, Adela. *Mark: A Commentary*. Hermeneia. Minneapolis, MN: Fortress, 2007.

Secondary Literature

Aagaard, Anna Marie. "'My Eyes Have Seen Your Salvation.' On Likeness to God and Deification in Patristic Theology." *Religion & Theology* 17 (2010): 302–28.
Abrahams, Israel. *Studies in Pharisaism and the Gospels*. 2 vols. Library of Biblical Studies. New York: Ktav, 1967.
Abrams, Daniel. "The Boundaries of Divine Ontology: The Inclusion and Exclusion of Metatron in the Godhead." *HTR* 87 (1994): 291–321.
Alexander, Philip. "3 Enoch and the Talmud." *JSJ* 18 (1987): 40–68.
Allison, Dale. "The Baptism of Jesus and a New Dead Sea Scroll." *BAR* 18 (1992): 58–60.
———. *The New Moses: A Matthean Typology*. Minneapolis, MN: Fortress, 1993.
———. "Behind the Temptations of Jesus: Q 4:1–13 and Mark 1:12–13." In *Authenticating the Activities of Jesus*. Edited by B. D. Chilton and C. Evans, 195–213. NTTS 28.2. Leiden: Brill, 2002.
Anderson, Gary. "The Exaltation of Adam and the Fall of Satan." In *Literature on Adam and Eve. Collected Essays*. Edited by G. Anderson, M. Stone, and J. Tromp, 83–110. SVTP 15. Brill: Leiden, 2000.
Ashton, John. *Understanding the Fourth Gospel*. Oxford: Clarendon Press, 1991.
Assefa, Daniel. *L'Apocalypse des animaux (1 Hen 85–90): une propagande militaire? Approches narrative, historico-critique, perspectives théologiques*. JSJSS 120. Leiden: Brill, 2007.
Balentine, Samuel. *The Hidden God: The Hiding of the Face of God in the Old Testament*. Oxford: Oxford University Press, 1983.
Barr, James. "Theophany and Anthropomorphism in the Old Testament." In *Congress Volume. Oxford 1959*. Edited by G. W. Anderson, 31–38. VTSup 7. Leiden: Brill, 1960.
Barrett, Charles Kingsley. *The Holy Spirit and the Gospel Tradition*. London: SPCK, 1947.
Bauckham, Richard. "Jesus and the Wild Animals (Mark 1:13): A Christological Image for an Ecological Age." In *Jesus of Nazareth: Lord and Christ: Essays on the Historical Jesus and New Testament Christology*. Edited by J. B. Green and M. Turner, 3–21. Grand Rapids, MI: Eerdmans, 1994.
———. "The Throne of God and the Worship of Jesus." In *The Jewish Roots of Christological Monotheism*. Edited by C. C. Newman, J. R. Davila, and G. S. Lewis, 43–69. JSJSS 63. Leiden: Brill, 1999.
———. *Jesus and the God of Israel: God Crucified and Other Essays on the New Testament's Christology of Divine Identity*. Milton Keynes/Grand Rapids, MI: Paternoster/Eerdmans, 2008.
———. "Moses as 'God' in Philo of Alexandria: A Precedent for Christology?" In *The Spirit and Christ in the New Testament and Christian Theology: Essays in Honor of Max Turner*. Edited by I. H. Marshall, 246–65. Grand Rapids, MI: Eerdmans, 2012.

Beale, Gregory. *The Temple and the Church's Mission: A Biblical Theology of the Dwelling Place of God*. NSBT 17. Downers Grove, IL: Apollos, 2004.

Becker, Joachim. *Gottesfurcht im Alten Testament*. AnBib 25. Rome: St. Martin's Press, 1965.

Begg, Christopher. "Josephus's Portrayal of the Disappearances of Enoch, Elijah, and Moses." *JBL* 109 (1990): 691–93.

Belleville, Linda. *Reflections of Glory: Paul's Polemical Use of the Moses-Doxa Tradition in 2 Corinthians 3.1–18*. JSNTSS 52. Sheffield: Sheffield Academic Press, 1991.

Bendoraitis, Kristian. *"Behold, the Angels Came and Served Him": A Compositional Analysis of Angels in Matthew*. London/New York: Bloomsbury, 2015.

Betz, Hans Dieter. "Jesus' Baptism and the Origins of the Christian Ritual." In *Ablution, Initiation, and Baptism: Late Antiquity, Early Judaism, and Early Christianity*, Edited by D. Hellholm, T. Vegge, Ø. Norderval, and C. Hellholm, 377–96. BZNW 176. Berlin: Walter de Gruyter, 2011.

Blenkinsopp, Joseph. "Deuteronomic Contribution to the Narrative in Genesis-Numbers: A Test-Case." In *Those Elusive Deuteronomists. The Phenomenon of Pan-Deuteronomism*. Edited by L. S. Schearing and S. L. McKenzie, 84–115. JSOTSS 268. Sheffield: Sheffield Academic Press, 1999.

Bloch-Smith, Elizabeth. "'Who is the King of Glory?' Solomon's Temple and Its Symbolism." In *Scripture and Other Artifacts. Essays on the Bible and Archeology in Honor of Philip J. King*. Edited by P. King, M. Coogan, J. Cheryl Exum, and L. Stager, 19–31. Louisville: Westminster, 1994.

Bockmuehl, Markus. "'The Form of God' (Phil 2:6): Variations on a Theme of Jewish Mysticism." *JTS* 48 (1997): 1–23.

———. "The Baptism of Jesus as 'Super-Sacrament' of Redemption." *Theology* 115 (2012): 83–91.

Bohak, Gideon. *Joseph and Aseneth and the Jewish Temple in Heliopolis*. EJL 10. Atlanta, GA: Scholars, 1996.

Boobyer, George Henry. *St. Mark and the Transfiguration Story*. Edinburgh: T&T Clark, 1942.

Borsch, Frederick. *The Son of Man in Myth and History*. London: SCM Press, 1967.

Böttrich, Christfried. "Apocalyptic Tradition and Mystical Prayer in the Ladder of Jacob." *JSP* 23 (2014): 290–306.

Boyarin, Daniel. "Two Powers in Heaven; or, the Making of a Heresy." In *The Idea of Biblical Interpretation: Essays in Honor of James L. Kugel*. Edited by H. Najman and J. H. Newman, 331–70. JSJSS 83. Leiden: Brill, 2003.

———. *Border Lines: The Partition of Judaeo-Christianity*. Philadelphia, PA: University of Pennsylvania Press, 2004.

———. "Beyond Judaisms: Meṭaṭron and the Divine Polymorphy of Ancient Judaism." *JSJ* 41 (2010): 323–65.

———. "Is Metatron a Converted Christian." *Judaïsme Ancien-Ancient Judaism* 1 (2013): 13–62.

Brock, Sebastian. "St Ephrem on Christ as Light in Mary and in the Jordan: Hymni de Ecclesia 36." *ECR* 7 (1975): 79–88.

———. "Clothing Metaphors as a Means of Theological Expression in Syriac Tradition." In *Typus, Symbol, Allegorie bei den östlichen Vätern und ihren Parallelen im Mittelalter*. Edited by M. Schmidt, 11–38. Regensburg: Friedrich Pustet, 1982.

———. *The Luminous Eye: The Spiritual World of St. Ephrem*. Kalamazoo, MI: Cistercian Publications, 1992.

Bunta, Silviu. *Moses, Adam and the Glory of the Lord in Ezekiel the Tragedian: On the Roots of a Merkabah Text*. PhD diss. Marquette University, 2005.

———. "The Likeness of the Image: Adamic Motifs and *Tselem* Anthropology in Rabbinic Traditions about Jacob's Image Enthroned in Heaven." *JSJ* 37 (2006): 55–84.

Capes, David. "Intertextual Echoes in the Matthean Baptismal Narrative." *BBR* 9 (1999): 37–49.

Chester, Andrew. *Messiah and Exaltation: Jewish Messianic and Visionary Traditions and New Testament Christology*. WUNT 207. Tübingen: Mohr Siebeck, 2007.

Chilton, Bruce. *Rabbi Paul: An Intellectual Biography*. New York: Doubleday, 2004.

Christman, Angela. "*What Did Ezekiel See?*" *Christian Exegesis of Ezekiel's Vision of the Chariot from Irenaeus to Gregory the Great*. BAC 4. Boston, MA: Brill, 2005.

Clements, Ronald. *God and Temple: The Idea of the Divine Presence in Ancient Israel*. Philadelphia, PA: Fortress, 1965.

Clifford, Richard. *The Cosmic Mountain in Canaan and the Old Testament*. Cambridge, MA: Harvard University Press, 1972.

Coats, George. *Moses: Heroic Man, Man of God*. JSOTSS 57. Sheffield: JSOT Press, 1988.

Coblentz Bautch, Kelley. *A Study of the Geography of 1 Enoch 17–19: "No One Has Seen What I Have Seen."* JSJSS 81. Leiden: Brill, 2003.

Cohn, Robert. "The Mountains and Mount Zion." *Judaism* 26 (1977): 97–115.

Collins, John. *The Apocalyptic Vision of the Book of Daniel*, Harvard Semitic Monographs 16. Missoula: Scholars Press, 1977.

———. *The Scepter and the Star. The Messiahs of the Dead Sea Scrolls and Other Ancient Literature*. New York: Doubleday, 1995.

———. *The Apocalyptic Imagination: An Introduction to Jewish Apocalyptic Literature*. 2nd ed. Grand Rapids, MI: Eerdmans, 1998.

———. "Enoch and the Son of Man: A Response to Sabino Chialà and Helge Kvanvig." In *Enoch and the Messiah Son of Man: Revisiting of the Book of Parables*. Edited by G. Boccaccini, 216–27. Grand Rapids, MI: Eerdmans, 2007.

Coutts, Joshua. *The Divine Name in the Gospel of John: Significance and Impetus*. WUNT 2.447. Tübingen: Mohr Siebeck, 2017.

Cox, Ronald. *By the Same Word: Creation and Salvation in Hellenistic Judaism and Early Christianity*. BZNW 145. Berlin: Walter de Gruyter, 2007.

Cullmann, Oscar. *The Christology of the New Testament*. Philadelphia, PA: Westminster, 1963.

Dan, Joseph. "Anafiel, Metatron and the Creator." *Tarbiz* 52 (1982): 447–57 [in Hebrew].

———. *The Ancient Jewish Mysticism*. Tel-Aviv: MOD Books, 1993.

Daniélou, Jean. "Le symbolisme eschatologique de la Fête des Tabernacles." *Irénikon* 31 (1958): 19–40.

———. *The Lord of History: Reflections on the Inner Meaning of History*. London: Longmans, 1958.

Davies, John Gordon. *He Ascended into Heaven: A Study in the History of Doctrine*. London: Lutterworth Press, 1958.

Davila, James. "Of Methodology, Monotheism and Metatron: Introductory Reflections on Divine Mediators and the Origins of the Worship of Jesus." In *The Jewish Roots of Christological Monotheism: Papers from the St. Andrews Conference on the Historical Origins of the Worship of Jesus*. Edited by C. C. Newman, J. R. Davila, and G. S. Lewis, 3–20. JSJSS 63. Leiden: Brill, 1999.

———. *Descenders to the Chariot: The People Behind the Hekhalot Literature*. JSJSS 70. Leiden: Brill, 2001.

———. "Review of *A Transparent Illusion: The Dangerous Vision of Water in Hekhalot Mysticism: A Source-Critical and Tradition-Historical Inquiry* by C. R. A. Morray-Jones." *JBL* 121 (2002): 585–88.

Davis, Carl Judson. *The Name and Way of the Lord: Old Testament Themes, New Testament Christology*. JSNTSS 129. Sheffield: Sheffield Academic Press, 1996.

De Jonge, Marinus. *God's Final Envoy: Early Christology and Jesus' Own View of His Mission*. Grand Rapids, MI: Eerdmans, 1998.

De Vaux, Roland. *Ancient Israel: Its Life and Institutions*. Grand Rapids, MI: Eerdmans, 1997.

Dearman, Andrew. "Theophany, Anthropomorphism, and the *Imago Dei*: Some Observations about the Incarnation in Light of the Old Testament." In *The Incarnation: An Interdisciplinary Symposium on the Incarnation of the Son of God*. Edited by S. T. Davis, D. Kendall, and G. O'Collins, 31–46. Oxford: Oxford University Press, 2004.

Dennis, Geoffrey. "The Use of Water as a Medium for Altered States of Consciousness in Early Jewish Mysticism: A Cross-Disciplinary Analysis." *AC* 19 (2008): 84–106.

Deutsch, Nathaniel. *The Gnostic Imagination: Gnosticism, Mandaeism, and Merkabah Mysticism*. Leiden: Brill, 1995.

———. *Guardians of the Gate. Angelic Vice Regency in Late Antiquity*. BSJS 22. Leiden: Brill, 1999.

Dixon, Edward. "Descending Spirit and Descending Gods: A 'Greek' Interpretation of the Spirit's 'Descent as a Dove' in Mark 1:10." *JBL* 128 (2009): 759–80.

Donaldson, Terence. *Jesus on the Mountain: A Study in Matthean Theology*. JSNTSS 8. Sheffield: JSOT, 1985.

Drijvers, Han and Reinink, Gerrit Jan. "Taufe und Licht. Tatian, Ebionäerevangelium und Thomasakten." In *Text and Testimony: Essays on New Testament and Apocryphal Literature in Honour of A. F. J. Klijn*. Edited by T. Baarda, A. Hilhorst, G. P. Luttikhuizen, and A. S. van der Woude, 91–110. Kampen: J. H. Kok, 1988.

Dunn, James. *Jesus and the Spirit: A Study of the Religious and Charismatic Experience of Jesus and the First Christians as Reflected in the New Testament*. London: SCM, 1975.

———. *Christology in the Making: A New Testament Inquiry into the Origins of the Doctrine of the Incarnation*. Philadelphia, PA: Westminster, 1980.

———. *The Partings of the Ways Between Christianity and Judaism and Their Significance for the Character of Christianity*. London: SCM, 1991.

Dupont, Jacques. "L'arrière-fond biblique du récit des tentations de Jésus." *NTS* 3 (1957): 287–304.

Eichrodt, Walther. *Theology of the Old Testament*. 2 vols. Philadelphia, PA: The Westminster Press, 1967.

Eltester, Friedrich Wilhelm. *Eikon im Neuen Testament*. BZNW 23. Berlin: Töpelmann, 1958.

Eskola, Timo. *Messiah and the Throne: Jewish Merkabah Mysticism and Early Christian Exaltation Discourse*. WUNT 142. Tübingen: Mohr Siebeck, 2001.

Fallon, Francis. *The Enthronement of Sabaoth*. Leiden: Brill, 1978.

Ferguson, Everett. *Baptism in the Early Church. History, Theology, and Liturgy in the First Five Centuries*. Grand Rapids, MI: Eerdmans, 2009.

Feuillet, André. "L'épisode de la tentation d'après l'Évangile selon Saint Marc (I,12–13)." *EstBib* 19 (1960): 49–73.

Fishbane, Michael. "Form and Reformulation of the Biblical Priestly Blessing." *JAOS* 103 (1983): 115–21.

Fletcher-Louis, Crispin. "4Q374: A Discourse on the Sinai Tradition: The Deification of Moses and Early Christology." *DSD* 3 (1996): 236-52.

———. *Luke-Acts: Angels, Christology and Soteriology*. WUNT 2.94. Tübingen: Mohr Siebeck, 1997.

———. "The Worship of Divine Humanity as God's Image and the Worship of Jesus." In *The Jewish Roots of Christological Monotheism. Papers from the St. Andrews Conference on the Historical Origins of the Worship of Jesus*. Edited by C. Newman, J. Davila, and G. Lewis, 112-28. JSJSS 63. Leiden: Brill, 1999.

———. *All the Glory of Adam: Liturgical Anthropology in the Dead Sea Scrolls*. STDJ 42. Leiden: Brill, 2002.

———. *Jesus Monotheism. Volume 1: Christological Origins. The Emerging Consensus and Beyond*. Eugene, OR: Cascade Books, 2015.

Fossum, Jarl. "Jewish-Christian Christology and Jewish Mysticism." *VC* 37 (1983): 263-69.

———. *The Name of God and the Angel of the Lord. Samaritan and Jewish Concepts of Intermediation and the Origin of Gnosticism*. WUNT 36. Tübingen: Mohr Siebeck, 1985.

———. *The Image of the Invisible God: Essays on the Influence of Jewish Mysticism on Early Christology*. NTOA 30. Fribourg: Universitätsverlag Freiburg Schweiz. Göttingen: Vanderhoeck & Ruprecht, 1995.

———. "The Adorable Adam of the Mystics and the Rebuttals of the Rabbis." In *Geschichte-Tradition-Reflexion. Festschrift für Martin Hengel zum 70. Geburtstag*. Edited by H. Cancik, H. Lichtenberger, and P. Schäfer, 1.529-39. 3 vols. Tübingen: Mohr Siebeck, 1996.

———. "Dove." In *Dictionary of Deities and Demons in the Bible*. Edited by K. van der Toorn, B. Becking, and P. W. van der Horst, 264. 2nd ed. Leiden: Brill, 1999.

———. "Glory." In *Dictionary of Deities and Demons in the Bible*. Edited by K. van der Toorn, B. Becking, and P. W. van der Horst, 352. 2nd ed. Leiden: Brill. 1999.

Gallusz, Laszlo. *The Throne Motif in the Book of Revelation*. LNTS 487. London: T&T Clark, 2014.

Gathercole, Simon. *The Preexistent Son: Recovering the Christologies of Matthew, Mark, and Luke*. Grand Rapids, MI: Eerdmans, 2006.

Gero, Stephen. "The Spirit as Dove at the Baptism of Jesus." *NovT* 18 (1976): 17-35.

Gibson, Jeffrey. *Temptations of Jesus in Early Christianity*. JSNTSS 112. Sheffield: Sheffield Academic Press, 1995.

Gieschen, Charles. *Angelomorphic Christology: Antecedents and Early Evidence*. AGAJU 42. Leiden: Brill, 1998.

———. "The Divine Name in the Ante-Nicene Christology." *VC* 57 (2003): 115-58.

Goshen Gottstein, Alon. "The Body as Image of God in Rabbinic Literature." *HTR* 87 (1994): 171-95.

———. *The Sinner and the Amnesiac: The Rabbinic Invention of Elisha Ben Abuya and Eleazar Ben Arach*. Stanford, CA: Stanford University Press, 2000.

———. "Jewish-Christian Relations and Rabbinic Literature – Shifting Scholarly and Relational Paradigms: The Case of Two Powers." In *Interaction Between Judaism and Christianity in History, Religion, Art, and Literature*. Edited by M. Poorthuis, J. J. Schwartz, and J. Turner, 15-44. JCPS 17. Leiden: Brill, 2009.

Goulder, Michael. "Elijah with Moses, or a Rift in the Pre-Markan Lute." In *Christology, Controversy and Community: New Testament Essays in Honour of David R. Catchpole*. Edited by D. G. Horrell and C. M. Tuckett, 193-208. NovTSup 99. Leiden: Brill, 2000.

Graupner, Axel and Wolter, Michael. *Moses in Biblical and Extra-Biblical Traditions.* BZAW 372. Berlin: Walter de Gruyter, 2007.
Green, Arthur. *Keter: The Crown of God in Early Jewish Mysticism.* Princeton, NJ: Princeton University Press, 1997.
Grelot, Pierre. "La géographie mythique d'Hénoch et ses sources orientales." *RB* 65 (1958): 33–69.
Gurtner, Daniel. *The Torn Veil: Matthew's Exposition of the Death of Jesus.* Cambridge: Cambridge University Press, 2007.
Hägerland, Tobias. *Jesus and the Forgiveness of Sins: An Aspect of His Prophetic Mission.* SNTSMS 150. Cambridge: Cambridge University Press, 2011.
Hagner, Donald. "The Vision of God in Philo and John: A Comparative Study." *JETS* 14 (1971): 81–93.
Hahn, Ferdinand. *Christologische Hoheitstitel. Ihre Geschichte im frühen Christentum.* FRLANT 83. 3rd ed. Göttingen: Vandenhoeck & Ruprecht, 1966.
Halperin, David. *The Merkabah in Rabbinic Literature.* New Haven, CT: Yale University Press, 1980.
———. *The Faces of the Chariot: Early Jewish Responses to Ezekiel's Vision.* TSAJ 16. Tübingen: Mohr Siebeck, 1988.
Hannah, Darrell. *Michael and Christ: Michael Traditions and Angel Christology in Early Christianity.* WUNT 2.109. Tübingen: Mohr Siebeck, 1999.
———. "The Throne of His Glory: The Divine Throne and Heavenly Mediators in Revelation and the Similitudes of Enoch." *ZNW* 94 (2003): 68–96.
Haran, Menahem. "The Shining of Moses's Face: A Case Study in Biblical and Ancient Near Eastern Iconography [Exod 34:29–35; Ps 69:32; Hab 3:4]." In *In the Shelter of Elyon.* Edited by W. B. Barrick and J. R. Spencer, 159–73. JSOTSS 31. Sheffield: Sheffield Academic Press, 1984.
Harlow, Daniel. "Idolatry and Alterity: Israel and the Nations in the Apocalypse of Abraham." In *The "Other" in Second Temple Judaism. Essays in Honor of John J. Collins.* Edited by D. C. Harlow, M. Goff, K. M. Hogan, and J. S. Kaminsky, 302–30. Grand Rapids, MI: Eerdmans, 2011.
Heidler, Johannes. "Die Verwendung von Psalm 22 im Kreuzigungsbericht des Markus: ein Beitrag zur Frage nach der Christologie des Markus." In *Christi Leidenspsalm: Arbeiten zum 22. Psalm. Festschrift zum 50. Jahr des Bestehens des Theologischen Seminars "Paulinum" Berlin.* Edited by H. Genest, 26–34. Neukirchen-Vluyn: Neukirchener Verlag, 1996.
Heil, John Paul. *The Transfiguration of Jesus: Narrative Meaning and Function of Mark 9:2–8, Matt 17:1–8 and Luke 9:28–36.* AnBib 144. Rome: Editrice Pontificio Istituto Biblico, 2000.
Helleman, Wendy. "Philo of Alexandria on Deification and Assimilation to God." *SPhA* 2 (1990): 51–71.
Hengel, Martin. *Studies in Early Christology.* Edinburg: T&T Clark, 1995.
Héring, Jean. *Le Royaume de Dieu et sa venue. Étude sur l'espérance de Jésus et de l'apôtre Paul.* Paris: Alcan, 1937.
Himmelfarb, Martha. *Ascent to Heaven in Jewish and Christian Apocalypses.* New York/Oxford: Oxford University Press, 1993.
Holladay, Carl R. *Theios Aner in Hellenistic Judaism: A Critique of the Use of This Category in New Testament Christology.* Missoula, MT: Scholars, 1977.
Hooker, Morna. "'What Doest Thou Here, Elijah?' A Look at St Mark's Account of the Transfiguration." In *The Glory of Christ in the New Testament: Studies in Christology*

in Memory of George Bradford Caird. Edited by L. D. Hurst and N. T. Wright, 59–70. Oxford: Clarendon Press, 1987.

Horstmann, Maria. *Studien zur Markinischen Christologie: Mk 8.27–9.13 als Zugang zum Christusbild des zweiten Evangeliums*. NTAbh 6. Münster: Aschendorff, 1969.

Huizenga, Leroy. *The New Isaac: Tradition and Intertextuality in the Gospel of Matthew*. NovTSup 131. Leiden: Brill, 2009.

Hultgren, Stephen. *Narrative Elements in the Double Tradition: A Study of Their Place within the Framework of the Gospel Narrative*. BZNW 113. Berlin/New York: Walter de Gruyter, 2002.

Hurowitz, Victor. "Inside Solomon's Temple." *Bible Review* 10.2 (1994): 24–36.

Hurtado, Larry. *One Lord, One God: Early Christian Devotion and Ancient Jewish Monotheism*. Philadelphia, PA: Fortress, 1988.

———. *Lord Jesus Christ: Devotion to Jesus in Earliest Christianity*. Grand Rapids, MI: Eerdmans, 2005.

Idel, Moshe. "Enoch is Metatron." *Imm* 24–25 (1990): 220–40.

———. *Ben: Sonship and Jewish Mysticism*. London: Continuum, 2007.

———. "The Changing Faces of God and Human Dignity in Judaism." In *Moshe Idel: Representing God*. Edited by H. Tirosh-Samuelson and A. W. Hughes, 103–22. LCJP 8. Leiden: Brill, 2014.

Jackson, Howard. "The Death of Jesus in Mark and the Miracle from the Cross." *NTS* 33 (1987): 23–31.

Jastrow, Marcus. *A Dictionary of the Targumim, the Talmud Babli and Yerushalmi, and the Midrashic Literature*. 2 vols. New York: Judaica Press, 1996.

Jeremias, Joachim. "Nachwort zum Artikel von H.-G. Leder." *ZNW* 54 (1963): 278–79.

———. "Adam." In *Theological Dictionary of the New Testament*. Edited by G. Kittel and G. W. Bromiley, 1.141–43. 10 vols. Grand Rapids, MI: Eerdmans, 1964.

———. *New Testament Theology*. New York: Charles Scribner's Sons, 1971.

Jervell, Jacob. *Imago Dei: Gen 1, 26f. im Spätjudentum, in der Gnosis und in den paulinischen Briefen*. FRLANT 76. Göttingen: Vandenhoeck & Ruprecht, 1960.

Johnstone, William. "Reactivating the Chronicles Analogy in Pentateuchal Studies, with Special Reference to the Sinai Pericope in Exodus." *ZAW* 99 (1987): 16–37.

Keck, Leander. "The Spirit and the Dove." *NTS* 17 (1970–1971): 41–67.

Kibbe, Michael. *Godly Fear or Ungodly Failure? Hebrews 12:18–29 and the Sinai Theophanies*. Berlin: Walter de Gruyter, 2016.

Kim, Seyoon. *The Origin of Paul's Gospel*. WUNT 2.4. Tübingen: Mohr Siebeck, 1981.

Köhler, Ludwig. "Die Grundstelle der Imago-Dei-Lehre, Genesis 1, 26." *ThZ* 4 (1948): 16–22.

Kraus, Wolfgang. "Die Bedeutung von Dtn 18,15–18 für das Verständnis Jesu als Prophet." *ZNW* 90 (1999): 153–76.

Kugel, James. *In Potiphar's House: The Interpretive Life of Biblical Texts*. San Francisco, CA: Harper Collins, 1990.

———. "The Ladder of Jacob." *HTR* 88 (1995): 209–27.

———. *Traditions of the Bible: A Guide to the Bible as It Was at the Start of the Common Era*. Cambridge, MA: Harvard University Press, 1998.

Kvanvig, Helge. "The Son of Man in the Parables of Enoch." In *Enoch and the Messiah Son of Man: Revisiting of the Book of Parables*. Edited by G. Boccaccini, 179–215. Grand Rapids, MI: Eerdmans, 2007.

Laderman, Shulamit. *Images of Cosmology in Jewish and Byzantine Art: God's Blueprint of Creation*. JCPS 25. Leiden: Brill, 2013.

Lee, Simon. *Jesus' Transfiguration and the Believers' Transformation: A Study of the Transfiguration and Its Development in Early Christian Writings*. WUNT 2.265. Tübingen: Mohr Siebeck, 2009.

Leloir, Louis. *Le témoignage d'Éphrem sur le Diatessaron*. CSCO 227. Subsidia 19. Louvain: Secretariat du CorpusSCO, 1962.

Lentzen-Deis, Fritzleo. *Die Taufe Jesu nach den Synoptikern: Literarkritische und gattungsgeschichtliche Untersuchungen*. FTS 4. Frankfurt/M.: Knecht, 1970.

Lesses, Rebecca. *Ritual Practices to Gain Power: Angels, Incantations, and Revelation in Early Jewish Mysticism*. HTS 44. Harrisburg: Trinity Press, 1998.

Lieber, Andrea. "Voice and Vision: Song as a Vehicle for Ecstatic Experience in Songs of the Sabbath Sacrifice." In *Of Scribes and Sages: Early Jewish Interpretation of Scripture*. Edited by C. A. Evans, 2.51–58. 2 vols. London/New York: T&T Clark, 2004.

Lierman, John. *The New Testament Moses: Christian Perceptions of Moses and Israel in the Setting of Jewish Religion*. WUNT 2.173. Tübingen: Mohr Siebeck, 2004.

Litwa, David. "The Deification of Moses in Philo of Alexandria." *SPhA* 26 (2014): 1–27.

———. *Iesus Deus: The Early Christian Depiction of Jesus as a Mediterranean God*. Minneapolis, MN: Fortress, 2014.

Lohfink, Gerhard. *Die Himmelfahrt Jesu: Untersuchungen zu den Himmelfahrts- und Erhöhungstexten bei Lukas*. SANT 26. Munich: Kösel, 1971.

Lourié, Basil. "Review of A. Kulik's *Retroverting Slavonic Pseudepigrapha*." *JSP* 15.3 (2006): 229–37.

Mach, Michael. "From Apocalypticism to Early Jewish Mysticism." In *The Encyclopedia of Apocalypticism*. Edited by J. J. Collins, 1.229–64. 3 vols. New York: Continuum, 1998.

MacRae, George. *Some Elements of Jewish Apocalyptic and Mystical Tradition and Their Relation to Gnostic Literature*. 2 vols. PhD diss. University of Cambridge, 1966.

Malbon, Elizabeth. *Narrative Space and Mythic Meaning in Mark*. San Francisco, CA: Harper and Row, 1986.

Marcus, Joel. *The Way of the Lord: Christological Exegesis of the Old Testament in the Gospel of Mark*. Edinburgh: T&T Clark, 1992.

———. "Jesus' Baptismal Vision." *NTS* 41 (1995): 512–21.

Martin, Ralph. *Carmen Christi: Philippians ii. 5–11 in Recent Interpretation and in the Setting of Early Christian Worship*. SNTSMS 4. Cambridge: Cambridge University Press, 1967.

Mathewson, David. "The Apocalyptic Vision of Jesus According to the Gospel of Matthew: Reading Matthew 3:16–4:11 Intertextually." *Tyndale Bulletin* 62 (2011): 89–108.

McDonnell, Kilian. "Jesus' Baptism in the Jordan." *TS* 56 (1995): 209–36.

———. *The Baptism of Jesus in the Jordan: The Trinitarian and Cosmic Order of Salvation*. Collegeville, MN: Liturgical Press, 1996.

McGrath, James. *The Only True God: Early Christian Monotheism in Its Jewish Context*. Urbana, IL: University of Illinois Press, 2012.

McGrath, James and Truex, Jerry. "Early Jewish and Christian Monotheism: A Select Bibliography." In *Early Jewish and Christian Monotheism*. Edited by L. T. Stuckenbruck and W. E. S. North, 235–42. JSNTSS 263. London: T&T Clark, 2004.

McGuckin, John. *The Transfiguration of Christ in Scripture and Tradition*. New York: Edwin Mellen, 1986.

McPolin, James. *The Name of the Father and of the Son in the Johannine Writings*. PhD diss. Pontifical Biblical Institute, 1971.

Meeks, Wayne. *The Prophet-King: Moses Traditions and the Johannine Christology*. NovTSup 14. Leiden: Brill, 1967.

———. "Moses as God and King." In *Religions in Antiquity. FS Erwin Ramsdall Goodenough*. Edited by J. Neusner, 354–71. SHR 14. Leiden: Brill, 1968.
Meier, John. *A Marginal Jew: Rethinking the Historical Jesus 2: Mentor, Message, and Miracles*. New York: Doubleday, 1994.
. Merrill Willis, Amy. *Dissonance and the Drama of Divine Sovereignty in the Book of Daniel*. Library of Hebrew Bible/Old Testament Studies. London: T&T Clark, 2010.
———. "Heavenly Bodies: God and the Body in the Visions of Daniel." In *Bodies, Embodiment, and Theology of the Hebrew Bible*. Edited by S. T. Kamionkowski and W. Kim, 13–37. New York: T&T Clark, 2010.
Mettinger, Tryggve. *The Dethronement of Sabaoth. Studies in the Shem and Kabod Theologies*. ConBOT 18. Lund: Wallin & Dalholm, 1982.
Meye Thompson, Marianne. "Jesus. 'The One Who Sees God.'" In *Israel's God and Rebecca's Children: Christology and Community in Early Judaism and Christianity: Essays in Honor of Larry W. Hurtado and Alan F. Segal*. Edited by D. Capes, A. DeConick, H. Bond, and T. Miller, 215–26. Waco, TX: Baylor University Press, 2007.
Meyers, Carol. "Sea, Molten." In *Anchor Bible Dictionary*. Edited by D. N. Freedman, 5.1061-62. 6 vols. New York: Doubleday, 1992.
Miller, Michael. *The Name of God in Jewish Thought: A Philosophical Analysis of Mystical Traditions from Apocalyptic to Kabbalah*. New York: Routledge, 2015.
Moorhead, John. "The Spirit and the World." *GOTR* 26 (1981): 113–17.
Morgenstern, Julian. "Moses with the Shining Face." *HUCA* 2 (1925): 1–27.
Morray-Jones, Chistopher. "Hekhalot Literature and Talmudic Tradition: Alexander's Three Test Cases." *JSJ* 22 (1991): 1–39.
———. "Paradise Revisited (2 Cor 12:1–12): The Jewish Mystical Background of Paul's Apostolate. Part 2: Paul's Heavenly Ascent and its Significance." *HTR* 86 (1993): 265–92.
———. *A Transparent Illusion. The Dangerous Vision of Water in Hekhalot Mysticism: A Source-Critical and Tradition-Critical Inquiry*. JSJSS 59. Leiden: Brill, 2002.
Moses, A. D. A. *Matthew's Transfiguration Story and Jewish-Christian Controversy*. JSNTSS 122. Sheffield: Academic Press, 1996.
Moss, Candida. "The Transfiguration: An Exercise in Markan Accommodation." *BibInt* 12 (2004): 72–73.
Motyer, Stephen. "The Rending of the Veil: A Markan Pentecost." *NTS* 33 (1987): 155–57.
Myers, Susan. *Spirit Epicleses in the Acts of Thomas*. WUNT 2.281. Tübingen: Mohr Siebeck, 2010.
Neirynck, Frans. "Minor Agreements: Matthew—Luke in the Transfiguration Story." In *Orientierung an Jesus: Zur Theologie der Synoptiker. Festschrift für Josef Schmid*. Edited by P. Hoffmann, N. Brox, and W. Pesch, 253–66. Freiburg: Herder, 1973.
Neis, Rachel. "Embracing Icons: The Face of Jacob on the Throne of God." *Images: A Journal of Jewish Art and Visual Culture* 1 (2007): 36–54.
Newman, Carey. *Paul's Glory-Christology: Tradition and Rhetoric*. NovTSup 69. Leiden: Brill, 1992.
Nissinen, Martti. "Sacred Springs and Liminal Rivers: Water and Prophecy in the Ancient Eastern Mediterranean." In *Thinking of Water in the Early Second Temple Period*. Edited by E. Ben Zvi and C. Levin, 29–48. BZAW 461. Berlin/Boston: Walter de Gruyter, 2014.
Olson, Daniel. *A New Reading of the Animal Apocalypse of 1 Enoch: "All Nations Shall be Blessed."* SVTP 24. Leiden: Brill, 2013.

Orlov, Andrei Aleksandrovich. "The Face as the Heavenly Counterpart of the Visionary in the Slavonic Ladder of Jacob." In *Of Scribes and Sages: Early Jewish Interpretation and Transmission of Scripture*. Edited by C. A. Evans, 2.59–76. 2 vols. SSEJC 9. London: T&T Clark, 2004.

———. *The Enoch-Metatron Tradition*. TSAJ 107. Tübingen: Mohr Siebeck, 2005.

———. "Vested with Adam's Glory: Moses as the Luminous Counterpart of Adam in the Dead Sea Scrolls and the Macarian Homilies." *Christian Orient* 4.10 (2006): 498–513.

———. "Pteromorphic Angelology in the Apocalypse of Abraham." *CBQ* 71 (2009): 830–42.

———. "The Sacerdotal Traditions of 2 Enoch and the Date of the Text." In *New Perspectives on 2 Enoch: No Longer Slavonic Only*. Edited by A. A. Orlov, G. Boccaccini, J. Zurawski, 103–16. SJS 4. Leiden: Brill, 2012.

———. *Divine Scapegoats: Demonic Mimesis in Early Jewish Mysticism*. Albany, NY: SUNY, 2015.

———. *The Greatest Mirror: Heavenly Counterparts in the Jewish Pseudepigrapha*. Albany, NY: SUNY, 2017.

———. *Yahoel and Metatron: Aural Apocalypticism and the Origins of Early Jewish Mysticism*. TSAJ 169. Tübingen: Mohr Siebeck, 2017.

Osborn. Eric. *The Emergence of Christian Theology*. Cambridge: Cambridge University Press, 1993.

Painter, John. *The Quest for the Messiah*. 2nd ed. Nashville, TN: Abingdon, 1993.

Palachuvattil, Joy. *"He Saw": The Significance of Jesus' Seeing Denoted by the Verb Eiden in the Gospel of Mark*. TG 84. Rome: Editrice Pontificia Università Gregoriana, 2002.

Petersen, William. *Tatian's Diatessaron: Its Creation, Dissemination, Significance and History in Scholarship*. VCS 25. Leiden: Brill, 1994.

Pokorný, Petr. "The Temptation Stories and Their Intention." *NTS* 20 (1973–1974): 115–27.

Propp, William. "The Skin of Moses' Face – Transfigured or Disfigured?" *CBQ* 49 (1987): 375–86.

Quispel, Gilles. "Ezekiel 1:26 in Jewish Mysticism and Gnosis." *VC* 34 (1980): 1–13.

———. "Genius and Spirit." In *Gnostica, Judaica, Catholica. Collected Essays of Gilles Quispel*. Edited by J. van Oort, 103–18. NHMS 55. Leiden: Brill, 2008.

Radice, Roberto. "Philo's Theology and Theory of Creation." In *The Cambridge Companion to Philo*. Edited by A. Kamesar, 124–45. Cambridge: Cambridge University Press, 2009.

Ramsey, Michael. *The Glory of God and the Transfiguration of Christ*. London: Longmans, Green and Co., 1949.

Refoulé, François. "Jésus, nouveau Moïse, ou Pierre, nouveau Grand Prêtre? (Mt 17,1-9; Mc 9,2-10)." *RTL* 24 (1993): 145–62.

Reindl, Joseph. *Das Angesicht Gottes im Sprachgebrauch des Alten Testaments*. ETS 25. Leipzig: St. Benno, 1970.

Richter, Sandra. *The Deuteronomic History and the Name Theology: lešakkēn šemô šām in the Bible and the Ancient Near East*. BZAW 318. Berlin: Walter de Gruyter, 2002.

Riesenfeld, Harald. *Jésus transfiguré: L'arrière-plan du récit évangélique de la transfiguration de Notre-Seigneur*. Copenhagen: Ejnar Munksgaard, 1947.

Rodriguez, Ángel Manuel. "Sanctuary Theology in the Hebrew Cultus and in Cultic-Related Texts." *AUSS* 24 (1986): 127–45.

Rowland, Christopher. "The Visions of God in Apocalyptic Literature." *JSJ* 10 (1979): 137–54.

———. *The Open Heaven: A Study of Apocalyptic in Judaism and Early Christianity.* New York: Crossroad, 1982.

———. "John 1:51, Jewish Apocalyptic and Targumic Tradition." *NTS* 30 (1984): 498–507.

Rowland, Christopher and Morray-Jones, Christopher. *The Mystery of God: Early Jewish Mysticism and the New Testament.* CRINT 12. Leiden: Brill, 2009.

Ruffatto, Kristine. "Polemics with Enochic Traditions in the Exagoge of Ezekiel the Tragedian." *JSP* 15 (2006): 195–210.

———. "Raguel as Interpreter of Moses' Throne Vision: The Transcendent Identity of Raguel in the Exagoge of Ezekiel the Tragedian." *JSP* 17 (2008): 121–39.

———. *Visionary Ascents of Moses in Pseudo-Philo's Liber Antiquitatum Biblicarum: Apocalyptic Motifs and the Growth of Visionary Moses Tradition.* PhD diss. Marquette University, 2010.

Runia, David. "God and Man in Philo of Alexandria." *JTS* 39 (1988): 48–75.

———. "The Beginnings of the End: Philo of Alexandria and Hellenistic Theology." In *Traditions of Theology: Studies in Hellenistic Theology, Its Background and Aftermath.* Edited by D. Frede and A. Laks, 281–312. PA 89. Leiden: Brill, 2002.

Sabbe, Maurice. "La rédaction du récit de la Transfiguration." In *La venue du Messie.* Edited by E. Massaux, 65–100. RechBib 6. Paris: Desclée de Brouwer, 1962.

Sacchi, Paolo. "The 2005 Camaldoli Seminar on the Parables of Enoch: Summary and Prospects for Future Research." In *Enoch and the Messiah Son of Man: Revisiting of the Book of Parables.* Edited by G. Boccaccini, 499–512. Grand Rapids, MI: Eerdmans, 2007.

Schäfer, Peter. *Hekhalot-Studien.* TSAJ 19. Tübingen: Mohr Siebeck, 1988.

———. *The Origins of Jewish Mysticism.* Tübingen: Mohr Siebeck, 2009.

Scholem, Gershom. *Jewish Gnosticism, Merkabah Mysticism, and Talmudic Tradition.* 2nd ed. New York: Jewish Theological Seminary of America, 1965.

———. *On the Mystical Shape of the Godhead.* New York: Schocken, 1976.

Schremer, Adiel. "Midrash, Theology, and History: Two Powers in Heaven Revisited." *JSJ* 39 (2008): 230–54.

———. *Brothers Estranged: Heresy, Christianity and Jewish Identity in Late Antiquity.* Oxford: Oxford University Press, 2010.

Schultze, Wilhelm August. "Der Heilige und die wilden Tiere. Zur Exegese von Mc 1,13b." *ZNW* 46 (1955): 280–83.

Schwienhorst-Schönberger, Ludger. *Das Bundesbuch (Ex 20,22–23,33). Studien zu seiner Entstehung und Theologie.* BZAW 188. Berlin: Walter de Gruyter, 1990.

Scott, Charles Anderson. *Christianity According to St Paul.* Cambridge: Cambridge University Press, 1927.

Scott, Ian. "Is Philo's Moses a Divine Man?" *SPhA* 14 (2002): 87–111.

Scott, Steven Richard. "The Binitarian Nature of the Book of Similitudes." *JSP* 18 (2008): 55–78.

Segal, Alan. *Two Powers in Heaven: Early Rabbinic Reports about Christianity and Gnosticism.* SJLA 25. Leiden: Brill, 1977.

———. "Judaism, Christianity and Gnosticism." In *Anti-Judaism in Early Christianity. Volume 2: Separation and Polemic.* Edited by S. G. Wilson, 133–61. Waterloo, ON: Wilfrid Laurier University Press, 1986.

———. *Paul the Convert: The Apostolate and Apostasy of Saul the Pharisee.* New Haven, CT: Yale University Press, 1990.

———. "Paul and the Beginning of Jewish Mysticism." In *Death, Ecstasy, and Other Worldly Journeys*. Edited by J. Collins and M. Fishbane, 95–122. Albany, NY: SUNY, 1995.

———. "Paul's Thinking about Resurrection in its Jewish Context." *NTS* 44 (1998): 400–19.

———. "'Two Powers in Heaven' and Early Christian Trinitarian Thinking." In *The Trinity: An Interdisciplinary Symposium on the Trinity*. Edited by S. T. Davis, D. Kendall, and G. O'Collins, 73–95. Oxford: Oxford University Press, 1999.

Seppälä, Serafim. "Baptismal Mystery in St. Ephrem the Syrian and *Hymnen de Epiphania*." In *Ablution, Initiation, and Baptism: Late Antiquity, Early Judaism, and Early Christianity*, Edited by D. Hellholm, T. Vegge, Ø. Norderval, and C. Hellholm, 1139–77. BZNW 176. Berlin: Walter de Gruyter, 2011.

Smith, Mark. "'Seeing God' in the Psalms: The Background to the Beatific Vision in the Hebrew Bible." *CBQ* 50 (1988): 171–83.

———. *God in Translation: Deities in Cross-Cultural Discourse in the Biblical World*. FAT 57. Tübingen: Mohr Siebeck, 2008.

Smith, Morton. "The Image of God. Notes on the Hellenisation of Judaism with Especial Reference to Goodenough's Work on Jewish Symbols." *BJRL* 40 (1958): 473–512.

Sommer, Benjamin. *The Bodies of God and the World of Ancient Israel*. New York: Cambridge University Press, 2009.

Stone, Michael. "The Fall of Satan and Adam's Penance: Three Notes on the Books of Adam and Eve." In *Literature on Adam and Eve. Collected Essays*. Edited by G. Anderson, M. Stone, and J. Tromp, 43–56. SVTP 15. Brill: Leiden, 2000.

Strauss, David Friedrich. *The Life of Jesus Critically Examined*. Philadelphia, PA: Fortress, 1972.

Stroumsa, Gedaliahu. "Forms of God: Some Notes on Metatron and Christ." *HTR* 76 (1983): 269–88.

Stuckenbruck, Loren. *Angel Veneration and Christology. A Study in Early Judaism and in the Christology of the Apocalypse of John*. WUNT 2.70. Tübingen: Mohr Siebeck, 1995.

Suter, David. "Enoch in Sheol: Updating the Dating of the Book of Parables." In *Enoch and the Messiah Son of Man: Revisiting the Book of Parables*. Edited by G. Boccaccini, 415–43. Grand Rapids, MI: Eerdmans, 2007.

Tabor, James. "'Returning to the Divinity': Josephus's Portrayal of the Disappearances of Enoch, Elijah, and Moses." *JBL* 108 (1989): 225–38.

Teppler, Yaakov. *Birkat HaMinim: Jews and Christians in Conflict in the Ancient World*. TSAJ 120. Tübingen: Mohr Siebeck, 2007.

Thompson, George. "Called—Proved—Obedient: A Study in the Baptism and Temptation Narratives of Matthew and Luke." *JTS* 11 (1960): 1–12.

Tuschling, Ruth. *Angels and Orthodoxy: A Study in their Development in Syria and Palestine from the Qumran Texts to Ephrem the Syrian*. STAC 40. Tübingen: Mohr Siebeck, 2007.

Ulansey, David. "The Heavenly Veil Torn: Mark's Cosmic 'Inclusio.'" *JBL* 110 (1991): 123–25.

Van den Broek, Roelof. "The Cathars: Medieval Gnostics?" In *Gnosis and Hermeticism from Antiquity to Modern Times*. Edited by R. van den Broek, and W. J. Hanegraaff, 87–108. SUNY Series in Western Esoteric Traditions. Albany, NY: SUNY, 1997.

Van der Horst, Pieter. "Moses' Throne Vision in Ezekiel the Dramatist." *JJS* 34 (1983): 21–29.

———. "Some Notes on the Exagoge of Ezekiel." *Mnemosyne* 37 (1984): 354–75.

Van Henten, Jan Willem. "Moses as Heavenly Messenger in Assumptio Mosis 10:2 and Qumran Passages." *JJS* 54 (2003): 216–27.

VanderKam, James. *From Revelation to Canon: Studies in Hebrew Bible and Second Temple Literature*. Leiden: Brill, 2000.

Vargas-Machuca, Antonio. "La tentación de Jesús según Mc. 1,12–13 ¿Hecho real o relato de tipo haggádico?" *EE* 48 (1973): 163–90.

Vermes, Geza. *Jesus the Jew: A Historian's Reading of the Gospels*. Philadelphia, PA: Fortress, 1981.

Vigne, Daniel. *Christ au Jourdain: Le Baptême de Jésus dans la tradition judéo-chrétienne*. Paris: Gabalda, 1992.

Von Heijne, Camilla Hélena. *The Messenger of the Lord in Early Jewish Interpretations of Genesis*. BZAW 42. Berlin: Walter de Gruyter, 2010.

Von Rad, Gerhard. *Studies in Deuteronomy*. London: SCM Press, 1953.

Weinfeld, Moshe. *Deuteronomy and the Deuteronomic School*. Oxford: Clarendon Press, 1972.

Weitzman, Steven. "Sensory Reform in Deuteronomy." In *Religion and the Self in Antiquity*. Edited by D. Brakke, M. Satlow, and S. Weitzman, 123–39. Bloomington, IN: Indiana University Press, 2005.

Wilson, Ian. *Out of the Midst of the Fire: Divine Presence in Deuteronomy*. SBLDS 151. Atlanta, GA: Scholars, 1995.

Wilson, Stephen. *Related Strangers: Jews and Christians*. Minneapolis, MN: Fortress, 1995.

Winston, David. "Philo's Conception of the Divine Nature." In *Neoplatonism and Jewish Thought*. Edited by L. E. Goodman, 21–42. Albany, NY: SUNY, 1992.

Witherington, Ben. *The Christology of Jesus*. Minneapolis, MN: Fortress, 1990.

Wolfson, Elliot. *Through a Speculum That Shines: Vision and Imagination in Medieval Jewish Mysticism*. Princeton, NJ: Princeton University Press, 1994.

———. *Along the Path: Studies in Kabbalistic Myth, Symbolism, and Hermeneutics*. Albany, NY: SUNY, 1995.

Yarbro Collins, Adela and Collins, John. *King and Messiah as Son of God: Divine, Human, and Angelic Messianic Figures in Biblical and Related Literature*. Grand Rapids, MI: Eerdmans, 2008.

Index of Names

Aagaard, A. M.   159
Abrahams, I.   167
Abrams, D.   63
Alexander, P.   28, 56, 62, 64–5, 67–70, 134, 176, 185
Allison, D.   89, 90–3, 118, 123, 127, 130, 132–3, 135, 137–8, 145, 150–1, 164, 167–8, 177, 185–6
Andersen, F.   29, 36, 107–8, 135
Anderson, G.   11, 24–7, 33, 79, 135
Ashton, J.   6
Assefa, D.   100
Attridge, H.   142

Balentine, S.   106
Barr, J.   11, 13
Barrett, C. K.   167, 177
Bauckham, R.   13, 52, 93, 120, 186
Beale, G.   172
Becker, J.   131
Begg, C.   98
Belleville, L.   121, 125, 127
Bendoraitis, K.   183
Betz, H. D.   178
Blanc, C.   54
Blenkinsopp, J.   140
Bloch-Smith, E.   173
Bockmuehl, M.   45, 150, 177, 189
Bohak, G.   172
Boobyer, G. H.   79, 116, 143
Borsch, F.   83
Böttrich, C.   32, 56–7
Boyarin, D.   6, 16, 63, 64, 75, 141
Braude, W.   61
Brock, S.   90, 156, 158, 159, 161
Bunta, S. N.   19, 31, 96

Capes, D.   145, 147, 149–50, 166, 168
Charles, R. H.   32, 109, 114, 136, 141, 177
Chester, A.   80, 81, 115–16, 119, 149
Chilton, B.   177, 185
Christman, A.   145–7

Clements, R.   40, 111
Clifford, R.   111
Coats, G.   93
Coblentz Bautch, K.   111–12
Cohn, R.   111
Collins, J. J.   11, 16, 22, 30–1, 38, 49, 80, 89, 132, 154
Colson, F. H.   98, 102
Coutts, J.   142
Cowley, A. E.   121
Cox, R.   103
Cranfield, C.   109, 123, 136, 140, 143, 167
Cullmann, O.   91

Dan, J.   66
Danby, H.   115
Daniélou, J.   113, 169
Davies, J. G.   83
Davies, W. D.   89, 91–3, 118, 127, 130, 132, 135, 137–8, 145, 150–1, 164, 167–8, 177, 186
Davila, J.   7, 13, 36, 64–5, 73–4, 135
Davis, C. J.   80, 84
Dearman, A.   83–4
De Jonge, M.   6, 160
Denis, A.-M.   28, 54
Dennis, G. W.   151
Deutsch, N.   35–6, 51, 68, 70
De Vaux, R.   113
Dillmann, A.   113
Dixon, E.   180
Donaldson, J.   90, 154
Donaldson, T.   111, 113, 137
Dörries, H.   175
Drijvers, H.   155
Dunn, J.   6, 81, 89
Dupont, J.   185

Eichrodt, W.   106–7
Eltester, F. W.   189
Epstein, I.   1, 72, 172, 191

Index of Names

Eskola, T.   111
Evans, C.   46, 57, 89, 92, 109, 119, 185

Fallon, F.   111
Falls, T.   154
Ferguson, E.   154, 156, 157
Ferrar, W. J.   90
Feuillet, A.   185
Fishbane, M.   80, 106
Fitzmyer, J.   86–7, 128, 163
Fletcher-Louis, C.   21, 24, 38, 100–1, 184, 187
Forbes, N.   32
Fossum, J.   19, 50–3, 57, 76, 93, 96, 116, 121–2, 125, 127, 137, 140, 142–3, 176, 179–80, 189
France, R. T.   145, 163, 182
Freedman, H.   58, 60, 72, 75–6, 152–3, 172–3
Friedlander, G.   36

Gallusz, L.   19, 111
García Martínez, F.   101, 108
Gathercole, S.   110–11, 120
Gero, S.   169
Gibson, J.   186
Gieschen, C.   114, 141
Gnilka, J.   145, 185
Goshen Gottstein, A.   71, 127
Goulder, M.   91
Graupner, A.   93
Gray, T.   147
Green, A.   94, 122, 186
Grelot, P.   113
Guelich, R.   148, 177–8, 182, 186
Guggenheimer, H.   72
Gundry, R.   135–6, 145
Gurtner, D.   165

Hägerland, T.   91
Hagner, D.   93, 145
Hahn, F.   178
Halperin, D.   45, 47, 71–2, 152–3
Hannah, D.   15–16, 19–20, 141
Haran, M.   94
Harlow, D.   49
Heidler, J.   165
Heil, J. P.   86–7, 94, 117, 119–20, 132, 179
Helleman, W.   93

Hengel, M.   38, 76
Héring, J.   189
Himmelfarb, M.   132
Holladay, C.   28, 93
Hooker, M.   109–10, 115–17, 120, 128
Horstmann, M.   113
Huizenga, L.   89, 92–3, 130, 132–3
Hultgren, S.   183
Hurowitz, V.   171
Hurtado, L.   2, 6, 17, 20, 30–1, 52–3, 93, 149

Idel, M.   36, 37, 77, 142

Jackson, H.   112, 165
Jacobson, H.   28–9, 125
Jastrow, M.   19
Jeremias, J.   177, 185–6
Jervell, J.   32, 189
Johnston, E.   157, 158
Johnstone, W.   140
Juel, D. H.   163
Jülicher, A.   155

Kapstein, I.   61
Keck, L.   81, 167
Kee, H.   160
Kibbe, M.   129
Kim, S.   43, 152
Kiraz, G.   161, 162
Knibb, M.   17–18, 20, 23, 31, 51
Köhler, L.   12
Kraus, W.   91
Kugel, J.   6, 55, 57, 60–1
Kulik, A.   46, 56, 180–1
Kvanvig, H.   22

Laderman, S.   168–9
Lane, W.   163
Lattke, M.   169
Lauterbach, J.   152
Lee, S.   21, 89, 118, 123, 144
Leloir, L.   155
Lesses, R.   151
Lieber, A.   46
Lierman, J.   91, 93, 99
Litwa, D.   89, 102–4
Lods, A.   113
Lohfink, G.   83

Lourié, B. 181
Lunt, H. 55, 57
Luz, U. 82, 113–14, 125, 133, 137, 145

McCarthy, C. 156
Macdonald, J. 121–2
McDonnell, K. 154, 158–9, 161–2, 168, 170–1, 174
McGrath, J. 6–7
McGuckin, J. 83, 91, 109, 129, 136, 140
Mach, M. 38
McNamara, M. 126
McPolin, J. 142
MacRae, G. 172
McVey, K. 158
Malbon, E. 165
Maloney, G. 175
Marcus, J. 89, 93, 95, 97, 99, 102, 104, 108, 116, 121–2, 129–30, 139, 141, 143–4, 148, 160–1, 163, 165, 167, 176–8, 183, 187
Marcus, R. 128
Martin, R. 38, 76, 131, 167, 189
Mathewson, D. 145, 147, 151, 173–4, 181–2
Meeks, W. 28, 30, 32, 91, 93, 97, 128
Meier, J. 145
Merrill Willis, A. 14–15, 43
Mettinger, T. 13, 40, 42, 44, 142
Meyers, C. 173
Meye Thompson, M. 149
Milik, J. T. 32
Miller, M. 63
Minov, S. 56
Moorhead, J. 181
Morfill, W. R. 32–3
Morgenstern, J. 94
Morray-Jones, C. 29–30, 47, 62, 68, 70, 73–5, 89, 151, 163, 168
Morris, L. 130
Moses, A. D.A. 109–10, 113, 137–8
Moss, C. 89
Motyer, S. 165
Mras, K. 54
Myers, S. 155–6

Neirynck, F. 86
Neis, R. 57

Neusner, J. 30, 71, 76
Newman, C. 7, 13, 79–81, 184
Newman, J. H. 6, 54
Nickelsburg, G. 17–18, 20, 22–3, 112
Nissinen, M. 151
Nolland, J. 130, 145

Odeberg, H. 69, 70
Olson, D. 100
Orlov, A. A. 3, 28, 32, 57, 63, 85, 105, 120, 126–7, 179, 183
Osborn, E. 6
Osborne, G. R. 130

Painter, J. 6
Palachuvattil, J. 168, 176–7
Petersen, W. 155–6
Philonenko, M. 46, 48
Philonenko-Sayar, B. 46, 48
Pokorný, P. 185
Propp, W. 94

Quispel, G. 96, 175

Radice, R. 103
Ramsey, M. 94, 116, 129, 136, 144
Refoulé, F. 93
Reindl, J. 106
Reinink, G. J. 155
Resch, A. 54
Richter, S. 40
Riesenfeld, H. 113
Roberts, A. 90, 154
Robinson, J. A. 54
Rodriguez, Á. M. 111
Rowland, C. 29–30, 47, 50–3, 57, 81, 89, 119, 124, 133, 145, 163, 168, 180
Ruffatto, K. 28, 30, 98, 101–2, 125
Runia, D. 93, 103

Sabbe, M. 113
Sabourin, L. 145
Sacchi, P. 17
Schäfer, P. 36, 65–6, 71–2, 74, 76
Scheck, T. 145–6
Schlüter, M. 36
Schneemelcher, W. 155

Scholem, G.   34, 45, 74
Schremer, A.   6
Schultze, W. A.   185
Schwienhorst-Schönberger, L.   140
Scott, C. A.   79
Scott, I. W.   93
Scott, S. R.   6
Segal, A.   5–6, 8–9, 26, 52, 62, 64, 76, 79, 80, 82–3, 149
Seppälä, S.   162
Shutt, R.   172
Simon, M.   58, 60–1, 72, 75–7, 110, 123, 127–8, 144, 152–3, 172
Smith, J. Z.   54
Smith, M.   32
Smith, M. S.   6, 106
Snell, B.   28
Sommer, B.   12
Sperling, H.   61, 153
Stone, M. E.   24–7, 33, 135
Strauss, D. F.   90
Stroumsa, G.   189
Stuckenbruck, L.   6, 134
Suter, D.   17

Tabor, J.   98, 110, 162
Taylor, V.   167
Teppler, Y.   6
Thackeray, H.   98
Thompson, G.   183
Thomson, R.   161, 170
Tigchelaar, E.   101, 108
Tishby, I.   175
Truex, J.   6

Turner, D.   6, 93, 145, 186
Tuschling, R.   6

Ulansey, D.   164, 165

Valavanolickal, K.   159
Van den Broek, R.   174–5
Van der Horst, P.   28, 30, 54, 176, 179
VanderKam, J. C.   17–18, 20–3, 131
Van Henten, J. W.   93
Vargas-Machuca, A.   185
Vermes, G.   91
Vigne, D.   154–5
Von Heijne, C. H.   57, 141
Von Mutius, H. G.   36
Von Rad, G.   40

Weinfeld, M.   11, 12, 39–40, 42–4
Weitzman, S.   41, 43–5
Wertheimer, S.   77
Whitaker, G. H.   98, 102
White, S.   160
Williams, F.   112, 155
Wilson, I.   39–40, 42–3
Wilson, S.   6, 9
Winston, D.   103
Witherington, B.   145
Wolfson, E.   12, 38–9, 41, 55, 59, 64
Wolter, M.   93

Yarbro Collins, A.   87, 89, 92, 94, 108, 109–10, 114, 116, 118, 123, 138, 140, 164–5, 168

Index of Subjects

Aaron   90, 109, 124, 126, 132, 176
Abarim   98
Abihu   109
Abraham   45–8, 52–4, 105, 160, 176, 180–2
abyss   31
Adam   12, 14, 24–7, 31–4, 36, 39, 45, 58, 66, 75–7, 89, 96, 100–1, 122, 126–8, 131, 135, 158–9, 171, 174–5, 183–8
   his authority over animals   14
   his veneration   25–6
   as icon of the deity   25–6
   as image of God   24–7
   as second power   25–6
Adam Christology   174
Adamic typology   183, 185–7
Aher (Elisha ben Avuyah)   1–2, 16, 62–9, 71–2, 75–6, 138, 191
altar   48, 171
Amram   29–30, 35, 89, 94, 100–1, 121, 134
Anafiel   65, 67–70
Ancient of Days   10, 14–16, 23, 38, 45, 49, 51, 68, 116, 119–20, 123
angelic opposition   27, 58–9, 61, 66, 184, 187
angelic veneration   13, 24, 26–7, 31–5, 66, 75, 126, 135, 184, 187
angelification   22, 100–2
Angel of the Lord   50, 140–2, 189
   as mediator of God's absence   141–2
   as mediator of the Name   142
angelus interpres   18, 59, 112, 185
anthropomorphism   11–14, 38–9, 45, 47, 64
Ark   39, 42
ascent   62, 74, 92, 95, 97–8, 101, 103–4, 121, 125, 135, 153, 166, 175, 190
aural ideology   2–3, 8–10, 15, 23, 25, 38, 40–9, 51, 53–4, 56, 58, 62–4, 69, 74–5, 81–8, 94, 128–9, 132–3, 136–42, 144, 148, 150–1, 176–7, 182, 190–1
authority   2, 8–10, 13–14, 17, 20, 38, 52, 64–5, 67, 76, 88, 104, 123, 140–1, 187
Azazel   21

Babylon   60–1, 146
Babylonians   147
baptism   2, 8, 23, 82, 88–90, 123, 137–8, 145–51, 153–71, 175–83, 187–91
bat qol   1–2, 83, 138–9, 168, 176–7, 190–1
Ben Azzai   71–2, 75
Ben Zoma   71–3, 75, 167–8
blood   99, 172

Chaldeans   152
chaos   73, 168–71, 173
Chariot   2, 42, 45–7, 51–2, 63, 82, 115, 135, 145, 152–3, 180
Chebar   82, 145–7, 151–3, 163, 188, 191
Cherubim   13, 40, 42
clothing metaphors   85–6, 116–20, 137
cloud   50, 64, 83, 85–7, 90, 92–3, 96, 98, 108–10, 121–2, 132–3, 136–8
commandments   41, 43
complementary two powers   8, 26–7, 84, 88
crown   10, 28–30, 32, 65–8, 95, 122

Dan   185
danger motif   44
David   45, 47, 90–1, 147, 152, 164, 166
Deuteronomi(sti)c school   11–12, 39–45, 140–2
diaspora   130
Diotima   104
dove   145–50, 153–4, 166–9, 173–83, 191
dualism   163

Index of Subjects

Eden   128, 158–9, 173–4, 183, 187
Edom   60–1
Egypt   101, 176
Eleazar   71, 98
Elijah   44, 46, 83, 85–7, 90–2, 94, 97–8, 109, 110, 115–17, 120, 128–30, 132
Enoch   14, 18–19, 21–4, 26, 28, 30, 32–5, 65, 81, 97–8, 105–8, 112, 119, 131–2, 134–5, 151
   as "Beloved"   37
   heavenly counterpart of   19, 21
   as icon of the deity   35
   as image of God   35–6
   as second power   21, 32, 34–5, 107
   veneration of   33–4, 66
Ephraim   157–9, 162, 185
Esau   59–61
eschatology   113
Eve   186
evil   1, 62, 191
Ezra   113, 118

fear motif   28, 60–1, 65, 67–9, 86–7, 92, 98, 130–5, 137
First Adam   185
flood   66

Gabriel   21, 32, 37–8, 99
Garden of Eden   12, 72, 86, 128, 131
Gilead   185
glorification   97–8, 118, 143, 160–2, 189
Greece   60–1

Hayyot   14, 47, 122, 152–3
Head of Days   17–18, 21–4, 51
heavenly counterpart   21, 31, 56–7
heresy   5, 7, 9, 63–4, 68, 75
Hermon   36, 112
Herod   17, 172
Holy Land   147
Holy of Holies   13, 164
Holy Spirit   38, 145–6, 158–9, 161, 167–8, 174–5, 177–8
honey   71–3
Horeb   44–6, 129
hypostasis   30, 40, 141

idol of jealousy   48

image *(tselem)*   18–20, 24, 26, 32, 35–7, 55–7, 59, 93, 96, 104, 124, 126–7, 174–5, 182, 184, 186, 189
impurity   169
invisibility   2, 15, 26, 37, 47, 63–4, 81, 83–4, 102, 117, 128, 140, 143, 148, 170, 172, 182, 190–1
Io   104
iqonin   13, 19, 23–4, 32, 57–8, 124–6, 135, 182
Isaac   54, 89, 93, 130–3, 160, 185
Israelites   43–4, 79, 100, 108, 124, 132, 141–2

Jacob   19–20, 23–4, 26, 35–7, 45, 54–61, 89, 105, 126, 131, 139
   angelic opposition to   58–61
   his *iqonin*   57
   as image of God   57
   as second power   54–61
James   85–6, 109
Jericho   185
Jerusalem   32, 38, 40, 52, 72, 77, 87, 113, 141, 164–5, 179, 188
Jerusalem Temple   32, 38, 164
Jesus   1–2, 5–9, 13, 15, 21, 23–7, 35, 52, 58, 79–98, 102–91
   enthronement of   111–14
   as Face of God   123–8
   as Image of God   123–8, 182–8
   iqonin of   123–8
   as Last Adam   185
   as mediator of the Name   142–3
   veneration of   133–6, 187
John the Baptist   149–50, 154
Jordan   146–7, 151, 153–7, 159–63, 166, 168–71, 174, 183, 187–8
Joshua   98, 109, 125, 160
Judas   100
judgment   10, 20–1, 30–1, 48, 52, 120

Kavod   1–3, 12–15, 18–19, 29, 35, 40, 42, 46, 48–50, 52–3, 56, 75, 77, 82–5, 87, 89, 93–4, 96, 103, 105–7, 110–11, 113, 115, 118, 129–30, 136, 138–9, 143–5, 148, 151–5, 157, 164, 166, 171–3, 179–81, 184–5, 188–9, 191

Kavod Christology   84–5, 89
Kenaz   100

Last Adam   185
Lesser YHWH   66, 105
likeness language   12–13, 24–5, 31, 36, 39, 48–9, 57, 76, 106, 135, 151, 153, 173, 175, 180–1
Logos   102–4
Lord of Spirits   18–20

Maccabean revolt   100
magi   135–6
Manasseh   185
manna   160
Media   60–1
messiah   6, 17, 19, 22, 81, 89, 111, 113, 116, 119, 149, 169, 176, 178–9
metamorphosis   21, 24, 28, 35, 38, 46, 65–6, 85–6, 91–2, 94, 97, 99, 101, 105, 107, 110, 114–21, 125, 132, 135, 162, 178, 190
Metatron   1–2, 7, 19, 21–2, 24, 28, 35, 38, 51, 62, 70, 75–7, 84, 88, 99, 120, 134–5, 138, 184
   crown of   66
   enthronement of   65
   as "Lesser YHWH"   66
   as Prince of the Divine Presence   67, 69, 134
   as replica of the deity   63
   as scribe   67
   as second power   65
   veneration of   66
   as vice-regent   67
Michael, archangel   21, 24–6, 32, 99, 112, 135, 141
mirror   48, 68, 94, 118, 124, 151–4, 185, 188
Moab   185
molten sea   172–3
monotheism   1, 3, 13, 102
Mosaic typology   102, 104–5, 108, 121, 123
Moses   23, 28–32, 41–5, 50, 64, 80–3, 85–7, 89–110, 113–16, 120–30, 132, 134, 136–40, 142, 153, 160, 162, 176, 185, 190–1
   crown of   122, 128–32
   his angelification   100–4

his divinization   30, 100–4
his enthronement   95–6
his glorification   97–100
his translation to heaven   97–100
as image of God   32, 124–8
iqonin of   124–8
as mediator of the Name   121–2
as second Adam   128
as second power   28–32
standing of   114
veneration of   31–2
mysteries   65, 72, 146

Nadab   109
Naphtali   185
Nathaniel   168
Nebo   98, 185
Negeb   185
"new Moses"   92–4, 105, 123
Noah   101
Noble Man   38

ocularcentric ideology   2–3, 9–10, 13–15, 20, 23, 28, 32, 38–9, 41, 44–56, 58, 62–6, 69–71, 75, 77, 81, 83–8, 94–5, 118, 120, 129, 133, 136–8, 141, 144, 147–50, 176, 178–9, 182, 184, 187–91
Ophannim   47
oppositional two powers   7–8, 62–77

Palestine   6, 82, 130
panim (face)   34–7, 42, 105–7, 115, 124, 139
Pardes   71, 73–4, 167
Pargod   184
parousia   80, 84, 144
Passover   146
peekaboo, angelic   135
Peter   83, 85–7, 109, 129–30, 133
Phanuel   21
Pharaoh   101, 103, 108
prayer   40, 42, 48, 86, 150
Prince of the Divine Presence   67, 69, 134
Promised Land   56, 185
prophetic Christology   83, 91
protoplast   24–7, 31, 36, 75–6, 125, 127, 131, 174, 184, 186
psychopomp   185
pteromorphic   164, 176–82, 188

qedushah 47

Raguel 28–9
Raphael 21
Red Sea 152, 160
resurrection 80, 97–8, 100, 103, 108, 113–15, 123, 143, 161, 179
robe of glory 159
Romans 146–7

Sabbath 16, 45–6, 109, 128
sacrifice 42, 48
salvation 81, 109, 168, 178, 186
Sammael 99
Satan 25–7, 33–4, 136, 158, 161, 184–8
   his quest for worship 185
   as second power 185
scepter 28, 30, 52, 95
Second Adam 128
"second power" 2–3, 7–8, 10, 12–16, 18–31, 34–5, 37–8, 48–51, 53, 58, 62–3, 65–7, 69–71, 75–7, 83–5, 88–9, 93, 95, 102, 105, 107, 111, 114–15, 120, 124–6, 129–30, 133–5, 137, 148–9, 159, 166, 175–6, 179–85, 187–8, 190–1
secrets 17, 30, 37, 115, 121–2, 168
Serapiel 49
Seth 186
Shekinah 65, 67, 69, 79, 91–2, 126, 137
Shem ideology 13, 40, 42, 46, 75, 129, 141–2
Sinai 28, 41, 43, 45, 80, 82–3, 89–92, 94–104, 108–10, 112, 114–16, 121–6, 128–9, 136, 138–40, 145, 151, 162, 181–2, 191
Socrates 104
Solomon 40, 168–9, 171, 173
Son of Man 10, 14–24, 29, 51, 81, 83, 85–6, 97, 114–15, 120, 143–4, 168, 191
   as heavenly counterpart 21
   as second power 10–24
spatial symbolism 40–1, 89, 153, 166, 176, 182
spirit 79, 81, 93, 118, 147–50, 155–61, 165–71, 174–83

Standing One 114
stars 18, 28, 31, 60, 100, 120, 122, 131
Story of the Four 71, 73, 75, 167

tabernacle 92
Tabor 98, 110, 162
Terah 48
theophany 9–10, 15–18, 22, 23, 28–9, 38, 41, 43–4, 46, 49–50, 54, 63, 68, 83–4, 89, 92, 94–5, 110–12, 116, 124, 126, 130–3, 136–7, 139, 144–5, 147–52, 154, 157, 163–4, 166, 182, 184, 187
Tigris 151–2
Torah 63, 71–2, 101
torn heaven 146, 163–4, 166, 177, 188
torn Temple's curtain 164–6, 188
transfiguration 2, 8, 15, 21, 23, 35, 82–3, 85–97, 99, 103–51, 162, 176–9, 182, 190–1
two powers 1–3, 5–10, 13–29, 32, 34–5, 37–8, 45, 49–50, 54, 58, 61–2, 65–8, 75–7, 82–5, 88, 93, 95, 102, 111, 114, 124, 126, 130, 135, 137–9, 145, 148–9, 166–7, 175, 177, 182–4, 187, 190–1

Ulai 152
Upper Face 56, 139
Uriel 37, 54

Voice 2–3, 9, 40, 42–3, 46, 56, 58, 62–3, 69, 74–5, 77, 88, 130, 133, 136–9, 142, 175–6, 182, 190
Vrevoil 37

Wisdom 51
worship 7, 12–13, 25–6, 48, 96, 109–10, 135–6, 187–8

Yahoel 3, 46, 49, 50–3, 58, 68, 70, 84, 89, 120, 180–2
   pteromorphic shape of 180–1
   as second power 49–53

Zion 111, 113
Zoar 185

Index of References

Hebrew Bible

Genesis
1:2-6	167
1:26	48
1:26-27	36
1:26-28	14
1:27	12, 127
2:7	12, 24
2:14	186
3	131
3:8	12
15:14	176
18:13	45
28	45
28:12	55, 61
28:13	59
32:31	44

Exodus
1–2	101
7:1	101, 103
19	43
19–24	129
19:9	35, 105
19:11	181
19:16-18	35, 105
20:4	43
20:18-19	43
20:19	41
20:21	104
23–24	80
23:20-22	140, 142
23:21-22	141
24	92, 108
24–31	138
24:1-2	90
24:1-9	109
24:9-10	111
24:9-11	43
24:9-18	90
24:10	45, 49
24:12	110
24:15-18	110, 136
24:16	108–9, 138
24:16-18	111
33	42–3
33–34	138
33:1-3	141
33:18-20	139
33:18-23	35, 106–7
33:20	44
34	92, 129
34:3	110
34:5	35, 105
34:9	123
34:29-30	124, 132
34:29-35	90, 104, 125
34:35	124, 132

Numbers
10:33-36	40
12:5	64
12:7-8	153

Deuteronomy
1–5	41
1:21	43
2:31	43
3	42
4:6	43
4:10	43
4:12	41, 43
4:12-24	43
4:15	41
4:24	44
4:32	41
4:33	44
4:36	40, 43
5:22-27	44
5:24	44
5:25-28	41
5:31	114
9:3	44
10:1-5	40
10:14	63
12–26	40
18:15	92, 139–40
26:15	40
34:1-4	185
34:6	97

Judges
5:20	31
13:22	44

2 Samuel
7:14	113

1 Kings
7:23-25	173
8:12-13	11
19	129
19:11-13	44, 46
22:19	11

2 Kings
16:17	173
25:13	173

1 Chronicles
18:8	173

2 Chronicles
4:2	173

Job
38:7	31

Psalms
2:7	113, 177
17:15	107
19:2	64
48:2	113
99:1-5	113
104:2	118

116:15	71–3	17:22-24	113	4:9-10	135
146:10	113	20:33	113	4:11	187
		27–28	14	7:28	123
Proverbs		34:23-31	113	16:27	83
25:16	71–2	47:1-8	171	17:1-9	86
				17:2	116–17, 124–5
Ecclesiastes		*Daniel*		17:5	43, 119, 137–8
5:5	71–3	7	13, 14, 23–4, 37–8, 45, 49, 61, 116, 191	17:6	133, 136
Song of Songs				17:9	115, 137
1:4	71			18:26	136
		7:1-2	120	20:33	130
Isaiah		7:2-3	17		
6	11	7:9	16, 29, 50–2, 83, 119–20	*Mark*	
6:5	44			1:9-11	148
11:2	177–8	7:9-10	14, 68	1:10	163, 166, 180, 183
24:33	113	7:9-14	9, 11, 17		
40:18	39	7:10	63, 120	1:10-11	165
40:25	39	7:13	16, 17, 18	1:12-13	161, 186
42:1	91, 177–8	7:13-14	17, 95	1:13	187
46:5	39	7:14	15	3:17	150
52:7	113	7:16	95	3:27	161
61:1	178	8:2	152	8:27	114
63:10–64:1	178	8:10	31	8:31	115
63:14	180	8:17-18	131	8:34	83
		10:4	151–2	8:38	120, 143–4
Jeremiah		10:5-6	50, 52	9:1	115
3:22	65	10:6	119	9:2	114, 116
8:19	113	10:7-9	131	9:2-3	109
30:10	60–1	10:9	133	9:2-7	87
52:17	173	10:9-12	134	9:2-8	43, 91, 110, 144
		10:18-19	134		
Ezekiel		12:3	118	9:2-10	85, 100
1	11, 13, 14, 45, 47–8, 52, 173			9:3	116
		Micah		9:6	132
1:1	145, 163–4	4:6	113	9:7	122, 138–9, 176
1:1-3	152	5:2-4	113		
1:4	119			9:9	114–15
1:13	147	*Zechariah*		9:9-10	97
1:15	14	14:8-11	113	10:51	130
1:26	46, 49, 80			15:38	166
1:26-28	50, 52–3, 111	**New Testament**		15:38-39	164–5
1:27	180				
2:1	133	*Matthew*			
2:2	174	3:1-17	123	*Luke*	
3:22-24	11	3:13	146	3:18–4:2	156
8	52	3:16	148, 163, 166, 174, 183	3:21	87, 163
8:2-4	179			3:21-22	150
10:1	11, 111	3:17	138, 183	3:21-23	146
12	51	4:9	136	3:22	148, 183

3:38	183	3:8-10	80	1:12	137
4:1	182	3:18	80, 116, 118, 144	1:13	50
5:16	87			3:12	181
6:12	87	4:4	80	4:1	163
9:18	87	4:6	80	4:3	50
9:26	83	12	81	10:1	181
9:28-37	86	12:1-12	75	12:12	181
9:29	119, 124–5			13:13	181
9:32	87, 133	*Galatians*		19:10	135
9:34	132	3:27	157	19:11	148, 163
9:36	115			22:1-2	172
11:1	87	*Ephesians*		22:8-9	135
22:41	87	1:17	79		
23:46	876				
24:49	177	*Philippians*		**Apocrypha**	
		2:6	189		
John		2:6-11	118	*Tobit*	
1:18	45, 83, 149	2:7	143	13:11	113
1:29-34	150	3:21	80		
1:32	183			*Wisdom of Solomon*	
1:32-33	148	*Colossians*		9:4	51
1:51	163, 168	1:15	45, 81, 83		
4:24	83	1:27	80	*2 Maccabees*	
5:37	149	3:4	80	2:7 136	
6:46	149				
		2 Thessalonians		**Pseudepigrapha**	
Acts		1:9-10	80		
2:17–18:33	177	2:14	81	*Apocalypse of Abraham*	
7:56	148, 163			8	45
10:11	148, 163	*1 Timothy*		8:1	46
10:25-26	135	1:11	80	9	46, 137
22:9	150	1:17	45, 81	11:2-3	180
		3:16	80	11:2-8	49
Romans		6:16	83	17:1	53
1:4	179			18	51
1:20	45, 81	*Titus*		18:1-4	53
5:12-21	186	2:13	80	18:1-5	53
6:4	80			18:2	46
9:23	80	*James*		18:2-3	138
12:2	116	2:1	79	18:3	47
				18:12–19:1	47
1 Corinthians		*1 Peter*		18:13-14	53
2:8	79	4:14	79	19:1	53
15:42-50	186			19:5	47
15:43-53	118	*2 Peter*		25:1-6	48
		1:16-17	88		
2 Corinthians				*Apocalypse of Zephaniah*	
3	117	*Revelation*		8:3	119
3:7-18	91	1	123		

2 Baruch

2	151
22:1	148
40:1-4	113
51:3	118
59:11	91

3 Baruch

4	33

1 Enoch

1	21
1:4	112
13	22
13:7	151
14	14, 22, 107
14–36	30
14:8	119
14:9-14	69, 131
14:11-17	119
14:18-23	11
14:18-24	45
14:20	124
14:20-21	106, 119
18	113
18:6-8	111
18:8	112
18:18	113
20:5	112
24:2–26:6	113
24:3	112
24–25	113
25:3	112
38:2	21
39:14	119
45:3	19, 20, 30
46:1	51
46:1-2	18, 22
46:1-3	17
46:3-8	18
47:3	17, 19
48:10	19
51:1	19
51:3	19, 20, 30
52:4	19, 21
52:6-9	21
53:6-7	21
55:4	19, 20, 30
60:2	11, 19
61:8	19, 20, 30
62:2-6	20
62:5	19
62:15	119
62:15-16	118
69:27-29	19
69:29	29
70:27	20
70–71	22
71	14, 23
71:9-14	21, 23
71:10	51
72–82	30
77:1	112
86:3-4	31
88:1	31
89:36	100
90:2	11
90:6-9	100
90:9	100
90:9-20	100
90:12	100
90:24	31

2 Enoch

1:6-8	134
21–22	32, 33
22	22, 105, 134, 139
22:5	135
22:6	33
22:8	119
22:10	119
22:10–24:4	37
24	38
37	107
39	105
39:3-6	34–5, 106–7
39:5	29
44:1	36
64:2-4	108

4 Ezra

7:97	118
13	113

Joseph and Aseneth

2:17-20	172
14:1-3	164

Jubilees

1:17-29	113
3:9	186
4:21	30
15:27	102

Ladder of Jacob

1:3-10	55
1:4-7	56
1:5	57, 59
2:1-3	56

Letter of Aresteas

89–91	172

Martyrdom and Ascension of Isaiah

7:25	106

Odes of Solomon

24	168
24:1-9	169

Prayer of Joseph

54	

Primary Adam Books

12:1	27
13:2	24–5, 27
13:2–14:1	25
14:1	26
14:2–15:1	26
15:2	25
25:3	45

Sibylline Oracles

3:716-720	113
7.81-84	154

Testament of Abraham

7:3	181

Testament of Judah

24:2	148

Testament of Levi

2:6	148
18	161
18:6	179

18:6-7	160	*Virt.*		Ber.	
18:10	186	72–79	103	3a	168, 176
		76	103		
Dead Sea Scrolls				Hag.	
4Q374	101, 108	Pseudo-Philo		14b	72
4Q377	101			15a	1, 2, 15, 62–3,
4Q381	184	*LAB*			65, 67–8, 70,
4Q405	46	9:8-13	101		76, 88, 137,
4Q504	127	12:1	91, 100, 125		167, 177, 191
4Q521	167	19:16	99		
		27:10	100	Hul.	
Hellenistic Jewish Authors				91b	59
		Targums			
Exagoge of Ezekiel the				Sotah	
Tragedian		*Targum Pseudo-Jonathan*		12a	102
67–90	28				
75–80	122	Exodus		Sukkah	
77–78	30	34:29-30	126	51b	172
		Targum to the Song of Songs			
Josephus		2:12	168, 176	**Midrashim**	
Ant.		**Mishnah, Tosefta, and**		*Midrash Rabbah*	
3.96-97	98	**Talmuds**		Genesis Rabbah	
4.326	98			5:4	75
7.365	187	*Mishnah*		8:10	27, 76
				11	128
Philo		Hag.		65:21	15
		2:1	74, 115	68:12	58–9
Decal.					
64	135	*Tosefta*		Exodus Rabbah	
				23:14	152
Legat.		Hag.			
116	135	2:3-4	71	Leviticus Rabbah	
				1:14	153
Mos. 1–2		Sotah		6:3	15
1.57	116	13:2	177	20:2	127
1.158	102			29:2	60
2.70	91	*Palestinian Talmud*			
2.280	116			Numbers Rabbah	
2.288	103	Ber.		13:19	172
2.288–291	97	1:12	15		
				Deuteronomy Rabbah	
QE 1–2		Hag.		11	91
2.29	103	77b	72	11:3	127
2.40	103			11:10	99, 102
2.46	128	*Babylonian Talmud*			
				Song of Songs Rabbah	
Sacr.		B. Bat.		1:27	72
9	103	75a	91, 125		

Other Midrashim (arranged alphabetically)

Midrash Gedullat Moshe
99

Midrash Tadshe
4   127

Midrash Tehillim
78:6   61

Pesikta de Rab Kahana
1:1   77-6

Pesikta Rabbati
22:6   15

Pirke de R. Eliezer
35   36
48   102

Mystical and Other Later Works

Alphabet of R. Akiba
77

Visions of Ezekiel
152

Zohar
I.149b   61
II.82b   153
III.43a-b   75

Hekhalot

Hekhalot Rabbati
§164   35-6
§§258-259   73

Hekhalot Zutarti
§338   72
§§338-348   73-4
§§407-408   73

Merkavah Rabbah
§671   72

§§671-673   73
§672   64, 67-9

Sefer Hekhalot/3 Enoch
4   135
4:5-10   66
6:1   69
7-11   65
12-15   66
15B:5   134
16   68, 70, 177
16:1-5   65, 67
18:24   15
45:1-4   184

Samaritan Sources

Defter
                 121

Memar Marqah
1.9   121-2
2.12   121
4.1   121
4.4   121
4.7   121
6.3   122

Christian and Gnostic Sources

Acts of Thomas
112   175

Aphrahat

Demonstrations
6.14   158

Cave of Treasures
2:10-24   33

Enthronement of Michael
                 33

Ephrem the Syrian

Commentary on the Diatessaron
156

Hymns on the Church
36.3   161
36.5-6   90
36.5-9   162

Hymns on Epiphany
9.12   162
12.1   158-9
12.2-4   158
14.32   156

Hymns on Nativity
22.39   158

Epiphanius of Salamis

Pan.
30.13.7   155

Eusebius of Caesarea

Praep. ev.
3:2 90

Gregory the Great

Hom. Ez.
I.2.5   147

Gospel of Bartholomew
4   33

Gospel of Ebionites
                 155

Gospel of Hebrews
                 155

Gospel of Philip
71:16-21   186

Gospel of Truth
38:6-7   142
39:19-27   143

Irenaeus

Haer.
4.20.9   90
5.21.2   185-6

Jerome

Comm. Ezech.
1.3a   146
1.4.53-68   146

Justin

Dial.
88.3   154
103   185–6

Macarian Homilies

Collection II
11.6   175
12.6   175
30.3–30.5   174
30.6   175

Origen

Cels.
2.71   150

Comm. Jo.
1.31   150

Hom. Ezech.
1.4.5–9   145

Hom. Jes. Nav.
4.2   160

Preaching of Paul
         154

Tatian

Diatessaron
         155

Teaching of St. Gregory
412–414   170
425   161

Qur'an
2:31-39   33
7:11-18   33
15:31-48   33
17:61-65   33
18:50   33
20:116–23   33
38:71-85   33

www.ingramcontent.com/pod-product-compliance
Lightning Source LLC
Chambersburg PA
CBHW052036300426
44117CB00012B/1852